Practice Exercises for Intermediate Microeconomic Theory

Tools and Step-by-Step Examples

Eric Dunaway, John C. Strandholm, Ana Espinola-Arredondo, and Felix Muñoz-Garcia

The MIT Press

Cambridge, Massachusetts

London, England

ISBN: 978-0-262-53985-2

10 9 8 7 6 5 4 3 2 1

Contents

Preface

This text presents detailed answer keys to all 140 self-assessment exercises and to the 173 odd-numbered end-of-chapter exercises in *Intermediate Microeconomic Theory: Tools and Step-by-Step Examples*. These answer keys are relatively detailed and provide a step-by-step approach that students can easily read on their own. These exercises cover material often discussed during a semester-long intermediate microeconomics course using algebra in most exercises and basic calculus in some exercises. The exercises can also be a good introduction to students interested in continuing their education pursuing graduate studies in economics or finance. In general, the book covers exercises from consumer theory, theory of the firm, game theory, imperfectly competitive markets, contract theory, and concludes with externalities and public goods.

Each exercise is labeled with a title and a superscript, A, B, or C, indicating a relative difficulty level, with A being the easiest and C being the hardest. The name of each exercise indicates the topic that the question covers and gives instructors and students a reference to associate the exercise with. Many answers include additional intuition not asked for in the original exercise with the goal to make students better understand the interpretation of mathematical results. Exercises follow the order in which they are presented in the chapter, and the last exercises in each chapter may combine multiple topics from the chapter or be more difficult than the first exercises in that chapter.

Organization of the book. Each chapter starts with worked-out solutions to the self-assessment exercises, which follow a similar approach to the examples in *Intermediate Microeconomic Theory: Tools and Step-by-Step Examples*, but consider different values or functional forms, thus being relatively easy to solve for students with different mathematical backgrounds. Following the answers to the self-assessment exercises, we presnet solutions to the odd-numbered end-of-chapter exercises.

Starting with chapter 2, the first four chapters cover the core of consumer theory, starting with preferences and utility (chapter 2); building to optimal consumer choice (chapter 3); then investigating substitution and income effects (chapter 4); and finally measuring welfare changes from price changes using consumer surplus, compensating variation, and equivalent variation in chapter 5. Chapter 6 looks at consumer choices under uncertainty focusing on risk preferences, insurance, and prospect theory. Theory of the firm is studied through the analysis of production functions and the firm's cost minimization problem in chapters 7 and 8, respectively. Chapter 9 brings both sides of the market together through partial equilibrium (for one good) and general equilibrium (for multiple goods). Chapter 10 introduces monopoly markets, and chapter 11 looks at how monopolies can price discriminate to increase their profits and bundle their product offerings. The next five chapters cover the interaction of different agents through a game theoretic perspective. We first offer a basic introduction to game theory, starting with simultaneous-move games (chapter 12) and following with sequential-move and repeated games (chapter 13). Chapter 14 gives a glimpse into industrial organization studying markets with few firms, known as imperfect competition. Chapters 15 and 16 look at more advanced topics using games of asymmetric information to understand equilibrium bidding strategies in auctions (chapter 15) and moral hazard and adverse selection in contracts (chapter 16). The book concludes by presenting exercises on externalities and public goods (chapter 17).

How to use the book. This book can be used in a few different ways. Some instructors may present some of the worked-out answers in class, as additional examples to illustrate the main definitions and theory. Instructors can also assign worked-out answers as a primer for their own homework assignments (that may include the even-numbered exercises). Students can use the text as a resource for practice exercises for exams or to refresh on the math tools, economic theory, and intuition.

The following table suggests, as an example, exercises that instructors can assign (around four exercises per chapter). For easier reference, these exercises are ranked by difficulty: easy, moderate, and challenging. Self-assessment exercises can also be recommended as a basic introduction to the main topics in each chapter.

Chapter	Easy	Moderate	Challenging
Chapter 2	5,7,17,19	1,3,13	9,11,15
Chapter 3	1,3,5,13	7,15,19	9,11,17
Chapter 4	7,9,15,17	1,3,11	5,13,19
Chapter 5	1,3,5,15	7,9,13	11,17,19,21
Chapter 6	1,3,5,19	9,11,15	7,13,17
Chapter 7	3,7,9,11	5,13,17	1,15,19
Chapter 8	7,17,19,21	9,11,13,15	1,3,5
Chapter 9	1,5,7,9	3,11,13	15,17,19,21
Chapter 10	3,7,17,19	1,5,9,13	11,15,21
Chapter 11	3,11,15	1,5,7,9	13,17,19
Chapter 12	1,7,15,21	3,5,13,17	9,11,19
Chapter 13	1,3,7,9	5,11,15,21	13,17,19
Chapter 14	1,5,17,21,23	3,7,11,13	9,15,19,25
Chapter 15	1,9,13,21	5,7,11,15	3,17,19
Chapter 16	1,3,19,21	7,9,11,13	5,15,17
Chapter 17	3,13,15,19	1,5,7	9,11,17

Suggested end-of-chapter exercises per chapter.

Acknowledgments. *Eric:* I would like to thank my wife, Haley, and his daughters, Lucille, Sophie, and Erica, for their endless support during his journey through academia. Thank you to my adviser, Felix Munoz-Garcia, as well as all those who went out of their way to teach me about both economics and life, with special mention to Jill McCluskey, Ron Mittelhammer, Mark Gibson, Ana Espinola-Arredondo, Raymond Batina, Kelley Cullen, and Michael Carroll. Finally, to my colleagues John Strandholm, Christopher Clarke, and Casey Bolt, thank you for the countless nights of discussion and challenging me to be better.

John: I would first like to thank my coauthors for the support and confidence in writing these exercises. Thank you to Christopher Clarke for moral support and helpful comments. To my adviser, Ana Espinola-Arredondo, and my microeconomic teachers who shared their passion on this great subject: Matthew Oliver, John Tschirhart, Klaas van't Veld, Felix Munoz-Garcia, and Jill McCluskey. I use your classes as a model for my own classes, and you provided inspiration for the exercises in this book. Thank you to my first teachers, my parents, John and Lori Strandholm, for instilling the importance of education and compassion in my teaching. Finally, to my wife, Sarah, for encouraging and supporting me on the late nights and weekends, and keeping me grounded. Thank you so much.

Ana and Felix: We would like to thank our teachers and advisers at the University of Barcelona, and then at the University of Pittsburgh, for instilling a passion for research and teaching. We thank our colleagues at Washington State University for their encouragement during the development of this book, and to several cohorts of students for practiced and provided feedback on these and similar exercises. We must also thank many teaching assistants who helped correct many of these exercises. Finally, we thank our family and friends for their constant support and encouragement.

Chapter 2 - Consumer Preferences and Utility

2.1 Solutions to Self-Assessment Exercises

Self-assessment exercise #2.1

SA 2.1 Consider now that Eric prefers bundle $A = (1, 1)$ to $B = (2, 1)$. Assume that this ranking holds for any two bundles we present to him, where only the amount of good x increases from bundle A to B. Are Eric's preferences monotonic? Are they strictly monotonic? What if he prefers bundle $A = (3, 3)$ to $B = (2, 2)$, and a similar ranking holds for any two bundles where the amount of both goods decreases from A to B?

- *First type of preferences.* Since Eric prefers bundle A to B, bundle A has fewer units of good x than bundle B, and both bundles have the same amount of good y, his preferences violate monotonicity and strict monotonicity.

  - Recall that, for monotonicity to hold, Eric should weakly prefer (that is, strictly prefer or be indifferent to) the bundle that contains more units of either good (x or y). Since he prefers the bundle with fewer units of x and the same amount of y, his preferences are nonmonotonic. Intuitively, Eric treats good x as a bad, preferring fewer units of it. As a remark, note that if Eric weakly preferred bundles with more units of x but the same amount of y, we would still not be able to say that monotonicity holds. For monotonicity, we would need Eric to weakly prefer bundles with more units of x or more of y.

  - For strict monotonicity to hold, Eric should strictly prefer bundles with more units of either good (x or y) but, as discussed above, he prefers the bundle with fewer units of good x (bundle A), implying that his preferences do not satisfy strict monotonicity either. A similar remark as for monotonicity applies here: if Eric strictly preferred bundles with more units of x but the same amount of y, we would still not be able to say that strict monotonicity holds. For that, we need to know that Eric strictly prefers bundles with more units of x, more of y, or both.

- *Second type of preferences.* He now prefers bundle A to bundle B, but in this case bundle A has more of each good than bundle B. As such, Eric's preferences are monotonic, but we cannot guarantee that his preferences are strictly monotonic. For his preferences to satisfy strict monotonicity, we would need to make sure that Eric prefers bundle A to B when only good x or only good y is increased.

Self-assessment exercise #2.2

SA 2.2 Assume that Eric prefers bundles with more units of good x but fewer units of y. If he cannot consume negative amounts of either good, can you find a bliss point (i.e., a bundle where he is satiated)? Given your answer, do Eric's preferences satisfy nonsatiation? What about monotonicity?

14

- Since good y is viewed as a bad by Eric, he would prefer to consume zero units of good y. That being said, Eric would always view a bundle with more of good x as at least as good as a bundle with less of good x. Thus, there does not exist a bliss point, as Eric can always identify bundles with higher amounts of good x. Since there does not exist a bliss point, Eric's preferences satisfy nonsatiation. However, as one of the goods is a bad, his preferences do not satisfy monotonicity. Recall that, for preferences to satisfy monotonicity, the consumer needs to prefer more units of good x, good y, or both. In this case, Eric prefers less of good y, violating monotonicity.

Self-assessment exercise #2.3

SA 2.3 Consider again bundles $A = (40, 30)$ and $B = (20, 30)$ from example 2.3, and assume that Chelsea's utility function is $u(x, y) = 2x + 3y$. Does she prefer bundle A, or B, or is she indifferent between them? What if her preferences are represented with utility function $v(x, y) = 4x + 6y$? What if they are represented with $v'(x, y) = 4x - 6y$? *Hint*: Utility function $v'(x, y)$ is not an increasing transformation of Chelsea's original utility function $u(x, y)$.

- *First utility function.* With Chelsea's utility function $u(x, y) = 2x + 3y$, bundle A yields a utility level of

$$u(40, 30) = (2 \times 40) + (3 \times 30) = 80 + 90 = 170$$

whereas bundle B only yields a utility level of

$$u(20, 30) = (2 \times 20) + (3 \times 30) = 40 + 90 = 130.$$

  – Since bundle A provides a higher utility level than bundle B, Chelsea prefers bundle A to bundle B.

- *Second utility function.* We now consider the alternative utility function $v(x, y) = 4x + 6y$, which is just a monotonic transformation of $u(x, y)$; that is, $v(x, y) = 2(2x + 3y) = 2u(x, y)$. In this context, bundle A yields a utility level of

$$v(40, 30) = (4 \times 40) + (6 \times 30) = 160 + 180 = 340$$

and bundle B yields a utility level of

$$v(20, 30) = (4 \times 20) + (6 \times 30) = 80 + 180 = 260.$$

  – That is, Chelsea's utility level from bundles A and B doubled relative to her utility with the first utility function $u(x, y) = 2x + 3y$. However, the utility ranking remains unchanged, implying that bundle A still provides a higher utility level than bundle B, and thus must be more preferred.

- *Third utility function.* Last, with utility function $v'(x, y) = 4x - 6y$, bundle A provides a utility level of

$$v'(40, 30) = (4 \times 40) - (6 \times 30) = 160 - 180 = -20$$

15

while bundle B provides a utility level of

$$v'(20, 30) = (4 \times 20) - (6 \times 30) = 80 - 180 = -100.$$

- Even though both utilities are negative in this case, we only concern ourselves with whichever number is higher. Since bundle A provides a higher utility level than bundle B, it is still the most preferred bundle.

Self-assessment exercise #2.4

SA 2.4 Consider that Eric's utility function is $u(x, y) = 2x + 3y$, which is just an example of $u(x, y) = ax + by$, where $a = 2$ and $b = 3$. Following the steps in example 2.4, show that this utility function satisfies completeness, transitivity, monotonicity, strict monotonicity, and nonsatiation, as summarized in table 2.1. Then consider one of Eric's friends, John, who has a utility function $u(x, y) = \min\{2x, 3y\}$. Following the steps in example 2.4, show that the utility function satisfies all the properties in table 2.1, except for strict monotonicity.

- Starting with Eric's utility function:
  - *Completeness.* Like in example 2.4, as long as we can specify two bundles $A = (x_A, y_A)$ and $B = (x_B, y_B)$ and rank them such that either $u(x_A, y_A) \geq u(x_B, y_B)$, $u(x_B, y_B) \geq u(x_A, y_A)$, or both, completeness is satisfied. For any values of x and y, we obtain a real value for the utility function $u(x, y) = 2x + 3y$, so we can compare any pair of bundles by simply comparing the utility values. Thus, $u(x, y)$ satisfies completeness.
  - *Transitivity.* Again, for every three bundles A, B and C, where $u(x_A, y_A) \geq u(x_B, y_B)$ and $u(x_B, y_B) \geq u(x_C, y_C)$, we must have that $u(x_A, y_A) \geq u(x_C, y_C)$ for transitivity to hold. Just like we did for completeness, we can translate any pair of values for x and y into a corresponding utility value, then rank them accordingly. Thus, transitivity holds by definition.
  - *Strict Monotonicity.* An increase in either the value of x or y for Eric's utility function leads to a strictly higher value of his utility. Thus, strict monotonicity holds.
  - *Monotonicity.* Since Eric's utility function is strictly monotonic, it is also monotonic. Intuitively, if we increase both the values of x and y in Eric's utility function, Eric receives a strictly higher utility level.
  - *Nonsatiation.* It is satisfied by monotonicity. If we increase Eric's bundle from (x, y) to $(x + b, y + a)$ for any positive values of a and b (i.e., increasing the amount of good x by b units, and the amount of good y by a units), Eric receives a strictly higher utility level. Thus, Eric never reaches a bliss point and his preferences satisfy nonsatiation.

- For John's utility function, we follow a similar process.
  - *Completeness.* For completeness to hold, we need that, for any two bundles $A = (x_A, y_A)$ and $B = (x_B, y_B)$, we can rank them such that either $u(x_A, y_A) \geq u(x_B, y_B)$, $u(x_B, y_B) \geq u(x_A, y_A)$, or both. For any real values of

16

x and y, we obtain a real value for the utility function $u(x, y) = \min\{2x, 3y\}$, and can compare any pair of bundles by simply comparing their utility values. Thus, $u(x, y)$ satisfies completeness.

- *Transitivity.* Since we can translate any possible bundle into a numerical utility value, we can rank them appropriately. If bundle A is preferred to bundle B and bundle B is preferred to bundle C, then $u(x_A, y_A) > u(x_B, y_B)$ and $u(x_B, y_B) > u(x_C, y_C)$. This implies that $u(x_A, y_A) > u(x_C, y_C)$ and thus bundle A must be preferred to bundle C and $u(x, y)$ satisfies transitivity.

- *Strict Monotonicity.* John's utility function does not satisfy strict monotonicity. Suppose $x = 1$ and $y = 10$. John's utility level is

$$u(1, 10) = \min\{2(1), 3(10)\} = \min\{2, 30\} = 2.$$

If we increase the amount of good y to 11 units, we obtain the same utility value:

$$u(1, 11) = \min\{2(1), 3(11)\} = \min\{2, 33\} = 2.$$

Intuitively, John prefers to consume goods x and y in fixed proportions, and increasing an overly proportioned good (good y in this case) does not increase John's utility. Since an increase of one component of John's bundle does not necessarily lead to a more preferred bundle, John's utility function does not satisfy strict monotonicity.

- *Monotonicity.* If we increase both the values of x and y in John's utility function, the lesser between $2x$ and $3y$ must increase as well. To see this point with our above example, consider bundle $(1, 10)$, which yields a utility level of

$$u(1, 10) = \min\{2(1), 3(10)\} = \min\{2, 30\} = 2,$$

and bundle $(2, 11)$, where both goods increased by one unit, which yields a utility level

$$u(2, 11) = \min\{2(2), 3(11)\} = \min\{4, 33\} = 4.$$

Thus, John reaches a strictly higher utility level and his utility function satisfies monotonicity.

- *Nonsatiation.* Since John's utility function satisfies monotonicity, it satisfies nonsatiation. If we increase John's bundle from (x, y) to $(x + b, y + a)$ for any positive values of a and b (i.e., increasing the amount of good x by b units, and the amount of good y by a units), the lesser of $2x$ and $3y$ must also increase and John receives a strictly higher utility level. Thus, John never reaches a bliss point and his preferences satisfy nonsatiation.

Self-assessment exercise #2.5

SA 2.5 Chelsea's utility function is $u(x, y) = 5x + 2y$. Find the marginal utility for goods x and y. Repeat your analysis, assuming that her utility function is $u(x, y) = 5x - 2y$. Interpret.

- *First utility function, $u(x, y) = 5x + 2y$.* To calculate the marginal utilities, we simply differentiate the utility function with respect to both goods x and y.
  - For good x, marginal utility is $MU_x = \frac{\partial u(x,y)}{\partial x} = 5$, which implies that Chelsea's utility increases by 5 for every additional unit of x she consumes.
  - For good y, marginal utility is $MU_y = \frac{\partial u(x,y)}{\partial y} = 2$, which similarly implies that Chelsea's utility increases by 2 for every additional unit of y she consumes.
- *Second utility function, $u(x, y) = 5x - 2y$.* We repeat the same process.
  - For good x, marginal utility is $MU_x = \frac{\partial u(x,y)}{\partial x} = 5$, which again implies that Chelsea's utility increases by 5 for every additional unit of x she consumes.
  - For good y, marginal utility is $MU_y = \frac{\partial u(x,y)}{\partial y} = -2$, which similarly implies that Chelsea's utility *decreases* by 2 for every additional unit of y she consumes. This implies that good y is a bad in this case.

Self-assessment exercise #2.6

SA 2.6 Are the expressions of MU_x and MU_y that you found in self-assessment 2.5 decreasing or increasing?

- For both cases in self-assessment 2.5, we find that marginal utility is neither decreasing nor increasing. In fact, if we differentiate each marginal utility by its respective variable, it is equal to zero. In other words, marginal utilities are not a function of the amount of good x or y (they are just numbers!).

  This implies that Chelsea values each unit of either good at the same rate, regardless of how many units of each good x or y she consumes. Intuitively, her enjoyment (or unenjoyment) of these goods does not increase or decrease as she consumes more units of them.

Self-assessment exercise #2.7

SA 2.7 Repeat example 2.7, but using utility function $u(x, y) = x^{1/3}y^{2/3}$ and utility level $u = 16$.

- As in example 2.7, we know that a utility level of $u = 16$ entails that $x^{1/3}y^{2/3} = 16$. To find our indifference curve, we must solve this expression for the variable in the vertical axis (good y).
  - First, we divide both sides of this expression by $x^{1/3}$, to obtain $y^{2/3} = \frac{16}{x^{1/3}}$.
  - From here, we must raise both sides of this expression to the $\frac{3}{2}$ power. This provides the equation for our indifference curve of $y = \frac{16^{3/2}}{x^{1/2}}$, or more compactly,
  $$y = \frac{64}{\sqrt{x}}.$$
- As before, we can choose a few different values of x:
  - For $x = 4$ units, y becomes $y = \frac{64}{\sqrt{4}} = 32$ units;
  - For $x = 9$ units, y becomes $y = \frac{64}{\sqrt{9}} = 21.33$ units; and

– For $x = 16$ units, y becomes $y = \frac{64}{\sqrt{16}} = 16$ units.

Figure 2.1 plots these three bundles in the positive quadrant and connects them to form our indifference curve for $u = 16$.

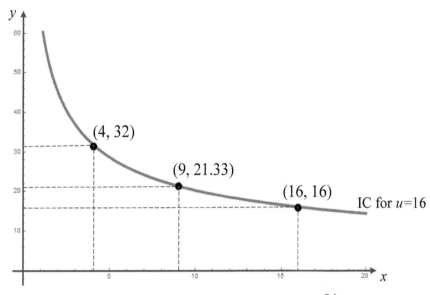

Figure 2.1. Indifference curve $y = \dfrac{64}{\sqrt{x}}$.

Self-assessment exercise #2.8

SA 2.8 Consider a consumer with utility function $u(x, y) = 3y + 2x$ who seeks to reach a utility level $u = 20$. Solve for y to find her indifference curve. Is it increasing or decreasing? What if her utility function is $u(x, y) = 3y - 2x$?

- *First utility function.* For a utility function of $u(x, y) = 3y + 2x$ and a utility level of $u = 20$, we know that his indifference curve entails $3y + 2x = 20$. We can find his indifference curve by solving this expression for y.

  – Subtracting both sides of this equation by $2x$ gives $3y = 20 - 2x$.
  – Next, we divide both sides by 3 to obtain his indifference curve,

$$y = \frac{20}{3} - \frac{2}{3}x.$$

This indifference curve is clearly decreasing in x, as depicted in figure 2.2.

19

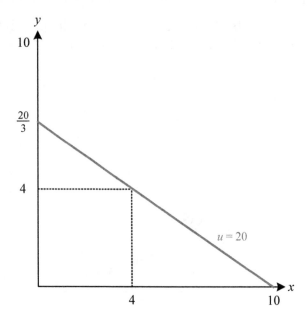

Figure 2.2. Indifference curve $y = \frac{20}{3} - \frac{2}{3}x$.

- *Second utility function.* For the second utility function of $u(x, y) = 3y - 2x$ and utility level of $u = 20$, we follow the same steps as before and solve for y to derive his indifference curve.

  - Adding $2x$ to both sides of this equation gives $3y = 20 + 2x$.
  - Last, we divide both sides by 3 to obtain the new indifference curve,

  $$y = \frac{20}{3} + \frac{2}{3}x.$$

  Since this indifference curve has a positive slope, it is actually increasing in x, as depicted in figure 2.3.

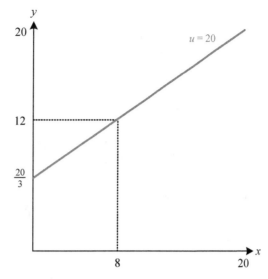

Figure 2.3. Indifference curve $y = \frac{20}{3} + \frac{2}{3}x$.

- This should make sense, as good x is a bad. In this case, our consumer would rather consume bundles with more of good y and less of good x. Intuitively, our consumer moves from a lower utility curve to a higher utility curve by moving upward and to the left. The leftward movement corresponds with good x's status as a bad. This effect is depicted in figure 2.4, as it shows the consumer's movement from $u = 20$ to a higher indifference curve at $u = 40$.

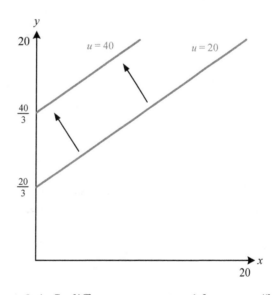

Figure 2.4. Indifference curves with x as a "bad."

Self-assessment exercise #2.9

SA 2.9 Eric's utility function is $u(x,y) = x^{1/3}y^{2/3}$. Find his MRS and show whether it is increasing or decreasing in x. Repeat your analysis for Pam's utility function, $u(x,y) =$

$3x + 2y$, and for Maria's utility function, $u(x, y) = 3x - 2y$.

- *Eric's utility function, $u(x, y) = x^{1/3}y^{2/3}$.* For Eric's utility function, we begin by calculating his marginal utilities.

  - For good x, $MU_x = \frac{\partial u(x,y)}{\partial x} = \frac{1}{3}x^{-2/3}y^{2/3}$; and for good y, $MU_y = \frac{\partial u(x,y)}{\partial y} = \frac{2}{3}x^{1/3}y^{-1/3}$.

  - Next, we use these marginal utilities to calculate the marginal rate of substitution,

  $$MRS_{x,y} = \frac{MU_x}{MU_y} = \frac{\frac{1}{3}x^{-2/3}y^{2/3}}{\frac{2}{3}x^{1/3}y^{-1/3}} = \frac{x^{-2/3}y^{2/3}}{2x^{1/3}y^{-1/3}}.$$

  We can further simplify this by remembering that when we divide similar bases raised to exponents, we simply subtract the exponents. That is, $MRS_{x,y} = \frac{y^{\frac{2}{3}-\left(-\frac{1}{3}\right)}}{2x^{\frac{1}{3}-\left(-\frac{2}{3}\right)}}$, or after rearranging

  $$MRS_{x,y} = \frac{y}{2x}.$$

  - Since x appears in the denominator of the $MRS_{x,y}$, we know that the $MRS_{x,y}$ is decreasing in x. Alternatively, we could differentiate the marginal rate of substitution for x,

  $$\frac{\partial MRS_{x,y}}{\partial x} = -\frac{y}{2x^2} < 0,$$

  which also implies that it is decreasing in x. Graphically, this indicates that Eric's indifference curves are bowed-in toward the origin, entailing that Eric is willing to substitute good y for x at a decreasing rate.

- *Pam's utility function, $u(x, y) = 3x + 2y$.* For Pam's utility function, we follow the same steps.

  - Starting with marginal utilities, $MU_x = \frac{\partial u(x,y)}{\partial x} = 3$ and $MU_y = \frac{\partial u(x,y)}{\partial y} = 2$.
  - We use these marginal utilities to calculate the marginal rate of substitution,

  $$MRS_{x,y} = \frac{MU_x}{MU_y} = \frac{3}{2}.$$

  - Since the marginal rate of substitution is not a function of x, it cannot be decreasing in x. In fact, the marginal rate of substitution does not vary with x at all in this case. Graphically, this means that Pam's indifference curves are straight lines, thus exhibiting a constant slope. Intuitively, this result means that Pam is willing to substitute good y for x at a constant rate.

- *Maria's utility function, $u(x, y) = 3x - 2y$.* Last, for Maria's utility function, we once again repeat the same steps.

  - Starting with marginal utilities, $MU_x = \frac{\partial u(x,y)}{\partial x} = 3$ and $MU_y = \frac{\partial u(x,y)}{\partial y} = -2$.
  - We use these marginal utilities to calculate our marginal rate of substitution,

  $$MRS_{x,y} = \frac{MU_x}{MU_y} = -\frac{3}{2}.$$

22

– Once again, the marginal rate of substitution is not a function of x, so it cannot be decreasing in x. In both Pam's and Maria's cases, they are always willing to trade a fixed amount of good x for good y. In this case, the $MRS_{x,y} = -\frac{3}{2}$, implying that Maria's indifference curves are positively sloped straight lines. In words, this result says that Maria is willing to substitute good y for x at a constant rate. In addition, she treats good y as a bad, implying that, if she received one more unit of good y, she would have to be compensated with $\frac{3}{2}$ units of good x to maintain her utility unchanged. (This does not happen when the consumer enjoys both goods, where more units of one of the goods means that the consumer has to give up units of the other good to keep her utility unaffected.)

Self-assessment exercise #2.10

SA 2.10 Chelsea's utility function is $u(x, y) = 3x + 2y$. Graph her indifference curve for utility levels $u = 10$ and $u = 20$.

- Since we know that Chelsea's utility function is $u(x, y) = 3x + 2y$ (a straight line) and her desired utility level is $u = 10$, we can find her utility curve by finding two bundles on this utility curve and connecting the dots.
  - *Indifference curve when reaching utility level $u = 10$.* If we set $x = 0$, we obtain $2y = 10$, and thus $y = 5$ units, which gives us our first bundle. If we then set $y = 0$, we find $3x = 10$, and thus $x = 3.33$ units, which gives us our second bundle.
  - *Indifference curve when reaching utility level $u = 20$.* We now perform the same steps as above, but assuming that Chelsea seeks to reach a utility level of $u = 20$. If we set $x = 0$, we obtain $2y = 20$, and thus $y = 10$ units, which gives us our first bundle. If we set $y = 0$, we have $3x = 20$, and thus $x = 6.66$ units, which gives us our second bundle.
  - Connecting the dots gives us our indifference curves, as detailed in figure 2.5.

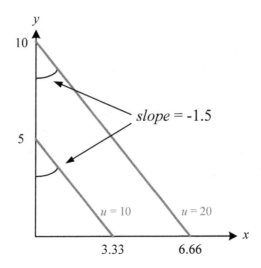

Figure 2.5. Chelsea's indifference curves.

23

Self-assessment exercise #2.11

SA 2.11 John's utility function is given by $u(x, y) = 3 \min\{x, 2y\}$. Graph his indifference curve for utility levels $u = 10$ and $u = 20$.

- John's utility function indicates that he views goods x and y as perfect complements. This implies that they must be consumed in fixed proportions to increase John's utility. We find this fixed proportion by examining the ratios of x and y within the brackets of the minimum function and set them equal to each other (i.e., $x = 2y$). Thus, John prefers to consume twice as much of good x as he does of good y, and our utility expands along the ray $y = 0.5x$.

  - *Indifference curve when reaching utility level $u = 10$.* We first focus on the ray crossing through the kinks of John's indifference curves. At the kinks, we know that two arguments inside the min operator coincide; that is, at $x = 2y$, or $y = \frac{1}{2}x$. We can then separately analyze points below the ray $y = \frac{1}{2}x$, which graphically starts at the origin with a slope of $\frac{1}{2}$, and points above this ray.

    * *Points below ray $y = \frac{1}{2}x$.* When John consumes bundles below the ray, he has too much of good x and not enough of good y. Thus, his utility is limited by the amount of good y. Using a utility level of $u = 10$, we can then focus on the units of good y (as they dictate John's utility for all points below ray $y = \frac{1}{2}x$), yielding

$$3(2y) = 10$$

    or, after solving for y, we find $y = 1.67$ units.

    * *Points above ray $y = \frac{1}{2}x$.* Likewise, when John consumes bundles above the ray $y = \frac{1}{2}x$, he has too much of good y and not enough of good x. With our utility level of $u = 10$, we have that

$$3x = 10,$$

    or $x = 3.33$ units. (Note that in this case the units of good x dictate John's utility.)

    * By combining these horizontal and vertical lines, we can derive John's indifference curve.

  - *Indifference curve when reaching utility level $u = 20$.* Repeating this analysis for $u = 20$, we can simply double all of our values as our fixed proportion is linear ($y = \frac{1}{2}x$). Thus, we have the horizontal line at $y = 3.33$ and the vertical line at $x = 6.66$, which combine to form John's indifference curve at $u = 20$.

  - The combined indifference curves are depicted in figure 2.6.

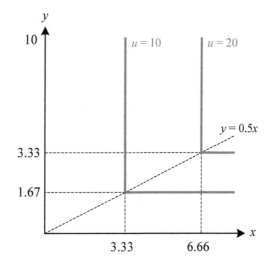

Figure 2.6. John's indifference curves.

Self-assessment exercise #2.12

SA 2.12 Maria's utility function is $u(x, y) = 5x^{1/2}y^{1/4}$. Graph her indifference curve for utility levels $u = 10$ and $u = 20$.

- Since Maria's utility function falls under the Cobb-Douglas classification, we know that her indifference curves are not linear, but are rather bowed-in toward the origin. As before, we can solve for y in Maria's utility function to find her indifference curves.

  – First, we divide both sides of $u(x, y) = 5x^{1/2}y^{1/4}$ by $5x^{1/2}$ to obtain

  $$y^{1/4} = \frac{u}{5x^{1/2}}.$$

  – Next we raise both sides of this equation to the fourth power to obtain our equation for Maria's indifference curves,

  $$y = \frac{u^4}{625x^2}.$$

  – Plugging in our different values for u gives us two different indifference curves,

  $$y = \frac{10,000}{625x^2} \quad \text{for } u = 10, \text{ and}$$
  $$y = \frac{160,000}{625x^2} \quad \text{for } u = 20.$$

  – We can plot these indifference curves by examining a few bundles that fall on these indifference curves:

    * For $u = 10$, if we set $x = 2$, we have that $y = 4$ units. Likewise, when $x = 4$, good y becomes $y = 1$ units.

25

* For $u = 20$, if we set $x = 4$, good y is $y = 16$ units. When $x = 8$, good y becomes $y = 4$ units.
* These bundles allow us to find a few relevant points along our indifference curves, which are depicted in figure 2.7.

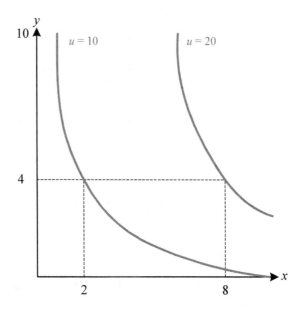

Figure 2.7. Maria's indifference curves.

Self-assessment exercise #2.13

SA 2.13 Consider Maria's utility function again, $u(x, y) = 5x^{1/2}y^{1/4}$. What is the utility elasticity of good x? And of good y? Interpret.

- *Utility elasticity of good x.* We can calculate Maria's utility elasticity of good x from the formula

$$
\begin{aligned}
\varepsilon_{u,x} &= \frac{\partial u(x,y)}{\partial x} \frac{x}{u(x,y)} \\
&= 5\frac{1}{2}x^{-1/2}y^{1/4}\frac{x}{5x^{1/2}y^{1/4}} \\
&= \frac{1}{2}\frac{y^{\frac{1}{4}-\left(\frac{1}{4}\right)}}{x^{\frac{1}{2}-\left(\frac{1}{2}\right)}} \\
&= \frac{1}{2}.
\end{aligned}
$$

This implies that a 1 percent increase in good x yields a 0.5 percent increase in Maria's utility.

- *Utility elasticity of good y.* Using the same process to calculate Maria's utility

26

elasticity of good y, we obtain

$$
\begin{aligned}
\varepsilon_{y,x} &= \frac{\partial u(x,y)}{\partial y} \frac{y}{u(x,y)} \\
&= 5\frac{1}{4}x^{1/2}y^{-3/4}\frac{y}{5x^{1/2}y^{1/4}} \\
&= \frac{1}{4}\frac{y^{-\frac{3}{4}+1-\frac{1}{4}}}{x^{\frac{1}{2}-\left(\frac{1}{2}\right)}} \\
&= \frac{1}{4}.
\end{aligned}
$$

In words, this result says that a 1 percent increase in good y corresponds with a 0.25 percent increase in Maria's utility.

Self-assessment exercise #2.14

SA 2.14 Eric's utility function is $u(x,y) = x^{1/3} + \frac{1}{4}y$. Find his MRS and depict his indifference curve for utility levels $u = 10$ and $u = 20$.

- Calculating Eric's marginal utilities for good x and y, we have $MU_x = \frac{1}{3}x^{-2/3}$ and $MU_y = \frac{1}{4}$. Therefore, his marginal rate of substitution is

$$
MRS_{x,y} = -\frac{MU_x}{MU_y} = -\frac{\frac{1}{3}x^{-2/3}}{\frac{1}{4}} = -\frac{4}{3}x^{-2/3}.
$$

- As before, we can depict Eric's indifference curves by solving for good y in his utility function:
  - First, we subtract $x^{1/3}$ from both sides of the equation, obtaining $\frac{1}{4}y = u - x^{1/3}$.
  - Last, we obtain the function for Eric's indifference curves by multiplying both sides of the equation by 4, yielding

$$
y = 4u - 4x^{1/3}.
$$

Plugging in our two values of u gives us indifference curves

$$
\begin{aligned}
y &= 40 - 4x^{1/3} \quad \text{for } u = 10, \text{ and} \\
y &= 80 - 4x^{1/3} \quad \text{for } u = 20.
\end{aligned}
$$

- Once again, we can derive a couple of bundles to help us draw these indifference curves.
  - For $u = 10$, if we set $x = 0$, good y becomes $y = 40$ units. Likewise, if $x = 8$, good y is $y = 32$ units.
  - For $u = 20$, if we set $x = 0$, good y becomes $y = 80$ units. When $x = 8$, good y is $y = 72$ units.

– Using these points, we can depict the indifference curves in figure 2.8.

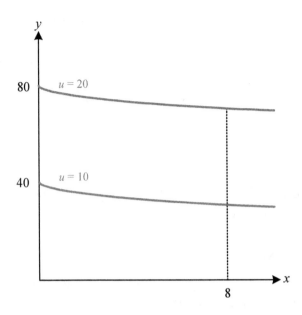

Figure 2.8. Eric's indifference curves.

Self-assessment exercise #2.15

SA 2.15 Ana's utility function is $u(x,y) = 5\,(x-2)^{1/2}\,(y-1)^{1/3}$. Find her marginal utilities and her MRS, and check if it is decreasing in x.

- Starting with Ana's marginal utilities, we must use the chain rule.

   – The marginal utility of good x is

   $$MU_x = \frac{\partial u(x,y)}{\partial x} = \frac{5}{2}(x-2)^{-1/2}(1)(y-1)^{1/3}.$$

   – Likewise, the marginal utility of good y is

   $$MU_y = \frac{\partial u(x,y)}{\partial y} = \frac{5}{3}(x-2)^{1/2}(y-1)^{-2/3}(1).$$

- Putting our two marginal utilities together, we can obtain her marginal rate of substitution,

   $$MRS_{x,y} = -\frac{MU_x}{MU_y} = -\frac{\frac{5}{2}(x-2)^{-1/2}(y-1)^{1/3}}{\frac{5}{3}(x-2)^{1/2}(y-1)^{-2/3}} = -\frac{2}{3}\frac{y-1}{x-2}.$$

   – Since good x (good y) appears solely in the denominator (numerator) of the marginal rate of substitution, the $MRS_{x,y}$ is decreasing (increasing) in good x (good y, respectively).

28

2.2 Solutions to End-of-Chapter Exercises

Exercise #2.1 - Indifference Curves[B]

2.1 Answer the following questions for each of the utility functions in table 2.1.

    (a) Find the marginal utility for good x and y, MU_x and MU_y.

- $u(x, y) = by$:

$$MU_x = \frac{\partial u(x, y)}{\partial x} = 0 \quad \text{and} \quad MU_y = \frac{\partial u(x, y)}{\partial y} = b.$$

Therefore, this consumer enjoys a constant and positive utility from additional units of good y, $MU_y = b$. (Recall that parameter b was assumed to be positive for all utility functions in table 2.1.) In contrast, the consumer does not care about the units of good x she has since her marginal utility is zero, $MU_x = 0$.

- $u(x, y) = ax$:

$$MU_x = \frac{\partial u(x, y)}{\partial x} = a \quad \text{and} \quad MU_y = \frac{\partial u(x, y)}{\partial y} = 0.$$

Therefore, this consumer enjoys a constant and positive utility from additional units of good x, $MU_x = a$. (Recall that parameter a was assumed to be positive for all utility functions in table 2.1.) In contrast, the consumer does not care about the units of good y she has since her marginal utility is zero, $MU_y = 0$.

- $u(x, y) = ax - by$:

$$MU_x = \frac{\partial u(x, y)}{\partial x} = a \quad \text{and} \quad MU_y = \frac{\partial u(x, y)}{\partial y} = -b.$$

Therefore, this consumer enjoys a constant and positive utility from additional units of good x, $MU_x = a$. (Recall that parameters a and b were assumed to be positive for all utility functions in table 2.1.) In contrast, the consumer receives a constant and negative utility from additional units of good y, $MU_y = -b$, which implies that good y is a bad.

- $u(x, y) = ax + by$:

$$MU_x = \frac{\partial u(x, y)}{\partial x} = a \quad \text{and} \quad MU_y = \frac{\partial u(x, y)}{\partial y} = b.$$

Therefore, this consumer enjoys a constant and positive utility from additional units of both goods x and y, $MU_x = a$ and $MU_y = b$, respectively. (Recall that parameters a and b were assumed to be positive for all utility functions in table 2.1.)

- $u(x, y) = A \min\{ax, by\}$:

$$MU_x = \frac{\partial u(x, y)}{\partial x} = Aa \ \text{ if } ax < by, \text{ but } MU_x = 0 \text{ otherwise, and}$$

$$MU_y = \frac{\partial u(x, y)}{\partial y} = Ab \ \text{ if } ax > by, \text{ but } MU_y = 0 \text{ otherwise.}$$

Therefore, this consumer only receives utility from the good that they have less of. When the consumer has relatively less of good x than good y (i.e., when $ax < by$), the consumer enjoys a constant and positive utility from additional units of good x, $MU_x = Aa$, and zero utility from additional units of good y, $MU_y = 0$. For example, if x represents left shoes and y denotes right shoes, and the consumer has more units of left shoes (x), then increasing the number of right shoes (y) can provide her with more pairs of shoes, thus increasing her utility.

On the contrary, when the consumer has relatively less of good y than good x (i.e., when $ax > by$), the consumer enjoys a constant and positive utility from additional units of good y, $MU_y = Ab$, and zero utility from additional units of good x, $MU_x = 0$.

- $u(x, y) = Ax^\alpha y^\beta$:

$$MU_x = \frac{\partial u(x, y)}{\partial x} = \alpha A x^{\alpha-1} y^\beta \quad \text{and} \quad MU_y = \frac{\partial u(x, y)}{\partial y} = \beta A x^\alpha y^{\beta-1}.$$

Therefore, this consumer enjoys a positive utility from additional units of both goods x and y, but the rate at which the utility increases changes depending on the relative consumption levels of both goods.

(b) Are these marginal utilities positive? Are they strictly positive? Connect your results with the properties of monotonicity and strict monotonicity.

- $u(x, y) = by$: In this case, only the marginal utility with respect to y is positive. Since the marginal utility of x is not positive, this utility function is monotonic, but not strictly monotonic; in fact, it is constant in x, implying that the indifference curve is straight (constant slope).
- $u(x, y) = ax$: In this case, only the marginal utility with respect to x is positive. Since the marginal utility of y is not positive, this utility function is monotonic, but not strictly monotonic; in fact, it is constant in x, implying that the indifference curve is straight (constant slope).
- $u(x, y) = ax - by$: In this case, the marginal utility with respect to y is negative. Thus, this utility function is neither monotonic nor strictly monotonic; in fact, it is constant in x, implying that the indifference curve is straight (constant slope).
- $u(x, y) = ax + by$: Since both marginal utilities are positive, this utility function is both monotonic and strictly monotonic; in fact, it is constant in x, implying that the indifference curve is straight (constant slope).
- $u(x, y) = A \min\{ax, by\}$: In this case, the marginal utilities for x and y are not strictly positive, but they are never negative, and one is always positive.

30

Thus, this utility function is monotonic, but not strictly monotonic.

- $u(x, y) = Ax^\alpha y^\beta$: Since both marginal utilities are positive, this utility function is both monotonic and strictly monotonic.

(c) Find $MRS = \frac{MU_x}{MU_y}$. Does MRS increase in the amount of good x?

- $u(x, y) = by$:

$$MRS_{x,y} = \frac{MU_x}{MU_y} = \frac{0}{b} = 0.$$

Therefore, differentiating $MRS_{x,y}$ with respect to x, we obtain

$$\frac{\partial MRS}{\partial x} = 0.$$

The marginal rate of substitution is not increasing in x.

- $u(x, y) = ax$:

$$MRS_{x,y} = \frac{MU_x}{MU_y} = \frac{a}{0}.$$

Therefore, the marginal rate of substitution is not increasing in x.

- $u(x, y) = ax - by$:

$$MRS_{x,y} = \frac{MU_x}{MU_y} = \frac{a}{-b} = -\frac{a}{b}.$$

Therefore, differentiating $MRS_{x,y}$ with respect to x, we obtain

$$\frac{\partial MRS}{\partial x} = 0.$$

The marginal rate of substitution is not increasing in x.

- $u(x, y) = ax + by$:

$$MRS_{x,y} = \frac{MU_x}{MU_y} = \frac{a}{b}.$$

Therefore, differentiating $MRS_{x,y}$ with respect to x, we obtain

$$\frac{\partial MRS}{\partial x} = 0.$$

The marginal rate of substitution is not increasing in x.

- $u(x, y) = A \min\{ax, by\}$:
  The marginal rate of substitution is not well defined when we have perfect complements. Intuitively, the indifference curve is vertical for all points to the left of the kink, horizontal for all points to the right of the kink, but undefined at the kink since we can draw infinitely many tangent lines at the kink, each with a different slope.

- $u(x, y) = Ax^\alpha y^\beta$:

$$MRS_{x,y} = \frac{MU_x}{MU_y} = \frac{\alpha A x^{\alpha-1} y^\beta}{\beta A x^\alpha y^{\beta-1}} = \frac{\alpha y}{\beta x}.$$

Therefore, differentiating $MRS_{x,y}$ with respect to x we obtain

$$\frac{\partial MRS}{\partial x} = -\frac{\alpha y}{\beta x^2} < 0.$$

The marginal rate of substitution is decreasing in x.

(d) Depict an indifference curve reaching a utility level of $u = 10$ and another of $u = 20$. Do the indifference curves cross either axis?

- $u(x, y) = by$: In this case, the indifference curves take the form $y = \frac{u}{b}$, which is unaffected by the value of x. Graphically, this means that indifference curves cross the vertical axis, as illustrated in figure 2.9.

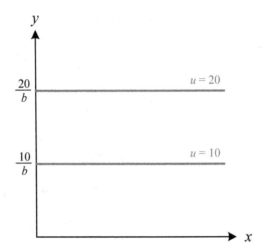

Figure 2.9. Horizontal indifference curves.

$u(x, y) = ax$: In this case, the indifference curves take the form $x = \frac{u}{a}$, which is unaffected by the value of y. Graphically, this means that indifference curves cross the horizontal axis of figure 2.10.

32

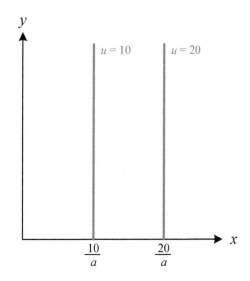

Figure 2.10. Vertical indifference curves.

- $u(x, y) = ax - by$: In this case, the indifference curve takes the form $y = \frac{u}{b} + \frac{a}{b}x$, which is increasing in the value of x. Intuitively, an increase in good x increases the individual's utility, so she needs to reduce her consumption of good y to maintain her utility unchanged. Graphically, this means that, as we move rightward (higher values of x in figure 2.11), we need to move downward (lower values of y) along a given indifference curve to keep the consumer's utility level unaffected.

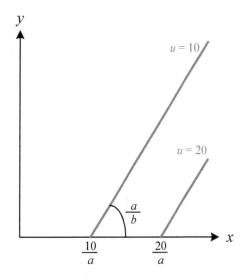

Figure 2.11. Perfectly "bad" substitutes.

- $u(x, y) = ax + by$: In this case, the indifference curve takes the form $y = \frac{u}{b} - \frac{a}{b}x$, which is decreasing in the value of x. Graphically, this means that indifference curves cross both axes. Intuitively, this consumer is completely indifferent with a proportional reduction of b units of good y in exchange for a units of

33

good x. It does not matter how much of either good they already have; they will always be indifferent between trades of that proportion. Figure 2.12 depicts two indifferent curves: one evaluated at $u = 10$, so its vertical intercept becomes $y = \frac{10}{b}$, and another evaluated at $u = 20$, with vertical intercept $y = \frac{20}{b}$.

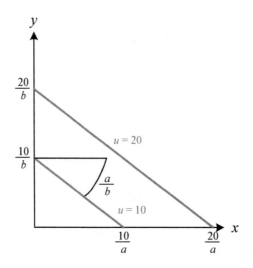

Figure 2.12. Perfect substitutes.

- $u(x, y) = A\min\{ax, by\}$: In this case, the indifference curves cross neither axis, as depicted in figure 2.13.

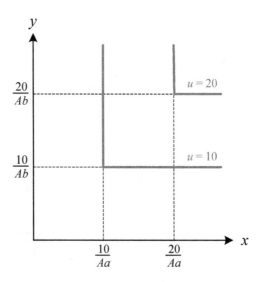

Figure 2.13. Perfect complements.

- $u(x, y) = Ax^{\alpha}y^{\beta}$: In this case, we can derive our indifference curves by solving this expression for y,

$$y = \left(\frac{u}{Ax^{\alpha}}\right)^{\frac{1}{\beta}}.$$

Intuitively, consumers' utility shifts outward as they consume more units of

34

either good x or good y. They are also willing to trade units of good x for units of good y, but the ratio they require to remain indifferent increases as they have less of their respective good. In addition, the parameters α and β determine how far the indifference curves shift as the consumption level of both good increases, as well as the relative curvature of the indifference curve. Figure 2.14 plots this curve evaluated at $u = 10$ and $u = 20$ where $A = 1$, $\alpha = 0.5$, and $\beta = 0.5$.

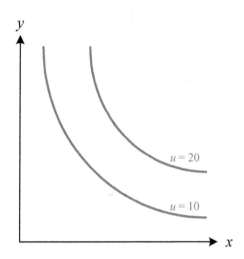

Figure 2.14. Cobb-Douglas preferences.

(e) Provide an example of goods that you think can be represented with each utility function in table 2.1.

- $u(x, y) = by$: Good x could be air, whereas good y is water.
- $u(x, y) = ax$: Good x could be water, whereas good y is air.
- $u(x, y) = ax - by$: Good x could be water, whereas good y is garbage.
- $u(x, y) = ax + by$: Goods x and y could be different brands of milk.
- $u(x, y) = A \min\{ax, by\}$: Goods x and y could be left shoes and right shoes, respectively.

Exercise #2.3 - One Way or Another[B]

2.3 Consider an individual with utility function

$$u(x, y) = \min\{x + 2y, 2x + y\}.$$

Plot her indifference curve at a utility level of $u = 10$ units. Interpret.

- For this utility function, goods x and y behave with aspects of both perfect substitutes and perfect complements. To plot this curve, we first treat this as if it were two separate curves,

$$x + 2y = 10 \quad \text{and} \quad 2x + y = 10.$$

35

Solving these both for y, we have

$$y = 5 - \frac{1}{2}x \quad \text{and} \quad y = 10 - 2x.$$

Figure 2.15 plots both curves.

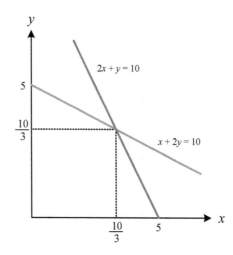

Figure 2.15. Substitutable complements–I.

Figure 2.16 combines the curves together, taking whichever curve is vertically above the other curve to form our indifference curve. This may seem counterintuitive since we are looking for the minimum of our respective functions. Intuitively, bundles with more of a single good (at the expense of the other good) reach a higher utility level when we are concerned about consuming our goods in a fixed proportion.

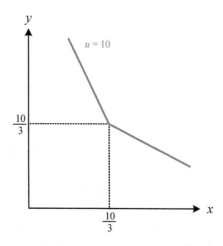

Figure 2.16. Substitutable complements–II.

Exercise #2.5 - Cobb-Douglas[A]

2.5 Consider an individual with the Cobb-Douglas utility function

$$u(x, y) = \sqrt{x}\sqrt{y}.$$

Assume that her income is $I = \$120$, the price of good x is $p_x = \$4$, and the price of good y is $p_y = \$10$.

(a) Find the marginal utility of good x, MU_x, and that of good y, MU_y.

- We calculate the marginal utilities by differentiating with respect to each respective variable,

$$MU_x = \frac{\partial u(x, y)}{\partial x} = \frac{\sqrt{y}}{2\sqrt{x}} \quad \text{and} \quad MU_y = \frac{\partial u(x, y)}{\partial y} = \frac{\sqrt{x}}{2\sqrt{y}}.$$

(b) Given the results in part (a), does this utility function satisfy monotonicity? What about strict monotonicity?

- Since both marginal utilities are strictly positive when the individual consumes a positive amount of both goods, this utility function satisfies both monotonicity and strict monotonicity. If the individual consumes zero units of one (or both) goods, the utility function satisfies monotonicity, but violates strict monotonicity.

(c) Using the marginal utilities you found in part (a), find the MRS.

- The marginal rate of substitution can be found by taking the ratio of our marginal utility with respect to x to our marginal utility with respect to y,

$$MRS_{x,y} = \frac{MU_x}{MU_y} = \frac{\frac{\sqrt{y}}{2\sqrt{x}}}{\frac{\sqrt{x}}{2\sqrt{y}}} = \frac{\sqrt{y}\left(2\sqrt{y}\right)}{\sqrt{x}\left(2\sqrt{x}\right)} = \frac{2y^{\frac{1}{2}+\frac{1}{2}}}{2x^{\frac{1}{2}+\frac{1}{2}}} = \frac{y}{x}.$$

Exercise #2.7 - Perfect Substitutes[A]

2.7 Consider a consumer with utility function $u(x, y) = ax + by$.

(a) For a given utility level $u(x, y) = 10$, find the equation of the indifference curve. (*Hint*: Set $u = 10$ and solve for y.)

- Setting our utility function equal to 10 yields,

$$ax + by = 10.$$

Solving for y, we obtain

$$y = \frac{10}{b} - \frac{a}{b}x$$

which is depicted in figure 2.17.

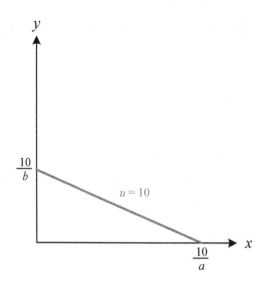

Figure 2.17. Plotting indifference curves.

To find the vertical intercept of this indifference curve, we simply set $x = 0$ and find $y = \frac{10}{b}$. Likewise, to find the horizontal intercept, we set $y = 0$ and find $x = \frac{10}{a}$.

(b) Find the marginal utilities MU_x and MU_y.

- We calculate the marginal utilities by differentiating with respect to each variable,

$$MU_x = \frac{\partial u(x, y)}{\partial x} = a \quad \text{and} \quad MU_y = \frac{\partial u(x, y)}{\partial y} = b.$$

(c) Find MRS. Does it increase in the amount of good x?

- The marginal rate of substitution can be found by taking the ratio of our marginal utility with respect to x to our marginal utility with respect to y,

$$MRS_{x,y} = \frac{MU_x}{MU_y} = \frac{a}{b}.$$

The marginal rate of substitution is constant, so it does not increase in the amount of good x.

(d) Does this utility function satisfy strict monotonicity? What about monotonicity? And local nonsatiation?

- Since both marginal utilities are strictly positive, this utility function satisfies both monotonicity and strict monotonicity. Since this utility function is monotonic, it also satisfies local nonsatiation.

Exercise #2.9 - Increasing Transformations[B]

2.9 Chelsea has the following Cobb-Douglas utility function: $u(x, y) = xy$. Assume that we apply any of the following transformations. Show that when we consider increasing transformations, Chelsea's ordering of bundles $A = (1, 2)$ and $B = (3, 8)$ is unaffected (i.e., she still prefers B to A). When we consider decreasing transformations, show that Chelsea's ordering of bundles A and B may be affected.

(a) $v(x, y) = [u(x, y)]^2$

- Chelsea's new utility function is

$$v(x, y) = [u(x, y)]^2 = x^2 y^2.$$

Plugging in her two bundles gives her utilities,

$$\text{Bundle } A \quad : \quad v(1, 2) = 1^2 2^2 = 4, \quad \text{and}$$
$$\text{Bundle } B \quad : \quad v(3, 8) = 3^2 8^2 = 576.$$

Since B still provides a higher utility than A, Chelsea's ordering of bundles is unaffected.

(b) $v(x, y) = \ln[u(x, y)]$

- Chelsea's new utility function is

$$v(x, y) = \ln[u(x, y)] = \ln(xy).$$

Plugging in her two bundles gives her utilities,

$$\text{Bundle } A \quad : \quad v(1, 2) = \ln(1 \times 2) = 1.097, \quad \text{and}$$
$$\text{Bundle } B \quad : \quad v(3, 8) = \ln(3 \times 8) = 3.178.$$

Since B still provides a higher utility than A, Chelsea's ordering of bundles is unaffected.

(c) $v(x, y) = 5[u(x, y)]$

- Chelsea's new utility function is

$$v(x, y) = 5[u(x, y)] = 5xy$$

Plugging in her two bundles gives her utilities,

$$\text{Bundle } A \quad : \quad v(1, 2) = 5 \times 1 \times 2 = 10, \quad \text{and}$$
$$\text{Bundle } B \quad : \quad v(3, 8) = 5 \times 3 \times 8 = 120.$$

Since B still provides a higher utility than A, Chelsea's ordering of bundles is unaffected.

(d) $v(x, y) = [u(x, y)]^{-1}$

- Chelsea's new utility function is

$$v(x, y) = [u(x, y)]^{-1} = \frac{1}{xy}.$$

Plugging in her two bundles gives her utilities,

$$\text{Bundle } A \quad : \quad v(1,2) = \frac{1}{1 \times 2} = \frac{1}{2}, \text{ and}$$
$$\text{Bundle } B \quad : \quad v(3,8) = \frac{1}{3 \times 8} = \frac{1}{24}.$$

Now, A provides a higher utility level than B, and thus Chelsea's ordering of bundles is reversed. This occurs because the transformation we apply on the utility function is not increasing.

(e) $v(x,y) = 7[u(x,y)] - 2$

- Chelsea's new utility function is

$$v(x,y) = 7[u(x,y)] - 2 = 7xy - 2.$$

Plugging in her two bundles gives her utilities,

$$\text{Bundle } A \quad : \quad v(1,2) = 7 \times 1 \times 2 - 2 = 12, \text{ and}$$
$$\text{Bundle } B \quad : \quad v(3,8) = 7 \times 3 \times 8 - 2 = 166.$$

Since B still provides a higher utility than A, Chelsea's ordering of bundles is unaffected. This utility transformation, despite having a -2, is still increasing in $u(x,y)$. Therefore, as long as the utility transformation is increasing in $u(x,y)$, we can guarantee the same ordering of bundles as with the original utility function.

Exercise #2.11 - Finding Properties–II^C

2.11 Repeat exercise 2.10, but assume now that Eric's preferences are represented with the following (Stone-Geary) utility function: $u(x,y) = 2\left(x^3 - 1\right)\left(y^2 - 2\right)$.

(a) Find Eric's marginal utility for books, MU_x, and for computers, MU_y.

- We calculate Eric's marginal utilities by differentiating with respect to each respective variable,

$$MU_x = \frac{\partial u(x,y)}{\partial x} = 6x^2(y^2 - 2) \quad \text{and} \quad MU_y = \frac{\partial u(x,y)}{\partial y} = 4(x^3 - 1)y.$$

(b) Are his preferences monotonic (i.e., weakly increasing in both goods)?

- Neither of Eric's marginal utilities are strictly positive. For instance, if $y < \sqrt{2}$, Eric's marginal utility with respect to x is negative. Likewise, if $x < 1$, Eric's marginal utility with respect to y is negative. Thus, Eric's preferences are not monotonic.

(c) For a given utility level $\bar{u}$, solve the utility function for y to obtain Eric's indifference curve.

- Setting Eric's utility at $\bar{u}$, we obtain

$$2\left(x^3 - 1\right)\left(y^2 - 2\right) = \bar{u}.$$

Solving Eric's utility function for y, first we divide both sides of this expression by $2(x^3 - 1)$, obtaining

$$y^2 - 2 = \frac{\bar{u}}{2\left(x^3 - 1\right)}.$$

Adding 2 to both sides of this expression yields

$$y^2 = \frac{\bar{u}}{2\left(x^3 - 1\right)} + 2,$$

and last, taking the square root of both sides of this expression, we have the equation for Eric's indifference curve,

$$y = \sqrt{\frac{\bar{u}}{2(x^3 - 1)} + 2}.$$

(d) Find Eric's MRS between x and y. Interpret your results.

- Eric's marginal rate of substitution can be found by taking the ratio of his marginal utility with respect to x to his marginal utility with respect to y,

$$MRS_{x,y} = \frac{MU_x}{MU_y} = \frac{6x^2(y^2 - 2)}{4(x^3 - 1)y} = \frac{3x^2(y^2 - 2)}{2(x^3 - 1)y}.$$

Eric's marginal rate of substitution implies that for each additional unit of books he receives, he must be compensated with a higher proportion of units of good computers in order to give up any further units of books.

(e) Are his preferences convex (i.e., bowed in toward the origin)?

- The convexity of Eric's preferences can be found by differentiating his marginal rate of substitution with respect to x,

$$\begin{aligned}
\frac{dMRS_{x,y}}{dx} &= \frac{12x(x^3 - 1)y(y^2 - 2) - 18x^4 y(y^2 - 2)}{[2(x^3 - 1)y]^2} \\
&= -\frac{6x(x^3 + 2)y(y^2 - 2)}{[2(x^3 - 1)y]^2},
\end{aligned}$$

which is negative $(x^3 - 1) > 0$ and $(y^2 - 2) > 0$, which simplifies to $x > 1$ and $y > \sqrt{2}$, and when $(x^3 - 1) < 0$ and $(y^2 - 2) < 0$, which simplifies to $x < 1$ and $y < \sqrt{2}$. In these two cases, Eric's preferences are convex.

- When, instead, $x < 1$ or $y < \sqrt{2}$ hold (but not both), Eric does not meet his minimum consumption requirements for one of the goods, and an increase in x increases his $MRS_{x,y}$, entailing that his preferences are concave (bowed-out from the origin).

(f) Consider a given utility level of 10 utils. Plot his indifference curve in this case.

- Plotting Eric's indifference curve, we obtain figure 2.18.

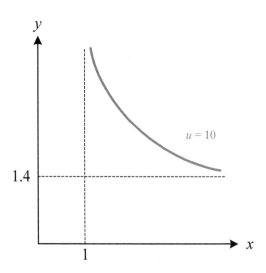

Figure 2.18. Stone-Geary preferences.

Exercise #2.13 - Finding Properties–IV^B

2.13 Repeat the previous exercise, but assume now that Eric's preferences are represented with the following utility function for two goods regarded as complements in consumption: $u(x, y) = \min\{3x, 4y\}$.

(a) Find Eric's marginal utility for books, MU_x, and for computers, MU_y.

- We calculate Eric's marginal utilities by differentiating with respect to each respective variable,

$$MU_x = \frac{\partial u(x, y)}{\partial x} = 3 \text{ if } 3x < 4y, \text{ but } MU_x = 0 \text{ otherwise,}$$

and

$$MU_y = \frac{\partial u(x, y)}{\partial y} = 4 \text{ if } 3x > 4y, \text{ but } MU_y = 0 \text{ otherwise.}$$

(b) Are his preferences monotonic (i.e., weakly increasing in both goods)?

- Since both of Eric's marginal utilities are weakly positive, his preferences are monotonic.

(c) For a given utility level, $\bar{u}$, solve the utility function for y to obtain Eric's indifference curve.

- Setting Eric's utility at $\bar{u}$, we obtain

$$\min\{3x, 4y\} = \bar{u}$$

If $3x < 4y$, we have $\min\{3x, 4y\} = 3x$. That is, $3x = \bar{u}$. Solving for x, we obtain the equation of the indifference curve in this case, $x = \frac{\bar{u}}{3}$. In contrast, when $3x > 4y$, we have $\min\{3x, 4y\} = 4y$. That is, $4y = \bar{u}$. Solving for y, we obtain the equation of the indifference curve, $y = \frac{\bar{u}}{4}$. Solving Eric's utility function for y, we have that his indifference curve is

$$\begin{cases} x = \frac{\bar{u}}{3} \text{ if } 3x < 4y, \text{ and} \\ y = \frac{\bar{u}}{4} \text{ if } 3x > 4y. \end{cases}$$

(d) Find Peter's MRS between x and y. Interpret your results.

- Eric's marginal rate of substitution can be found by taking the ratio of his marginal utility with respect to x to his marginal utility with respect to y,

$$MRS_{x,y} = \frac{MU_x}{MU_y} = \begin{cases} +\infty \text{ if } 3x < 4y, \text{ and} \\ 0 \text{ if } 3x > 4y. \end{cases}$$

Eric's marginal rate of substitution implies that he wants to consume books and computers in fixed amounts, specifically four books to three computers. Eric views these goods as perfect complements.

(e) Are his preferences convex (i.e., bowed in toward the origin)?

- Since Eric's indifference curves are L shaped, his preferences are convex.

(f) Consider a given utility level of 10 utils. Plot his indifference curve in this case.

- Plotting Eric's indifference curve, we obtain figure 2.19.

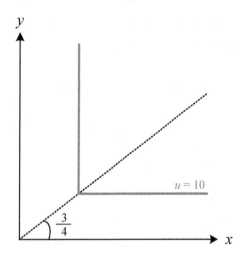

Figure 2.19. Perfect complements.

Exercise #2.15 - Guilty Preferences[B]

2.15 Repeat exercise 2.14, but assume that Peter's utility function is now

$$u(x, y) = 4x - (x - y);$$

that is, he suffers from guilt when he owns more books than his friend ($x > y$). Relative to envy aversion in exercise 2.14, guilt aversion reduces Peter's utility less dramatically. Stated in words, Peter cares more about feeling envy than about feeling guilt.

(a) Find Peter's marginal utility for the books he owns, MU_x, and for his friend's, MU_y.

- We calculate Peter's marginal utilities by differentiating with respect to each respective variable,

$$MU_x = \frac{\partial u(x,y)}{\partial x} = 3 \quad \text{and} \quad MU_y = \frac{\partial u(x,y)}{\partial y} = 1.$$

(b) Are his preferences monotonic (i.e., weakly increasing in both goods)?

- Since Peter's marginal utility is strictly positive in both goods, his preferences are monotonic.

(c) For a given utility level, $\bar{u}$, solve the utility function for y to obtain Peter's indifference curve.

- Setting Peter's utility at $\bar{u}$, we obtain

$$4x - (x - y) = \bar{u}.$$

Solving Peter's utility function for y, we have

$$y = \bar{u} - 3x.$$

(d) Find Peter's MRS between x and y. Interpret your results.

- Peter's marginal rate of substitution can be found by taking the ratio of his marginal utility with respect to x to his marginal utility with respect to y,

$$MRS_{x,y} = \frac{MU_x}{MU_y} = \frac{3}{1} = 3.$$

Peter's marginal rate of substitution implies that while he always wants to consume more of his own books, he wants his friend to consume more books too so he does not feel bad.

(e) Are his preferences convex (i.e., bowed in toward the origin)?

- The convexity of Peter's preferences can be found by differentiating his marginal rate of substitution with respect to x,

$$\frac{dMRS_{x,y}}{dx} = 0.$$

Since this is not negative, Peter's marginal rate of substitution is not decreasing in x, which implies that Peter's preferences are not convex.

(f) Consider a given utility level of 10 utils. Plot his indifference curve in this case.

- Plotting Peter's indifference curve, we obtain figure 2.20.

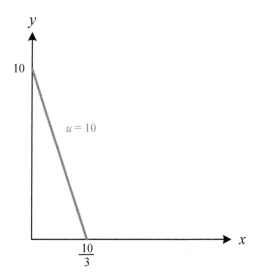

Figure 2.20. Guilty preferences.

To find the vertical intercept of this indifference curve, we simply set $x = 0$ and find $y = 10$. Likewise, to find the horizontal intercept, we set $y = 0$ and find $x = \frac{10}{3}$.

Exercise #2.17 - Protein Preferences[A]

2.17 John is out to dinner and is presented a menu of items that contains a beef dish and a chicken dish and John chooses the beef dish. Before the server walks away with John's order, she remembers that the menu is actually out of date, and a fish dish is available, as well.

(a) Suppose that John remains with his original order of the beef dish. What does this imply about John's preferences for all three dishes?

- This implies that John's preference ordering is either

$$Beef \succ Chicken \succ Fish$$

or

$$Beef \succ Fish \succ Chicken.$$

We are unable to determine whether John prefers chicken to fish or fish to chicken.

(b) Suppose that John switches his order to the fish dish. What does this imply about John's preferences for all three dishes?

- In this case, John's switch implies that

$$Fish \succ Beef \succ Chicken.$$

Switching to the fish dish is perfectly rational for John, since it was not available before.

45

(c) Suppose that John switches his order to the chicken dish. What does this imply about John's preferences for all three dishes?

- When John switches to the chicken dish, his preferences are now

$$Chicken \succ Beef \succ Chicken$$

which is an intransitivity. This would violate WARP and imply that John's preferences are not rational. As a note, we are unable to rank the fish dish anywhere, as there is nothing to compare it to.

Exercise #2.19 - Eating Pizza[A]

2.19 While out for dinner one night, Peter orders a large pepperoni pizza for himself. After eating the first slice, he remarks that the pizza is delicious, and he'll have another slice. Slices two and three continue to receive accolades, but less so, with Peter expressing that he is starting to feel full after the third slice. Peter decides to have a fourth slice, after which he decides that he is full and prefers to eat no more pizza.

(a) What is happening to Peter regarding his utility?

- Since Peter receives less additional satisfaction with each additional slice of pizza he eats, Peter is experiencing diminishing marginal utility.

(b) Suppose that Peter was dared to eat a fifth slice of pizza and accepted. Afterward, he complains that he feels ill and leaves for the bathroom (rather hurriedly). What has happened to Peter's utility?

- At this point, Peter's utility has decreased (as he is now sick). This would imply that Peter is experiencing negative marginal utility, as the next slice of pizza decreases his total utility.

Chapter 3 - Consumer Choice

3.1 Solutions to Self-Assessment Exercises

Self-assessment exercise #3.1

SA 3.1 Eric faces prices $p_x = \$13$ and $p_y = \$18$, and income $I = \$250$. Plot his budget line, finding the vertical and horizontal intercepts, and its slope. Interpret.

- With Eric's prices and income, we find that the equation of his budget line is

$$13x + 18y \leq 250.$$

If we let this equation hold with equality (i.e., $13x + 18y = 250$), we can solve it for y to help us plot the budget line.

- First, we subtract $13x$ from both sides of the equation, $18y = 250 - 13x$.
- Last, we divide both sides of the equation by 18 to obtain our budget line, $y = \frac{250}{18} - \frac{13}{18}x$, or

$$y = 13.89 - 0.72x.$$

- To help us plot this line, we can set $x = 0$ to find the vertical intercept, $y = 13.89$ units. Likewise, we can set $y = 0$ to find the horizontal intercept,

$$0 = 13.89 - 0.72x,$$

or $13.89 = 0.72x$ which, solving for x, yields $x = \frac{13.89}{0.72} = 19.23$ units. From here, we can connect the dots to obtain our budget line, as depicted in figure 3.1.

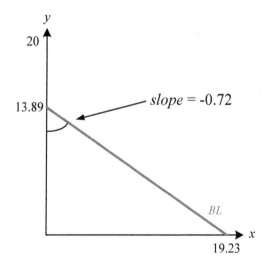

Figure 3.1. Budget line $y = 13.89 - 0.72x$.

- Interpreting this budget line, if Eric spends all of his income on good y, he is able to purchase 13.89 units of good y. Likewise, if Eric spends all of his income on good x, he is able to purchase 19.23 units of good x. He can purchase numerous other combinations of goods x and y, however, and starting from the case where he purchases 13.89 units of good y, for every unit of good x that Eric purchases, he must purchase 0.72 less units of good y.

Self-assessment exercise #3.2

SA 3.2 Consider self-assessment 3.1 again. If Eric's income increases to $I' = \$540$, find his budget line. What are the new vertical and horizontal intercepts? Does the slope of the budget line change?

- Since the income increased to $I' = \$540$, the equation for Eric's budget line becomes
$$13x + 18y \leq 540.$$

Again, by letting this equation hold with equality, we can solve it for y to help us analyze the slope of the budget line.

- Once again, we start by subtracting $13x$ from both sides of the equation, $18y = 540 - 13x$.
- Then we obtain our budget line by dividing both sides of the equation by 18, $y = \frac{540}{18} - \frac{13}{18}y$, or
$$y = 30 - 0.72x.$$

- With this new budget line, we can observe that it has exactly the same slope as the budget line where income was $I = \$250$. This is because the slope is determined by the relative prices (i.e., the price ratio $\frac{p_x}{p_y}$), which have not changed under this new budget line.

  - We can use the same technique as before to calculate our vertical and horizontal intercepts. Setting $x = 0$ provides our vertical intercept of $y = 30$ units. Setting $y = 0$ provides our horizontal intercept of $0 = 30 - 0.72x$, or after solving for x, $x = \frac{30}{0.72} = 41.53$ units. This new budget line is depicted with the original budget line from self-assessment 3.1 in figure 3.2.

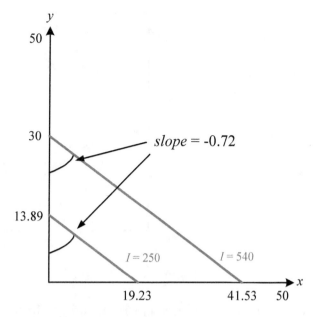

Figure 3.2. Budget line $y = 30 - 0.72x$.

Self-assessment exercise #3.3

SA 3.3 Consider Eric's situation in self-assessment 3.1 again. If the price of good x doubles from $p_x = \$13$ to $p'_x = \$26$, while p_y and I are unaffected, what is the new position of Eric's budget line? What if, instead, the price of good y doubles from $p_y = \$18$ to $p'_y = \$36$, while p_x and I are unchanged?

- *Price of good x doubles.* When the price of good x doubles, Eric's budget line becomes

$$26x + 18y \leq 250.$$

When this equation holds with equality, we can set one of our variables equal to zero to find our intercepts.

– Setting $x = 0$ provides our vertical intercept of $y = \frac{250}{18} = 13.89$ units. Likewise setting $y = 0$ provides our horizontal intercept of $x = \frac{250}{26} = 9.62$ units. This new budget line is depicted with the original budget line from self-assessment 3.1 in figure 3.3.

49

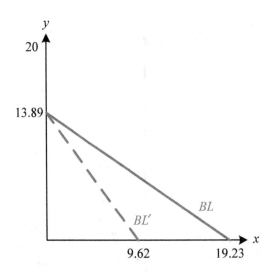

Figure 3.3. Budget line $y = 13.89 - 1.44x$.

– While the vertical intercept is unchanged from before, our horizontal intercept has been halved (which should make sense since the price doubled). As a result, the slope of our budget line doubles since now we must give up twice as much of a unit of good y to purchase one more unit of good x.

• *Price of good y doubles.* When the price of good y doubles, Eric's budget line now becomes

$$13x + 36y \leq 250.$$

Following the same steps as before, we can find the intercepts by letting this equation hold with equality and setting each of our variables equal to zero.

– Setting $x = 0$ provides our vertical intercept of $y = \frac{250}{36} = 6.94$ units. Once again setting $y = 0$ provides our horizontal intercept of $x = \frac{250}{13} = 19.23$ units. This new budget line is depicted with the original budget line from self-assessment exercise 3.1 in figure 3.4.

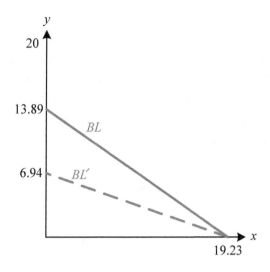

Figure 3.4. Budget line $y = 6.94 - 0.36x$.

- Now the horizontal intercept is unchanged from before while the vertical intercept has been halved due to the price of good y doubling. This causes the slope of the budget line to be halved as Eric no longer has to give up as much of good y to purchase one more unit of good x.

Self-assessment exercise #3.4

SA 3.4 Chelsea has utility function $u(x,y) = x^{1/2}y^{1/4}$, facing prices $p_x = \$3$ and $p_y = \$2$, and income $I = \$16$. Using the same steps as in example 3.2, find Chelsea's optimal consumption of goods x and y.

- *Step 1.* To solve for Chelsea's optimal consumption, first we must use the tangency condition, $\frac{MU_x}{MU_y} = \frac{p_x}{p_y}$.

  - For the left-hand side, we calculate the ratio of our marginal utilities, where $MU_x = \frac{\partial u(x,y)}{\partial x} = \frac{1}{2}x^{-1/2}y^{1/4}$ and $MU_y = \frac{\partial u(x,y)}{\partial y} = \frac{1}{4}x^{1/2}y^{-3/4}$. Therefore,

$$\frac{MU_x}{MU_y} = \frac{\frac{1}{2}x^{-1/2}y^{1/4}}{\frac{1}{4}x^{1/2}y^{-3/4}} = \frac{2y}{x}.$$

  - For the right-hand side, it is simply the ratio of the prices, $\frac{p_x}{p_y} = \frac{3}{2}$.
  - Setting them equal to one another gives

$$\frac{2y}{x} = \frac{3}{2},$$

  which we can rearrange to obtain $4y = 3x$. Since this contains both x and y we move on to step 2a.

- *Step 2a.* Next, we use Chelsea's budget line, $3x + 2y = 16$ and substitute $4y$ for

51

$3x$, obtaining

$$\underbrace{4y}_{3x} + 2y = 16.$$

- – Combining terms, we have $6y = 16$, and we can divide both sides of this equation to obtain the amount of good y that Chelsea consumes, $y = 2.67$ units. With a positive value of y, we can move on to step 4.

- **Step 4.** Last, we return to our tangency condition to determine how much of good x Chelsea consumes.

  - – Dividing both sides of the tangency condition by 3, we have $x = \frac{4}{3}y$. Plugging in our value for y gives

  $$x = \frac{4}{3}(2.67) = 3.56 \text{ units.}$$

Self-assessment exercise #3.5

SA 3.5 Repeat the analysis of example 3.3, but assume now that prices change to $p_x = \$2$ and $p_y = \$1$. How are the results affected?

- **Step 1.** Once again, we start by finding the tangency condition.

  - – Since nothing has changed about the utility functions, our ratio of marginal utilities is unchanged; that is,

  $$\frac{MU_x}{MU_y} = \frac{y+7}{x}.$$

  - – With our new prices, we have a new price ration, $\frac{p_x}{p_y} = \frac{2}{1} = 2$.
  - – Setting them equal to one another gives us

  $$\frac{y+7}{x} = 2,$$

  which rearranges to $y+7 = 2x$. Since we have both x and y in this expression, we move on to step 2a.

- **Step 2a.** Using our budget line, $2x + y = 10$, we substitute $y + 7$ for $2x$, obtaining

  $$\underbrace{(y+7)}_{2x} + y = 10,$$

  or $2y = 3$. Dividing both sides of this expression gives us our total consumption of good y, $y = \frac{3}{2} = 1.5$ units. Since this value is positive, we can jump to step 4.

- **Step 4.** Last, we use our tangency condition to find our value of x.

  - – Dividing both sides of the tangency condition by 2 gives us $x = \frac{1}{2}y + 3.5$.

Plugging in our value of $y = \frac{3}{2}$ yields

$$x = \frac{1}{2}\underbrace{\left(\frac{3}{2}\right)}_{y} + 3.5 = 4.25 \text{ units.}$$

- Intuitively, since good y has become much cheaper relative to good x, the consumer decides to incorporate some of good y into their consumption bundle.

Self-assessment exercise #3.6

SA 3.6 Eric's utility function is $u(x, y) = 3x + 4y$ and faces prices $p_x = \$1$ and $p_y = \$2.5$ and income $I = \$23$. Comparing his $MRS_{x,y}$ and the price ratio, find his optimal consumption of goods x and y.

- First, we need to calculate Eric's marginal rate of substitution,

$$MRS_{x,y} = \frac{MU_x}{MU_y} = \frac{3}{4} = 0.75,$$

and compare it to the ratio of prices,

$$\frac{p_x}{p_y} = \frac{1}{2.5} = \frac{2}{5} = 0.4.$$

- Since $\frac{3}{4} > \frac{2}{5}$, Eric receives more benefit by solely consuming good x. Alternatively, the "bang for the buck" he obtains from good x, $\frac{MU_x}{p_x} = \frac{3}{1} = 3$, is larger than that for good y, $\frac{MU_y}{p_y} = \frac{4}{2.5} = 1.6$, inducing him to keep increasing his purchases of good x, while reducing those of good y, until he only consumes the former.
- In this case, Eric can consume

$$x = \frac{I}{p_x} = \frac{23}{1} = 23 \text{ units}$$

of good x and no units of good y. This budget line and its associated maximum utility are depicted in figure 3.5.

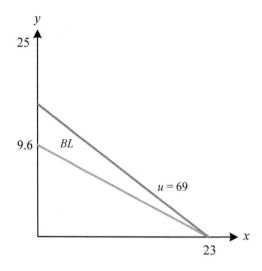

Figure 3.5. Perfect substitutes corner solution.

Self-assessment exercise #3.7

SA 3.7 John's utility function is $u(x, y) = 5\min\{2x, 3y\}$ and he faces prices $p_x = \$1$ and $p_y = \$2$ and income $I = \$100$. Using the previous argument, find his optimal consumption of goods x and y.

- Since we cannot define John's marginal rate of substitution, we must use the fact that John prefers to consume goods x and y in fixed proportions to maximize his utility (i.e., the two arguments inside the min operator must coincide, $2x = 3y$) or, after dividing both sides by 2,

$$x = \frac{3}{2}y.$$

This is the kink of John's indifference curves, as depicted in the following figure. This budget line and its associated maximum utility are depicted in figure 3.6.

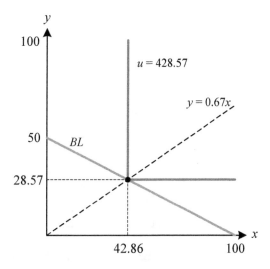

Figure 3.6. Perfect complements optimal consumption.

- Using the condition we found above, $x = \frac{3}{2}y$, and John's budget line, $x + 2y = 100$, we can substitute $\frac{3}{2}y$ for x, giving the equation

$$\underbrace{\frac{3}{2}y}_{x} + 2y = 100.$$

  - Combining terms on the left-hand side of the equation gives us $\frac{7}{2}y = 100$. Dividing both sides of this expression by $\frac{7}{2}$ provides our equilibrium consumption level of good y, $y = 28.57$ units.

- Returning to our condition for John's consumption bundle, $x = \frac{3}{2}y$, we can plug in our value of $y = 28.57$ to find our equilibrium consumption level of good x,

$$x = \frac{3}{2}\underbrace{(28.57)}_{y} = 42.86 \text{ units.}$$

Self-assessment exercise #3.8

SA 3.8 Consider figures 3.6a–3.6d again. Assume for each figure that bundle A lies at the crossing point between budget lines BL and BL'. How are the results of example 3.4 affected? What if B is the bundle lying at the crossing point between BL and BL'?

- When bundle A lies at the crossing point between budget lines BL and BL', it is always affordable under both sets of prices.

  - Figure 3.6a. Since both bundles are affordable under BL, the premise of WARP is satisfied. However, since bundle A is affordable under BL', WARP is violated.

55

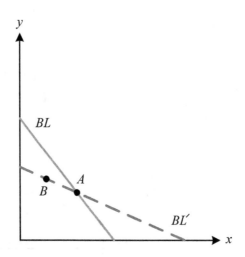

Figure 3.7a. Reproduction of figure 3.6a in the textbook.

- Figure 3.6b. Since both bundles are affordable under BL, the premise of WARP is satisfied. As before, since bundle A is affordable under BL', WARP is violated. See figure 3.7a for a visual explanation.

- Figure 3.6c. Since bundle B is not affordable under BL, the premise of WARP is not satisfied, so WARP is not violated.

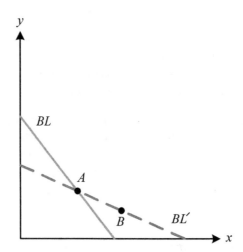

Figure 3.7b. Reproduction of figure 3.6c in the textbook.

- Figure 3.6d. Once again, since bundle B is not affordable under BL, the premise of WARP is not satisfied, so WARP is not violated. See figure 3.7b for a visual explanation.

- When bundle B lies at the crossing point between budget lines BL and BL', it is always affordable under both sets of prices.

  - Figure 3.6a. Since both bundles are affordable under BL, the premise of WARP is satisfied. Likewise, since bundle A is not affordable under BL', WARP holds.

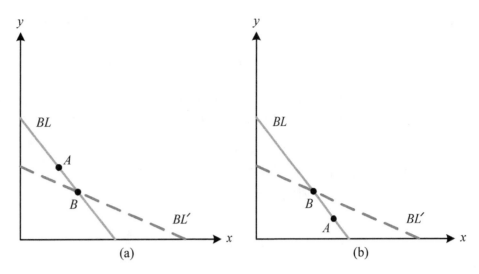

Figures 3.8a and 3.8b. Reproduction of figures 3.6a and 3.6b in the textbook.

- Figure 3.6b. Since both bundles are affordable under BL, the premise of WARP is satisfied. However, since bundle A is also affordable under BL', WARP is violated. See figure 3.8a for a visual explanation.

- Figure 3.6c. Since both bundles are affordable under BL, the premise of WARP is satisfied. Likewise, since bundle A is not affordable under BL', WARP holds.

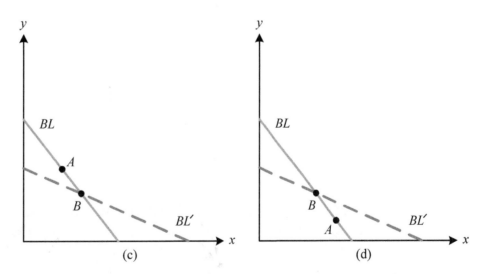

Figures 3.8c and 3.8d. Reproduction of figures 3.6c and 3.6d in the textbook.

- Figure 3.6d. Since both bundles are affordable under BL, the premise of WARP is satisfied. However, since bundle A is also affordable under BL', WARP is violated.

SA 3.9 Eric's utility function is $u(x,y) = x^{\frac{1}{2}}y^{\frac{1}{2}}$, and he faces prices $p_x = \$1$ and $p_y = \$3$, and has a utility target of $\bar{u} = 20$. Using the same steps as in example 3.7, solve Eric's EMP, finding his optimal purchases of goods x and y.

- *Step 1.* As in our utility maximization problems, we begin the expenditure minimization problem by finding Eric's tangency condition, $\frac{MU_x}{MU_y} = \frac{p_x}{p_y}$.

  - Calculating Eric's marginal utilities, we obtain $MU_x = \frac{\partial u(x,y)}{\partial x} = \frac{1}{2}x^{-\frac{1}{2}}y^{\frac{1}{2}}$ and $MU_y = \frac{\partial u(x,y)}{\partial y} = \frac{1}{2}x^{\frac{1}{2}}y^{-\frac{1}{2}}$. Combining these into our marginal rate of substitution gives

  $$MRS_{x,y} = \frac{MU_x}{MU_y} = \frac{\frac{1}{2}x^{-\frac{1}{2}}y^{\frac{1}{2}}}{\frac{1}{2}x^{\frac{1}{2}}y^{-\frac{1}{2}}} = \frac{y^{\frac{1}{2}+\left(-\frac{1}{2}\right)}}{x^{\frac{1}{2}+\left(-\frac{1}{2}\right)}} = \frac{y}{x}.$$

  - Next, we obtain our ratio of prices, $\frac{p_x}{p_y} = \frac{1}{3}$.
  - Setting them equal to one another, we have our tangency condition,

  $$\frac{y}{x} = \frac{1}{3}.$$

  Rearranging this expression gives $y = \frac{1}{3}x$, or $3y = x$. Since this result contains both x and y, we move on to step 2a.

- *Step 2a.* We don't have a budget line to work with this time, but we do have a desired utility level. Thus, we use the utility function set to that level as our second equation, $x^{\frac{1}{2}}y^{\frac{1}{2}} = 20$.

  - Substituting $3y$ for x gives

  $$\underbrace{(3y)^{\frac{1}{2}}}_{x}y^{\frac{1}{2}} = 20.$$

  We can distribute the exponent through the parenthesis to obtain

  $$(3)^{\frac{1}{2}}y^{\frac{1}{2}}y^{\frac{1}{2}} = 20,$$

  or, after simplifying, $1.73y = 20$. Dividing both sides of this expression by 1.73 provides our equilibrium consumption level of y, $y = \frac{20}{1.73} = 11.56$ units. Since this value is positive, we can skip ahead to step 4.

- *Step 4.* We can find our optimal purchase of good x by using the tangency condition, $x = 3y$.

  - Plugging in our value of $y = 11.56$, we obtain

  $$x = 3\underbrace{(11.56)}_{y} = 34.68 \text{ units.}$$

Self-assessment exercise #3.10

SA 3.10 John's utility function is $u(x, y) = 4x^{1/2} + 2y$, he faces prices $p_x = \$2$ and $p_y = \$3$, and has a utility target of $\bar{u} = 10$. Using the same steps as in example 3.8, solve John's EMP, finding his optimal purchases of goods x and y.

- *Step 1.* Once again, we begin the expenditure minimization problem by finding John's tangency condition, $\frac{MU_x}{MU_y} = \frac{p_x}{p_y}$.

  - Calculating John's marginal utilities, we obtain $MU_x = \frac{\partial u(x,y)}{\partial x} = 2x^{-1/2}$ and $MU_y = \frac{\partial u(x,y)}{\partial y} = 2$. Combining these into our marginal rate of substitution gives
  $$MRS_{x,y} = \frac{MU_x}{MU_y} = \frac{2x^{-1/2}}{2} = x^{-1/2}.$$

  - Next, we obtain our ratio of prices, $\frac{p_x}{p_y} = \frac{2}{3}$.

  - Setting them equal to one another, we have our tangency condition, $x^{-1/2} = \frac{2}{3}$. Since this expression only contains x, we move to step 2c.

- *Step 2c.* Rearranging this expression, we have $\sqrt{x} = \frac{3}{2}$. Squaring both sides gives our optimal purchase of good x,

$$x = \frac{9}{4} = 2.25 \text{ units.}$$

  - Now we substitute this value, $x = 2.25$, into our utility function, $4x^{1/2} + 2y = 10$ to obtain
  $$4\underbrace{(2.25)^{1/2}}_{x} + 2y = 10,$$

  or $6 + 2y = 10$, which further simplifies to $2y = 4$. We can now solve for y, to obtain the optimal purchase of good y, $y = 2$ units.

3.2 Solutions to End-of-Chapter Exercises

Exercise #3.1 - Budget Line[A]

3.1 Peter has an income of $I = \$100$, which he dedicates to purchasing soda and pizza. The price of soda is \$1 per can, while that of pizza is \$2 per slice.

(a) Find the equation of his budget line, and represent it graphically.

- We can find Peter's budget line by multiplying the quantity of soda (s) he purchases by its price (\$1), adding the multiplication of his quantity of pizza (p) he purchases by its price (\$2), and setting it equal to his income, \$100,

$$1s + 2p = 100.$$

With this line, it is easiest to plot it by finding Peter's vertical and horizontal intercepts. Starting with the vertical intercept (assuming we place our quantity of pizza on the vertical axis), we set $s = 0$, then solve for p to obtain

$$p = \frac{100}{2} = 50.$$

Likewise, to find Peter's horizontal intercept, we set $p = 0$, then solve for s to obtain

$$s = 100.$$

From here we connect these two points to obtain Peter's budget line, as illustrated in figure 3.9.

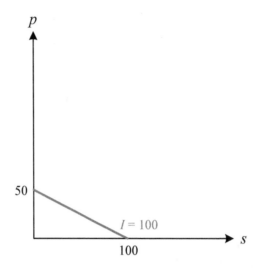

Figure 3.9. Budget line with $I = \$100$.

(b) How does Peter's budget set change when his income increases to $I' = \$150$?

- When Peter's income increases to $I' = \$150$, his budget line shifts outward. Previously unaffordable bundles now become affordable to him. We can plot this change by finding new vertical and horizontal intercepts for this expanded budget line,

$$s + 2p = 150.$$

Starting with the vertical intercept, we set $s = 0$, then solve for p to obtain

$$p = \frac{150}{2} = 75.$$

Likewise, to find Peter's horizontal intercept, we set $p = 0$, then solve for s to obtain

$$s = 150.$$

From here we connect these two points to obtain Peter's budget line, as illustrated in figure 3.10. Notably, Peter's budget set is the area that lays below the budget line, $s + 2p \leq 150$.

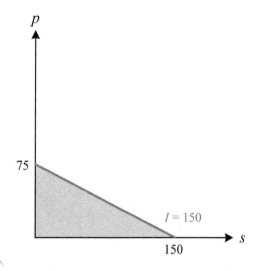

Figure 3.10. Budget line with $I = \$150$.

(c) Consider that the university that Peter attends subsidizes pizza, decreasing its price by $1. What is Peter budget set now?

- With the new price of pizza, Peter's budget line becomes

$$1s + 1p = 150.$$

which we plot by first locating his vertical and horizontal intercepts. Starting with the vertical intercept, we set $s = 0$, then solve for p to obtain

$$p = 150.$$

Likewise, to find Peter's horizontal intercept, we set $p = 0$, then solve for s to obtain

$$s = 150.$$

From here we connect these two points to obtain Peter's budget line, as illustrated in figure 3.11.

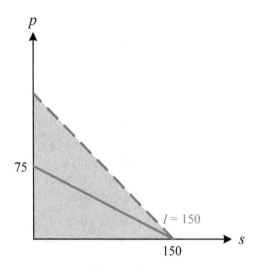

Figure 3.11. Effect of a price decrease.

The net result is that Peter's budget line has rotated outward along his pizza axis, making previously unaffordable bundles now affordable.

(d) What if, instead, the university gives Peter 25 vouchers that he can use to get 25 free slices of pizza?

- In this case, the slope of Peter's budget line does not change at all, but rather shifts upward by the free 25 slices of pizza provided by his university as depicted in figure 3.12.

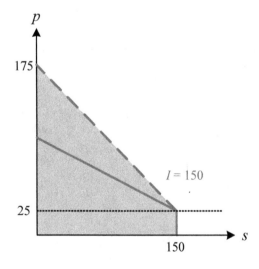

Figure 3.12. Pizza vouchers.

Exercise #3.3 - Composite Good[A]

3.3 Consider an individual with utility function $u(x, y) = (x + 3)y$, and income $I = \$30$. The price of good x is $p_x = \$2$, while that of good y is normalized to $p_y = \$1$ (that is, good y represents the money left for purchasing all other goods but x, which we refer as the "numeraire").

(a) Find the optimal consumption bundle of this individual. Evaluate his utility function at this optimal bundle.

- *Step 1.* To solve for our optimal consumption, first we must use the tangency condition, $\frac{MU_x}{MU_y} = \frac{p_x}{p_y}$.
  - For the left-hand side, we calculate the ratio of our marginal utilities, where $MU_x = \frac{\partial u(x,y)}{\partial x} = y$ and $MU_y = \frac{\partial u(x,y)}{\partial y} = x + 3$. Therefore,

  $$\frac{MU_x}{MU_y} = \frac{y}{x+3}.$$

  - For the right-hand side, it is simply the ratio of the prices, $\frac{p_x}{p_y} = \frac{2}{1}$.
  - Setting them equal to one another gives

  $$\frac{y}{x+3} = 2,$$

  which we can rearrange to obtain $y = 2x + 6$, or $x = \frac{1}{2}y - 3$. Since this contains both x and y, we move on to step 2a.

- *Step 2a.* Next, we use our budget line, $2x + y = 30$ and substitute $\frac{1}{2}y - 3$ for x, obtaining

  $$2 \underbrace{\left(\frac{1}{2}y - 3\right)}_{x} + y = 30.$$

  - Combining terms, we have $2y = 36$, and we can divide both sides of this equation to obtain the amount of good y that he consumes, $y = 18$ units. With a positive value of y, we can move on to step 4.

- *Step 4.* Last, we return to our tangency condition to determine how much of good x he consumes.
  - Plugging in his value for y gives $x = \frac{1}{2}(18) - 3 = 6$ units.

- Last, evaluating our utility by plugging in our equilibrium values,

  $$u(6, 18) = (6 + 3)(18) = 162.$$

(b) Assume now that his income was increased by \$10 (for a total of $I' = \$40$). What is his new optimal consumption bundle? What is the new utility level that he can reach?

- *Step 1.* To solve for our optimal consumption, first we must use the tangency condition, $\frac{MU_x}{MU_y} = \frac{p_x}{p_y}$.
  - For the left-hand side, we calculate the ratio of our marginal utilities, where $MU_x = \frac{\partial u(x,y)}{\partial x} = y$ and $MU_y = \frac{\partial u(x,y)}{\partial y} = x + 3$. Therefore,

  $$\frac{MU_x}{MU_y} = \frac{y}{x+3}.$$

- For the right-hand side, it is simply the ratio of the prices, $\frac{p_x}{p_y} = \frac{2}{1}$.
- Setting them equal to one another gives

$$\frac{y}{x+3} = 2,$$

which we can rearrange to obtain $y = 2x + 6$, or $x = \frac{1}{2}y - 3$. Since this contains both x and y, we move on to step 2a.

- *Step 2a.* Next, we use our budget line, $2x + y = 40$ and substitute $\frac{1}{2}y - 3$ for x, obtaining

$$2 \underbrace{\left(\frac{1}{2}y - 3\right)}_{x} + y = 40.$$

  - Combining terms, we have $2y = 46$, and we can divide both sides of this equation to obtain the amount of good y that he consumes, $y = 23$ units. With a positive value of y, we can move on to step 4.

- *Step 4.* Last, we return to our tangency condition to determine how much of good x he consumes.
  - Plugging in his value for y gives $x = \frac{1}{2}(23) - 3 = 8.5$ units.

- Last, evaluating our utility by plugging in our equilibrium values,

$$u(8.5, 23) = (8.5 + 3)(23) = 264.5.$$

(c) Assume now that the price of good x decreases in \$1, so its new price is $p'_x = \$1$. What is his new optimal consumption bundle? What is the new utility level that he can reach?

- *Step 1.* To solve for our optimal consumption, first we must use the tangency condition, $\frac{MU_x}{MU_y} = \frac{p_x}{p_y}$.
  - For the left-hand side, we calculate the ratio of our marginal utilities, where $MU_x = \frac{\partial u(x,y)}{\partial x} = y$ and $MU_y = \frac{\partial u(x,y)}{\partial y} = x + 3$. Therefore,

$$\frac{MU_x}{MU_y} = \frac{y}{x+3}.$$

  - For the right-hand side, it is simply the ratio of the prices, $\frac{p_x}{p_y} = \frac{1}{1}$.
  - Setting them equal to one another gives

$$\frac{y}{x+3} = 1,$$

which we can rearrange to obtain $y = x + 3$, or $x = y - 3$. Since this contains both x and y, we move on to step 2a.

- *Step 2a.* Next, we use our budget line, $x + y = 30$ and substitute $y - 3$ for x, obtaining

$$\underbrace{y - 3}_{x} + y = 30.$$

- Combining terms, we have $2y = 33$, and we can divide both sides of this equation to obtain the amount of good y that he consumes, $y = 16.5$ units. With a positive value of y, we can move on to step 4.

- *Step 4.* Last, we return to our tangency condition to determine how much of good x he consumes.

  - Plugging in his value for y gives $x = 16.5 - 3 = 13.5$ units.

- Last, evaluating our utility by plugging in our equilibrium values,

$$u(13.5, 16.5) = (13.5 + 3)(16.5) = 272.75.$$

(d) Assume that he receives a coupon allowing him to consume 4 units of good x for free. What is his new optimal consumption bundle? What is the new utility level that he can reach?

- Since he receives 4 units of good x for free, he is still able to allocate $30 between good x and good y. Those results will be identical to the results in part (a). Thus, his new utility is,

$$u(10, 18) = (10 + 3)(18) = 234.$$

(e) In which version of parts b–d is the consumer better off? That is, describe whether the consumer prefers the change in income from part (b), the change in prices from part (c), or the coupon from part (d).

- The consumer is better off in part (c), under the price change. This allows him to consume more of both goods, increasing his utility.

Exercise #3.5 - Expenditure Function[A]

3.5 Consider that a consumer's expenditure function is given by

$$e(p_x, p_y, u) = 3 \left(\frac{u p_x (p_y)^2}{4} \right)^{1/3}.$$

Find the demand for good y, $y(p_x, p_y, u)$. [*Hint*: Because

$$p_x h_x(p_x, p_y, u) + p_y h_y(p_x, p_y, u) = e(p_x, p_y, u),$$

you may differentiate $e(p_x, p_y, u)$ with respect to p_y to find $h_y(p_x, p_y, u)$.] The demand function you find is the one that solves the EMP. In this scenario, however, we find it without needing to solve the EMP. As we have information about expenditure function $e(p_x, p_y, u)$, we can find this demand function more directly by just differentiating $e(p_x, p_y, u)$ with respect to p_y.

- Differentiating the expenditure function with respect to the price of good y, p_y, we obtain

$$\frac{\partial e(p_x, p_y, u)}{\partial p_y} = y(p_x, p_y, u)$$

$$= 3\left(\frac{1}{3}\right)\left(\frac{up_x\,(p_y)^2}{4}\right)^{-2/3}\left(2\frac{up_xp_y}{4}\right),$$

which simplifies to

$$\frac{\partial e(p_x, p_y, u)}{\partial p_y} = \left(\frac{up_x\,(p_y)^2}{4}\right)^{-2/3}\left[\left(\frac{up_xp_y}{2}\right)^{-3/2}\right]^{-2/3}$$

$$= \left[\left(\frac{up_x\,(p_y)^2}{4}\right)\left(\frac{up_xp_y}{2}\right)^{-3/2}\right]^{-2/3}$$

$$= \left[\left(\frac{2^{3/2}up_x\,(p_y)^2}{4u^{3/2}(p_x)^{3/2}(p_y)^{3/2}}\right)\right]^{-2/3}$$

$$= \left[\left(\frac{p_y^{1/2}}{2^{1/2}u^{1/2}(p_x)^{1/2}}\right)\right]^{-2/3}$$

$$= \left(\frac{p_y}{2up_x}\right)^{-1/3}$$

$$= \left(\frac{2up_x}{p_y}\right)^{1/3}.$$

Exercise #3.7 - Cobb-Douglas–I^A

3.7 Eric has a monthly income of $I = \$500$ and a Cobb-Douglas utility function of the type $u(x, y) = x^{1/2}y^{1/2}$. The price for good x is \$1, and the price for good y is \$3.

(a) Find Eric's tangency condition, following step 1 of the utility maximization procedure.

- *Step 1.* To solve for Eric's optimal consumption, first we must use the tangency condition, $\frac{MU_x}{MU_y} = \frac{p_x}{p_y}$.
  - For the left-hand side, we calculate the ratio of our marginal utilities, where

$$MU_x = \frac{\partial u(x, y)}{\partial x} = \frac{1}{2}x^{-1/2}y^{1/2}, \text{ and}$$

$$MU_y = \frac{\partial u(x, y)}{\partial y} = \frac{1}{2}x^{1/2}y^{-1/2}.$$

Therefore,

$$\frac{MU_x}{MU_y} = \frac{\frac{1}{2}x^{-1/2}y^{1/2}}{\frac{1}{2}x^{1/2}y^{-1/2}} = \frac{y}{x}.$$

66

- For the right-hand side, it is simply the ratio of the prices, $\frac{p_x}{p_y} = \frac{1}{3}$.
- Setting them equal to one another gives

$$\frac{y}{x} = \frac{1}{3},$$

which we can rearrange to obtain $x = 3y$.

(b) Find Eric's equilibrium quantities for goods x and y.

- Since Eric's tangency condition contains both x and y, we move on to step 2a.
- *Step 2a.* Next, we use Eric's budget line, $x + 3y = 500$ and substitute $3y$ for x, obtaining

$$\underbrace{3y}_{x} + 3y = 500.$$

   - Combining terms, we have $6y = 500$, and we can divide both sides of this equation to obtain the amount of good y that Eric consumes, $y = 83.33$ units. With a positive value of y, we can move on to step 4.
- *Step 4.* Last, we return to our tangency condition to determine how much of good x Eric consumes.
   - Plugging in our value for y gives $x = 3(83.33) = 250$ units.

Exercise #3.9 - Cobb-Douglas–III^C

3.9 Eric has a Cobb-Douglas utility function of the type $u(x, y) = x^{1/2}y^{1/2}$. Suppose that Eric has a general value for his income, I, and general values for the prices of goods x and y (p_x and p_y, respectively).

(a) Find Eric's tangency condition, following step 1 of the utility maximization procedure.

- *Step 1.* To solve for Eric's optimal consumption, first we must use the tangency condition, $\frac{MU_x}{MU_y} = \frac{p_x}{p_y}$.
   - For the left-hand side, we calculate the ratio of our marginal utilities, where

$$MU_x = \frac{\partial u(x, y)}{\partial x} = \frac{1}{2}x^{-1/2}y^{1/2} \text{ and}$$
$$MU_y = \frac{\partial u(x, y)}{\partial y} = \frac{1}{2}x^{1/2}y^{-1/2}.$$

Therefore,
$$\frac{MU_x}{MU_y} = \frac{\frac{1}{2}x^{-1/2}y^{1/2}}{\frac{1}{2}x^{1/2}y^{-1/2}} = \frac{y}{x}.$$

   - For the right-hand side, it is simply the ratio of the prices, $\frac{p_x}{p_y}$.

– Setting them equal to one another gives

$$\frac{y}{x} = \frac{p_x}{p_y},$$

which we can rearrange to obtain $x = \frac{p_y}{p_x}y$.

(b) Find Eric's equilibrium quantities for goods x and y as a function of I, p_x, and p_y.

- Since Eric's tangency condition contains both x and y, we move on to step 2a.
- *Step 2a.* Next, we use Eric's budget line, $p_x x + p_y y = I$ and substitute $\frac{p_y}{p_x}y$ for x, obtaining

$$p_x \underbrace{\left(\frac{p_y}{p_x}y\right)}_{x} + p_y y = I.$$

– Combining terms, we have $2p_y y = I$, and we can divide both sides of this equation to obtain the amount of good y that Eric consumes, $y = \frac{I}{2p_y}$ units. With a positive value of y, we can move on to step 4.

- *Step 4.* Last, we return to our tangency condition to determine how much of good x Eric consumes.

– Plugging in our value for y gives $x = \frac{p_y}{p_x}\left(\frac{I}{2p_y}\right) = \frac{I}{2p_x}$ units.

(c) Compare your results with those in exercise 3.7 by setting $I = \$500$, $p_x = \$1$, and $p_y = \$3$. Are they identical?

- Plugging in our values,

$$x = \frac{500}{2(1)} = 250 \text{ units, and}$$

$$y = \frac{500}{2(3)} = 83.33 \text{ units,}$$

which is exactly the same result as in exercise 3.7.

Exercise #3.11 - Different Relationships^C

3.11 Eric has a weekly income of $I = \$50$ and a utility function of the type $u(x,y) = \frac{x^{1/2}}{y+1} = x^{1/2}(y+1)^{-1}$. The price for good x is \$1, and the price for good y is also \$1.

(a) Are x and y both goods? If not, which is a bad?

- In this situation, Eric's utility is increasing in good x, but decreasing in good y, making it a bad.

(b) Find Eric's tangency condition, following step 1 of the utility maximization procedure.

- *Step 1.* To solve for Eric's optimal consumption, first we must use the tangency condition, $\frac{MU_x}{MU_y} = \frac{p_x}{p_y}$.

- For the left-hand side, we calculate the ratio of our marginal utilities, where

$$MU_x = \frac{\partial u(x,y)}{\partial x} = \frac{1}{2}x^{-1/2}(y+1)^{-1}, \text{ and}$$

$$MU_y = \frac{\partial u(x,y)}{\partial y} = -x^{1/2}(y+1)^{-2}.$$

Therefore,

$$\frac{MU_x}{MU_y} = \frac{\frac{1}{2}x^{-1/2}(y+1)^{-1}}{-x^{1/2}(y+1)^{-2}} = -\frac{y+1}{2x}.$$

- For the right-hand side, it is simply the ratio of the prices, $\frac{p_x}{p_y} = \frac{1}{1}$.
- Setting them equal to one another gives

$$-\frac{y+1}{2x} = 1,$$

which we can rearrange to obtain $x = -\frac{1}{2}y - \frac{1}{2}$.

(c) Find Eric's equilibrium quantities for goods x and y.

- In this situation, Eric's utility function is misbehaved as his tangency condition implies that one of his equilibrium quantities must be negative. As such, it would make sense to set the "bad" good equal to zero since Eric will not want to consume it in equilibrium. Thus, we proceed to step 3.
- *Step 3.* Setting $y = 0$, we solve for Eric's equilibrium amount of good x by using his budget line,

$$x = 50 \text{ units.}$$

Exercise #3.13 - Perfect Complements–I[A]

3.13 John has a monthly income of $I = \$400$ and a utility function of the type $u(x,y) = \min\{2x, y\}$. The price of good x is \$3, while the price of good y is \$4.

(a) What is John's most preferred ratio of consuming good x to good y?

- Since John receives his utility as the lesser of $2x$ and y, he prefers to consume them in that ratio, $2x = y$, or $x = \frac{1}{2}y$.

(b) Find John's equilibrium quantities for goods x and y.

- What we derived for John in part (a) is essentially a tangency condition. Since John's tangency condition contains both x and y, we move on to step 2a.
- *Step 2a.* Next, we use John's budget line, $3x + 4y = 400$ and substitute $\frac{1}{2}y$ for x, obtaining

$$3\underbrace{\left(\frac{1}{2}y\right)}_{x} + 4y = 400.$$

- Combining terms, we have $\frac{11}{2}y = 400$, and we can divide both sides of this equation to obtain the amount of good y that John consumes, $y = 72.73$ units. With a positive value of y, we can move on to step 4.
- *Step 4.* Last, we return to our tangency condition to determine how much of good x John consumes.
  - Plugging in our value for y gives $x = \frac{1}{2}(72.73) = 36.36$ units.

Exercise #3.15 - Expenditure Minimization Problem[A]

3.15 Peter wishes to reach a utility level of $U = 50$ and has a Cobb-Douglas utility function of the type $u(x, y) = x^{0.4}y^{0.6}$. The price for good x is \$1, and the price for good y is \$4.

(a) Find Peter's tangency condition, following step 1 of the expenditure minimization procedure.
- *Step 1.* We begin the expenditure minimization problem by finding Peter's tangency condition, $\frac{MU_x}{MU_y} = \frac{p_x}{p_y}$.
  - Calculating Peter's marginal utilities, we obtain $MU_x = \frac{\partial u(x,y)}{\partial x} = 0.4x^{-0.6}y^{0.6}$ and $MU_y = \frac{\partial u(x,y)}{\partial y} = 0.6x^{0.4}y^{-0.4}$. Combining these into our marginal rate of substitution gives

$$MRS_{x,y} = \frac{MU_x}{MU_y} = \frac{0.4x^{-0.6}y^{0.6}}{0.6x^{0.4}y^{-0.4}} = \frac{2y}{3x}.$$

  - Next, we obtain our ratio of prices, $\frac{p_x}{p_y} = \frac{1}{4}$.
  - Setting them equal to one another, we have our tangency condition,

$$\frac{2y}{3x} = \frac{1}{4}.$$

Rearranging this expression gives $8y = 3x$, or $x = \frac{8}{3}y$.

(b) Find Peter's equilibrium quantities for goods x and y.
- Since this tangency condition contains both x and y, we move on to step 2a.
- *Step 2a.* We don't have a budget line to work with this time, but we do have a desired utility level. Thus, we use the utility function set to that level as our second equation, $x^{0.4}y^{0.6} = 50$.
  - Substituting $\frac{8}{3}y$ for x gives

$$\underbrace{\left(\frac{8}{3}y\right)}_{x}^{0.4} y^{0.6} = 50.$$

We can distribute the exponent through the parenthesis to obtain

$$\left(\frac{8}{3}\right)^{0.4} y^{0.4}y^{0.6} = 50,$$

or, after simplifying, $1.48y = 50$. Dividing both sides of this expression by 1.48 provides our equilibrium consumption level of y, $y^E = 33.78$ units. Since this value is positive, we can skip ahead to step 4.

- *Step 4.* We can find our optimal purchase of good x by using the tangency condition, $x = \frac{8}{3}y$.
  - Plugging in our value of $y^E = 33.78$, we obtain

$$x^E = \frac{8}{3}\underbrace{(33.78)}_{y} = 90.09 \text{ units.}$$

(c) How much income does Peter require to reach his target utility level?

- To find Peter's income requirement, we multiply his equilibrium quantities by their respective prices and add them together, obtaining

$$I = 1(90.09) + 4(33.78) = \$225.21.$$

Exercise #3.17 - Perfect Complements–II[B]

3.17 John wishes to reach a utility level of $U = 75$ and has a utility function of the type $u(x, y) = \min\{3x, 2y\}$. The price of good x is \$2, while the price of good y is \$3.

(a) What is John's most preferred ratio of consuming good x to good y?

- Since John receives his utility as the lesser of $3x$ and $2y$, he prefers to consume them in that ratio, $3x = 2y$, or $x = \frac{2}{3}y$.

(b) Find John's equilibrium quantities for goods x and y.

- What we derived for John in part (a) is essentially a tangency condition. Since John's tangency condition contains both x and y we move on to step 2a.
- *Step 2a.* We don't have a budget line to work with this time, but we do have a desired utility level. Thus, we use the utility function set to that level as our second equation, $\min\{3x, 2y\} = 75$.
  - Substituting $\frac{2}{3}y$ for x gives

$$\min\left\{3\underbrace{\left(\frac{2}{3}y\right)}_{x}, 2y\right\} = 75.$$

Distributing, we have,
$$\min\{2y, 2y\} = 75,$$

or, after simplifying, $2y = 75$. Dividing both sides of this expression by 2 provides our equilibrium consumption level of y,

$$y^E = 37.5 \text{ units.}$$

71

Since this value is positive, we can skip ahead to step 4.

- *Step 4.* We can find our optimal purchase of good x by using the tangency condition, $x = \frac{2}{3}y$.

  - Plugging in our value of $y = 37.5$, we obtain

$$x^E = \frac{2}{3}\underbrace{(37.5)}_{y} = 25 \text{ units.}$$

(c) How much income does John require to reach his target utility level?

- To find John's income requirement, we multiply his equilibrium quantities by their respective prices and add them together, obtaining

$$I = 2(25) + 3(37.5) = \$162.50.$$

Exercise #3.19 - Utility Maximization[B]

3.19 Suppose that you are in a situation where you can afford purchasing 3 units of good x and 4 units of good y. You discover that another affordable bundle of 5 units of good x and 2 units of good y causes you to reach the same level of utility. Assume that your utility function and budget line are both well behaved.

(a) Are you maximizing your utility by consuming your original bundle? Why or why not?

- No. Since you have two affordable bundles that allow you to reach the same utility level, your utility curve is not tangent to your budget line. This implies that you are not maximizing your utility.

(b) Propose an alternative, affordable bundle that would yield a higher utility level than either of the original bundles.

- Any linear combination of our two bundles would produce a higher utility level. Thus, a bundle with 4 units of good x and 3 units of good y would produce a higher utility level than either of the original bundles. This effect is illustrated in figure 3.13.

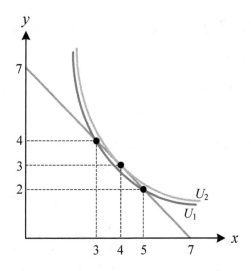

Figure 3.13. Multiple crossings.

Chapter 4 - Substitution and Income Effects

4.1 Solutions to Self-Assessment Exercises

Self-assessment exercise #4.1

SA 4.1 Assume that Eric's demand function for good x is $x = \frac{5I}{\sqrt{p_x} - 3p_y}$. Find the derivative $\frac{\partial x}{\partial I}$ and its sign, and interpret your results.

- Differentiating Eric's demand function with respect to his income,

$$\frac{\partial x}{\partial I} = \frac{5}{\sqrt{p_x} - 3p_y} > 0.$$

Since Eric's demand for good x is positive only when $\sqrt{p_x} - 3p_y > 0$, we can assume that its derivative with respect to income is also positive. This implies that good x is a normal good for Eric; as his income increases, his consumption of good x also increases.

Self-assessment exercise #4.2

SA 4.2 Consider again Eric's demand function $x = \frac{5I}{\sqrt{p_x} - 3p_y}$. Find his income elasticity $\varepsilon_{x,I}$, its sign, and interpret your results.

- We can calculate Eric's income elasticity using the standard formula,

$$\varepsilon_{x,I} = \frac{\partial x(p_x, p_y, I)}{\partial I} \frac{I}{x(p_x, p_y, I)},$$

and substituting in our result from self-assessment 4.1 for the derivative of good x with respect to income,

$$\varepsilon_{x,I} = \frac{5}{\sqrt{p_x} - 3p_y} \frac{I}{\frac{5I}{\sqrt{p_x} - 3p_y}}.$$

We can rearrange this expression to obtain

$$\varepsilon_{x,I} = \frac{5I\left(\sqrt{p_x} - 3p_y\right)}{5I\left(\sqrt{p_x} - 3p_y\right)} = 1 > 0,$$

since the numerator and denominator are exactly equal to one another, this expression simply reduces to 1. With a value of 1, the income elasticity implies that a 1 percent increase in income corresponds with a 1 percent increase in the demand for good x. This is consistent with good x being a normal good.

Self-assessment exercise #4.3

SA 4.3 Consider Maria's demand function $x = \frac{5I}{\sqrt{p_x}}$ and assume that her demand for good y is symmetric, so that $y = \frac{5I}{\sqrt{p_y}}$. Find Maria's income-consumption curve, and evaluate it

74

at prices $p_x = \$4$ and $p_y = \$9$.

- We can calculate Maria's income-consumption curve by taking the ratio of her demand for good y to her demand for good x,

$$\frac{y}{x} = \frac{\frac{5I}{\sqrt{p_y}}}{\frac{5I}{\sqrt{p_x}}}$$

$$= \frac{\sqrt{p_x}}{\sqrt{p_y}}.$$

Plugging in our prices, we find that the income-consumption curve is equal to $\frac{y}{x} = \frac{\sqrt{4}}{\sqrt{9}} = \frac{2}{3}$ at these prices. Intuitively, Maria prefers to consume goods x and y in fixed proportions based on their relative prices. As her income increases, the amount of x and y increase, but her preferred proportion does not change.

Self-assessment exercise #4.4

SA 4.4 Consider again Eric's demand function, $x = \frac{5I}{\sqrt{p_x}-3p_y}$. Solve for income I to find his Engel curve. Is its slope positive or negative? What does your result mean in terms of good x being normal or inferior?

- To find Eric's Engel curve, we must solve his demand function for his income, I.
  - First, we multiply both sides of the equation by the denominator, $\sqrt{p_x} - 3p_y$ to obtain $5I = x\left(\sqrt{p_x} - 3p_y\right)$.
  - Last, we divide both sides of the equation by 5 to obtain the Engel curve,

$$I = \frac{\sqrt{p_x} - 3p_y}{5}x > 0.$$

- Once again, since $\sqrt{p_x} - 3p_y$ must be positive for Eric to demand any of good x, the slope of the Engel curve must also be positive. Thus, the result is consistent with good x being a normal good for Eric.

Self-assessment exercise #4.5

SA 4.5 Consider again Eric's demand function, $x = \frac{5I}{\sqrt{p_x}-3p_y}$. Find the derivative $\frac{\partial x(p_x, p_y, I)}{\partial p_x}$, its sign, and interpret.

- For this analysis, it may be easier to rewrite Eric's demand for good x as $x = 5I\left(\sqrt{p_x} - 3p_y\right)^{-1}$. We can differentiate this expression for good x by using the chain rule,

$$\frac{\partial x(p_x, p_y, I)}{\partial p_x} = 5I(-1)\left(\sqrt{p_x} - 3p_y\right)^{-2}\left(\frac{1}{2\sqrt{p_x}}\right),$$

which rearranges to

$$\frac{\partial x(p_x, p_y, I)}{\partial p_x} = -\frac{5I}{2\sqrt{p_x}\left(\sqrt{p_x} - 3p_y\right)^2} < 0.$$

Since both the numerator and denominator of this expression are positive, we know that the derivative is negative. This implies that as the price of good x increases, the quantity demanded of good x decreases, which we should expect for a normal demand function.

Self-assessment exercise #4.6

SA 4.6 Consider again Eric's demand function, $x = \frac{5I}{\sqrt{p_x}-3p_y}$. Find its price elasticity ε_{x,p_x}, and interpret your result.

- Eric's price elasticity can be calculated using the standard formula,

$$\varepsilon_{x,p_x} = \frac{\partial x(p_x, p_y, I)}{\partial p_x} \frac{p_x}{x(p_x, p_y, I)},$$

and using our result for the derivative of the demand for good x with respect to its price from self-assessment 4.5, we have

$$\varepsilon_{x,p_x} = -\frac{5I}{2\sqrt{p_x}\left(\sqrt{p_x} - 3p_y\right)^2} \frac{p_x}{\frac{5I}{\sqrt{p_x}-3p_y}},$$

which we can rearrange to obtain

$$\varepsilon_{x,p_x} = -\frac{5I p_x \left(\sqrt{p_x} - 3p_y\right)}{10I \sqrt{p_x} \left(\sqrt{p_x} - 3p_y\right)^2}.$$

We can simplify this expression, dividing both the numerator and denominator by $5I\sqrt{p_x}\left(\sqrt{p_x} - 3p_y\right)$ to obtain

$$\varepsilon_{x,p_x} = -\frac{\sqrt{p_x}}{2\left(\sqrt{p_x} - 3p_y\right)},$$

which implies that as the price of good x increases by 1 percent, the quantity demanded of good x decreases by $\frac{\sqrt{p_x}}{2\left(\sqrt{p_x}-3p_y\right)}$ percent. This expression is negative if the term in the denominator is positive; that is, $\sqrt{p_x} > 3p_y$ has to be positive for demand for good x to be positive, or $\frac{\sqrt{p_x}}{3} > p_y$. We next present two numerical examples:

- *Good x is relatively expensive.* If $p_x = \$9$ and $p_y = \$\frac{1}{2}$ (which satisfies condition $\frac{\sqrt{p_x}}{3} > p_y$ since $\frac{\sqrt{9}}{3} = 1 > \frac{1}{2} = p_y$), this elasticity becomes

$$\varepsilon_{x,p_x} = -\frac{\sqrt{9}}{2\left(\sqrt{9} - \left(3 \times \frac{1}{2}\right)\right)} = -\frac{3}{2\left(3 - 1.5\right)} = -1,$$

  implying that a 1 percent increase in p_x increases the quantity demanded of good x proportionally (i.e., by 1 percent).
- *Good x is relatively inexpensive.* If, instead, prices are $p_x = \$2$ and $p_y = \$1$, condition $\frac{\sqrt{p_x}}{3} > p_y$ is violated since $\frac{\sqrt{2}}{3} = 0.47 < 1 = p_y$), this elasticity

becomes

$$\varepsilon_{x,p_x} = -\frac{\sqrt{2}}{2\left(\sqrt{2} - (3 \times 1)\right)} = \frac{3}{2\left(3 - \sqrt{2}\right)} \simeq 0.45,$$

meaning that, after a 1 percent increase in p_x, the consumer increases her quantity demanded for this product.

Overall, after a 1 percent increase in p_x, the consumer responds by reducing her quantity demanded when good x is relatively expensive (that is, when condition $\frac{\sqrt{p_x}}{3} > p_y$ holds; but increases her quantity demanded when good x is relatively inexpensive.

Self-assessment exercise #4.7

SA 4.7 Maria's demand function for good x is $x = \frac{5I}{\sqrt{p_x}}$, and her demand for good y is $y = \frac{5I}{\sqrt{p_y}}$. Find her price-consumption curve and interpret your results.

- We can calculate Maria's price-consumption curve by examining the ratio of her demand for good y to her demand for good x,

$$\frac{y}{x} = \frac{\frac{5I}{\sqrt{p_y}}}{\frac{5I}{\sqrt{p_x}}},$$

which we can rearrange to

$$\frac{y}{x} = \frac{5I\sqrt{p_x}}{5I\sqrt{p_y}} = \frac{\sqrt{p_x}}{\sqrt{p_y}}.$$

This has a similar interpretation as example 4.7. As the price of good x increases, the ratio of $\frac{y}{x}$ also increases, which implies that Maria shifts her consumption toward more of good y. The difference between this case and the case in example 4.7 is that the effect is not as strong; the ratio changes at the rate of the square roots of the prices.

Self-assessment exercise #4.8

SA 4.8 John's utility function is $u(x, y) = x^{1/3}y^{2/3}$, his income is $I = \$150$, and the price of good y is $p_y = \$1$. The price of good x decreases from $p_x = \$3$ to $p'_x = \$1$. Using the steps in example 4.8, find the substitution and income effects.

- Before applying the steps in example 4.8, it would be useful to calculate John's marginal rate of substitution,

$$MRS_{x,y} = \frac{MU_x}{MU_y} = \frac{\frac{1}{3}x^{-2/3}y^{2/3}}{\frac{2}{3}x^{1/3}y^{-1/3}} = \frac{y^{\frac{2}{3}+\frac{1}{3}}}{2x^{\frac{1}{3}+\frac{2}{3}}} = \frac{y}{2x}.$$

- *Finding initial bundle A.* With John's initial prices, his tangency condition, $\frac{MU_x}{MU_y} = \frac{p_x}{p_y}$ is $\frac{y}{2x} = \frac{3}{1}$. This expression rearranges to $y = 6x$. Inserting this expression into the budget line gives

$$3x + \underbrace{6x}_{y} = 150.$$

From here, we can divide both sides of this expression by 9 to obtain

$$x = \frac{150}{9} = 16.67 \text{ units.}$$

From John's tangency condition, we can solve for John's consumption of good y,

$$y = 6x = 6(16.67) = 100 \text{ units.}$$

This leads to John's initial bundle $A = (16.67, 100)$. This initial bundle is depicted in figure 4.1.

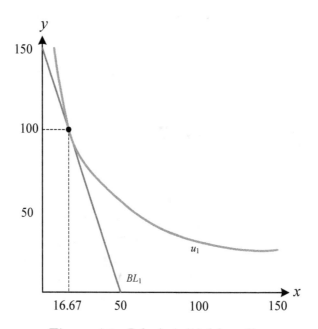

Figure 4.1. John's initial bundle.

- *Finding final bundle C.* Now with John's final prices, his tangency condition, $\frac{MU_x}{MU_y} = \frac{p_x}{p_y}$ is $\frac{y}{2x} = \frac{1}{1}$. Once again, we can rearrange this expression to obtain $y = 2x$. Inserting this expression into the new budget lines gives

$$x + \underbrace{2x}_{y} = 150.$$

As before, we can divide both sides of this expression by 3 to obtain $x = \frac{150}{3} = 50$ units. Using John's tangency condition, we can solve for John's consumption of good y, $y = 2x = 2(50) = 100$. This gives us John's final bundle $C = (50, 100)$. The final bundle, along with the initial bundle for comparison, is depicted in figure 4.2.

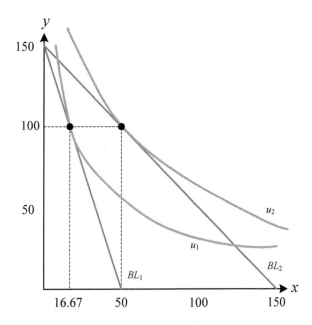

Figure 4.2. John's initial and final bundles.

- *Finding decomposition bundle B.* To break down John's change from his initial bundle to his final bundle, we need to satisfy both conditions as explained in example 4.8.

  - First, the decomposition bundle must reach the utility level John received under his initial bundle, which we can calculate by inserting bundle A into John's utility function,

$$(16.67)^{1/3}(100)^{2/3} = 55.04.$$

  Thus, John's decomposition bundle B must satisfy $x^{1/3}y^{2/3} = 55.04$.

  - Second, the decomposition bundle must be tangent to John's indifference curve. This happens where the slope of John's indifference curve is equal to the slope of his final budget line, which implies that we use the tangency condition from John's final bundle, $y = 2x$.

Substituting John's tangency condition into the first condition gives

$$x^{1/3}\underbrace{(2x)}_{y}{}^{2/3} = 55.04.$$

We can distribute the exponent through the parentheses to obtain

$$x^{1/3}2^{2/3}x^{2/3} = 55.04.$$

The left-hand side of this expression simplifies to $1.59x = 55.04$. Dividing both sides by 1.59 provides John's decomposition bundle value of good x,

$$x = \frac{55.04}{1.59} = 34.62 \text{ units.}$$

As before, we use John's tangency condition to find his decomposition value for good y,

$$y = 2x = 2(34.62) = 69.24 \text{ units.}$$

This gives us John's decomposition bundle $B = (34.62, 69.24)$. The decomposition bundle is added to our previous figure in figure 4.3.

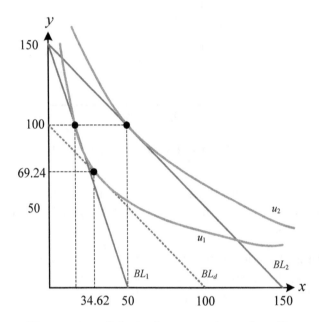

Figure 4.3. John's decomposition bundle.

- Last, we can calculate John's substitution and income effects by comparing the values of his different bundles:

$$\text{Substitution Effect:} \quad x_B - x_A = 34.62 - 16.67 = 17.95, \text{ and}$$
$$\text{Income Effect:} \quad x_C - x_B = 50 - 34.62 = 15.38.$$

which we depict in figure 4.4.

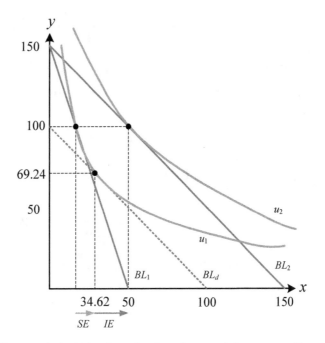

Figure 4.4. John's substitution and income effects.

Self-assessment exercise #4.9

SA 4.9 Chelsea's utility function is $u(x,y) = 3x + 4y^{1/2}$, her income is $I = \$220$, and $p_y = \$1$. The price of good x decreases from $p_x = \$3$ to $p'_x = \$2$. Using the steps in example 4.9, find the substitution and income effects.

- To begin our analysis, it is useful to consider Chelsea's marginal rate of substitution,

$$MRS_{x,y} = \frac{MU_x}{MU_y} = \frac{\frac{3}{2}x^{-1/2}}{4} = \frac{3}{8x^{1/2}}.$$

- *Finding initial bundle A.* Using Chelsea's initial prices, we can establish her tangency condition, $\frac{MU_x}{MU_y} = \frac{3}{1}$, as

$$\frac{3}{8x^{1/2}} = 3.$$

Solving this expression for x, we obtain

$$x = \left(\frac{1}{8}\right)^2 = \frac{1}{64} = 0.0156 \text{ units.}$$

Using Chelsea's budget line, we can substitute this result in to obtain

$$3\left(\frac{1}{64}\right) + y = 220.$$

81

Solving this expression for x, we obtain Chelsea's initial consumption of good y,

$$y = 220 - \frac{3}{64} = 219.95 \text{ units.}$$

This gives us Chelsea's initial bundle $A = (0.0156, 219.95)$.

- *Finding final bundle C.* Now with Chelsea's final prices, her tangency condition, $\frac{MU_x}{MU_y} = \frac{p_x}{p_y}$ is

$$\frac{3}{8x^{1/2}} = \frac{2}{1}.$$

Once again, we can solve this expression for x to obtain

$$x = \left(\frac{3}{16}\right)^2 = \frac{9}{256} = 0.0352 \text{ units.}$$

As before, we use Chelsea's budget line and substitute this result in to obtain

$$2\left(\frac{9}{256}\right) + y = 220.$$

Solving this expression for y, we obtain Chelsea's final consumption of good y,

$$y = 220 - \frac{18}{256} = 219.93 \text{ units,}$$

which provides Chelsea's final bundle $C = (0.0352, 219.93)$.

- *Finding decomposition bundle B.* Now we need to determine how Chelsea's bundle changes from her initial bundle to her final bundle, breaking them into the substitution and income effects. To calculate this, we need to satisfy both conditions as explained in example 4.9.

  - First, the decomposition bundle must reach the utility level Chelsea received under her initial bundle, which we can calculate by inserting bundle A into Chelsea's utility function,

  $$3(0.0156)^{1/2} + 4(219.95) = 880.18.$$

  Thus, Chelsea's decomposition bundle B must satisfy $3x^{1/2} + 4y = 880.18$.
  - Second, the decomposition bundle must be tangent to Chelsea's indifference curve. This happens where the slope of Chelsea's indifference curve is equal to the slope of her final budget line, which implies that we use the tangency condition from Chelsea's final bundle, $x = 0.0352$.

Substituting Chelsea's tangency condition into the first condition gives

$$3\left(\frac{9}{256}\right)^{1/2} + 4y = 880.18.$$

Since $3\left(\frac{9}{256}\right)^{1/2} = 0.5625$, we can solve this expression for good y to obtain,

$$x = \frac{880.18 - 0.5625}{4} = 219.90 \text{ units.}$$

This gives us Chelsea's decomposition bundle $B = (0.0352, 219.90)$.

- Last, we can calculate Chelsea's substitution and income effects by comparing the values of her different bundles:

$$\text{Substitution Effect:} \quad x_B - x_A = 0.0352 - 0.0156 = 0.0196, \text{ and}$$
$$\text{Income Effect:} \quad x_C - x_B = 0.0352 - 0.0352 = 0.$$

This result for Chelsea should make sense. Since the majority of her utility comes from consuming good y (the quasilinear parameter), Chelsea allocates all of her savings from the price change to purchasing more of good y. This leads to zero income effect with all of the gains due to Chelsea substituting from good y to good x.

4.2 Solutions to End-of-Chapter Exercises

Exercise #4.1 - Deriving Functions–I[A]

4.1 Consider an individual with a Cobb-Douglas utility function $u(x_1, x_2) = x_1 x_2$, facing an income $I = 100$ and prices p_1 and p_2 for goods 1 and 2, respectively.

(a) Find the demand function for each good.

- We can derive our demand functions using the same strategies from chapter 3.

- *Step 1.* To solve for our optimal consumption, first we must use the tangency condition, $\frac{MU_{x_1}}{MU_{x_2}} = \frac{p_1}{p_2}$.

  - For the left-hand side, we calculate the ratio of our marginal utilities, where $MU_{x_1} = \frac{\partial u(x_1, x_2)}{\partial x_1} = x_2$ and $MU_{x_2} = \frac{\partial u(x_1, x_2)}{\partial x_2} = x_1$. Therefore,

  $$\frac{MU_{x_1}}{MU_{x_2}} = \frac{x_2}{x_1}.$$

  - For the right-hand side, it is simply the ratio of the prices, $\frac{p_1}{p_2}$.
  - Setting them equal to one another gives

  $$\frac{x_2}{x_1} = \frac{p_1}{p_2},$$

  which we can rearrange to obtain $x_1 = \frac{p_2}{p_1} x_2$. Since our tangency condition contains both x_1 and x_2, we move on to step 2a.

- *Step 2a.* Next, we use our budget line, $p_1 x_1 + p_2 x_2 = I$ and substitute $\frac{p_2}{p_1} x_2$

83

for x_1, obtaining

$$p_1 \underbrace{\left(\frac{p_2}{p_1}x_2\right)}_{x_1} + p_2 x_2 = I.$$

– Combining terms, we have $2p_2 x_2 = I$, and we can divide both sides of this equation to obtain the demand function for good x_2,

$$x_2 = \frac{I}{2p_2} \text{ units.}$$

With a positive value of x_2, we can move on to step 4.

- *Step 4.* Last, we return to our tangency condition to determine the demand function for good x_1.

  – Plugging in our value for x_2 gives $x_1 = \frac{p_2}{p_1}\left(\frac{I}{p_2}\right) = \frac{I}{2p_1}$ units.

  – Last, plugging in our value for income of $I = \$100$, we have our final demand functions,

$$x_1 = \frac{100}{2p_1} = \frac{50}{p_1}, \text{ and}$$
$$x_2 = \frac{100}{2p_2} = \frac{50}{p_2}.$$

(b) Assume that the price of both goods increases by 10 percent. Find the new demand functions for each good.

- In this situation, we simply increase our prices by 10 percent, or multiply them by 1.1. The resulting demand functions are,

$$x_1 = \frac{50}{1.1p_1} = \frac{45.45}{p_1}, \text{ and}$$
$$x_2 = \frac{50}{1.1p_2} = \frac{45.45}{p_2}.$$

(c) Find the price-consumption curve of each good. Interpret.

- To find the price-consumption curve, we calculate the ratio of the demand for good x_2 to the demand for good x_1, obtaining,

$$\frac{x_2}{x_1} = \frac{\frac{50}{p_2}}{\frac{50}{p_1}}.$$

which simplifies to

$$\frac{x_2}{x_1} = \frac{p_1}{p_2}.$$

Intuitively, this price-consumption curve implies that as the price of good 1 increases, the ratio on the right-hand side increases, implying that the ratio on the left-hand side, $\frac{x_2}{x_1}$, must also increase, and more of good 2 is consumed relative to good 1. We see the same effect when the price of good 2

84

decreases, as it also increases the ratio on the right-hand side of the equation. In contrast, as either the price of good 1 decreases or the price of good 2 increases, the ratio on the right-hand side decreases, which implies that more of good 1 is consumed relative to good 2. Solving this expression for x_2, the we obtain

$$x_2 = \frac{p_1}{p_2} x_1,$$

which is depicted in figure 4.5.

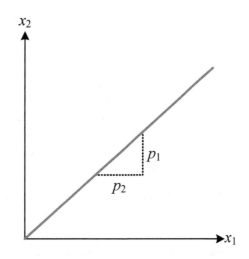

Figure 4.5. Price-consumption curve.

(d) Find the Engel curve of each good. Interpret.

- *Good 1*: Solving the demand function for good 1 for I, we obtain the Engel curve,

$$I = 2p_1 x_1.$$

This Engel curve has a positive slope, implying that demand increases with income and that good 1 is a normal good.

- *Good 2*: Solving the demand function for good 2 for I, we obtain the Engel curve,

$$I = 2p_2 x_2.$$

This Engel curve has a positive slope, implying that demand increases with income and that good 2 is a normal good. This curve is depicted in figure 4.6.

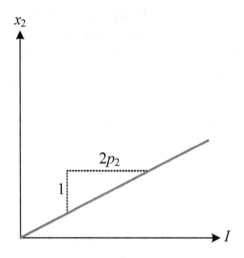

Figure 4.6. Engel curve.

Exercise #4.3 - Quasilinear Utility–I^B

4.3 Repeat your analysis in exercise 4.1, but assuming a quasilinear utility function $u(x_1, x_2) = \ln x_1 + x_2$.

(a) Find the demand function for each good.

- We can derive our demand functions using the same strategies from chapter 3.
- *Step 1.* To solve for our optimal consumption, first we must use the tangency condition, $\frac{MU_{x_1}}{MU_{x_2}} = \frac{p_1}{p_2}$.
  - For the left-hand side, we calculate the ratio of our marginal utilities, where $MU_{x_1} = \frac{\partial u(x_1, x_2)}{\partial x_1} = \frac{1}{x_1}$ and $MU_{x_2} = \frac{\partial u(x_1, x_2)}{\partial x_2} = 1$. Therefore,

$$\frac{MU_{x_1}}{MU_{x_2}} = \frac{\frac{1}{x_1}}{1} = \frac{1}{x_1}.$$

  - For the right-hand side, it is simply the ratio of the prices, $\frac{p_1}{p_2}$.
  - Setting them equal to one another gives

$$\frac{1}{x_1} = \frac{p_1}{p_2}.$$

  Since our tangency condition only contains x_1 we move on to step 2b.
- *Step 2b.* Now we solve our tangency condition for x_1. Rearranging terms, we obtain our demand for good 1,

$$x_1 = \frac{p_2}{p_1}.$$

Last, to find our demand for good 2, we plug our value of x_1 into our budget

86

line, $p_1 x_1 + p_2 x_2 = I$ to obtain,

$$p_1 \underbrace{\left(\frac{p_2}{p_1} \right)}_{x_1} + p_2 x_2 = I.$$

Rearranging terms,

$$p_2 x_2 = I - p_2,$$

and, dividing both sides by p_2, provides our demand function for good 2,

$$x_2 = \frac{I - p_2}{p_2}.$$

- Last, plugging in our value for income of $I = \$100$, we have our final demand functions,

$$x_1 = \frac{p_2}{p_1}, \text{ and}$$
$$x_2 = \frac{100 - p_2}{p_2}.$$

(b) Assume that the price of both goods increases by 10 percent. Find the new demand functions for each good.

- In this situation, we simply increase our prices by 10 percent, or multiply them by 1.1. The resulting demand functions are,

$$x_1 = \frac{1.1 p_2}{1.1 p_1} = \frac{p_2}{p_1}, \text{ and}$$
$$x_2 = \frac{100 - 1.1 p_2}{1.1 p_2}.$$

(c) Find the price-consumption curve of each good. Interpret.

- To find the price-consumption curve, we calculate the ratio of the demand for good x_2 to the demand for good x_1, obtaining,

$$\frac{x_2}{x_1} = \frac{\frac{100 - p_2}{p_2}}{\frac{p_2}{p_1}},$$

which simplifies to

$$\frac{x_2}{x_1} = \frac{p_1 (100 - p_2)}{(p_2)^2}.$$

Intuitively, this price-consumption curve implies that as the price of good 1 increases, the ratio on the right-hand side increases, implying that the ration on the left-hand side, $\frac{x_2}{x_1}$, must also increase, and more of good 2 is consumed relative to good 1. We see the same effect when the price of good 2 decreases, as it also increases the ratio on the right-hand side of the equation. In contrast, as either the price of good 1 decreases or the price of good 2 increases, the ratio on the right-hand side decreases, which implies that more of good 1 is consumed relative to good 2. Solving this expression for x_2, we obtain

$$x_2 = \frac{p_1(100 - p_2)}{(p_2)^2} x_1,$$

which is depicted in figure 4.7.

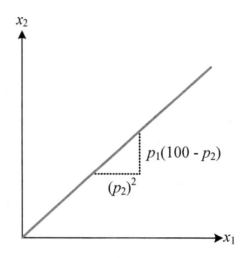

Figure 4.7. Price-consumption curve.

(d) Find the Engel curve of each good. Interpret.

- *Good 1*: Income does not affect the consumption of good 1 at all. This implies that good 1 is neither negative nor positive and is simply consumed based on relative prices.

- *Good 2*: Solving the demand function for good 2 for I, we obtain the Engel curve,

$$I = p_2 x_2 + p_2.$$

This Engel curve has a positive slope (with a positive intercept), implying that demand increases with income and that good 2 is a normal good.

Exercise #4.5 - Decomposition Bundles[B]

4.5 Consider an individual with an utility function $u(x, y) = x^2 y$, and facing prices $p_x = \$2$ and $p_y = \$4$.

(a) Assuming that his income is $I = \$800$, find the optimal consumption of goods x and y that maximizes his utility. That is, solve his UMP.

- We can derive our demand functions using the same strategies from chapter 3.

- *Step 1*. To solve for our optimal consumption, first we must use the tangency condition, $\frac{MU_x}{MU_y} = \frac{p_x}{p_y}$.

- For the left-hand side, we calculate the ratio of our marginal utilities, where $MU_x = \frac{\partial u(x,y)}{\partial x} = 2xy$ and $MU_y = \frac{\partial u(x,y)}{\partial y} = x^2$. Therefore,

$$\frac{MU_x}{MU_y} = \frac{2xy}{x^2} = \frac{2y}{x}.$$

- For the right-hand side, it is simply the ratio of the prices, $\frac{p_x}{p_y}$.
- Setting them equal to one another gives

$$\frac{2y}{x} = \frac{p_x}{p_y},$$

which we can rearrange to obtain $x = \frac{2p_y}{p_x}y$. Since our tangency condition contains both x and y, we move on to step 2a.

- *Step 2a.* Next, we use our budget line, $p_x x + p_y y = I$ and substitute $\frac{2p_y}{p_x}y$ for x, obtaining

$$p_x \underbrace{\left(\frac{2p_y}{p_x}y\right)}_{x} + p_y y = I.$$

- Combining terms, we have $3p_y y = I$, and we can divide both sides of this equation to obtain the demand function for good y,

$$y = \frac{I}{3p_y} \text{ units.}$$

With a positive value of y, we can move on to step 4.

- *Step 4.* Last, we return to our tangency condition to determine the demand function for good x.
  - Plugging in our value for y gives

$$x = \frac{2p_y}{p_x}\left(\frac{I}{3p_y}\right) = \frac{2I}{3p_x} \text{ units.}$$

- *Finding initial bundle A.* Plugging in our value for prices, $p_x = \$2$, $p_y = \$4$, and income of $I = \$800$, we have our initial bundle,

$$x = \frac{2(800)}{3(2)} = 266.67 \text{ units, and}$$

$$y = \frac{800}{3(4)} = 66.67 \text{ units.}$$

This implies that our initial bundle is $A = (266.67, 66.67)$.

(b) Consider now that the price of good y decreases from $p_y = \$4$ to $p_y' = \$3$. Find this consumer's new optimal consumption bundle. Then, identify the total effect of the price change, and decompose it into the substitution and income effects.

- *Finding final bundle C.* Now, we plug in the final prices $p_x = \$2$, $p_y' = \$3$, and

89

income of $I = \$800$ into our demand functions to obtain our final bundle,

$$x = \frac{2(800)}{3(2)} = 266.67 \text{ units, and}$$

$$y = \frac{800}{3(3)} = 88.89 \text{ units.}$$

This implies that our final bundle is $C = (266.67, 88.89)$.

- *Total effect.* To find the total effect, we simply take the difference between the final value of good y and the initial value of good y, obtaining,

$$TE = y_C - y_A = 88.89 - 66.67 = 22.22 \text{ units.}$$

- *Finding decomposition bundle B.* Recall that the decomposition bundle must satisfy two conditions:

  - Bundle B must reach the initial utility level. Plugging in our initial bundle A into the utility function provides a utility level of

  $$u(266.67, 66.67) = 266.67^2 \times 66.67 = 4,741,096.30.$$

  This implies that our decomposition bundle must satisfy

  $$x^2 y = 4,741,096.30.$$

  - Bundle B must be tangent to BL_d, the decomposition budget line that has the same slope as the final budget line. To find this tangency point, we plug in the final prices to our tangency condition from before,

  $$\frac{2y}{x} = \frac{p_1}{p_2'} = \frac{2}{3}.$$

  We can rearrange this expression to obtain $x = 3y$.
  - We now have a system of two equations and two unknowns. Substituting $3y$ for x in our utility function, we have

  $$\underbrace{(3y)^2}_{x} y = 4,741,096.30,$$

  which rearranges to $y^3 = 526,788.48$. Taking the cube root of both sides, we obtain our decomposition value of good y, $y = 80.76$ units. Last, we plug our value of y into the decomposition tangency condition to find x,

  $$x = 3(80.76) = 242.29 \text{ units.}$$

  This implies that our decomposition bundle is $B = (242.29, 80.76)$.

- *Substitution and income effects.* With our decomposition bundle found, we can calculate the substitution effect as the movement along our original utility

90

curve, from bundle A to bundle B,

$$SE = y_B - y_A = 80.76 - 66.67 = 14.09 \text{ units.}$$

Likewise, our income effect is the movement from our initial utility level to our final utility level, from bundle B to bundle C,

$$IE = y_C - y_B = 88.89 - 80.76 = 8.13 \text{ units.}$$

(c) Considering that the price of good y remains at $p_y = \$4$, assume that the consumer seeks to reach the same utility level as in part (a). Find the optimal consumption of goods x and y that minimizes his expenditure. That is, solve his EMP.

- We can derive our demand functions using the same strategies from chapter 3.
- *Step 1.* To solve for our optimal consumption, first we must use the tangency condition, $\frac{MU_x}{MU_y} = \frac{p_x}{p_y}$.
  - For the left-hand side, we calculate the ratio of our marginal utilities, where $MU_x = \frac{\partial u(x,y)}{\partial x} = 2xy$ and $MU_y = \frac{\partial u(x,y)}{\partial y} = x^2$. Therefore,

  $$\frac{MU_x}{MU_y} = \frac{2xy}{x^2} = \frac{2y}{x}.$$

  - For the right-hand side, it is simply the ratio of the prices, $\frac{p_x}{p_y}$.
  - Setting them equal to one another gives

  $$\frac{2y}{x} = \frac{p_x}{p_y},$$

  which we can rearrange to obtain $x = \frac{2p_y}{p_x}y$. Since our tangency condition contains both x and y, we move on to step 2a.
- *Step 2a.* Next, we use our utility curve, $x^2y = u$ and substitute $\frac{2p_y}{p_x}y$ for x, obtaining

  $$\underbrace{\left(\frac{2p_y}{p_x}y\right)^2}_{x} y = u.$$

  - Combining terms, we have $\frac{4(p_y)^2}{(p_x)^2}y^3 = u$, and we can divide both sides of this equation, then take a cube root to obtain the compensated demand function for good y,

  $$y = \left(\frac{(p_x)^2 u}{4(p_y)^2}\right)^{\frac{1}{3}} \text{ units.}$$

  With a positive value of y, we can move on to step 4.
- *Step 4.* Last, we return to our tangency condition to determine the demand function for good x.

– Plugging in our value for y gives

$$x = \frac{2p_y}{p_x} \left(\frac{(p_x)^2 u}{4(p_y)^2} \right)^{\frac{1}{3}}.$$

Moving all of the terms inside of the exponent, we have,

$$x = \left(\frac{8(p_y)^3}{(p_x)^3} \frac{(p_x)^2 u}{4(p_y)^2} \right)^{\frac{1}{3}},$$

and simplifying, we obtain,

$$x = \left(\frac{2p_y u}{p_x} \right)^{\frac{1}{3}} \text{ units.}$$

- *Finding initial bundle A.* Plugging in our value for prices, $p_x = \$2$, $p_y = \$4$, and desired utility level of $u = 4,741,096.30$ (from part (b)), we have our initial bundle,

$$x = \left(\frac{2p_y u}{p_x} \right)^{\frac{1}{3}} = \left(\frac{2(4)(4,741,096.30)}{2} \right)^{\frac{1}{3}} = 266.67 \text{ units, and}$$

$$y = \left(\frac{(p_x)^2 u}{4(p_y)^2} \right)^{\frac{1}{3}} = \left(\frac{2^2(4,741,096.30)}{4(4^2)} \right)^{\frac{1}{3}} = 66.67 \text{ units.}$$

This implies that our initial bundle is $A = (266.67, 66.67)$.

(d) As in part (b), assume that the price of good y decreases from $p_y = \$4$ to $p_y' = \$3$. Find this consumer's new optimal consumption bundle. Comparing your results from parts (c) and (d), argue that the total effect that we find when using the compensated demand (the result of the EMP) measures the substitution effect alone. Interpret.

- *Finding final bundle C.* Plugging in our value for prices, $p_x = \$2$, $p_y' = \$3$, and desired utility level of $u = 4,741,096.30$ (from part (b)), we have our final bundle,

$$x = \left(\frac{2p_y' u}{p_x} \right)^{\frac{1}{3}} = \left(\frac{2(3)(4,741,096.30)}{2} \right)^{\frac{1}{3}} = 242.29 \text{ units, and}$$

$$y = \left(\frac{(p_x)^2 u}{4(p_y')^2} \right)^{\frac{1}{3}} = \left(\frac{2^2(4,741,096.30)}{4(3^2)} \right)^{\frac{1}{3}} = 80.76 \text{ units.}$$

This implies that our final bundle is $C = (242.29, 80.76)$. Interestingly, our final bundle is identical to the decomposition bundle we found in part (b). Intuitively, we held our initial utility constant as we adjusted our prices, which is exactly the process used to calculate the decomposition bundle.

Exercise #4.7 - Income Effects[A]

4.7 Peter informs us that his demand for housing decreases when his income decreases. Can we infer from that information that, after an increase in the price of housing, Peter's demand will decrease?

- Yes, we can. From Peter's first statement, we know the housing is a normal good since his demand decreases as his income decreases. In addition, since the price of housing increases, we know that Peter's substitution effect will be negative along with his income effect (since housing is a normal good). This implies that Peter's total effect will be unambiguously negative, so his demand for housing must decrease after an increase in the price of housing.

Exercise #4.9 - Linear Demand[A]

4.9 Suppose that the demand for cookies (good x) was expressed as $x = 250 - 3p_x$, where p_x is the price of cookies.

(a) Calculate the price elasticity of demand.

- Using the formula for the price elasticity of demand,

$$\varepsilon_{x,p_x} = \frac{\partial x}{\partial p_x} \frac{p_x}{x}.$$

For the first term, we can differentiate the demand function to obtain,

$$\frac{\partial x}{\partial p_x} = -3.$$

In addition, we can substitute $250 - 3p_x$ for x in the price elasticity of demand formula, obtaining

$$\varepsilon_{x,p_x} = \frac{\partial x}{\partial p_x} \frac{p_x}{x} = -3\frac{p_x}{250 - 3p_x} = -\frac{3p_x}{250 - 3p_x}.$$

(b) For what prices is the demand for cookies elastic?

- The price elasticity of demand for cookies is elastic when it is less than -1. Thus, we simply need to solve the expression,

$$-\frac{3p_x}{250 - 3p_x} < -1.$$

Rearranging terms, we have $-6p_x < -250$. Dividing both sides of this expression by -6, we obtain our price $p_x > 41.67$.

(c) For what prices is the demand for cookies inelastic?

- The price elasticity of demand for cookies is inelastic when it is greater than -1. Thus, we simply need to solve the expression,

$$-3\frac{p_x}{250 - 3p_x} > -1.$$

Rearranging terms, we have $-6p_x > -250$. Dividing both sides of this expression by -6, we obtain our price $p_x < 41.67$.

Exercise #4.11 - Income Elasticity–I^B

4.11 Suppose that the demand for beef (good x) can be expressed as $x = \frac{2I-I^2}{p_x}$, where I is the consumer's income, measured in units of $\$100,000$.

(a) Calculate the income elasticity for beef.

- We calculate the income elasticity by applying our income elasticity formula,

$$\varepsilon_{x,I} = \frac{\partial x}{\partial I}\frac{I}{x},$$

where the left term can be obtained by differentiating the demand function with respect to I,

$$\frac{\partial x}{\partial I} = \frac{2-2I}{p_x}.$$

Last, we substitute $\frac{2I-I^2}{p_x}$ for x to obtain our income elasticity,

$$
\begin{aligned}
\varepsilon_{x,I} &= \frac{\partial x}{\partial I}\frac{I}{x} \\
&= \frac{2-2I}{p_x}\frac{I}{\frac{2I-I^2}{p_x}} \\
&= \frac{(2-2I)I}{p_x\frac{2I-I^2}{p_x}} \\
&= \frac{2I-2I^2}{2I-I^2}.
\end{aligned}
$$

(b) Provide an interpretation for the income elasticity for beef. For what values of I is beef a normal good?

- Looking at the numerator of the income elasticity, we have a normal good when it is positive,

$$2I - 2I^2 > 0$$

Dividing both sides by $2I$ and rearranging, this implies that beef is a normal good when $I < 1$. Intuitively, at low income levels, consumers increase their beef consumption as their income increases, but after a certain income level ($I > 1$), beef becomes an inferior good as consumers substitute into other high-quality foods like Wagyu. The Engel curve for beef is depicted in figure 4.8.

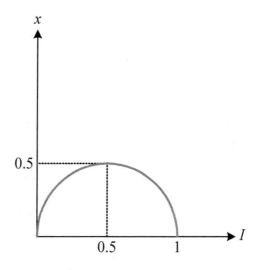

Figure 4.8. Engel curve.

Exercise #4.13 - Perfect Complements[B]

4.13 Consider an individual with utility function $u(x,y) = \min\{2x, 3y\}$, facing an income $I = 250$ and prices p_x and p_y for goods 1 and 2, respectively.

(a) Find the demand function for each good.

- We must first determine the preferred consumption ratio given that we have perfect complements. Since we receive our utility as the lesser of $2x$ and $3y$, he prefers to consume them in that ratio, $2x = 3y$, or $x = \frac{3}{2}y$. What we derived is essentially a tangency condition. Since our tangency condition contains both x and y, we move on to step 2a from the utility maximization procedure in chapter 3.

- *Step 2a.* Next, we use our budget line, $p_x x + p_y y = I$ and substitute $\frac{3}{2}y$ for x, obtaining

$$p_x \underbrace{\left(\frac{3}{2}y\right)}_{x} + p_y y = I.$$

  - Combining terms, we have $\left(\frac{3}{2}p_x + p_y\right)y = I$, and we can divide both sides of this equation to obtain the amount of good y that he consumes,

$$y = \frac{I}{\frac{3}{2}p_x + p_y}$$
$$= \frac{2I}{3p_x + 2p_y} \text{ units.}$$

  With a positive value of y, we can move on to step 4.

- *Step 4.* Last, we return to our tangency condition to determine how much of good x he consumes.

95

– Plugging in our value for y gives

$$x = \frac{3}{2}\left(\frac{2I}{3p_x + 2p_y}\right)$$

$$= \frac{3I}{3p_x + 2p_y} \text{ units.}$$

- Last, plugging in our value for income of $I = \$250$, we have our final demand functions,

$$x = \frac{750}{3p_x + 2p_y}, \text{ and}$$

$$y = \frac{500}{3p_x + 2p_y}$$

(b) Calculate the price elasticity of demand and income elasticities for both goods. Interpret.

- *Price elasticity of demand:*

  – *Good x.* Using the formula for the price elasticity of demand,

  $$\varepsilon_{x,p_x} = \frac{\partial x}{\partial p_x}\frac{p_x}{x}.$$

  For the first term, we can differentiate the demand function with respect to p_x to obtain,

  $$\frac{\partial x}{\partial p_x} = -\frac{9I}{(3p_x + 2p_y)^2}.$$

  In addition, we can substitute $\frac{3I}{3p_x+2p_y}$ for x in the price elasticity of demand formula, obtaining

  $$\varepsilon_{x,p_x} = \frac{\partial x}{\partial p_x}\frac{p_x}{x}$$

  $$= -\frac{9I}{(3p_x + 2p_y)^2}\frac{p_x}{\frac{3I}{3p_x+2p_y}}$$

  $$= -\frac{9Ip_x(3p_x + 2p_y)}{3I(3p_x + 2p_y)^2}$$

  $$= -\frac{3p_x}{3p_x + 2p_y}.$$

  The price elasticity of demand in this case is negative (as expected), but greater than -1, implying that the price elasticity of demand is inelastic. Thus, the consumer is not too sensitive to the price of good x.

  – *Good y.* Using the formula for the price elasticity of demand,

  $$\varepsilon_{y,p_y} = \frac{\partial y}{\partial p_y}\frac{p_y}{y}.$$

For the first term, we can differentiate the demand function with respect to p_y to obtain,

$$\frac{\partial y}{\partial p_y} = -\frac{4I}{(3p_x + 2p_y)^2}.$$

In addition, we can substitute $\frac{2I}{3p_x + 2p_y}$ for y in the price elasticity of demand formula, obtaining

$$
\begin{aligned}
\varepsilon_{y,p_y} &= \frac{\partial y}{\partial p_y}\frac{p_y}{y} \\
&= -\frac{4I}{(3p_x + 2p_y)^2}\frac{p_y}{\frac{2I}{3p_x + 2p_y}} \\
&= -\frac{4Ip_y(3p_x + 2p_y)}{2I(3p_x + 2p_y)^2} \\
&= -\frac{2p_y}{3p_x + 2p_y}.
\end{aligned}
$$

The price elasticity of demand in this case is negative (as expected), but greater than -1, implying that the price elasticity of demand is inelastic. Thus, the consumer is not too sensitive to the price of good y.

- *Income elasticity:*
  - *Good x.* Using the formula for the income elasticity,

$$\varepsilon_{x,I} = \frac{\partial x}{\partial I}\frac{I}{x}.$$

For the first term, we can differentiate the demand function with respect to I to obtain,

$$\frac{\partial x}{\partial I} = \frac{3}{3p_x + 2p_y}.$$

In addition, we can substitute $\frac{3I}{3p_x + 2p_y}$ for x in the price elasticity of demand formula, obtaining

$$
\begin{aligned}
\varepsilon_{x,I} &= \frac{\partial x}{\partial I}\frac{I}{x} \\
&= \frac{3}{3p_x + 2p_y}\frac{I}{\frac{3I}{3p_x + 2p_y}} \\
&= \frac{3I(3p_x + 2p_y)}{3I(3p_x + 2p_y)} = 1.
\end{aligned}
$$

With an income elasticity equal to 1, we know that this is a normal good, and that a 1 percent increase in income will correspond with a 1 percent increase in the consumption of good x, as we would expect with perfect complements.

– *Good y.* Using the formula for the income elasticity,

$$\varepsilon_{y,I} = \frac{\partial y}{\partial I}\frac{I}{y}.$$

For the first term, we can differentiate the demand function with respect to I to obtain,

$$\frac{\partial y}{\partial I} = \frac{2}{3p_x + 2p_y}.$$

In addition, we can substitute $\frac{2I}{3p_x+2p_y}$ for y in the price elasticity of demand formula, obtaining

$$
\begin{aligned}
\varepsilon_{y,I} &= \frac{\partial y}{\partial I}\frac{I}{y} \\
&= \frac{2}{3p_x + 2p_y}\frac{I}{\frac{2I}{3p_x+2p_y}} \\
&= \frac{2(3p_x + 2p_y)}{2(3p_x + 2p_y)} = 1.
\end{aligned}
$$

With an income elasticity equal to 1, we know that this is a normal good, and that a 1 percent increase in income will correspond with a 1 percent increase in the consumption of good y, as we would expect with perfect complements.

(c) Find the price-consumption curve of each good. Interpret.

- Using the price-consumption curve formula,

$$\frac{y}{x} = \frac{\frac{2I}{3p_x+2p_y}}{\frac{3I}{3p_x+2p_y}} = \frac{2}{3}.$$

The price-consumption curve is constant in this case, which corresponds to what we know about perfect complements. Intuitively, the consumer always wants to consume 2 units of good x with 3 units of good y, so the prices really do not matter to his relative consumption of the goods. This price-consumption curve is depicted in figure 4.9.

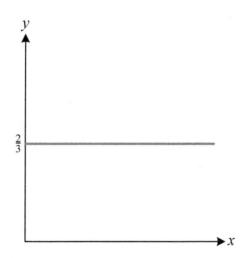

Figure 4.9. Flat price-consumption curve.

Exercise #4.15 - Deriving Functions–II^A

4.15 Consider an individual with the Cobb-Douglas utility function $u(x,y) = x^{0.4}y^{0.6}$, facing an income I and prices p_x and p_y for goods x and y, respectively.

   (a) Find the demand function for each good.

- We can derive our demand functions using the same strategies from chapter 3.
- *Step 1.* To solve for our optimal consumption, first we must use the tangency condition, $\frac{MU_x}{MU_y} = \frac{p_x}{p_y}$.
  - For the left-hand side, we calculate the ratio of our marginal utilities, where $MU_x = \frac{\partial u(x,y)}{\partial x} = 0.4x^{-0.6}y^{0.6}$ and $MU_{x2} = \frac{\partial u(x,y)}{\partial y} = 0.6x^{0.4}y^{-0.4}$. Therefore,
  $$\frac{MU_x}{MU_y} = \frac{0.4x^{-0.6}y^{0.6}}{0.6x^{0.4}y^{-0.4}} = \frac{2y}{3x}.$$
  - For the right-hand side, it is simply the ratio of the prices, $\frac{p_x}{p_y}$.
  - Setting them equal to one another gives
  $$\frac{2y}{3x} = \frac{p_x}{p_y},$$
  which we can rearrange to obtain $x = \frac{2p_y}{3p_x}y$. Since our tangency condition contains both x and y, we move on to step 2a.
- *Step 2a.* Next, we use our budget line, $p_x x + p_y y = I$ and substitute $\frac{2p_y}{3p_x}y$ for x, obtaining
$$p_x \underbrace{\left(\frac{2p_y}{3p_x}y\right)}_{x} + p_y y = I.$$

99

– Combining terms, we have $\frac{5p_y}{3}y = I$, and we can divide both sides of this equation to obtain the demand function for good y,

$$y = \frac{3I}{5p_y} \text{ units.}$$

With a positive value of y, we can move on to step 4.

- *Step 4.* Last, we return to our tangency condition to determine the demand function for good x_1.

– Plugging in our value for y gives

$$x = \frac{2p_y}{3}\left(\frac{3I}{5p_y}\right) = \frac{2I}{5p_x} \text{ units.}$$

(b) Find the price-consumption curve of each good. Interpret.

- Using the price-consumption curve formula,

$$\frac{y}{x} = \frac{\frac{3I}{5p_y}}{\frac{2I}{5p_x}} = \frac{3p_x}{2p_y}.$$

The price-consumption curve is increasing with increases in p_x or decreases in p_y. This curve is also decreasing with increases in p_y or decreases in p_x. Intuitively, as good x becomes more expensive, consumers respond by consuming more of good y relative to good x. In addition, the gravitation toward good y is stronger since the consumer has stronger preferences for good y. This manifests itself in the price-consumption curve as the slope is greater than 1. This price-consumption curve is depicted in figure 4.10.

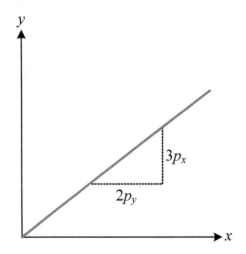

Figure 4.10. Price-consumption curve.

(c) Find the Engel curve of each good. Interpret.

100

- *Good x.* Solving the demand function for I,

$$I = \frac{5p_x}{2}x,$$

which has a constant, positive slope for all values of x. This implies that good x is a normal good.
- *Good y.* Solving the demand function for I,

$$I = \frac{5p_y}{3}y,$$

which has a constant, positive slope for all values of y. This implies that good y is a normal good.

Exercise #4.17 - Income Elasticity–II[A]

4.17 Suppose that the demand for good x can be expressed as $x = \frac{1}{2Ip_x}$, where p_x is the price of good x and I is the consumer's income.

(a) Calculate and interpret the income elasticity for good x.
- Using the formula for the income elasticity,

$$\varepsilon_{x,I} = \frac{\partial x}{\partial I}\frac{I}{x}.$$

For the first term, we can differentiate the demand function with respect to I to obtain,

$$\frac{\partial x}{\partial I} = -\frac{1}{2I^2 p_x}.$$

In addition, we can substitute $\frac{1}{2Ip_x}$ for x in the price elasticity of demand formula, obtaining

$$
\begin{aligned}
\varepsilon_{x,I} &= \frac{\partial x}{\partial I}\frac{I}{x} \\
&= -\frac{1}{2I^2 p_x}\frac{I}{\frac{1}{2Ip_x}} = -1.
\end{aligned}
$$

With a value of -1, this implies that good x is inferior. In fact, as the consumer's income increases by 1 percent, his consumption of good x decreases proportionally, 1 percent.

(b) Derive and plot the Engel curve for good x.
- Solving the demand function for I,

$$I = \frac{1}{2p_x x},$$

which has a negative slope for all values of x as depicted in figure 4.11. This implies that good x is an inferior good.

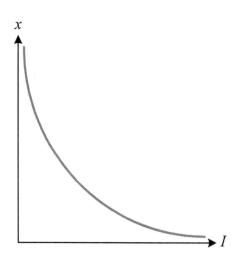

Figure 4.11. Engel curve.

Exercise #4.19 - Giffen Good?[B]

4.19 Suppose that you work in a hardware store in a community that is expecting a major hurricane in the next few days. To ration your plywood, you start to increase its price, but you find that with each price increase, more people seem to purchase your plywood. You begin to expect that your plywood may be a Giffen good.

(a) Provide an argument why plywood is a Giffen good under these circumstances.

- Since the quantity demanded for plywood is increasing along with the price, it implies that this good violates the Law of Demand, and is a Giffen good.

(b) Provide an alternative explanation for the increase in plywood sales.

- It is possible that consumer preferences for plywood are changing as rapidly as prices in anticipation of the hurricane. With rapidly changing preferences, the demand curve would be shifting outward, increasing the equilibrium quantity demanded and price of plywood without ever violating the Law of Demand.

Chapter 5 - Measuring Welfare Changes

5.1 Solutions to Self-Assessment Exercises

Self-assessment exercise #5.1

SA 5.1 Repeat the analysis in example 5.1, but considering now a demand function $p(q) = 11 - \frac{1}{3}q$. What is the change in CS when the price of good x decreases from \$4 to \$3?

- With the new demand function at a price of $p = \$4$, output is the level of q that solves $4 = 11 - \frac{1}{3}q$; that is, $q = 21$ units. Consumer surplus here is represented as area A in the figure with the area

$$CS = \frac{1}{2}(11 - 4)(21) = 73.5.$$

If prices fall to $p = \$3$, output will increase to $3 = 11 - \frac{1}{3}q$; that is, $q = 24$ units. Consumer surplus will increase by the size of areas B and C in the figure. This change in consumer surplus, ΔCS is

$$\Delta CS = B + C$$
$$= (4 - 3)(21) + \frac{1}{2}(4 - 3)(24 - 21)$$
$$= 21 + 1.5 = 22.5.$$

The increase in consumer surplus is 22.5, which produces a new consumer surplus of $73.5 + 22.5 = 96$.

Self-assessment exercise #5.2

SA 5.2 Repeat the analysis in example 5.2, but assume a demand function $x = \frac{3I}{2\sqrt{p_x}}$. Still assuming that the price of good x decreases from \$4 to \$3, what is the change in CS, ΔCS?

- The increase in consumer surplus here is represented by

$$\Delta CS = \int_3^4 \frac{3I}{2\sqrt{p_x}} dp_x$$
$$= \frac{3I}{2} \int_3^4 \frac{1}{\sqrt{p_x}} dp_x$$
$$= \frac{3I}{2} \, 2\sqrt{p_x}\Big|_3^4$$
$$= \frac{3I}{2} \left[2\sqrt{4} - 2\sqrt{3}\right] = 0.8I.$$

Self-assessment exercise #5.3

SA 5.3 Repeat the analysis in example 5.3, assuming the same utility function and $p_y = \$1$, but consider that income is $I = \$125$ and the price of good x decreases from $p_x = \$2$

to $p'_x = \$1$.

- First, we need to use the tangency condition to find the bundles at the initial and final prices. From $\frac{MU_x}{MU_y} = \frac{p_x}{p_y}$, we obtain $\frac{y}{x} = \frac{p_x}{p_y}$. This simplifies to $y = p_x x$ since $p_y = \$1$. We can insert this result into the budget line $p_x x + p_y y = I$, which, in this case is $p_x x + y = \$125$, we find

$$p_x x + \underbrace{p_x x}_{y = p_x x} = 125,$$

which simplifies to

$$2p_x x = 125.$$

Solving for x, we find that $x = \frac{125}{2p_x}$. We can then insert this back into the expression we found from the tangency condition, $y = p_x x$, to find the demand for good y; that is, $y = p_x \frac{125}{2p_x} = \frac{125}{2} = 62.5$ units.

Let us now consider that the price of good x decreases from $p_x = \$2$ to $p'_x = \$1$, while the price of good y remains fixed at $p_y = \$1$.

1. *Finding initial bundle A.* At the initial price $p_x = \$2$, the demand for good x is $x_A = \frac{125}{2 \cdot 2} = 31.25$ units.

2. *Finding final bundle C.* At the final price of $p'_x = \$1$, the demand for good x increases to $x_C = \frac{125}{2} = 62.5$ units.

3. *Finding decomposition bundle B.* At the decomposition bundle, the consumer must:

   (a) Reach the same utility level as with the initial bundle $A = (31.25, 62.5)$, which is

   $$u_A = 31.25 \cdot 62.5 = 1,953.125.$$

   Therefore, the amount of goods x and y that she consumes at the decomposition bundle B, (x_B, y_B), must also yield a utility level of $1,953.125$, which we can mathematically express as

   $$(x_B)(y_B) = 1,953.125.$$

   (b) The consumer's indifference curve must be tangent to the budget line; that is, $\frac{MU_x}{MU_y} = \frac{p_x}{p_y}$, or, in our context $y = p_x x$. Since, $p'_x = 1$, the tangency condition can be written as $y = x$. Substituting in the above equation

   $$u_B = (x_B)(y_B) = (x_B)(x_B) = 1,953.125,$$

   which simplifies first to $x_B^2 = 1,953.125$, and by taking the square root of each side, we find that $x_B = 44.19$. We can insert this into the tangency condition $y = x$, to find the amount of good y that the consumer has at bundle B, finding $y_B = 44.19$ units.

4. *Evaluating the CV.* The CV is given by $CV = I - I_B$, where $I = \$125$ is the consumer's income and I_B represents the income that the individual needs to purchase the decomposition bundle $B = (44.19, 44.19)$ at the final prices.

Specifically,

$$I_B = (\$1 \times 44.19) + (\$1 \times 44.19) = \$88.38.$$

Thus, the CV is

$$CV = I - I_B = \$100 - \$88.38 = \$11.62.$$

Therefore, after experiencing the price decrease, if we reduce the consumer's income by \$11.62, her utility level will coincide with that from before the price decrease.

Self-assessment exercise #5.4

SA 5.4 Repeat the analysis in example 5.4, assuming the same utility function and $p_y = \$1$, but consider that income is $I = \$125$, and the price of good x decreases from $p_x = \$2$ to $p'_x = \$1$.

- From self-assessment 5.3, we know that the initial bundle A is $A = (31.25, 62.5)$, the final bundle is $C = (62.5, 62.5)$, and the decomposition bundle is $B = (44.19, 44.19)$. The EV of this price decrease is given by $EV = I_E - I$, where $I = \$125$ is our original income and I_E represents the income she needs to purchase bundle E. We need to find bundle E, which must meet these conditions:

  1. Bundle E must reach the same utility level as the final bundle C. Since $C = (62.5, 62.5)$, its utility level is $u_C = 62.5 \cdot 62.5 = 3{,}906.25$. Therefore, bundle E must reach that same utility, or

  $$(x_E)(y_E) = 3{,}906.25.$$

  2. Bundle E must meet the tangency condition $\frac{MU_x}{MU_y} = \frac{p_x}{p_y}$. In this scenario, that entails $\frac{y}{x} = \frac{2}{1}$. This simplifies to $y = 2x$. Plugging this into the above expression $(x_E)(y_E) = 3{,}906.25$, we obtain

  $$x_E \underbrace{(2x_E)}_{y_E} = 3{,}906.25.$$

  This simplifies to $2(x_E)^2 = 3{,}906.25$, or $x_E^2 = \frac{3{,}906.25}{2} = 1{,}953.125$. Applying square roots to both sides, we find that

  $$x_E = \sqrt{1{,}953.125} = 44.19 \text{ units.}$$

  We can use the tangency condition, $y = 2x$, to find that the amount of good y that the individual consumes in bundle E; that is, $y_E = 2 \times 44.19 = 88.38$ units.

  Therefore, the income that the individual needs to purchase bundle $E = (44.19, 88.38)$ at the initial prices ($p_x = \$2$ and $p_y = \$1$) is

  $$I_E = (\$2 \times 44.19) + (\$1 \times 88.38) = \$176.76,$$

implying that her EV is

$$EV = I_E - I = \$176.76 - \$125 = \$51.76.$$

In words, before the price decrease, we would need to increase her income by $51.76 to help her reach the same utility level that she will enjoy after the price decrease.

Self-assessment exercise #5.5

SA 5.5 Repeat the analysis in example 5.5, assuming the same utility function and $p_y = \$1$, but consider that income is $I = \$125$, and that the price of good x decreases from $p_x = \$2$ to $p'_x = \$1$.

- We start by finding the demand function for goods x and y. In this context, the tangency condition is $\frac{MU_x}{MU_y} = \frac{p_x}{p_y}$ becomes $\frac{\frac{1}{\sqrt{x}}}{1} = \frac{p_x}{1}$, which simplifies to $x = \frac{1}{p_x^2}$, providing us with the demand function for good x. The demand function for good y starts by manipulating the budget line: $p_x x + p_y y = I$ becoming $p_x x + y = 125$ here. Inserting our result $x = \frac{1}{p_x^2}$ into the budget line, we obtain

$$p_x \frac{1}{p_x^2} + y = 125,$$

which simplifies to $\frac{1}{p_x} + y = 125$, which yields the demand function for good y,

$$y = 125 - \frac{1}{p_x}.$$

Now we can consider the price decrease of good x from $2 to $1 to find the increase in consumer welfare measured through CS, CV, and EV.

Finding the CS. To obtain the welfare change by using the CS, we need to integrate the demand function of good x between $2 and $1 as follows:

$$\begin{aligned}
\Delta CS &= \int_1^2 \frac{1}{p_x^2} dp_x \\
&= -\frac{1}{p_x}\Big|_1^2 \\
&= \left(-\frac{1}{2}\right) - \left(-\frac{1}{1}\right) = \frac{1}{2} = 0.5.
\end{aligned}$$

Finding the CV. We next find the change in consumer welfare measured through $CV = I - I_B$. We start by finding the income that the consumer needs to purchase bundle B, I_B. To do that, we first obtain bundles A, C, and B.

1. *Finding initial bundle A.* At initial prices $p_x = \$2$, the above demands for goods x and y simplify to $x_A = \frac{1}{p_x^2} = \frac{1}{2^2} = \frac{1}{4}$ and $y_A = 125 - \frac{1}{2} = \frac{498}{4} = 124.5$.

106

2. *Fining final bundle C.* At the final price $p'_x = \$1$, the demand for goods x and y change to $x_C = \frac{1}{p_x^2} = \frac{1}{1^2} = 1$ and $y_C = 125 - 1 = 124$.

3. *Finding decomposition bundle B.* At the decomposition bundle, the consumer must:

(a) Reach the same utility level as with the initial bundle A. Since we found that A is $A = (\frac{1}{4}, \frac{498}{4})$. This bundle yields a utility level of

$$u_A = 2\sqrt{\frac{1}{4}} + \frac{498}{4}$$
$$= \frac{502}{4} = 125.5.$$

Therefore, the decomposition bundle $B = (x_B, y_B)$ must yield a utility level of 125.5, which mathematically can be expressed as follows:

$$u_B = 2\sqrt{x_B} + y_B = 125.5$$

(b) The consumer's indifference curve must be tangent to the budget line at the final prices, $\frac{MU_x}{MU_y} = \frac{p'_x}{p'_y}$, which in this example means

$$\frac{\frac{1}{\sqrt{x_B}}}{1} = \frac{1}{1},$$

or $\sqrt{x_B} = 1$. Squaring both sides, we obtain $x_B = 1$. Substituting this result into the utility level we need to obtain for bundle B, $2\sqrt{1} + y_B = 125.5$, gives us $2 + y_B = 125.5$, which simplifies to $y_B = 123.5$. Finally, the income that the consumer needs to purchase the decomposition bundle $B = (1, 123.5)$ is

$$I_B = 1 + 123.5 = 124.5$$

4. *Evaluating the CV.* The CV is then given by

$$CV = I - I_B = 125 - 124.5 = 0.5$$

which coincides with the CS we found above.

Finding the EV. We now find the change in consumer welfare measured through the $EV = I_E - I$. We start by finding the income that the consumer needs to purchase bundle E, I_E.

1. Bundle E must reach the same utility level as the final bundle C. We already found that $C = (1, 124)$, which yields a utility level of

$$u_C = 2\sqrt{1} + 124 = 126.$$

Therefore, bundle $E = (x_E, y_E)$ must also yield a utility level of 126, which can be written mathematically as

$$u_E = 2\sqrt{x_E} + y_E = 126.$$

2. The consumer's indifference curve must be tangent to the budget line at the initial prices, $\frac{MU_x}{MU_y} = \frac{p_x}{p_y}$, which in this example means,

$$\frac{\frac{1}{\sqrt{x_E}}}{1} = \frac{2}{1},$$

or $\sqrt{\frac{1}{x_E}} = 2$. Squaring both sides and rearranging, we obtain $x_E = \frac{1}{4} = 0.25$. Substituting this result into $2\sqrt{x_E} + y_E = 126$, gives us

$$2\sqrt{\frac{1}{4}} + y_E = 126,$$

which simplifies to $\frac{2}{2} + y_E = 126$, and ultimately yields $y_E = 125$. Therefore, the income that the consumer needs to purchase bundle $E = (0.25, 125)$ is

$$I_E = 2(0.25) + 1(125) = 125.5.$$

3. *Evaluating the EV.* The EV is given by

$$EV = I_E - I = 125.5 - 125 = 0.5.$$

This result coincides with what we found for both CS and CV above due to the quasilinear utility function exhibited by the consumer.

Self-assessment exercise #5.6

SA 5.6 Repeat the analysis in example 5.6, assuming the same utility function and $p_y = \$1$, but consider that the price of good x decreases from $p_x = \$2$ to $p'_x = \$0.5$.

- Here, we can use the same demand function from the EMP; that is,

$$x^E(p_x, p_y, u) = \sqrt{u\frac{p_y}{p_x}} = \sqrt{833.33\frac{1}{p_x}} = 28.87\sqrt{\frac{1}{p_x}}.$$

To find the CV, we take the integral of the demand function between the prices; that is,

$$
\begin{aligned}
CV &= \int_{p'_x}^{p_x} x^E(p_x, p_y, u)\,dp_x \\
&= \int_{0.5}^{2} 28.87\sqrt{\frac{1}{p_x}}\,dp_x \\
&= \int_{0.5}^{2} 28.87(p_x)^{-1/2}\,dp_x.
\end{aligned}
$$

The integral of $(p_x)^a$ is $\frac{p_x^{a+1}}{a+1}$ (power rule for integration), implying that the integral of $(p_x)^{-1/2}$ is $\frac{p_x^{-1/2+1}}{-\frac{1}{2}+1} = \frac{p_x^{1/2}}{\frac{1}{2}} = 2p_x^{1/2}$. Therefore, the above integral becomes

$$
\begin{aligned}
CV &= 28.87 \times 2\sqrt{p_x}\big|_{0.5}^{2} \\
&= 57.74 \times \sqrt{p_x}\big|_{0.5}^{2} \\
&= 57.74 \left[\sqrt{2} - \sqrt{0.5}\right] \approx 40.83.
\end{aligned}
$$

Self-assessment exercise #5.7

SA 5.7 Repeat the analysis in example 5.7, assuming the same utility function and $p_y = \$1$, but consider that the price of good x decreases from $p_x = \$2$ to $p_x' = \$0.5$.

- Using the same utility function and level as example 5.7, have a demand function $x^E(p_x, p_y, u') = \sqrt{u'\frac{p_y}{p_x}} = \sqrt{1250\frac{1}{p_x}} = 25\sqrt{\frac{2}{p_x}}$. Therefore, EV becomes

$$
\begin{aligned}
CV &= \int_{p_x'}^{p_x} x^E(p_x, p_y, u')dp_x \\
&= \int_{0.5}^{2} 25\sqrt{\frac{2}{p_x}}\,dp_x \\
&= 25\sqrt{2} \int_{0.5}^{2} \sqrt{\frac{1}{p_x}}\,dp_x \\
&= 25\sqrt{2} \int_{0.5}^{2} (p_x)^{-1/2}dp_x.
\end{aligned}
$$

The integral of $(p_x)^a$ is $\frac{p_x^{a+1}}{a+1}$ (power rule for integrals), implying that the integral of $(p_x)^{-1/2}$ is $\frac{p_x^{-1/2+1}}{-\frac{1}{2}+1} = \frac{p_x^{1/2}}{\frac{1}{2}} = 2p_x^{1/2}$. Therefore, the above integral becomes

$$
\begin{aligned}
CV &= 25\sqrt{2} \times 2\sqrt{p_x}\big|_{0.5}^{2} \\
&= 50\sqrt{2} \times \sqrt{p_x}\big|_{0.5}^{2} \\
&= 50\sqrt{2} \left[\sqrt{2} - \sqrt{0.5}\right] = 50.
\end{aligned}
$$

5.2 Solutions to End-of-Chapter Exercises

Exercise #5.1 - Changes in CS^A

5.1 Patricia wants to measure the change in CS when the market price for doughnuts increases to $14.50 (box of a dozen doughnuts). She needs your help! Consider that the demand for doughnuts is $p(q) = 15 - \frac{1}{2}q$, and the supply is $p = 7q$.

- First, we need to find the initial price and quantity for which a box of doughnuts was sold. We can do this by setting demand equal to supply

$$
15 - \frac{1}{2}q = 7q,
$$

which simplifies to $15 = 7.5q$ and finally $q = 2$ units. Plugging $q = 2$ into demand gives a price of

$$p(2) = 15 - \frac{1}{2}2 = \$14.$$

Initial consumer surplus is then

$$CS = \frac{1}{2}(15 - 14)2 = 1.$$

- If the price increases to \$14.50, then the quantity demanded becomes

$$p(q) = 15 - \frac{1}{2}q = \$14.50,$$

or $15 - 14.5 = \frac{1}{2}q$, which simplifies to $0.5 = 0.5q$, or $q = 1$ units. In other words, when the price increases from \$14 to \$14.50, quantity demanded decreases from 2 to 1 unit. New consumer surplus is then

$$CS' = \frac{1}{2}(15 - 14.50) \times 1 = \frac{1}{4}.$$

Summarizing, if the price increases from \$14 to \$14.50, Patricia loses consumer surplus

$$CS' - CS = \frac{1}{4} - 1 = -\frac{3}{4}.$$

Exercise #5.3 - CS and Changing Prices[A]

5.3 Every spring, John goes to a local co-op to buy seeds to plant in his field. He has been keeping track of prices of seeds and the number of tons of seeds that he buys each year and estimates his demand curve to be $p(q) = 300 - 10q$. Last year, John paid \$150 per ton of seeds. This year, he noticed that the price went down to \$100. Unfortunately, John didn't take any economics courses in college, so he doesn't know how to quantify his welfare improvement. Help John find his CS from this price decrease.

- Last year, John paid \$150 per ton of seed and purchased the amount as given by his demand curve

$$\$150 = 300 - 10q,$$

or $q = 15$ units, with corresponding consumer surplus

$$CS = \frac{1}{2}(300 - 150)15 = 1,125.$$

- When the price decreases to \$100, he buys according to

$$\$100 = 300 - 10q,$$

or $q = 20$ units, with corresponding consumer surplus

$$CS' = \frac{1}{2}(300 - 100)20 = 2,000.$$

Therefore, John's consumer surplus increases by

$$CS' - CS = 2000 - 1125 = 875.$$

Exercise #5.5 - CS and Nonlinear Demand–I[A]

5.5 Jean has a Cobb-Douglas utility function that yields a demand for jeans of $j = \frac{I}{2p_j}$. Jean has an income of $100, and jeans have a price of $25.

(a) What is the change in CS if the price of jeans increases from $25 to $30?

- We can represent the change in consumer surplus here as

$$\Delta CS = \int_{30}^{25} \frac{100}{2p_j} dp_j = 50 \int_{30}^{25} \frac{1}{p_j} dp_j.$$

Since the integral of $\frac{1}{p_j}$ is $\int \frac{1}{p_j} dp_j = \ln p_j$, we obtain that

$$\begin{aligned} \Delta CS &= 50 \int_{30}^{25} \frac{1}{p_j} dp_j \\ &= 50 \times \ln p_j |_{30}^{25} = -9.11. \end{aligned}$$

(b) What is the change in CS if the price of jeans decreases from $25 to $20?

- In this case, we can represent the change in consumer surplus as

$$\begin{aligned} \Delta CS &= \int_{20}^{25} \frac{100}{2p_j} dp_j \\ &= 50 \int_{20}^{25} \frac{1}{p_j} dp_j \\ &= 50 \times \ln p_j |_{20}^{25} = 11.16. \end{aligned}$$

Exercise #5.7 - Calculating CV[B]

5.7 Redo the analysis from example 5.3, but now assume that p_y changes from $p_y = \$1$ to $p_y' = \$2$, while $p_x = \$1$.

- We can borrow from example 5.3, using the same tangency condition $\frac{y}{x} = \frac{p_x}{p_y}$, or $x = p_y y$ since $p_x = \$1$. Substituting this expression into the budget line $p_x x + p_y y = I$, we obtain $2p_y y = 100$, which yields the demand for good y, $y = \frac{100}{2p_y} = \frac{50}{p_y}$, and demand for good x,

$$x = p_y y = p_y \frac{50}{p_y} = 50 \text{ units.}$$

(a) *Finding initial bundle A.* At the initial price of $p_y = 1$, the demand for good y is $y_A = \frac{50}{1} = 50$ units.

(b) *Finding final bundle C.* At the final price of $p'_y = 2$, the demand for good y is $y_A = \frac{50}{2} = 25$ units.

(c) *Finding the decomposition bundle B.* At the decomposition bundle, the consumer must:

1. Reach the same utility level as with the initial bundle $A = (50, 50)$. This bundle yields a utility level of

$$u_A = 50 \times 50 = 2500.$$

The decomposition bundle must also yield a utility level of 2500, which we can write as

$$(x_B)(y_B) = 2500.$$

2. The consumer's indifference curve must be tangent to the budget line, $\frac{y}{x} = \frac{p_x}{p'_y}$, or $x = 2y$. Substituting this into the equation above,

$$(y_B)(2y_B) = 2500.$$

Simplifying, we get that $y_B = \sqrt{1250} \simeq 35.36$ units. We can insert this into the tangency condition to find that

$$x_B = 2y_B = 2 \times 35.36 = 70.71 \text{ units}.$$

The decomposition bundle is $B = (35.36, 70.71)$.

3. *Evaluating the CV.* The CV is given by $CV = I - I_B$, where $I = \$100$ and I_B is

$$I_B = (2 \times 35.36) + 70.71 = 141.42.$$

The CV is

$$CV = I - I_B = 100 - 141.42 = -41.42.$$

After the price increase, we increase the consumer's income by \$41.42, and her utility level coincides with that before the price increase.

Exercise #5.9 - CV with Cobb-Douglas Utility Function^B

5.9 Chris has a demand for books (b) and other goods (y) that follows the Cobb-Douglas utility function $u(b, y) = y\sqrt{b}$, and an income of $I = \$50$. Find Chris's CV if the price of books decreases from $p_b = \$2$ to $p'_b = \$1$.

- For this demand, the tangency condition $\frac{MU_b}{MU_y} = \frac{p_b}{p_y}$, or $\frac{y}{2\sqrt{b}\sqrt{b}} = \frac{p_b}{p_y}$, which simplifies to $y = 2p_b b$ since $p_y = \$1$. Substituting this into the budget line $p_b b + p_y y = I$ we obtain $p_b b + 2p_b b = 50$, which simplifies to $3p_b b = 50$, and demand for books b is $b = \frac{50}{3p_b}$. Demand for other good y is

$$y = 2p_b \frac{50}{3p_b} = \frac{100}{3} = 33.33.$$

(a) *Finding initial bundle A.* At the initial price of $p_b = 2$, the demand for books is $b_A = \frac{50}{3\times2} = 8.33$ books.

(b) *Finding final bundle C.* At the final price of $p'_b = 1$, the demand for books is $y_A = \frac{50}{3\times1} = 16.66$ books.

(c) *Finding the decomposition bundle B.* At the decomposition bundle, the consumer must:

1. Reach the same utility level as with the initial bundle $A = (8.33, 33.33)$. This bundle yields a utility level of

$$u_A = 33.33\sqrt{8.33} = 96.20.$$

   The decomposition bundle must also yield a utility level of 96.20, which we can write as

$$(y_B)\sqrt{b_B} = 96.20.$$

2. The consumer's indifference curve must be tangent to the budget line, $y = 2p'_b b$, or $y = 2b$ since $p'_b = \$1$. Substituting this into the equation above,

$$(2b_B)\sqrt{b_B} = 96.20.$$

   Simplifying, we obtain $b_B^{3/2} = \frac{96.20}{2} = 48.1$. Solving for b_B, we get

$$b_B = 40.1^{2/3} \simeq 13.22 \text{ units.}$$

   We can insert this into the tangency condition to find that

$$y_B = 2b_B = 2 \times 13.22 = 26.44 \text{ units.}$$

   The decomposition bundle is, then, $B = (13.22, 26.44)$.

3. *Evaluating the CV.* The CV is given by $CV = I - I_B$, where $I = \$50$ and I_B is

$$I_B = 13.22 + 26.44 = 39.66.$$

   The *CV* is

$$CV = I - I_B = 50 - 39.66 = 10.34.$$

   After the price decrease, we decrease Chris's income by $10.34, and his utility level coincides with that before the price decrease.

Exercise #5.11 - CV with General Price Change[C]

5.11 Let's investigate the impact of a generic change in price. Consider a consumer with the Cobb-Douglas utility $u(x, y) = xy$, an income of $I = 100$, and a normalized price of good y at $p_y = \$1$. What is the CV of a change in the price of x from p_x to p'_x? For simplicity, you can assume that $p_x = 1$. Dividing both prices by p_x, we can more compactly express the initial price as $\frac{p_x}{p_x} = \$1$, and the final price as $\frac{p'_x}{p_x} = p$. Intuitively, when $p > 1$, we have that $p'_x > p_x$, so good x becomes more expensive, and when $0 < p < 1$, we have that $p'_x < p_x$ and good x is cheaper.

- Borrowing from the analysis in example 5.3, we will still have that $y = 50$ units and the demand for good x is $x = \frac{50}{p_x}$.

  (a) *Finding the initial bundle A.* At the initial price of $p_x = \$1$, the demand for good x is $x_A = \frac{50}{1} = 50$ units.

  (b) *Finding the final bundle C.* At the new price of p'_x, the demand for good x is $x_A = \frac{50}{p'_x}$ units.

  (c) *Finding the decomposition bundle B.* At the decomposition bundle, the consumer must:

    1. Reach the same utility level as with the initial bundle $A = (50, 50)$. This bundle yields a utility level of

       $$u_A = 50 \times 50 = 2,500.$$

       The decomposition bundle must also yield a utility level of 2,500, which we can write as

       $$(x_B)(y_B) = 2,500.$$

    2. The consumer's indifference curve must be tangent to the budget line, $\frac{MU_x}{MU_y} = p$, or $\frac{y}{x} = \frac{p}{1}$, which simplifies to $y = px$. Substituting this into the equation above,

       $$(x_B)\underbrace{(px_B)}_{y_B} = 2,500.$$

       Simplifying, we get that $x_B = \frac{50}{\sqrt{p}}$. We can insert this into the tangency condition to find that

       $$y_B = px_B = p\underbrace{\frac{50}{\sqrt{p}}}_{x_B} = 50\sqrt{p}.$$

       The decomposition bundle is, therefore, $B = \left(\frac{50}{\sqrt{p}}, 50\sqrt{p}\right)$.

    3. *Evaluating the CV.* The CV is given by $CV = I - I_B$, where $I = \$100$ and I_B is

       $$I_B = \left(p\frac{50}{\sqrt{p}}\right) + (50\sqrt{p}) = 50\sqrt{p} + 50\sqrt{p} = 100\sqrt{p}.$$

       Therefore, the CV is

       $$CV = I - I_B = 100 - 100\sqrt{p} = 100\left(1 - \sqrt{p}\right).$$

       Therefore, when $p < 1$, which occurs when good x becomes cheaper, $p'_x < p_x$ since $p = \frac{p'_x}{p_x}$, the above expression is positive entailing that $CV > 0$. In words, we would need to take income away from the consumer after the price decrease to make her as well off as before this price change. In contrast, when $p > 1$, good x becomes more expensive, $p'_x > p_x$, implying that $CV < 0$. In this case, we would need to give income to the consumer to make her as well off as she becomes after the price increase.

Exercise #5.13 - EV with Cobb-Douglas Demand–II[B]

5.13 Consider a consumer with the Cobb-Douglas demand $u(x, y) = x\sqrt{y}$, with income $I = \$100$, and the price of good y is normalized at $p_y = \$1$. Calculate the EV of the change in price of good x from $p_x = \$5$ to $p'_x = \$10$.

- We can borrow the tangency condition from the previous problem to find the demand for each good; that is, $y = 2p_x x$, and $x = \frac{I}{3p_x}$. The final bundle is

$$x_C = \frac{100}{3 \times 10} = 3.33 \text{ units},$$

and

$$y_C = 2 \times 10 \times 3.33 = 66.66 \text{ units}.$$

Bundle E must reach the utility level of the final bundle $u_C = 66.66\sqrt{3.33} = 121.64$; that is,

$$y_E \sqrt{x_E} = 121.64.$$

Bundle E must also be a tangency point; that is, $y = 2p_x x$. Plugging this into the above requirement,

$$2p_x x_E \sqrt{x_E} = 121.64,$$

which simplifies to $2(5)x_E^{3/2} = 121.64$, or $x_E^{3/2} = 12.164$, and finally $x_E = 5.29$ units. The tangency point tells us that

$$y_E = 2(5)x_E = 10(5.29) = 52.9 \text{ units}.$$

The income needed to purchase this bundle is

$$I_E = (5 \times 5.29) + 52.9 = \$79.35.$$

Thus, EV is

$$EV = I_E - I = 79.35 - 100 = -20.65.$$

In words, before the price increase, we decrease the consumer's income by $20.65, we help her reach the same utility level she will enjoy after the price increase.

Exercise #5.15 - EV with Different Income[A]

5.15 Redo the analysis from example 5.4, but now assume that $I = \$200$. How does the increase in income affect EV?

- From exercise 5.8, we know that the final bundle C is $C = (50, 100)$. The utility from this bundle is $u_C = 50 \times 100 = 5,000$. Bundle E must reach this level of utility; that is, $u_E = x_E y_E = 5,000$. The tangency point E must meet is $y = 3x$. Plugging this into the utility expression, we obtain

$$x_E(3x_E) = 5,000,$$

115

simplifying to $3x_E^2 = 5000$, or $x_E = 40.82$ units. From the tangency point,

$$y_E = 3 \times 40.82 = 122.46 \text{ units.}$$

The income needed to obtain this bundle is

$$I_E = 3(40.82) + 122.46 = 244.92.$$

Therefore, EV is

$$EV = I_E - I = 244.92 - 200 = 44.92.$$

Therefore, if we increase the consumer's income by $44.92, she will be able to obtain the same utility level as that after the price change.

Exercise #5.17 - CS, CV, and EV with No Income Effects–I[B]

5.17 Repeat the analysis from example 5.5, but now assume a generic increase in the price of good x, from p_x to p_x'. For simplicity, you can assume that $p_x = 1$. Dividing both prices by p_x, we can more compactly express the initial price as $\frac{p_x}{p_x} = \$1$, and the final price as $\frac{p_x'}{p_x} = p$. Intuitively, when $p > 1$, we have that $p_x' > p_x$, so good x becomes more expensive, and when $0 < p < 1$, we have that $p_x' < p_x$ and good x is cheaper.

- Since there are no income effects, CS, CV, and EV will all coincide, for any change in the price of good x. Therefore, by finding CS, we will also have CV and EV. From example 5.5, the demand for good x is $x = \frac{1}{p_x^2}$.

- The welfare change given by CS is

$$\begin{aligned} \Delta CS &= \int_{p_x'}^{1} \frac{1}{p_x^2} dp_x \\ &= -\frac{1}{p_x} \Big|_{p_x'}^{1} \\ &= -1 + \frac{1}{p_x'}. \end{aligned}$$

- **Finding CV.** The initial bundle A will be $x = \frac{1}{1^2} = 1$ unit, and $y = 100 - \frac{1}{1} = 99$ units. The decomposition bundle B needs to reach the same utility as bundle A at the new price p_x'; that is, $u_A = 2\sqrt{1} + 99 = 101$. Therefore, bundle B must meet

$$101 = 2\sqrt{x_B} + y_B.$$

The bundle must also be a tangency point, or, here $x_B = \frac{1}{p_x'^2}$. Plugging this into the utility condition, $101 = 2\sqrt{\frac{1}{p_x'^2}} + y_B$, which simplifies to $101 - \frac{2}{p_x'} = y_B$. The income needed to purchase this bundle is

$$
\begin{aligned}
I_B &= p'_x \frac{1}{p'^2_x} + \left(101 - \frac{2}{p'_x} \right) \\
&= 101 - \frac{1}{p'_x}.
\end{aligned}
$$

CV is calculated by

$$
\begin{aligned}
CV &= I - I_B \\
&= 100 - \underbrace{\left(101 - \frac{1}{p'_x} \right)}_{I_B} \\
&= -1 + \frac{1}{p'_x}.
\end{aligned}
$$

- **Finding EV.** The final bundle will be $x_C = \frac{1}{p'^2_x}$ and $y_C = 100 - \frac{1}{p'_x}$. Bundle E must reach the same level of utility as bundle C; that is,

$$
\begin{aligned}
u_C &= 2 \sqrt{ \underbrace{\frac{1}{p'^2_x}}_{x_C} + \underbrace{\left(100 - \frac{1}{p'_x} \right)}_{y_C} } \\
&= 100 + \frac{1}{p'_x}.
\end{aligned}
$$

Therefore, bundle E must meet the condition that

$$
100 + \frac{1}{p'_x} = 2\sqrt{x_E} + y_E.
$$

It must also meet the tangency condition at the initial prices; that is, $x_E = \frac{1}{1^2} = 1$. Plugging this into the utility condition, $100 + \frac{1}{p'_x} = 2\sqrt{1} + y_E$, we find that $y_E = 98 + \frac{1}{p'_x}$. The income needed for this bundle is

$$
I_E = 1 + 98 + \frac{1}{p'_x} = 99 + \frac{1}{p'_x}.
$$

Therefore, EV is calculated by

$$
\begin{aligned}
EV &= I_E - I \\
&= \underbrace{\left(99 + \frac{1}{p'_x} \right)}_{I_E} - 100 \\
&= -1 + \frac{1}{p'_x}.
\end{aligned}
$$

Therefore, we can see that if utility is quasilinear, then all three measures of welfare change coincide,

$$CS = CV = EV.$$

Exercise #5.19 - Alternative Representation of CV^B

5.19 Consider a consumer with utility $u(x, y) = x^{0.75}y^{0.25}$.

(a) Find the demand for goods x and y by solving the consumer's EMP.

- First, we need to satisfy the tangency condition, $\frac{MU_x}{MU_y} = \frac{p_x}{p_y}$, which is

$$\frac{0.75x^{-0.25}y^{0.25}}{0.25x^{0.75}y^{-0.75}} = \frac{p_x}{p_y}.$$

This simplifies to

$$\frac{3y}{x} = \frac{p_x}{p_y}.$$

Solving for y, we obtain

$$y = \frac{xp_x}{3p_y}.$$

Second, we know the consumer must reach a utility level u so that $u = x^{0.75}y^{0.25}$. Inserting $y = \frac{xp_x}{3p_y}$ into the utility target yields

$$u = x^{0.75} \underbrace{\left(\frac{xp_x}{3p_y}\right)^{0.25}}_{y}$$

which simplifies to

$$u = x\left(\frac{p_x}{3p_y}\right)^{0.25}.$$

Solving for x yields the demand for good x

$$x^E(p_x, p_y, u) = u\left(\frac{3p_y}{p_x}\right)^{0.25}.$$

We can plug this into the equation we found for good y from the tangency condition, $y = \frac{xp_x}{3p_y}$, to find demand for good y

$$y = \frac{\overbrace{u\left(\frac{3p_y}{p_x}\right)^{0.25}}^{x^E} p_x}{3p_y},$$

118

which first simplifies to

$$y = u \left(\frac{3p_y}{p_x} \right)^{0.25} \frac{p_x}{3p_y}.$$

Finally, one more simplification yields the demand for good y

$$y^E(p_x, p_y, u) = u \left(\frac{p_x}{3p_y} \right)^{0.75}.$$

(b) Calculate the CV for a price increase from $p_x = \$1$ to $p'_x = \$2$, where $u = 10$ and $p_y = \$1$.

- At $u = 10$ and $p_y = \$1$, demand for good x is

$$
\begin{aligned}
x^E(p_x, p_y, u) &= 10 \left(\frac{3(1)}{p_x} \right)^{0.25} \\
&= 13.16 \left(\frac{1}{p_x} \right)^{0.25}.
\end{aligned}
$$

The CV becomes the integral of the demand function between prices $p_x = \$1$ and $p'_x = \$2$; that is,

$$
\begin{aligned}
CV &= \int_{p_x}^{p'_x} x^E(p_x, p_y, u) dp_x \\
&= \int_1^2 13.16 \left(\frac{1}{p_x} \right)^{0.25} dp_x \\
&= 13.16 \int_1^2 (p_x)^{-0.25} dp_x.
\end{aligned}
$$

The integral of $(p_x)^a$ is $\frac{p_x^{a+1}}{a+1}$ (power rule for integration), implying that the integral of $(p_x)^{-0.25}$ is $\frac{p_x^{-0.25+1}}{-0.25+1} = \frac{p_x^{0.75}}{0.75} = 1.33 (p_x)^{0.75}$. Therefore, the above integral becomes

$$
\begin{aligned}
CV &= 13.16 \times 1.33 (p_x)^{0.75} \Big|_1^2 = \\
&= 17.5(2^{0.75} - 1^{0.75}) \\
&= \$11.93.
\end{aligned}
$$

This means that, after the price increase, we need to give the consumer $11.93 to make her as well off as she was before the price increase.

(c) Calculate the CV of the price change for good x, but use the demand function of good y to see how the consumer's welfare in her purchases of good y is affected by a more expensive good x.

119

- At $u = 10$ and $p_y = \$1$, demand for good y is

$$
\begin{aligned}
y^E(p_x, p_y, u) &= 10 \left(\frac{p_x}{3(1)} \right)^{0.75} \\
&= 4.39 p_x^{0.75}.
\end{aligned}
$$

The CV becomes the integral of the demand function between prices $p_x = \$1$ and $p_x' = \$2$; that is,

$$
\begin{aligned}
CV &= \int_{p_x}^{p_x'} y^E(p_x, p_y, u) dp_x \\
&= \int_1^2 4.39 p_x^{0.75} dp_x \\
&= 4.39 \int_1^2 p_x^{0.75} dp_x.
\end{aligned}
$$

The integral of $(p_x)^a$ is $\frac{p_x^{a+1}}{a+1}$ (power rule for integration), implying that the integral of $(p_x)^{0.75}$ is $\frac{p_x^{0.75+1}}{0.75+1} = \frac{p_x^{1.75}}{1.75} = 0.57 (p_x)^{1.75}$. Therefore, the above integral becomes

$$
\begin{aligned}
CV &= 4.39 \times 0.57 (p_x)^{1.75} \Big|_1^2 \\
&= 2.5 \left(2^{1.75} - 1^{1.75} \right) \\
&= \$5.90.
\end{aligned}
$$

This means that, after the price increase, we need to give the consumer $\$5.90$ to make her as well off as she was before the price increase in her purchases of good y.

Exercise #5.21 - Alternative Representation of EV^B

5.21 Consider a consumer with a utility function $u(x, y) = x^{0.75} y^{0.25}$.

(a) Find the demand for goods x and y by solving the consumer's EMP.

- First, we need to satisfy the tangency condition, $\frac{MU_x}{MU_y} = \frac{p_x}{p_y}$, which is

$$
\frac{0.75 x^{-0.25} y^{0.25}}{0.25 x^{0.75} y^{-0.75}} = \frac{p_x}{p_y}.
$$

This simplifies to

$$
\frac{3y}{x} = \frac{p_x}{p_y}.
$$

Solving for y, we obtain

$$
y = \frac{x p_x}{3 p_y}.
$$

120

Second, we know the consumer must reach a utility level u so that $u = x^{0.75}y^{0.25}$. Inserting $y = \frac{xp_x}{3p_y}$ into the utility target yields

$$u = x^{0.75}\underbrace{\left(\frac{xp_x}{3p_y}\right)^{0.25}}_{y}$$

which simplifies to

$$u = x\left(\frac{p_x}{3p_y}\right)^{0.25}.$$

Solving for x yields the demand for good x

$$x^E(p_x, p_y, u) = u\left(\frac{3p_y}{p_x}\right)^{0.25}.$$

We can plug this into the equation we found for good y from the tangency condition, $y = \frac{xp_x}{3p_y}$, to find demand for good y

$$y = \frac{\overbrace{u\left(\frac{3p_y}{p_x}\right)^{0.25}}^{x^E}p_x}{3p_y},$$

which first simplifies to $y = u\left(\frac{3p_y}{p_x}\right)^{0.25}\frac{p_x}{3p_y}$. Finally, one more simplification yields the demand for good y

$$y^E(p_x, p_y, u) = u\left(\frac{p_x}{3p_y}\right)^{0.75}.$$

(b) Calculate the EV for a price increase from $p_x = \$1$ to $p'_x = \$2$, where the new utility is $u' = 5$ and $p_y = \$1$.

- At $u' = 5$ and $p_y = \$1$, demand for good x is

$$x^E(p_x, p_y, u') = 5\left(\frac{3(1)}{p_x}\right)^{0.25} = 6.58\left(\frac{1}{p_x}\right)^{0.25}.$$

The EV becomes the integral of the demand function between prices $p_x = \$1$

and $p'_x = \$2$; that is,

$$
\begin{aligned}
EV &= \int_{p_x}^{p'_x} x^E(p_x, p_y, u') dp_x \\
&= \int_1^2 6.58 \left(\frac{1}{p_x}\right)^{0.25} dp_x \\
&= 6.58 \int_1^2 (p_x)^{-0.25} dp_x.
\end{aligned}
$$

The integral of $(p_x)^a$ is $\frac{p_x^{a+1}}{a+1}$ (power rule for integration), implying that the integral of $(p_x)^{-0.25}$ is $\frac{(p_x)^{-0.25+1}}{-0.25+1} = \frac{p_x^{0.75}}{0.75} = 1.33\,(p_x)^{0.75}$. Therefore, the above integral becomes

$$
\begin{aligned}
EV &= 6.58 \times 1.33\,(p_x)^{0.75}\Big|_1^2 \\
&= 6.58\left[1.33(2^{0.75} - 1^{0.75})\right] \\
&= 8.75(2^{0.75} - 1^{0.75}) \\
&= \$5.97.
\end{aligned}
$$

This means that we need to take $\$5.97$ from the consumer to make her as well off as she is after the price increase. Note that the CV from exercise 5.9 and the EV from exercise 5.10 do not coincide. As discussed in the chapter, this occurs when income effects are present, which happens for Cobb-Douglas utility functions.

(c) Calculate the EV of the price change in good x, but use the demand function of good y to see how the consumer's welfare in her purchases of good y is affected by a more expensive good x.

- At $u' = 5$ and $p_y = \$1$, demand for good y is

$$
\begin{aligned}
y^E(p_x, p_y, u') &= 5\left(\frac{p_x}{3(1)}\right)^{0.75} \\
&= 2.19 p_x^{0.75}.
\end{aligned}
$$

The EV becomes the integral of the demand function between prices $p_x = \$1$ and $p'_x = \$2$; that is,

$$
\begin{aligned}
EV &= \int_{p_x}^{p'_x} y^E(p_x, p_y, u') dp_x \\
&= \int_1^2 2.19 p_x^{0.75} dp_x \\
&= 2.19 \int_1^2 (p_x)^{1.75} dp_x.
\end{aligned}
$$

The integral of $(p_x)^a$ is $\frac{p_x^{a+1}}{a+1}$ (power rule for integration), implying that the integral of $(p_x)^{0.75}$ is $\frac{(p_x)^{0.75+1}}{0.75+1} = \frac{p_x^{1.75}}{1.75} = 0.57\,(p_x)^{1.75}$. Therefore, the above integral becomes

$$
\begin{aligned}
EV &= 2.19 \times 0.57\,(p_x)^{1.75}\Big|_1^2 \\
&= 1.25[2^{1.75} - 1^{1.75}] \\
&= \$2.95.
\end{aligned}
$$

This means that we need to take \$2.95 from the consumer to make her as well off as she is after the price increase of good x in her purchases of good y.

Chapter 6 - Choice under Uncertainty

6.1 Solutions to Self-Assessment Exercises

Self-assessment exercise #6.1

SA 6.1 Consider the lottery in example 6.1, but assume now that outcome A provides you with a payoff of $800, while outcome C only gives you $12. How is the EV of the lottery affected? Interpret.

- With our new values, we still have a 10 percent chance of receiving outcome A ($800), a 60 percent chance of receiving outcome B ($20), and a 30 percent chance of receiving outcome C ($12). We can calculate our expected value of this lottery by multiplying each outcome by its associated probability,

$$
\begin{aligned}
EV &= (0.1 \times \$800) + (0.6 \times \$20) + (0.3 \times \$12) \\
&= \$80 + \$12 + \$3.6 \\
&= \$95.6.
\end{aligned}
$$

Naturally, this expected value is much higher than the expected value calculated in example 6.1. Even though the probability of outcome A happening did not change, since its monetary value increased significantly the lottery will pay out more money on average. We can see this effect by the much higher number in outcome A's contribution to the expected value of this lottery.

Self-assessment exercise #6.2

SA 6.2 Consider the risky lottery in example 6.2. If outcome A yields $800 rather than $90, how is the variance of the lottery affected? Interpret.

- To calculate the variance of the risky lottery in example 6.2 with our new value for outcome A, we must first calculate its expected value, which we do by multiplying each possible outcome by its respective probability,

$$
\begin{aligned}
EV &= (0.1 \times \$800) + (0.6 \times \$20) + (0.3 \times \$60) \\
&= \$110.
\end{aligned}
$$

- Next, we calculate the variance of our lottery by taking the difference between each outcome and the expected value, squaring that difference, multiplying that square by its respective probability, and then adding them together.

$$
\begin{aligned}
Var_{Risky} &= 0.1 \times (\$800 - \$110)^2 + 0.6 \times (\$20 - \$110)^2 + 0.3 \times (\$60 - \$110)^2 \\
&= \$53,220,
\end{aligned}
$$

which is over 87 times larger than the original variance for the risky lottery ($609). Since outcome A provides a much higher amount of money now, we can expect the spread of outcomes to increase dramatically.

Self-assessment exercise #6.3

SA 6.3 Consider the scenario in example 6.3, but assume that the individual's utility function changes to $u(I) = I^{1/3}$. What is his EU from the risky lottery? What about from the safe lottery?

- *Risky lottery.* To calculate the expected utility for the risky lottery, we follow the same steps as before, where we multiply each utility outcome by its respective probability,

$$
\begin{aligned}
EU_{Risky} &= (0.1 \times 90^{1/3}) + (0.6 \times 20^{1/3}) + (0.3 \times 60^{1/3}) \\
&= 3.25.
\end{aligned}
$$

- *Safe lottery.* Once again, we multiply each utility outcome by its respective probability,

$$
\begin{aligned}
EU_{Safe} &= (0.5 \times 30^{1/3}) + (0.5 \times 48^{1/3}) \\
&= 3.37.
\end{aligned}
$$

- In both of these situations, we find that the individual's expected utilities are lower than what was observed in example 6.3 in the textbook. Intuitively, our individual receives less utility for all income values with this new utility function, which impacts their expected utility.

Self-assessment exercise #6.4

SA 6.4 Consider the scenario in example 6.4, but assume that the individual's utility function is $u(I) = 5I^3$. What is his EU from the risky lottery? What about from the safe lottery? Which lottery yields the highest EU? Interpret.

- *Risky lottery.* As in our previous problems, we calculate the expected utility for the risky lottery by multiplying each utility outcome by its respective probability,

$$
\begin{aligned}
EU_{Risky} &= 0.1 \times (5 \times 90^3) + 0.6 \times (5 \times 20^3) + 0.3 \times (5 \times 60^3) \\
&= 712,500.
\end{aligned}
$$

- *Safe lottery.* Once again, we multiply each utility outcome by its respective probability,

$$
\begin{aligned}
EU_{Safe} &= 0.5 \times (5 \times 30^3) + 0.5 \times (5 \times 48^3) \\
&= 343,980.
\end{aligned}
$$

- In this situation, the risky lottery actually receives the highest expected utility. Since this consumer is risk loving, the thrill of the chance at winning $90 (or even $60) weighs significantly on his expected utility, making the lower payoff of $20 seem far less significant. This leads to the consumer preferring the risky lottery over the safe lottery.

Self-assessment exercise #6.5

SA 6.5 Consider the scenario in example 6.5, but assuming that the individual's utility function is $u(I) = 2 + 5I$. What is her EU from the risky lottery? What about from the safe lottery? Which lottery yields the highest EU? Interpret.

- *Risky lottery.* As in our previous problems, we calculate the expected utility for the risky lottery by multiplying each utility outcome by its respective probability,

$$
\begin{aligned}
EU_{Risky} &= 2 + (0.1 \times 5 \times 90) + (0.6 \times 5 \times 20) + (0.3 \times 5 \times 60) \\
&= 197.
\end{aligned}
$$

- *Safe lottery.* Once again, we multiply each utility outcome by its respective probability,

$$
\begin{aligned}
EU_{Safe} &= 2 + (0.5 \times 5 \times 30) + (0.5 \times 5 \times 48) \\
&= 197.
\end{aligned}
$$

- In this situation, both lotteries have the exact same expected utility. Intuitively, since the consumer is neither risk averse nor risk loving, she does not mind either lottery, as she understands that on average she will receive the same monetary amount.

Self-assessment exercise #6.6

SA 6.6 Consider the scenario in example 6.6, but assume now that $EV = \$42$ and $EU = 6$. Find the RP and interpret your result.

- Using the same steps as in example 6.6, we know that $u(EV - RP) = EU$. Substituting in our utility function and values, we have

$$
\sqrt{\$42 - RP} = 6.
$$

Squaring both sides of this expression gives $42 - RP = 36$. We can solve this expression for RP to obtain our risk premium,

$$
RP = \$42 - \$36 = \$6.
$$

This result implies that the consumer is willing to pay \$6 to avoid taking this risk of the lottery, which is consistent with the individual being risk averse as expected by her concave utility function $u(I) = \sqrt{I}$.

Self-assessment exercise #6.7

SA 6.7 Consider an individual with the utility function $u(I) = I^2$. We find that $EV = \$42$ and $EU = 1,822$. What is her RP from the lottery? What is her CE? Compare the CE and RP and interpret your result.

- First, we must calculate this individual's risk premium. Recall that $u(EV - RP) = EU$. Substituting in our utility function and values, we have

$$(\$42 - RP)^2 = 1,822.$$

Taking the square root of both sides of this expression gives $42 - RP = 42.68$. We can solve this expression for RP to obtain our risk premium,

$$RP = 42 - 42.68 = -\$0.68.$$

This result implies that our consumer is not willing to pay anything to avoid taking this risk. This negative risk premium implies that our individual is risk loving (as suggested by their utility function). Using our formula to calculate this individual's certainty equivalent,

$$
\begin{aligned}
CE &= EV - RP \\
&= 42 - (-\$0.68) = \$42.68.
\end{aligned}
$$

In this case, our individual's certainty equivalent is also above their risk premium, implying that again, they are risk loving. Since their certainty equivalent is above their risk premium, this individual would have to receive money to not take the risk.

Self-assessment exercise #6.8

SA 6.8 Consider an individual with utility function $u(I) = 2I^{1/3}$. Using the same steps as in example 6.8, find her AP coefficient. Interpret.

- To find this individual's Arrow-Pratt coefficient of risk aversion, we must first calculate the first and second derivatives of her utility function,

$$
\begin{aligned}
u' &= \frac{\partial u(I)}{\partial I} = \frac{2}{3}I^{-2/3} \\
u'' &= \frac{\partial^2 u(I)}{\partial I^2} = -\frac{4}{9}I^{-5/3}.
\end{aligned}
$$

From here, we can apply the formula to find the AP coefficient,

$$
\begin{aligned}
AP &= -\frac{u''}{u'} \\
&= -\frac{-\frac{4}{9}I^{-5/3}}{\frac{2}{3}I^{-2/3}} \\
&= \frac{2}{3I} > 0.
\end{aligned}
$$

Since the AP coefficient is positive, this implies that our individual is risk averse.

6.2 Solutions to End-of-Chapter Exercises

Exercise #6.1 - Expected Utility[A]

6.1 Scientists are evaluating the impact of climate change on the production of apples in the Yakima region in Washington State. After analyzing the data on temperature during the last fifty years, they have identified three cases:

(a) low impact, which can occur with probability 5 percent.

(b) medium impact, with probability 45 percent.

(c) high impact, with probability 50 percent.

A low-impact scenario implies profits for the agriculture industry of $\pi = \$85$ million, the medium-impact yields profits of $\pi = \$5$ million, and the high-impact scenario implies negative profits of $\pi = \$900$ million. Consider a farmer who is risk averse and her utility function is concave and equal to

$$u(\pi) = 10 + 3 \times (\pi)^{\frac{1}{3}}.$$

Calculate the EU for this farmer and discuss whether she should support measures to deal with climate change.

- The expected utility for this farmer is calculated by the weighted average

$$EU = (0.05) \underbrace{\left[10 + 3 \times (85)^{\frac{1}{3}} \right]}_{\text{low impact}} + (0.45) \underbrace{\left[10 + 3 \times (5)^{\frac{1}{3}} \right]}_{\text{medium impact}} + (0.50) \underbrace{\left[10 + 3 \times (-900)^{\frac{1}{3}} \right]}_{\text{high impact}}$$

$$= 1.16 + 6.81 - 9.48 = -1.51.$$

Since the farmer's expected utility is negative as a result of the probability of being impacted by climate change, she should support measures to deal with climate change. If this effort is costless, it would make sense for the farmer to support such measures. If the support has costs, then she would want to compare the expected benefits of the support with the costs of the support.

Exercise #6.3 - EV and Variance–II[B]

6.3 You are looking at two firms as an investment opportunity.

- For the first firm, you know that with probability 0.7, your investment will mature to a profit of $45 million, and with probability 0.3, your investment will mature to a loss of $30 million.

- For the second firm, you know that with probability 0.8, your investment will mature to a profit of $30 million, and with probability 0.2, your investment will mature to a loss of $7.5 million.

(a) Calculate the EV of each investment.

- *First firm.* The expected value of investing in the first firm is

$$EV_1 = (0.7 \times \$45) - (0.3 \times \$30)$$
$$= 31.5 - 9$$
$$= \$22.5 \text{ million.}$$

- *Second firm.* The expected value of investing in the second firm is

$$EV_2 = (0.8 \times \$30) - (0.2 \times \$7.5)$$
$$= 24 - 1.5$$
$$= \$22.5 \text{ million.}$$

(b) Calculate the variance of each investment.

- *First firm.* The variance of investing in the first firm is

$$Var_1 = 0.7(\$45 - \$22.5)^2 + 0.3(-\$30 - \$22.5)^2$$
$$= 0.7(\$22.5)^2 + 0.3(-\$52.5)^2$$
$$= 0.7(506.25) + 0.3(2756.25)$$
$$= \$1,181.25 \text{ million.}$$

- *Second firm.* The variance of investing in the second firm is

$$Var_2 = 0.8(\$30 - \$22.5)^2 + 0.2(-\$7.5 - \$22.5)^2$$
$$= 0.8(\$7.5)^2 + 0.2(-\$30)^2$$
$$= 0.8(56.25) + 0.2(900)$$
$$= \$225 \text{ million.}$$

(c) If you had the opportunity to invest in only one of these firms, which would you pick and why?

- Each investment has the same expect value; however, the investment in the second firm offers the lower variance. The risk neutral investor would likely invest in the second firm due to the lower variance, but a more risky individual may choose to invest in the first firm.

Exercise #6.5 - Expected Utility–II[A]

6.5 Consider the situation in exercise 6.2, but suppose now that your utility function is

$$u(\pi) = (50 + \pi)^2,$$

where π is the profit from your investments.

(a) Calculate the EU of each investment.

- *First firm.* The expected utility is calculated as

$$EU_1 = 0.7\,(50 + 45)^2 + 0.3\,(50 - 30)^2$$
$$= 0.7\,(95)^2 + 0.3\,(20)^2$$
$$= 6437.5.$$

- *Second firm.* The expected utility is calculated as

$$EU_2 = 0.8\,(50 + 30)^2 + 0.2\,(50 - 7.5)^2$$
$$= 0.8\,(80)^2 + 0.2\,(42.5)^2$$
$$= 5481.25.$$

(b) Based on your utility level, if you had the opportunity to invest in only one of these firms, which would you pick, and why?

- We pick the investment opportunity that has the largest expected utility; that is, we would invest in the first firm. Even though each lottery has the same expected value, the utility function values the chance of the higher payoff (and riskier investment) of the first firm more than the second firm.

Exercise #6.7 - Risk Aversion^B

6.7 Suppose that you took part in a lottery that had a chance to increase, decrease, or have no effect on your level of income. With probability 0.5, your income remains at its original level, \$500. With probability 0.2, your income increases to \$700, and with probability 0.3, your income decreases to \$400. Your utility function is

$$u(I) = I^{0.7},$$

where I denotes your income level.

(a) Using only the utility function, show that your risk preferences are risk averse.

- We know that utility functions following the form $u(I) = a + bI^\gamma$ are concave where a and b are positive, and $\gamma \in (0, 1)$. For our utility function, $a = 0$, $b = 1$, and $\gamma = 0.7$. This fits the requirements for a concave utility function, which means that we are risk averse.

(b) Calculate both your EU and the utility equivalent of the EV of your income.

- *Expected utility.* The expected utility of our income is

$$EU = 0.5(500^{0.7}) + 0.2(700^{0.7}) + 0.3(400^{0.7})$$
$$= 0.5(77.50) + 0.2(98.08) + 0.3(66.29)$$
$$= 78.25.$$

- *Utility of expected value.* First, we need to find our expected income; that is,

$$EV = (0.5 \times \$500) + (0.2 \times \$700) + (0.3 \times \$400)$$
$$= \$250 + \$140 + \$120$$
$$= \$510.$$

Our utility at the expected value is

$$u(510) = 510^{0.7} = 78.58.$$

(c) Using the results from part (b), show that your risk preferences are risk averse.

- To show that we are risk averse, we need that $u(EV) > EU$, which holds in this case since

$$78.58 = u(EV) > EU = 78.25.$$

(d) Suppose now that you had the option to either accept this lottery, or walk away with your initial $500. Should you accept the lottery? Why or why not?

- With our initial income, our utility is

$$u(500) = 500^{0.7} = 77.50.$$

Since this is less than our expected utility from accepting the lottery ($EU = 78.25$), we should accept the lottery.

Exercise #6.9 - Risk Loving[B]

6.9 Suppose that you took part in a lottery that had a chance to increase, decrease, or have no effect on your level of income. With probability 0.3, your income remains at its original level, $200. With probability 0.2, your income increases to $300, and with probability 0.5, your income decreases to $0. Your utility function is

$$u(I) = I^{2.5},$$

where I denotes your income level.

(a) Using only the utility function, show that your risk preferences are risk loving.

- We know that utility functions following the form $u(I) = a + bI^{\gamma}$ are convex if $a, b > 0$ and $\gamma > 1$. For our utility function, $a = 0$, $b = 1$, and $\gamma = 2.5$. This fits the requirements for a convex utility function, which means that we are risk loving.

(b) Calculate both your EU and the utility equivalent of the EV of your income.

- *Expected utility.* The expected utility of our income is

$$EU = 0.3(200^{2.5}) + 0.2(300^{2.5}) + 0.5(0^{2.5})$$
$$= 0.3(565, 685) + 0.2(1, 558, 846) + 0.5(0)$$
$$= 481, 475.$$

- *Utility of expected value.* First, we need to find our expected income; that is,

$$EV = (0.3 \times \$200) + (0.2 \times \$300) + (0.5 \times \$0)$$
$$= \$60 + \$60 + 0$$
$$= \$120.$$

Our utility at the expected value is

$$u(120) = 120^{2.5} = 157,744.$$

(c) Using the results from part (b), show that your risk preferences are risk loving.

- To show that we are risk loving, we need that $u(EV) < EU$, which holds in this case since
$$157,744 = u(EV) < EU = 481,475.$$

(d) Suppose now that you had the option to either accept this lottery, or walk away with your initial \$200. Should you accept the lottery? Why or why not?

- With our initial \$200, our utility is

$$u(200) = 200^{2.5} = 565,685.$$

Even though we are risk loving, there is not enough of a potential gain from the lottery, so we prefer to not accept the lottery and stay at our initial income.

Exercise #6.11 - Risk Neutrality^B

6.11 Suppose that you took part in a lottery that had a chance to increase, decrease, or have no effect on your level of income. With probability 0.4, your income remains at its original level, \$400. With probability 0.4, your income increases to \$800, and with probability 0.2, your income decreases to \$200. Your utility function is

$$u(I) = 125 + 3I,$$

where I denotes your income level.

(a) Using only the utility function, show that your risk preferences are risk neutral.

- Risk neutrality arises with linear utility functions. The utility function $u(I) = 125 + 3I$ is linear in income; therefore, we are risk neutral.

(b) Calculate both your EU and the utility equivalent of the EV of your income.

- *Expected utility.* The expected utility of our income is

$$EU = 0.4(125 + 3(400)) + 0.4(125 + 3(800)) + 0.2(125 + 3(200))$$
$$= 0.4(1,325) + 0.4(2,525) + 0.2(725)$$
$$= 1,685.$$

- *Utility of expected value.* First, we need to find our expected income; that is,

$$EV = (0.4 \times \$400) + (0.4 \times \$800) + (0.2 \times \$200)$$
$$= \$160 + \$320 + \$40$$
$$= \$520$$

Our utility at the expected value is

$$u(520) = 125 + 3(520) = 1,685.$$

Since we are risk neutral, our expected utility coincides with the utility of the expected value.

(c) Using the results from part (b), show that your risk preferences are risk neutral.

- To show that we are risk neutral, we need that $u(EV) = EU$, which holds in this case since
$$1,685 = u(EV) = EU = 1,685.$$

(d) Suppose now that you had the option to either accept this lottery, or walk away with your initial $400. Should you accept the lottery? Why or why not?

- Our utility at $400 is

$$u(400) = 125 + 3(400) = 1,325.$$

Because our utility at our initial income is less than our expected utility from the lottery, we should accept the lottery, which has expected utility of 1,685.

Exercise #6.13 - Contracting an Illness[B]

6.13 Consider a situation where you are faced with a risky situation. You currently have $100,000 available for consumption, and with a 90 percent probability, you would suffer no illness. You have a 9 percent chance, however, of contracting a case of influenza, leading to the loss of $10,000 in consumption. In addition, there is a 1 percent chance that this is a severe illness, leading to the loss of $50,000 in consumption. Your utility from consumption is

$$U(C) = C^{0.4},$$

where C is your consumption level.

(a) What is your attitude toward risk? How do you know this?

- We know that utility functions following the form $u(I) = a + bI^\gamma$ are concave if $a, b > 0$ and $\gamma \in (0, 1)$. For our utility function, $a = 0$, $b = 1$, and $\gamma = 0.4$. This fits the requirements for a concave utility function, which means that we are risk averse.

(b) Suppose that you could purchase insurance against influenza. What is your CE?

- Our certainty equivalent is

$$CE = EV - RP.$$

We first need to calculate expected value; that is,

$$EV = (0.9 \times \$100,000) + (0.09 \times (\$100,000 - \$10,000)) + (0.01 \times (\$100,000 - \$50,000))$$

which simplifies to

$$EV = (0.9 \times \$100,000) + (0.09 \times \$90,000) + (0.01 \times \$50,000)$$
$$= \$90,000 + \$8,100 + \$500$$
$$= \$98,600$$

Therefore, our certainty equivalent is

$$CE = 98,600 - RP.$$

(c) What is the maximum premium that you are willing to pay for insurance against influenza?

- The maximum we are willing to pay for insurance against influenza is the difference between our utility at our initial income less the insurance premium (IP) and our expected utility. We first need to find our expect utility, which is

$$EU = 0.9(100,000^{0.4}) + 0.09(90,000^{0.4}) + 0.01(50,000^{0.4})$$
$$= 0.9(100) + 0.09(95.87) + 0.01(75.79)$$
$$= 99.39.$$

The utility from purchasing insurance is

$$u(100,000 - IP) = (100,000 - IP)^{0.4}.$$

Setting the above expression equal to our expected utility of 99.39, we find that

$$(100,000 - IP)^{0.4} = \underbrace{99.39}_{EU}.$$

Taking each side to the 1/0.4 power, we get that

$$100,000 - IP = 98,482.$$

Solving for IP, we find that the maximum we would pay for insurance is

$$IP = \$1,519.$$

(d) What is your risk premium? How does this compare with your risk premium if you were risk neutral?

- *Risk averse.* The maximum we are willing to pay for insurance against influenza is the risk premium RP, which we can find by solving $u(CE) = EU$, or

$$u(98,600 - RP) = 99.39.$$

134

With our utility function, this equation becomes

$$(98,600 - RP)^{0.4} = 99.39.$$

Taking each side to the $\frac{1}{0.4}$ power, we obtain

$$98,600 - RP = 98,482,$$

and solving for RP, we find that

$$RP = \$118.$$

- *Risk neutral.* If we were risk neutral, with a utility of $u(I) = I$ (a linear utility function), our expected utility coincides with the expected value, i.e.,

$$\begin{aligned} EU &= (0.9 \times \$100,00) + (0.09 \times \$90,000) + (0.01 \times \$50,000) \\ &= \$90,000 + \$8,100 + \$500 \\ &= \$98,600. \end{aligned}$$

Therefore, to find our risk premium in this case, we solve

$$u(98,600 - RP) = 98,600.$$

Given that our utility function is $u(I) = I$, this equation becomes

$$98,600 - RP = 98,600,$$

and our risk premium is \$0. If we were risk neutral, we would have a lower risk premium than if we are risk averse.

Exercise #6.15 - Not Purchasing Full Insurance[B]

6.15 Consider Adam's situation in exercise 6.14, except now each unit of insurance costs \$0.11.

(a) What is Adam's expected utility from buying a units of insurance?

- In the case that Adam does not suffer a loss, his utility is a function of his wealth minus the amount of insurance he purchases; that is, $\sqrt{100 - 0.11a}$.
- In the case that Adam suffers the loss, his utility is a function of his wealth minus the loss and the insurance premium plus the insurance reimbursement: $\sqrt{100 - 0.11a - 25 + a} = \sqrt{75 + 0.89a}$.
- Therefore, Adam's expected utility function, which accounts for the probability he is in each state, is

$$EU = 0.9\underbrace{\sqrt{100 - 0.11a}}_{\text{No loss}} + 0.1\underbrace{\sqrt{75 + 0.89a}}_{\text{Loss}}.$$

(b) How many units of insurance, a, does Adam purchase in this scenario?

135

- Adam buys the units of insurance a that maximize his expected utility EU, as found in part (a); that is,

$$\max_a \ 0.9\sqrt{100 - 0.11a} + 0.1\sqrt{75 + 0.89a}.$$

Differentiating with respect to a yields

$$0.5(-0.11)0.9(100 - 0.11a)^{-1/2} + 0.5(0.89)0.1(75 + 0.89a)^{-1/2} = 0.$$

This simplifies first to

$$-0.0495(100 - 0.11a)^{-1/2} + 0.0445(75 + 0.89a)^{-1/2} = 0,$$

Adding the first term to the right-hand side and dividing by 0.0495, we obtain

$$0.89899(75 + 0.89a)^{-1/2} = (100 - 0.11a)^{-1/2},$$

and taking each side to the -2 power yields

$$1.237(75 + 0.89a) = (100 - 0.11a).$$

Simplifying first to $92.78 + 1.1a = 100 - 0.11a$, and then to

$$7.22 = 1.21a,$$

we can divide each side by 1.21 to ultimately find that Adam purchases $a = 5.97$ units. In this case, the insurance premium is not actuarially fair as the premium (\$0.11) is larger than its expected payoff, $0.1 \times \$1 = \$0.10$. This induces Adam to not fully insure against his potential loss (i.e., $a < 25$).

Exercise #6.17 - Arrow-Pratt Coefficient–II[B]

6.17 Consider an individual with the utility function $u(I) = \exp^I$, where exp denotes the exponential function and I is an individual's income level.

(a) Calculate the Arrow-Pratt coefficient of risk aversion.
- We first need to calculate the first two derivatives, u' and u'':

$$u' = \exp^I \quad \text{and}$$
$$u'' = \exp^I.$$

The Arrow-Pratt coefficient of risk aversion is

$$AP \equiv -\frac{u''}{u'} = -\frac{\exp^I}{\exp^I} = -1.$$

(b) Based on your results from part (a), what is this individual's attitude toward risk?
- This individual's utility function is convex since the AP coefficient is negative. Therefore, the individual is risk loving.

Exercise #6.19 - Prospect Theory–I[B]

6.19 Suppose that your initial wealth is $W = \$50$, and your utility function is $u(W) = \sqrt{W}$. While out on a walk one day, you notice a $5 bill on the ground and pick it up.

(a) By how much does your utility increase?

- Our initial utility is

$$u(50) = \sqrt{50} = 7.07.$$

  After finding the $5, our utility increases to

$$u(55) = \sqrt{55} = 7.42.$$

  This leaves an increase in utility of

$$7.42 - 7.07 = 0.35.$$

(b) Suppose now that while walking home with your $55, you are stopped by a police officer for jaywalking and fined $5. By how much does your utility decrease? How does your utility now compare with your original utility?

- Our decrease in utility is then

$$u(50) - u(55) = 7.07 - 7.42$$
$$= -0.35.$$

(c) Repeat part (a), but suppose now that your utility function is $u(W, W_0) = \sqrt{W - W_0}$ when you increase your wealth, where W_0 represents your wealth before the event occurs (your reference point), and $u(W, W_0) = -(W - W_0)^2$ when you decrease your wealth.

- When we find the $5, our utility is

$$u(55, 50) = \sqrt{55 - 50}$$
$$= \sqrt{5} = 2.24.$$

(d) Repeat part (b) with the utility function in part (c).

- When we lose the $5 to the jaywalking ticket, our utility is

$$u(50, 55) = -(55 - 50)^2$$
$$= -(5)^2 = -25.$$

(e) Compare the results of parts (b) and (d). Under which situation are you worse off? Why?

- We can see that we are worse off with the reference-dependent utility function. Under the first utility function, we felt the same magnitude of a utility change regardless if it was a gain or a loss. Under the reference-dependent utility, since losses have convex utility and gains have concave utility, the loss of $5 has a greater magnitude than if we were to gain $5.

Exercise #6.21 - Gambling[A]

6.21 Suppose that you have a situation where your grandfather enjoys spending all his free time (and money) playing the slot machines at his local casino. When you confront him, he explains to you that he is risk loving, and he can't give up the thrill of taking a gamble. With what you know about risk premiums, how could you persuade your grandfather to curtail his gambling habits?

- The risk premium for a risk lover is negative. This means that to make the individual indifferent between playing the lottery and taking the certain outcome, we need to increase the expected value of the lottery. One option would be to pay him for the time he is gambling. This has the effect of increasing his expected value from gambling, which, consequently, could make him stop gambling if we paid him enough.

Chapter 7 - Production Functions

7.1 Solutions to Self-Assessment Exercises

Self-assessment exercise #7.1

SA 7.1 Consider the firm discussed in example 7.1, but assume that its production function is $q = 5K^{1/3}L^{2/3}$. Which is the largest amount of output q that the firm can produce using $L = 9$ and $K = 4$ inputs? What if the production function changes to $q = 7K + 4L$? What if it changes to $q = 5\min\{2K, 3L\}$? What if it changes to $q = 4K^{1/2} + 3L$?

- The production function tells us the greatest output we can produce for a given set of inputs. Thus, we need to plug $L = 9$ and $K = 4$ into each of our production functions:

  $\rightarrow q = 5K^{1/3}L^{2/3} = 5 \times \left(4^{1/3}9^{2/3}\right) = 34.34$ units of output.

  $\rightarrow q = 7K + 4L = 7(4) + 4(9) = 64$ units of output.

  $\rightarrow q = 5\min\{2K, 3L\} = 5\min\{2 \times 4, 3 \times 9\} = 5\min\{8, 27\} = 5 \times 8 = 40$ units of output.

  $\rightarrow q = 4K^{1/2} + 3L = \left(4 \times 4^{1/2}\right) + (3 \times 9) = 8 + 27 = 35$ units of output.

Self-assessment exercise #7.2

SA 7.2 Consider the firm in example 7.2, but assume now that its production function changes to $q = 7L^{1/3} + 4L - 2$. Find the average product, AP_L, and the labor at which AP_L reaches its maximum.

- We first obtain the average product,

$$
\begin{aligned}
AP_L &= \frac{q}{L} = \frac{7L^{1/3} + 4L - 2}{L} \\
&= \frac{7}{L^{2/3}} + 4 - \frac{2}{L}.
\end{aligned}
$$

The AP_L reaches its maximum when its derivative with respect to labor is zero, $\frac{\partial AP_L}{\partial L} = 0$; that is,

$$
\frac{\partial AP_L}{\partial L} = -\frac{14}{3L^{5/3}} + \frac{2}{L^2} = 0.
$$

Rearranging, yields

$$
\frac{14}{3L^{5/3}} = \frac{2}{L^2}.
$$

Moving all terms with L to the left-hand side of the equality, we obtain

$$
\frac{L^2}{L^{5/3}} = \frac{6}{14}.
$$

which simplifies to $L^{1/3} = \frac{6}{14}$. Powering both sides by 3, we find

$$L = \frac{27}{343} \approx 0.079 \text{ workers.}$$

Therefore, the AP_L curve reaches its maximum at $L = 0.079$ workers.

Self-assessment exercise #7.3

SA 7.3 Consider the firm in example 7.3, but assume that the firm's production function changes to $q = 7L^{1/3} + 4L - 2$. Find the marginal product, MP_L, and check if it increases or decreases in labor.

- The marginal product curve is

$$MP_L = \frac{\partial q}{\partial L} = \frac{7}{3}L^{-2/3} + 4.$$

To check if it increases or decreases in L, we need to take the derivative with respect to L:

$$\frac{\partial MP_L}{\partial L} = -\frac{14}{9}L^{-5/3},$$

which is negative for all values of L. Therefore, as L increases, MP_L decreases.

Self-assessment exercise #7.4

SA 7.4 Consider the firm in self-assessments 7.2 and 7.3. Using the same steps as in example 7.4, find the point at which MP_L crosses the AP_L curve.

- In self-assessment 7.2 we found that AP_L reaches its maximum at $L = \frac{27}{343} \approx 0.079$ workers. At this value of L, $AP_L = \frac{7}{L^{2/3}} + 4 - \frac{2}{L}$ becomes

$$
\begin{aligned}
AP_L(0.079) &= \frac{7}{0.079^{2/3}} + 4 - \frac{2}{0.079} \\
&= 16.7.
\end{aligned}
$$

If we evaluate $MP_L = \frac{7}{3}L^{-2/3} + 4$ at $L = \frac{27}{343} \approx 0.079$ workers, we find that

$$
\begin{aligned}
MP_L(0.079) &= \frac{7}{3}(0.079)^{-2/3} + 4 \\
&= 16.7,
\end{aligned}
$$

confirming that MP_L crosses the AP_L at its maximum point.

Self-assessment exercise #7.5

SA 7.5 Consider the firm in example 7.5, but assume that it seeks to produce $q = 200$ units. What is the firm's isoquant now? What if its production function changes to $q =$

$L^{1/3}K^{2/3}$? Interpret your results.

- *First production function.* Inserting $q = 200$ into the left-hand side of the production function, we obtain $200 = 5L^{1/2}K^{1/2}$, and dividing each side by 5, we obtain $40 = L^{1/2}K^{1/2}$. Squaring both sides yields $1600 = KL$, and solving for K we obtain the isoquant

$$K = \frac{1600}{L}.$$

- *Second production function.* Inserting $q = 200$ into the left-hand side of the new production function, we obtain $200 = L^{1/3}K^{2/3}$. Now, we need to solve for capital K, first by cubing both sides, which yields $200^3 = LK^2$. Dividing each side by L gives us $K^2 = \frac{200^3}{L}$. Finally, taking the square root of each side gives us

$$K = \frac{200^{3/2}}{L^{1/2}}.$$

- *Comparison.* The isoquant of both production functions approaches each of the axes without touching them, but that of the second production function approaches the L-axes more quickly than the first production function.

Self-assessment exercise #7.6

SA 7.6 Consider a firm with production function $q = 4L^{1/3}K^{2/3}$. Using the same steps as in example 7.6, find this firm's MRTS. Interpret your results.

- First, we need to find the marginal product of labor and capital, as follows:

$$
\begin{aligned}
MP_L &= \frac{\partial q}{\partial L} = \frac{4}{3}L^{-2/3}K^{2/3}, \text{ and} \\
MP_K &= \frac{\partial q}{\partial K} = \frac{8}{3}L^{1/3}K^{-1/3}.
\end{aligned}
$$

Therefore, the $MRTS$ is

$$MRTS = \frac{MP_L}{MP_K} = \frac{\frac{4}{3}L^{-2/3}K^{2/3}}{\frac{8}{3}L^{1/3}K^{-1/3}} = \frac{K^{\frac{2}{3}-\left(\frac{1}{3}\right)}}{2L^{\frac{1}{3}-\left(\frac{2}{3}\right)}} = \frac{K}{2L}.$$

This means that the isoquant is half as steep as the slope of the isoquant in example 7.6, so that the isoquant will become "flatter" more quickly as L increases.

Self-assessment exercise #7.7

SA 7.7 Consider a firm with production function $q = 5L + 2K$. Using the same steps as in example 7.7, find this firm's MRTS. Assume now that its production function changes to $q' = 5L + 4K$. What is the firm's MRTS now? How does it compare to the initial MRTS? Interpret your results in terms of capital productivity.

141

- Using the formula $MRTS = \dfrac{a}{b}$, the $MRTS = \dfrac{5}{2}$ for the first production function q, and $MRTS = \dfrac{5}{4}$ for the second production function q'. This means that the isoquant for q' is less steep than the isoquant for q; hence, capital has become relatively more productive.

Self-assessment exercise #7.8

SA 7.8 Consider a firm with production function $q = 5L + 2K$. If the firm seeks to produce $q = 230$ units, find the isoquant, its vertical and horizontal intercept, and its slope.

- Solving for K in our production function $230 = 5L + 2K$ yields the isoquant

$$K = \frac{230}{2} - \frac{5}{2}L.$$

Its vertical axis will be where $K = \dfrac{230}{2} = 115$, and its horizontal axis will be at the level of L that solves $0 = \dfrac{230}{2} - \dfrac{5}{2}L$; that is, $L = \dfrac{230}{5} = 46$ workers. The slope is constant and is equal to the $MRTS$, $\dfrac{5}{2}$.

Self-assessment exercise #7.9

SA 7.9 Consider a firm with production function $q = 5\min\{3L, K\}$. If the firm seeks to produce $q = 200$ units of output, find and depict the isoquant.

- The fixed-proportion production function has an L-shaped isoquant. The vertical line will be at

$$L = \frac{q}{Aa} = \frac{200}{5 \times 3} = 13.33 \text{ workers.}$$

The horizontal line will be at

$$K = \frac{q}{Ab} = \frac{200}{5} = 40 \text{ units of capital.}$$

The kink of all isoquants will occur at the point where the two arguments inside the min $\{\cdot\}$ operator are equal to each other; that is, $3L = K$ in this production function. Since we have $q = 200$, this kink happens at $K = 40$ units of capital and $L = \dfrac{200}{5 \times 3} = 13.33$ workers.

Self-assessment exercise #7.10

SA 7.10 Consider a firm with production function $q = 5L^{1/3}K^{2/3}$. Find the firm's MRTS. Then, assuming that the firm seeks to produce $q = 220$ units of output, find and depict the isoquant.

- The $MRTS$ is

$$MRTS = \frac{MP_L}{MP_K} = \frac{\frac{5}{3}L^{-2/3}K^{2/3}}{\frac{10}{3}L^{1/3}K^{-1/3}} = \frac{K^{\frac{2}{3}-\left(\frac{1}{3}\right)}}{2L^{\frac{1}{3}-\left(\frac{2}{3}\right)}} = \frac{K}{2L}.$$

- To find the isoquant, we need to solve $200 = 5L^{1/3}K^{2/3}$ for K. Dividing each side by 5 gives us $40 = L^{1/3}K^{2/3}$. Cubing both sides yields $40^3 = LK^2$. Next, divide by L to get $K^2 = \dfrac{40^3}{L}$, and square-root each side to get the isoquant

$$K = \frac{40^{3/2}}{L^{1/2}}.$$

This isoquant will approach both axes, but never cross them; however, it will approach the K-axis more quickly than the L-axis.

Self-assessment exercise #7.11

SA 7.11 Consider a firm with the production function $q = 5L^{1/3}K^{2/3}$. Use the same steps as in example 7.8 to find if this production function exhibits increasing, decreasing, or constant returns to scale. What if the firm's production function changes to $q = 7L + 8K$? What if it changes to $q = 3\min\{L, 2K\}$?

- $q = 5L^{1/3}K^{2/3}$: If we increase all inputs by λ, we get

$$5(\lambda L)^{1/3}(\lambda K)^{2/3} = 5\lambda^{1/3}L^{1/3}\lambda^{2/3}K^{2/3} = \lambda^{1/3+2/3}5L^{1/3}K^{2/3} = \lambda\underbrace{\left(5L^{1/3}K^{2/3}\right)}_{q} = \lambda q.$$

The resulting increase in output is the same as the increase in the input, so this production function exhibits constant returns to scale.

- $q = 7L + 8K$: If we increase all inputs by λ, we get

$$7\lambda L + 8\lambda K = \lambda\underbrace{(7L + 8K)}_{q} = \lambda q.$$

Again, the resulting increase in output is the same as the increase in the input, so this production function exhibits constant returns to scale.

- $q = 3\min\{L, 2K\}$: If we increase all inputs by λ, we get

$$3\min\{\lambda L, 2\lambda K\} = \lambda\underbrace{3\min\{L, 2K\}}_{q} = \lambda q.$$

Again, the resulting increase in output is the same as the increase in the input, so this production function exhibits constant returns to scale.

Self-assessment exercise #7.12

SA 7.12 Consider a firm with the production function $q = 7L + 2K$, which changes to $q = 7L + 5K$. Is the firm experiencing technological progress?

- Technological progress would mean that

$$7L + 2K < 7L + 5K.$$

This simplifies to $2K < 5K$, and further to $2 < 5$, which always holds. Therefore, the firm experienced technological progress.

Self-assessment exercise #7.13

SA 7.13 Consider the firm in self-assessment 7.12. Find the MRTS before and after the technological change. Is this change labor saving, capital saving, or neutral?

- For linear production functions, the $MRTS = \dfrac{a}{b}$. Before the technological progress, the $MRTS_{pre} = \dfrac{7}{2}$, and after the $MRTS_{post} = \dfrac{7}{5}$. It is clear that the

$$MRTS_{pre} > MRTS_{post} \quad \text{since} \quad \frac{7}{2} > \frac{7}{5},$$

hence the technological progress is labor saving, since it can fire some workers and hire capital to become more productive.

7.2 Solutions to End-of-Chapter Exercises

Exercise #7.1 - Properties of Production Functions[B]

7.1 A firm uses only one input, labor (L), to produce output with production function $q(L) = 3L^2 + 0.5L - 0.6L^3$.

(a) *Total product.* For which values of L does the total product curve $q(L)$ increase or decrease? For which values is it concave or convex in labor?

- To answer the first part, we need to examine the sign of the derivative,

$$\frac{\partial q(L)}{\partial L} = 6L + 0.5 - 1.8L^2.$$

The total product is increasing when $6L + 0.5 - 1.8L^2 > 0$. Solving for the roots of this quadratic expression, we find that $\frac{\partial q(L)}{\partial L} = 0$ at $L = \{-0.08, 3.4\}$. At $L = 0$, $\frac{\partial q(L)}{\partial L} = 0.5 > 0$, so, for $0 < L < 3.4$, the total product is increasing. For $L > 3.4$, total product is decreasing.

To check concavity, we need to investigate the sign of the second derivative,

$$\frac{\partial^2 q(L)}{\partial L^2} = 6 - 3.6L.$$

Solving $6 - 3.6L > 0$, we can see that $\frac{\partial^2 q(L)}{\partial L^2} > 0$ when $L < \frac{6}{3.6} \simeq 1.67$ workers. Therefore, total product is convex in labor for $L < 1.67$, and concave in labor for $L > 1.67$. Intuitively, labor exhibits increasing returns to scale when $L < 1.67$, but decreasing returns otherwise. Figure 7.1 depicts total, marginal and average product.

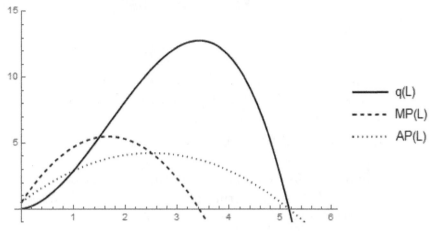

Figure 7.1. Total, marginal, and average product.

(b) *Marginal product.* For which values of L does the marginal product curve $\frac{\partial q(L)}{\partial L}$ increase or decrease? For which values is it concave or convex in labor?

- The marginal product curve is

$$MP_L = \frac{\partial q(L)}{\partial L} = 6L + 0.5 - 1.8L^2.$$

  Marginal product increases when $\frac{\partial^2 q(L)}{\partial L^2} = 6 - 3.6L > 0$. Following part (a), marginal product increases when $L < 1.67$, and decreases when $L > 1.67$.

- To evaluate the concavity of the marginal product curve, we need to look at the second derivative of the marginal product curve (which is the same as the third derivative of the total product curve), $\frac{\partial^3 q(L)}{\partial L^3} = -3.6 < 0$ for all L, meaning that the marginal product curve is concave.

(c) *Average product.* For which values of L does the average product curve $\frac{q(L)}{L}$ increase or decrease? For which values is it concave or convex in labor?

- First, the average product is

$$AP_L = \frac{q(L)}{L} = 3L + 0.5 - 0.6L^2.$$

  The $AP(L)$ increases when $\frac{\partial AP(L)}{\partial L} = 3 - 1.2L > 0$. Simplifying, the $AP(L)$ increases when $L < 3/1.2 = 2.5$, and decreases when $L > 2.5$.

- To evaluate the concavity of the average product curve, we need to look at the sign of the second derivative of $AP(L)$,

$$\frac{\partial^2 AP_L}{\partial L^2} = -1.2 < 0$$

145

for all L. This means that the average product curve is concave.

(d) Find the value of L where the marginal product curve crosses the total product curve, and where it crosses the average product curve.

- The marginal product curve crosses the total product curve at $MP(L) = q(L)$, or
$$3L^2 + 0.5L - 0.6L^3 = 6L + 0.5 - 1.8L^2.$$

This simplifies to
$$0.6L^3 - 4.8L^2 + 5.5L + 0.5 = 0,$$

which has three roots: $L = \{-.08, 1.49, 6.59\}$. The marginal product curve crosses the total product curve at $L = 1.49$ (the only point where production is positive of the three points).

- The marginal product and average product curves cross at the minimum of the average product curve, or where $\frac{\partial AP_L}{\partial L} = 0$. Solving $3 - 1.2L = 0$, we find that the marginal and average product curves cross at $L = 2.5$. We can verify this by evaluating each curve at $L = 2.5$, and find that $MP(2.5) = AP(2.5) = 4.25$.

Exercise #7.3 - Where the MP and AP Curves Cross[A]

7.3 A firm has the production function $q = 50L - 2L^2 - 10$. At what level of labor do the marginal product and average product curves cross?

- For this production function,

$$MP_L = \frac{\partial q}{\partial L} = 50 - 4L, \text{ and}$$
$$AP_L = \frac{q}{L} = 50 - 2L - \frac{10}{L}.$$

To find where these two expressions cross, we set $MP_L = AP_L$, or

$$50 - 4L = 50 - 2L - \frac{10}{L},$$

which simplifies to $2L = \frac{10}{L}$, and further to $L^2 = 5$. Applying square roots to both sides leaves us with our answer $L = \sqrt{5} \simeq 2.24$ units of labor. Figure 7.2 depicts marginal and average product.

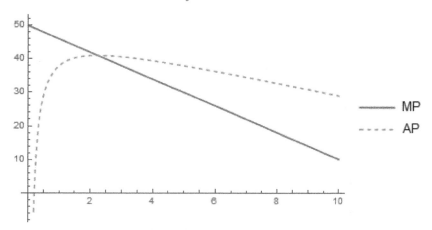

Figure 7.2. Marginal and average product curves.

Exercise #7.5 - MP and Changing Capital[B]

7.5 A firm produces stickers, s, using capital and labor in its production, with the production function $s = 10K + 20L^2 - K^3L^3$. Does the marginal product of labor increase or decrease as capital increases?

- The marginal product is

$$MP_L = \frac{\partial s}{\partial L} = 40L - 3K^3L^2.$$

To find how the marginal product of labor changes with respect to capital, we take a derivative with respect to capital:

$$\frac{\partial MP_L}{\partial K} = -9K^2L^2.$$

Since $K^2L^2 > 0$ for all levels of capital and labor, it must be that $\frac{\partial MP_L}{\partial K} < 0$. This means that the marginal product of labor decreases as capital increases. Intuitively, every worker becomes less productive as the firm acquires more capital (maybe every worker has a new computer and gets more frequently distracted browsing the internet). Figure 7.3 depicts marginal product evaluated at two levels of capital.

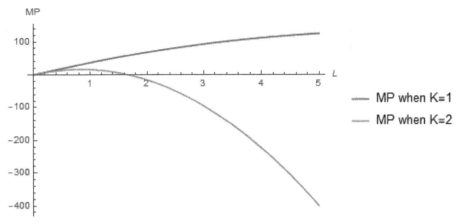

Figure 7.3. Marginal product curve at different levels of capital.

Exercise #7.7 - Linear Production and MRTS^A

7.7 Jack produces water bottles and wants to know more about his production function. He finds that it follows the function $q(K, L) = 20K + 30L + 10KL$. Find the marginal products of labor and capital, as well as the MRTS.

- First, the marginal product of labor is

$$MP_L = \frac{\partial q}{\partial L} = 30 + 10K,$$

and that of capital is

$$MP_K = \frac{\partial q}{\partial K} = 20 + 10L.$$

Then, the $MRTS_{K,L}$ is

$$MRTS_{K,L} = \frac{MP_L}{MP_K} = \frac{30 + 10K}{20 + 10L}.$$

Exercise #7.9 - Returns to Scale–I^A

7.9 Do the following production functions exhibit increasing, decreasing, or constant returns to scale?

(a) $q = 5K^{0.7}L^{0.3}$.

- Increasing both inputs by a common factor of λ yields

$$5(\lambda K)^{0.7}(\lambda L)^{0.3} = 5\lambda^{0.7}K^{0.7}\lambda^{0.3}L^{0.3} = \lambda^1 \underbrace{\left(5K^{0.7}L^{0.3}\right)}_{q} = \lambda q.$$

This implies that this production function exhibits constant returns to scale.

(b) $q = K^{0.5}L^{0.6}$.

- Increasing both inputs by a common factor of λ yields

$$(\lambda K)^{0.5}(\lambda L)^{0.6} = \lambda^{0.5}K^{0.5}\lambda^{0.6}L^{0.6} = \lambda^{1.1}\underbrace{\left(K^{0.5}L^{0.6}\right)}_{q} = \lambda^{1.1}q.$$

This implies that this production function exhibits increasing returns to scale as $\lambda^{1.1}q > \lambda q$.

(c) $q = 2K + 4L$.

- Increasing both inputs by a common factor of λ yields

$$2(\lambda K) + 4(\lambda L) = \lambda\underbrace{(2K + 4L)}_{q} = \lambda q.$$

This implies that this production function exhibits constant returns to scale.

Exercise #7.11 - Decreasing Marginal Returns[A]

7.11 A bakery that specializes in cupcakes has the production function for cupcakes of $c = 10L - 0.5L^2$ in their current space. What is the firm's marginal product? At what amount of labor does the firm's output begin to decrease (i.e., when does there start to be "too many cooks in the kitchen")?

- The bakery's marginal product is

$$MP_L = \frac{\partial q}{\partial L} = 10 - L.$$

To find where the firm's output begins to decrease, we want to find the point on the MP_L curve that is equal to zero and is negative for values of labor greater than that value. Setting $MP_L = 0$ yields $10 - L = 0$, which gives us $L = 10$ units. It is easy to check that for $L > 10$ workers, $MP_L < 0$.

Exercise #7.13 - Choosing Production[A]

7.13 Eric is a manager of a firm that produces playing cards. He is investing in a new technology and has two options with the resulting production functions: (a) $q = 10L^{0.5}K^{0.5}$, and (b) $q = 10(L^{0.5} + K^{0.5})$. If the firm has 100 units of capital, when would Eric prefer technology (a) over technology (b)?

- Figure 7.4 depicts both production functions. Eric will prefer technology (a) over (b) if
$$10L^{0.5}K^{0.5} > 10(L^{0.5} + K^{0.5}) \quad \text{at } K = 100.$$

Plugging in for capital leaves our inequality at

$$10L^{0.5}(100)^{0.5} > 10(L^{0.5} + (100)^{0.5})$$

or, after rearranging, $100L^{0.5} > 10(L^{0.5} + 10)$. Dividing by 10 leaves $10L^{0.5} > L^{0.5} + 10$, and combining like terms, we get $9L^{0.5} > 10$. Finally, we get that technology (a) is preferred to (b) if $L > \frac{100}{81} \simeq 1.23$ units of labor. Overall, if Eric hires more than 1.23 units of labor, he will be more productive with technology (a).

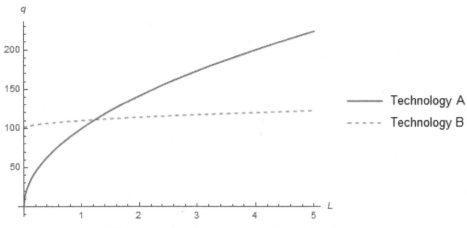

Figure 7.4. Two production functions.

Exercise #7.15 - CES Production Function and Marginal Products[B]

7.15 Find the marginal products of labor and capital for the CES production function $q = \left(aL^{\frac{\sigma-1}{\sigma}} + bK^{\frac{\sigma-1}{\sigma}}\right)^{\frac{\sigma}{\sigma-1}}$.

- The marginal product of labor is (using the chain rule)

$$MP_L = \frac{\partial q}{\partial L} = \frac{\sigma}{\sigma-1}\left(aL^{\frac{\sigma-1}{\sigma}} + bK^{\frac{\sigma-1}{\sigma}}\right)^{\frac{\sigma}{\sigma-1}-1}\left(\frac{\sigma-1}{\sigma}aL^{\frac{\sigma-1}{\sigma}-1}\right)$$

$$= \left(aL^{\frac{\sigma-1}{\sigma}} + bK^{\frac{\sigma-1}{\sigma}}\right)^{\frac{\sigma-\sigma+1}{\sigma-1}} aL^{\frac{\sigma-1-\sigma}{\sigma}}$$

$$= \left(aL^{\frac{\sigma-1}{\sigma}} + bK^{\frac{\sigma-1}{\sigma}}\right)^{\frac{1}{\sigma-1}} aL^{\frac{-1}{\sigma}}.$$

- The marginal product of capital is (using the chain rule)

$$MP_K = \frac{\partial q}{\partial L} = \frac{\sigma}{\sigma-1}\left(aL^{\frac{\sigma-1}{\sigma}} + bK^{\frac{\sigma-1}{\sigma}}\right)^{\frac{\sigma}{\sigma-1}-1}\left(\frac{\sigma-1}{\sigma}bK^{\frac{\sigma-1}{\sigma}-1}\right)$$

$$= \left(aL^{\frac{\sigma-1}{\sigma}} + bK^{\frac{\sigma-1}{\sigma}}\right)^{\frac{\sigma-\sigma+1}{\sigma-1}} bK^{\frac{\sigma-1-\sigma}{\sigma}}$$

$$= \left(aL^{\frac{\sigma-1}{\sigma}} + bK^{\frac{\sigma-1}{\sigma}}\right)^{\frac{1}{\sigma-1}} bK^{\frac{-1}{\sigma}}.$$

Exercise #7.17 - Choosing Factors of Production[B]

7.17 Ashley is a producer of water purifiers for use in remote African villages and relies heavily on donations and volunteers in her production of water purifiers. In 1 hour, a worker can make 5 purifiers with 10 units of capital, or 2 workers can make 10 purifiers with 15 units of capital. As of Thursday evening, Ashley has 20 committed volunteers (for 5 hours on Saturday) and 100 units of capital. Ashley has 24 hours to round up more volunteers, more capital, or both. What should she do?

- If we divide 100 by 15 units of capital, we can get 6 groups of capital for 12 workers to produce 10 purifiers per hour and 1 person who can make 5 purifiers per hour with the last 10 units of capital. The total amount of purifiers this group could make with this organization is 65 purifiers per hour. This means that there are 7 leftover workers who aren't producing anything.

  If she were to use the other production function, she could have 10 workers each with 10 units of capital make a total of 50 purifiers, but 10 workers will be left over, not producing.

- Regardless of which production combination she uses, her lack of capital is limiting. Therefore, she should spend her time increasing her capital donations. Once she finds 60 units of capital (enough to have 10 groups of 2 workers each with 15 units of capital), she can round up both labor and capital.

Exercise #7.19 - Comparing MRTS^C

7.19 Tony and Chris are studying for exams to be certified public accountants (CPAs). Tony prefers reading laws and regulations (R), while Chris prefers practicing audits (A). Tony's score follows the function $S_T = 10A^{0.65}R^{0.35}$, while Chris's score follows $S_C = 10A^{0.4}R^{0.6}$.

(a) At what point will their MRTS between practicing audits and reading regulations be equal?

- Tony's MRTS is

$$MRTS_T^T = \frac{MP_A}{MP_R} = \frac{6.5A^{-0.35}R^{0.35}}{3.5A^{0.65}R^{-0.65}} = \frac{6.5R}{3.5A}.$$

Chris's MRTS is

$$MRTS_C^C = \frac{MP_A}{MP_R} = \frac{6A^{-0.6}R^{0.6}}{6A^{0.4}R^{-0.4}} = \frac{3R}{2A}.$$

The two MRTS will be equal when

$$\frac{6.5R}{3.5A} = \frac{3R}{2A}$$
$$\frac{6.5}{3.5} = \frac{3}{2},$$

which cannot happen since $\frac{6.5}{3.5} > \frac{3}{2}$. This means that Tony, who prefers audits, has a higher MRTS between audits and reading regulations. In other words, he will need to read more regulations to make up for one less audit to keep the same score relative to Chris.

(b) Tony and Chris went to college together and know that each of them is studying for the CPA exam, and they plan to study together. Their score functions change

151

by adding a variable representing the time they spend studying together, T, such that $S_T = 10A^{0.65}R^{0.35}+T^{0.5}$ and $S_C = 10A^{0.4}R^{0.6}+T^{0.5}$. Find the MRTS between the time spent studying together and their preferred method of studying. Can we tell who is willing to give up more of his preferred method of studying to study together? If so, who?

- Tony's $MRTS_{G,A}^T$ is

$$MRTS_{G,A}^T = \frac{MP_A}{MP_G} = \frac{6.5A^{-0.35}R^{0.35}}{0.5G^{-0.5}} = \frac{13R^{0.35}G^{0.5}}{A^{0.35}}.$$

Chris's $MRTS_{G,R}^C$ is

$$MRTS_{G,R}^C = \frac{MP_R}{MP_G} = \frac{6A^{0.4}R^{-0.4}}{0.5G^{-0.5}} = \frac{12A^{0.4}G^{0.5}}{R^{0.4}}.$$

The student with the bigger MRTS will be more willing to give up more of his preferred method of studying to study together:

$$MRTS_{G,A}^T > MRTS_{G,R}^C$$
$$\frac{13R^{0.35}G^{0.5}}{A^{0.35}} > \frac{12A^{0.4}G^{0.5}}{R^{0.4}}$$
$$13R^{0.75}G^{0.5} > 12A^{0.75}G^{0.5}$$
$$13R^{0.75} > 12A^{0.75}$$
$$1.1R > A.$$

If Tony and Chris both spend the same amount of time studying audits and regulations, then Tony will be more willing to give up more of his preferred method of studying if $1.1R > A$, otherwise, we would need to input each of their times studying each method into their respective MRTS to find who is more willing to study together.

Chapter 8 - Cost Minimization

8.1 Solutions to Self-Assessment Exercises

Self-assessment exercise #8.1

SA 8.1 Consider the firm in example 8.1, but assume that wages double to $w = \$20$. Find the firm's isocost in this scenario, and interpret how it changed relative to that in figure 8.1a.

- The equation for the isocost line is $TC = wL + rK$. From example 8.1, we have that the firm incurs a total cost $TC = \$200$ and the price of every unit of capital is $r = \$15$, so the new isocost line is

$$200 = 20L + 15K.$$

Solving for K, we find that
$$K = \frac{200}{15} - \frac{20}{15}L.$$

- *Vertical intercept.* The vertical intercept is the same as in example 8.1; that is, $\frac{200}{15} \simeq 13.3$.

- *Slope.* However, the slope has changed to $\frac{20}{15} = \frac{4}{3}$, which is twice as steep as from example 8.1 where the slope was $\frac{2}{3}$. This is a direct result of labor being twice as expensive as in the example. This means that the new isocost will lie below the one from example 8.1, indicating that we can hire fewer units of labor and capital.

- *Horizontal intercept.* We can also see this result by finding the horizontal intercept. Setting the above isocost line equal to zero (since $K = 0$), we obtain

$$0 = \frac{200}{15} - \frac{20}{15}L.$$

Solving for L, we find the horizontal intercept, $L = 10$ workers. Relative to figure 8.1a in the textbook, the firm can hire half of the workers ($L = 10$ rather than $L = 20$) since their wage doubled.

Self-assessment exercise #8.2

SA 8.2 Repeat the analysis in example 8.2, but assume that wages decrease to $w = \$20$. How are the results in example 8.2 affected?

- Our production function is $q = L^{1/2}K^{1/2}$, and we want to reach an output of $q = 100$ with input prices $w = \$20$ and $r = \$10$.

Step 1. First, we set the tangency condition $\frac{MP_L}{MP_K} = \frac{w}{r}$, which yields

$$\frac{\frac{1}{2}L^{-1/2}K^{1/2}}{\frac{1}{2}L^{1/2}K^{-1/2}} = \frac{20}{10},$$

or rearranging, $\frac{K}{L} = 2$. Solving for K simplifies to $K = 2L$. Since this result contains both K and L, we move on to step 2a.

Step 2a. Inserting our result from step 1, $K = 2L$, into the output target of the firm, $q = 100$, $100 = L^{1/2}K^{1/2}$, we obtain

$$100 = L^{1/2}\underbrace{(2L)^{1/2}}_{K}.$$

Rearranging, we obtain $100 = 2^{1/2}L$, and, solving for L, $L = \frac{100}{2^{1/2}} \simeq 70.71$ workers. Since we have a positive amount of workers, we can move on to step 4.

Step 4. Last, we can plug this result into the tangency condition $K = 2L$, to find that

$$K = 2 \times 70.71 = 141.42 \text{ units of capital.}$$

Summary. The cost-minimizing input combination is then

$$(L, K) = (70.71, 141, 42).$$

Compared to example 8.2, we use more labor and less capital since labor became relatively cheaper. However, labor is still twice as expensive as capital, yet just as productive, so we still use more capital than labor in our production decisions.

Self-assessment exercise #8.3

SA 8.3 Repeat the analysis in example 8.3, but assuming that wages decrease to $w = \$20$. How are the results in example 8.3 affected?

- The firm's production function is $q = 2L + 8K$, and we want to reach an output level of $q = 100$ with input prices $w = \$20$ and $r = \$10$.

Step 1. First, we set the tangency condition $\frac{MP_L}{MP_K} = \frac{w}{r}$, which yields

$$\frac{2}{8} = \frac{20}{10}.$$

This equality cannot hold since each side yields a different number (i.e., $0.25 < 2$). Since our tangency conditions contains no input, we move on to step 2c.

Step 2c. We obtained that $\frac{2}{8} = 0.25 < 2 = \frac{20}{10}$, which entails that $\frac{MP_L}{MP_K} < \frac{w}{r}$, or, after cross-multiplying,

$$\frac{MP_L}{w} < \frac{MP_K}{r}.$$

As a consequence, the firm will only purchase capital and no labor, so that $L = 0$.

Step 4. Inserting $L = 0$ into the output target of the firm $100 = 2L + 8K$, yields

$$100 = 2(0) + 8K.$$

Solving for K, we obtain $K = \frac{100}{8} = 12.5$ units of capital.

Summary. The cost-minimizing input combination is

$$(L, K) = (0, 12.5),$$

thus coinciding with that in example 8.3. Even though labor is cheaper here, we do not use it because capital is still more productive per dollar spent on it; that is, capital shows a higher "bang for the buck" than labor even after purchasing as many units of capital as the firm can afford.

Self-assessment exercise #8.4

SA 8.4 Repeat the analysis in example 8.4, but assume that the firm's production function changes to $q = 4L^{1/3}K^{1/2}$. How are the results in example 8.4 affected? Interpret the results.

- We will follow the same procedure as in example 8.4:

Step 1. We first find the tangency condition $\frac{MP_L}{MP_K} = \frac{w}{r}$, which yields

$$\frac{\frac{4}{3}L^{-2/3}K^{2/3}}{\frac{8}{3}L^{1/3}K^{-1/3}} = \frac{w}{r}.$$

Rearranging, we find $\frac{K}{2L} = \frac{w}{r}$, which solving for K simplifies to $K = \frac{2wL}{r}$. Since this result contains both inputs K and L, we move on to step 2a.

Step 2a. We now insert our result from step 1, $K = \frac{2wL}{r}$, into the output target of the firm, $q = 4L^{1/3}K^{2/3}$, to obtain

$$q = 4L^{1/3}\underbrace{\left(\frac{2wL}{r}\right)^{2/3}}_{K}.$$

This simplifies first to $q = 4\left(\frac{2w}{r}\right)^{2/3}L^{1/3}L^{2/3}$, combining L-terms, we get

$$q = 4\left(\frac{2w}{r}\right)^{2/3}L.$$

Solving for L, we find the firm's labor demand

$$L = \frac{q}{4\left(\frac{2w}{r}\right)^{2/3}} = \frac{q(r)^{2/3}}{2^{8/3}(w)^{2/3}}.$$

Step 4. Last, we plug labor demand into the tangency condition, $K = \frac{2wL}{r}$, to find that capital demand is

$$K = \frac{2w}{r}\frac{q(r)^{2/3}}{2^{8/3}(w)^{2/3}} = \frac{qw^{1-\frac{2}{3}}}{2^{\frac{8}{3}-1}r^{1-\frac{2}{3}}} = \frac{q(w)^{1/3}}{2^{5/3}(r)^{1/3}}.$$

Summary. We now compare the labor demand in example 8.4, $L = \frac{q\sqrt{r}}{\sqrt{w}}$, against that in this

155

exercise, $L' = \frac{q(r)^{2/3}}{2^{8/3}(w)^{2/3}}$. To show that $L > L'$, we need that $\frac{q\sqrt{r}}{\sqrt{w}} > \frac{q(r)^{2/3}}{2^{8/3}(w)^{2/3}}$ holds. Multiplying each side by $\frac{1}{\sqrt{r}}$ and $2^{8/3}w^{2/3}$, the inequality becomes

$$\frac{2^{8/3}w^{2/3}}{w^{1/2}} > \frac{r^{2/3}}{r^{1/2}},$$

and simplifying one more step yields $2^{8/3}w^{1/6} > r^{1/6}$. We can now take the 6th power of each side to find that $2^{16}w > r$, where $2^{16} = 65,536$. We can then conclude that labor demand is smaller than in example 8.3 if $65,536 > \frac{r}{w}$. In words, the firm hires fewer workers when facing production function $q = 4L^{1/3}K^{2/3}$ than with $q = L^{1/2}K^{1/2}$ as long as capital is not much more costly than labor; that is, input ratio $\frac{r}{w}$ can be larger than one, or a large number, but not be larger than $65,536$. Otherwise, the firm hires more workers with the new production function.

A similar approach can be used to find that capital demand is smaller with the new production when $2^{22}w > r$.

Self-assessment exercise #8.5

SA 8.5 Repeat the analysis in example 8.5, but assume that the firm's production function changes to $q = 3L + 8K$. How are the results in example 8.5 affected? Interpret.

- We follow the steps in example 8.5.

Step 1. We first find the tangency condition $\frac{MP_L}{MP_K} = \frac{w}{r}$, which yields

$$\frac{3}{8} = \frac{w}{r}.$$

This result does not contain either input, K or L, so we now move on to step 2c.

Step 2c. Comparing the marginal product per dollar across inputs, we obtain that

$$\frac{MP_L}{w} < \frac{MP_K}{r} \quad \text{if} \quad \frac{3}{8} < \frac{8}{r},$$

i.e., $\frac{3}{8} < \frac{w}{r}$, which induces the firm to hire no workers, $L = 0$. Otherwise, the marginal product per dollar spent on labor is higher than that on capital, entailing that the firm hires no capital, $K = 0$.

Step 4. If $\frac{3}{8} < \frac{w}{r}$ holds, the firm hires no workers, $L = 0$, which we can insert into the output target $q = 3L + 8K$, yielding

$$q = 3 \underbrace{(0)}_{L=0} + 8K.$$

Solving for K, we obtain a demand for capital of $K = \frac{q}{8}$ units of capital.

If, instead, $\frac{3}{8} > \frac{w}{r}$ holds, the firm hires no capital, $K = 0$, and its demand for labor is found by inserting $K = 0$ into the output target, with yields

$$q = 3L + 8 \underbrace{(0)}_{K=0}.$$

Solving for L, we find $L = \frac{q}{3}$ workers.

Summary. The results here are very similar to those in example 8.5. However, the marginal product of labor has increased, meaning that the firm is willing to switch to only using labor, and no capital, at a relatively more expensive wage rate (a higher $\frac{w}{r}$).

Self-assessment exercise #8.6

SA 8.6 Consider the labor and capital demands found in self-assessment 8.4. Find the total cost function TC, and then evaluate it at input prices $w = \$40$ and $r = \$10$. Compare it against $TC = 40q$, which we found in example 8.6. Interpret.

- The labor and capital demands we found in self-assessment 8.4 were $L = \dfrac{q(r)^{2/3}}{2^{8/3}(w)^{2/3}}$ and $K = \dfrac{q(w)^{1/3}}{2^{5/3}(r)^{1/3}}$. Total cost is

$$TC = wL^* + rK^* = w\underbrace{\frac{q(r)^{2/3}}{2^{8/3}(w)^{2/3}}}_{L^*} + r\underbrace{\frac{q(w)^{1/3}}{2^{5/3}(r)^{1/3}}}_{K^*}$$

$$= w^{1/3}\frac{q(r)^{2/3}}{2^{8/3}} + r^{2/3}\frac{q(w)^{1/3}}{2^{5/3}}$$

$$= qr^{2/3}w^{1/3}\frac{1}{2^{8/3}} + qr^{2/3}w^{1/3}\frac{1}{2^{5/3}}$$

$$= qr^{2/3}w^{1/3}\underbrace{\left(\frac{1}{2^{8/3}} + \frac{1}{2^{5/3}}\right)}_{\simeq 0.472}$$

$$\simeq 0.472qr^{2/3}w^{1/3}.$$

If we evaluate it at input prices $w = \$40$ and $r = \$10$, we obtain

$$TC = 0.234q\underbrace{(10)^{2/3}}_{r}\underbrace{(40)^{1/3}}_{w} \simeq 7.524q.$$

If we compare this total cost to $TC = 40q$, we find that, at any output level q, the firm faces a lower total cost than in example 8.6.

Self-assessment exercise #8.7

SA 8.7 Consider the labor and capital demands found in self-assessment 8.5. Find the total cost function TC in this scenario, and compare it against $TC = r\frac{q}{8}$, found in example 8.7. Interpret.

157

- In self-assessment 8.5, we found that input demands were $L = 0$ and $K = \frac{q}{8}$ if $\frac{3}{8} < \frac{w}{r}$, but became $L = \frac{q}{3}$ and $K = 0$ if $\frac{3}{8} > \frac{w}{r}$.

- Therefore, when input prices satisfy $\frac{3}{8} < \frac{w}{r}$, total costs are

$$TC = w \underbrace{0}_{L} + r \underbrace{\frac{q}{8}}_{K} = r\frac{q}{8},$$

which increase in both the output q and the price of capital r, but do not change when the price of labor w changes.

- If, instead, input prices satisfy $\frac{3}{8} > \frac{w}{r}$, then the firm uses only labor, and total costs become

$$TC = w \underbrace{\frac{q}{3}}_{L} + r \underbrace{0}_{K} = w\frac{q}{3},$$

which increase in both output q and wages w, but are unaffected by the price of capital r.

- In the case where the firm uses only capital, so $TC = r\frac{q}{8}$, total cost coincides with that in example 8.7. This happens because the productivity of capital is the same in each production function, and we are only using capital to produce output.

Self-assessment exercise #8.8

SA 8.8 Repeat the analysis in example 8.8, but assume that capital is fixed at $K = 50$ units. Find the firm's demand for labor, and its short-run cost function STC. Assume the same input prices as in example 8.8, $w = \$40$ and $r = \$10$, and compare STC against the firm's long-run total cost $TC = 40q$.

- In the short run, capital is fixed at $\bar{K} = 50$ units. To find the cost-minimizing units of labor, we plug $\bar{K} = 50$ into the firm's production function, as follows

$$q = L^{1/2} \underbrace{50}_{\bar{K}=50}{}^{1/2}.$$

We now solve for L. First, square both sides to obtain $q^2 = 50L$, and solving for L, we find the short-run demand for labor

$$L = \frac{q^2}{50},$$

which is increasing in output q. In this context, the short-run total cost becomes

$$STC = wL^* + r\bar{K} = w\frac{q^2}{50} + r50.$$

If we consider input prices $w = \$40$ and $r = \$10$, this short-run total cost simplifies to

$$STC = \$500 + \frac{4}{5}q^2.$$

This short-run cost still lies above the long-run total cost of $TC = 40q$, but is shifted to the left and down, being tangent to the TC curve at $q = 25$. At low levels of output, it will cheaper to produce with capital set at $\bar{K} = 50$, whereas at higher levels of output, it will be cheaper to produce with capital set at $\bar{K} = 150$. This happens because, at low levels of output, we use inputs at a ratio closer to what is efficient in the long run than if capital was at $\bar{K} = 50$.

Self-assessment exercise #8.9

SA 8.9 Assume a firm with total cost $TC = 30q^2$. Find its average and marginal cost functions, and depict them against q.

- The firm's average cost is

$$AC = \frac{TC}{q} = \frac{30q^2}{q} = 30q$$

and its marginal cost is

$$MC = \frac{\partial TC}{\partial q} = 60q.$$

Graphically, the average cost curve $AC = 30q$ is a straight line from the origin with a slope of 30. The marginal cost curve, $MC = 60q$, is a straight line from the origin with a slope of 60, thus being twice as steep as the average cost curve.

Self-assessment exercise #8.10

SA 8.10 Consider a firm with total cost $TC = 5 + 30q^2$. Find its output elasticity, and interpret your results.

- The output elasticity in this case is

$$\varepsilon_{TC,q} = \frac{\partial TC}{\partial q}\frac{q}{TC} = 60q\frac{q}{5 + 30q^2} = \frac{12q^2}{1 + 6q^2}$$

Intuitively, if the firm increases its output by 1 percent, total cost increases by $\frac{12q^2}{1 + 6q^2}$ percent. This number is increasing in q, which means that a 1 percent increase in output yields a larger percentage increase in total costs as the firm's output increases.

- As a practice, you can plot the ratio $\varepsilon_{TC,q} = \frac{12q^2}{1 + 6q^2}$ as a function of q, which starts at a height of approximately $\varepsilon_{TC,q} = 1.71$ when $q = 1$, and rapidly increases to $\varepsilon_{TC,q} = 1.99$ for all $q > 10$ units.

Self-assessment exercise #8.11

SA 8.11 Consider a firm with total cost $TC = 5 + 2q + q^3$. Find the average cost curve $AC(q)$ and its minimum point. Interpret your results in terms of economies of scale.

- To find the minimum of average cost, we first need to find average cost

$$AC = \frac{TC}{q} = \frac{5}{q} + 2 + q^2.$$

Next, we can find the minimum of average by setting the derivative of average cost equal to zero; that is,

$$\frac{\partial AC}{\partial q} = -\frac{5}{q^2} + 2q = 0,$$

Rearranging, we obtain $2q = \frac{5}{q^2}$, or $q^3 = \frac{5}{2}$. Taking the cube root of both sides yields an output of

$$q = \left(\frac{5}{2}\right)^{1/3} \simeq 1.357 \text{ units.}$$

For all levels of output less than $q = 1.357$, the AC curve is decreasing, thus exhibiting economies of scale. For output levels greater than $q = 1.357$, the firm suffers from diseconomies of scale.

Self-assessment exercise #8.12

SA 8.12 Consider the scenario in example 8.12. Does the soda company benefit from economies of scope when $\alpha = 2$, $\beta = 3$, and $q_1 = q_2 = 4$ units?

- From example 8.12, the firm experiences economies of scope if its total cost from producing both types of sodas is lower than the sum of producing each type of soda independently; that is,

$$(3 - \alpha)q_1 + (4 - \alpha)q_2 + (10 + \beta) < [3q_1 + 10] + [4q_2 + 10].$$

If $\alpha = 2$, $\beta = 3$, and $q_1 = q_2 = 4$ units, this inequality becomes

$$(3 - 2)4 + (4 - 2)4 + (10 + 3) < [3(4) + 10] + [4(4) + 10].$$
$$4 + (2)4 + 13 < 12 + 10 + 16 + 10$$
$$25 < 48.$$

Therefore, the firm benefits from economies of scope. If we obtained a larger number on the left- than in the right-hand side, the firm would suffer from diseconomies of scope.

Self-assessment exercise #8.13

SA 8.13 Consider a firm with $AVC(E) = \frac{10}{E^{1/2}}$. Find the experience elasticity of the firm, and the slope of its experience curve. Interpret.

- The experience elasticity is

$$
\begin{aligned}
\varepsilon_{AVC<E} &= \frac{\partial AVC}{\partial E} \frac{E}{AVC} \\
&= -\frac{5}{E^{3/2}} \frac{E}{\frac{10}{E^{1/2}}} \\
&= -\frac{E^{3/2}}{2E^{3/2}} = -\frac{1}{2}.
\end{aligned}
$$

In words, this means that a 1 percent increase in the firm's production experience E decreases its average variable costs by 0.5 percent.

- The slope of the experience curve is

$$
\begin{aligned}
\text{Slope of experience curve} &= \frac{AVC(2E)}{AVC(E)} \\
&= \frac{\frac{10}{(2E)^{1/2}}}{\frac{10}{E^{1/2}}} = \frac{10E^{1/2}}{10(2E)^{1/2}} \\
&= \frac{1}{2^{1/2}} \simeq 0.71
\end{aligned}
$$

Intuitively, when the production experience doubles (from E to $2E$), the firm's average cost decreases by a factor of 0.71.

8.2 Solutions to End-of-Chapter Exercises

Exercise #8.1 - Cost Minimization for Cobb-Douglas[B]

8.1 Consider a firm with the Cobb-Douglas production function $f(K, L) = 4K^{1/2}L^{1/3}$, where K denotes units of capital and L represents units of labor. Assume that the firm faces input prices of $r = \$10$ per unit of capital, and $w = \$7$ per unit of labor.[1]

(a) Solve the firm's cost-minimization problem, to obtain the combination of inputs (labor and capital) that minimizes the firm's cost of producing a given amount of output, q.

- The tangency condition $\frac{MP_L}{MP_K} = \frac{w}{r}$ is

$$
\frac{\frac{4}{3}K^{1/2}L^{-2/3}}{2K^{-1/2}L^{1/3}} = \frac{7}{10}
$$

which simplifies to

$$
\frac{2}{3}\frac{K}{L} = \frac{7}{10}
$$

This contains both L and K, so we solve for K:

$$
K = \frac{7}{10}\frac{3}{2}L = \frac{21}{20}L
$$

---

[1]The firm sells every unit of output at a price $p > 0$.

We can insert this back into the firm's output target $q = 4K^{1/2}L^{1/3}$, to find that

$$q = 4 \underbrace{\left(\frac{21}{20}L\right)^{1/2}}_{K} L^{1/3}$$

rearranging,

$$q = 4\left(\frac{21}{20}\right)^{1/2} L^{2/6+3/6},$$

where we need to solve for L:

$$L^{5/6} = \frac{q}{4}\left(\frac{20}{21}\right)^{1/2}$$

$$L = \left(\frac{q}{4}\left(\frac{20}{21}\right)^{1/2}\right)^{6/5}$$

$$L = \left(\frac{q}{4}\right)^{6/5}\left(\frac{20}{21}\right)^{3/5} \simeq 0.184q^{6/5}.$$

This is the firm's labor demand. Plugging this back into the tangency condition,

$$K = \frac{21}{20}\left(\frac{q}{4}\right)^{6/5}\left(\frac{20}{21}\right)^{3/5}$$

which simplifies to

$$K = \left(\frac{q}{4}\right)^{6/5}\left(\frac{21}{20}\right)^{2/5} \simeq 0.193q^{6/5}$$

which is the firm's demand for capital.

(b) Use your results from part (a) to find the firm's cost function. This is its long-run total cost, as all inputs can be altered.

- Plugging back into the cost function, we get

$$C = wL + rK = 7\underbrace{\left(\frac{q}{4}\right)^{6/5}\left(\frac{20}{21}\right)^{3/5}}_{L} + 10\underbrace{\left(\frac{q}{4}\right)^{6/5}\left(\frac{21}{20}\right)^{2/5}}_{K}.$$

If we simplify this numerically, we get

$$C \simeq 3.218q^{6/5}.$$

(c) Find the firm's marginal cost function, and its average cost function. Interpret.

- The firm's marginal cost is

$$MC = \frac{dC}{dq} = \frac{6}{5}3.218q^{1/5} \simeq 3.862q^{1/5}.$$

Each additional unit the firm produces will cost about $3.862q^{1/5}$, which increases as q increases.

The firm's average cost is

$$AC = \frac{C}{q} = \frac{3.218q^{6/5}}{q} = 3.218q^{1/5}.$$

This average cost lies below the marginal cost, but has the same shape. Figure 8.1 depicts marginal and average costs.

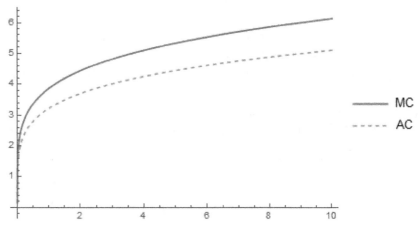

Figure 8.1. Marginal and average cost curves.

(d) Assume now that the amount of capital is held fixed at $\overline{K} = 3$ units. Solve the firm's cost-minimization problem again to find the amount of labor that minimizes the firm's cost.

- If $\overline{K} = 3$, the firm's cost-minimizing amount of labor satisfies

$$q = 4 \underbrace{(3)}_{\overline{K}}^{1/2} L^{1/3}.$$

Solving for L, we find that

$$L^{1/3} = \frac{q}{4(3)^{1/2}}$$

$$L = \left(\frac{q}{4(3)^{1/2}}\right)^3$$

$$L = \frac{q^3}{64(3)^{3/2}} \simeq 0.003q^3.$$

(e) Use your results from part (c) to find the firm's short-run cost function (since in the short run the firm can only alter the amount of labor, but without changing the units of capital).

- Plugging the previous result into the firm's total cost, we get

$$C = 7\underbrace{(0.003q^3)}_{L} + 10\underbrace{(3)}_{K} = 0.021q^3 + 30.$$

Exercise #8.3 - Properties of a Cost Function[B]

8.3 A firm has the following cost function:

$$TC(q) = 2q^3 - \frac{1}{3}q^2 + \frac{1}{2}q + \frac{9}{10},$$

where q denotes units of output. Intuitively, the first three terms on the right side capture the firm's variable cost, because they depend on the output the firm produces, whereas the last term represents its fixed cost, as it is not a function of output q.

(a) *Total cost.* For which output q does the total cost curve $TC(q)$ increase or decrease? For which values is it concave or convex in output?

- We need to look at the derivative:

$$\frac{dC}{dq} = 6q^2 - \frac{2}{3}q + \frac{1}{2}.$$

This is always greater than 0, which means that the total cost curve is always increasing. To evaluate the concavity, we look at the second derivative:

$$\frac{d^2C}{dq^2} = 12q - \frac{2}{3}.$$

Setting equal to zero and solving for q, we can find that the second derivative is positive for $q > \frac{1}{18}$, which is where the total cost curve is convex. For $q < \frac{1}{18}$, the total cost curve is concave.

(b) *Marginal cost.* For which output q does the marginal cost curve $\frac{\partial TC(q)}{\partial q}$ increase or decrease? For which values is it concave or convex in output?

- We found marginal cost in the last problem, $MC = 6q^2 - \frac{2}{3}q + \frac{1}{2}$, and its derivative, $12q - \frac{2}{3}$, which tells us that marginal cost is increasing for $q > \frac{1}{18}$. The second derivative of marginal cost, $\frac{d^2MC}{dq^2} = 12 > 0$ means that the marginal cost curve is convex.

(c) *Average cost.* For which output q does the average cost curve $AC(q) = \frac{TC(q)}{q}$ increase or decrease? For which values is it concave or convex in output?

- Average cost is

$$\frac{C(q)}{q} = 2q^2 - \frac{1}{3}q + \frac{1}{2} + \frac{9}{10q}.$$

The derivative of average cost is

$$\frac{dAC}{dq} = 4q - \frac{1}{3} - \frac{9}{10q^2}.$$

164

Solving for when this equals zero, we find that the average cost is decreasing for $q < 0.52$ but increasing for $q > 0.52$. The second derivative tells us about its concavity:

$$\frac{d^2 AC}{dq^2} = 4 + \frac{18}{10q},$$

which is always positive, so average cost is convex.

(d) *Average variable cost.* For which output q does the average variable cost curve $AC(q)$ increase or decrease? For which values is it concave or convex in output?

- The variable cost is part of costs that varies with output: $2q^3 - \frac{1}{3}q^2 + \frac{1}{2}q$. Therefore, average variable cost is:

$$AVC = 2q^2 - \frac{1}{3}q + \frac{1}{2}.$$

The derivative will tell us when it increases or decreases:

$$\frac{dAVC}{dq} = 4q - \frac{1}{3}.$$

Setting equal to zero and solving, we find that average variable cost decreases when $q < \frac{1}{12} \simeq 0.083$, and increases at larger values of q. The second derivative, $\frac{d^2 AVC}{dq^2} = 4$, tells us that the average variable cost is convex.

(e) Find the value of q where the marginal cost curve crosses the total cost curve, where it crosses the average cost curve, and where it crosses the average variable cost curve.

- The marginal cost curve crosses the average cost and average variable cost curves at their lowest points, which we have already calculated. Marginal and average costs cross at $q = 0.52$, while marginal and average variable costs cross at $q = 0.083$.

Exercise #8.5 - CMP for Cobb-Douglas Production–I^C

8.5 Consider a Cobb-Douglas production function $q = AL^\alpha K^\beta$, where $A, \alpha, \beta > 0$. Assume that input prices are w for labor and r for capital.

(a) Find labor demand $L(q, w, r)$.

- We first set the tangency condition $\frac{MP_L}{MP_K} = \frac{w}{r}$, which yields

$$\frac{\beta A K^\alpha L^{\beta-1}}{\alpha A K^{\alpha-1} L^\beta} = \frac{w}{r},$$

which simplifies to

$$\frac{\beta K}{\alpha L} = \frac{w}{r}, \text{ or, } K = \frac{\alpha w}{\beta r} L.$$

We can plug this into the output target for the firm, $q = K^\alpha L^\beta$, to obtain

$$q = A \left(\frac{\alpha w}{\beta r} L \right)^\alpha L^\beta,$$

rearranging, yields

$$q = A \left(\frac{\alpha w}{\beta r} \right)^\alpha L^{\alpha+\beta},$$

or

$$L^{\alpha+\beta} = \frac{q}{A} \left(\frac{\beta r}{\alpha w} \right)^\alpha.$$

Solving for L, we get the firm's labor demand

$$L = \left(\frac{q}{A} \right)^{\frac{1}{\alpha+\beta}} \left(\frac{\beta r}{\alpha w} \right)^{\frac{\alpha}{\alpha+\beta}}.$$

(b) Find capital demand $K(q, w, r)$.

- We can plug labor demand back into the tangency condition for the demand for capital

$$K = \frac{\alpha w}{\beta r} \underbrace{\left(\frac{q}{A} \right)^{\frac{1}{\alpha+\beta}} \left(\frac{\beta r}{\alpha w} \right)^{\frac{\alpha}{\alpha+\beta}}}_{L}$$

$$= \left(\frac{\beta r}{\alpha w} \right)^{-1} \left(\frac{q}{A} \right)^{\frac{1}{\alpha+\beta}} \left(\frac{\beta r}{\alpha w} \right)^{\frac{\alpha}{\alpha+\beta}}$$

$$= \left(\frac{q}{A} \right)^{\frac{1}{\alpha+\beta}} \left(\frac{\beta r}{\alpha w} \right)^{\frac{\alpha}{\alpha+\beta}-1}.$$

Since $\frac{\alpha}{\alpha+\beta} - 1 = \frac{\alpha-(\alpha+\beta)}{\alpha+\beta} = -\frac{\beta}{\alpha+\beta}$, the above expression becomes

$$K = \left(\frac{q}{A} \right)^{\frac{1}{\alpha+\beta}} \left(\frac{\beta r}{\alpha w} \right)^{-\frac{\beta}{\alpha+\beta}}$$

which can be written as

$$K = \left(\frac{q}{A} \right)^{\frac{1}{\alpha+\beta}} \left(\frac{\alpha w}{\beta r} \right)^{\frac{\beta}{\alpha+\beta}}.$$

(c) Find total cost $TC(q)$.

- The firm's cost function is found by plugging our input demands into total cost

$$C(q, w, r) = wL^* + rK^*,$$

$$= w \underbrace{\left(\frac{q}{A}\right)^{\frac{1}{\alpha+\beta}} \left(\frac{\beta r}{\alpha w}\right)^{\frac{\alpha}{\alpha+\beta}}}_{L} + r \underbrace{\left(\frac{q}{A}\right)^{\frac{1}{\alpha+\beta}} \left(\frac{\alpha w}{\beta r}\right)^{\frac{\beta}{\alpha+\beta}}}_{K}$$

$$= w^{\frac{\beta}{\alpha+\beta}} \left(\frac{q}{A}\right)^{\frac{1}{\alpha+\beta}} \left(\frac{\beta r}{\alpha}\right)^{\frac{\alpha}{\alpha+\beta}} + r^{\frac{\alpha}{\alpha+\beta}} \left(\frac{q}{A}\right)^{\frac{1}{\alpha+\beta}} \left(\frac{\alpha w}{\beta}\right)^{\frac{\beta}{\alpha+\beta}}$$

$$= \left(\frac{q}{A}\right)^{\frac{1}{\alpha+\beta}} \left(r^{\frac{\alpha}{\alpha+\beta}} w^{\frac{\beta}{\alpha+\beta}} \left(\frac{\beta}{\alpha}\right)^{\frac{\alpha}{\alpha+\beta}} + r^{\frac{\alpha}{\alpha+\beta}} w^{\frac{\beta}{\alpha+\beta}} \left(\frac{\alpha}{\beta}\right)^{\frac{\beta}{\alpha+\beta}} \right)$$

$$= \left(\frac{q}{A}\right)^{\frac{1}{\alpha+\beta}} r^{\frac{\alpha}{\alpha+\beta}} w^{\frac{\beta}{\alpha+\beta}} \left(\left(\frac{\beta}{\alpha}\right)^{\frac{\alpha}{\alpha+\beta}} + \left(\frac{\alpha}{\beta}\right)^{\frac{\beta}{\alpha+\beta}} \right).$$

Since $\left(\frac{\beta}{\alpha}\right)^{\frac{\alpha}{\alpha+\beta}} = \left(\frac{\alpha}{\beta}\right)^{-\frac{\alpha}{\alpha+\beta}}$, we can write total cost as

$$C(q, w, r) = \left(\frac{q}{A}\right)^{\frac{1}{\alpha+\beta}} r^{\frac{\alpha}{\alpha+\beta}} w^{\frac{\beta}{\alpha+\beta}} \left(\left(\frac{\alpha}{\beta}\right)^{-\frac{\alpha}{\alpha+\beta}} + \left(\frac{\alpha}{\beta}\right)^{\frac{\beta}{\alpha+\beta}} \right).$$

(d) Find average cost and marginal cost, $AC(q)$ and $MC(q)$. Show under which conditions on α and β these costs are constant in q and coincide between them.

- First, let's simplify the notation, let $T = r^{\frac{\alpha}{\alpha+\beta}} w^{\frac{\beta}{\alpha+\beta}} \left(\left(\frac{\alpha}{\beta}\right)^{-\frac{\alpha}{\alpha+\beta}} + \left(\frac{\alpha}{\beta}\right)^{\frac{\beta}{\alpha+\beta}} \right)$ since it is constant in q. This allows us to write the cost function as

$$C(q, w, r) = \left(\frac{q}{A}\right)^{\frac{1}{\alpha+\beta}} T$$

Average cost is

$$\frac{C(q, w, r)}{q} = \frac{1}{q} \left(\frac{q}{A}\right)^{\frac{1}{\alpha+\beta}} T,$$

$$= q^{\frac{1-\alpha-\beta}{\alpha+\beta}} \left(\frac{1}{A}\right)^{\frac{1}{\alpha+\beta}} T.$$

Marginal cost is

$$\frac{\partial C(q, w, r)}{\partial q} = \frac{1}{\alpha+\beta} q^{\frac{1-\alpha-\beta}{\alpha+\beta}} \left(\frac{1}{A}\right)^{\frac{1}{\alpha+\beta}} T.$$

The two terms coincide and are constant in q if $\alpha + \beta = 1$ (the firm exhibits constant returns to scale); that is,

$$AC = MC = \left(\frac{1}{A}\right)T,$$

which is constant in q.

Exercise #8.7 - Explicit and Implicit Costs[A]

8.7 Calculate the explicit and implicit costs of finishing your education. (*Hint:* Your university's financial aid page should have estimates on tuition and cost of living, but the opportunity cost of your degree may be harder to estimate.)

- The *explicit* costs of finishing your education should be given to you through your school's financial aid website. If you have one year left of school, the estimated year total may be $30,000. This estimate (usually) includes living expenses and transportation costs.

- The *implicit*, or opportunity, cost of your last year in school may be harder to estimate. This would include the wages you are giving up by not working full-time. You can find some information on the Bureau of Labor Statistics website, which has data on over 800 occupations in different locations. For example, a retail sales worker would make approximately $25,000 in the next year.

Exercise #8.9 - CMP with Cobb-Douglas Production–II[B]

8.9 Jared is a manager for a local coffee roaster. He hires labor at a rate of $20 per hour, and capital costs $15 per hour. His production function of pounds of coffee beans follows $q = 2K^{0.25}L^{0.75}$.

(a) If Jared wants to produce 10 pounds of coffee beans per hour, how much labor and capital should he employ?

- The tangency condition $\frac{MP_L}{MP_K} = \frac{w}{r}$ is

$$\frac{1.5K^{0.25}L^{-0.25}}{0.5K^{-0.75}L^{0.75}} = \frac{20}{15},$$

which simplifies to

$$\frac{3K}{L} = \frac{4}{3}.$$

Solving for K, we have

$$K = \frac{4}{9}L.$$

Plugging this into the Jared's output, we find

$$10 = 2\underbrace{\left(\frac{4}{9}L\right)^{0.25}}_{K}L^{0.75} = 2\left(\frac{4}{9}\right)^{0.25}L.$$

168

Solving for L, we get

$$L = \frac{10}{2} \left(\frac{9}{4}\right)^{0.25} \simeq 6.12.$$

Using the tangency condition to find K, we get

$$K = \frac{4}{9} \frac{10}{2} \left(\frac{9}{4}\right)^{0.25} \simeq 2.72.$$

Jared should hire 6.12 units of labor and 2.72 units of capital to make 10 pounds of coffee.

(b) What if the price of capital increases to \$20?

- If the price of labor increases to \$20, the tangency condition changes to

$$\frac{3K}{L} = \frac{20}{20},$$

or, $K = \frac{1}{3}L$. Plugging this into Jared's output, we get

$$10 = 2 \underbrace{\left(\frac{1}{3}L\right)^{0.25}}_{K} L^{0.75} = 2 \left(\frac{1}{3}\right)^{0.25} L.$$

Solving for L, we get

$$L = \frac{10}{2} (3)^{0.25} \simeq 6.58.$$

Plugging this back into the tangency condition, we get

$$K = \frac{1}{3} \frac{10}{2} (3)^{0.25} \simeq 2.19.$$

Therefore, if the price of capital increases, Jared hires more labor and less capital.

Exercise #8.11 - Cobb-Douglas Production and Input Demand[B]

8.11 Let's revisit our local coffee roaster Jared, with production function $q = 2K^{0.25}L^{0.75}$. Find Jared's input demand for labor and capital without assuming specific values for the price of labor and capital, w and r, respectively.

- The tangency condition $\frac{MP_L}{MP_K} = \frac{w}{r}$ is

$$\frac{1.5K^{0.25}L^{-0.25}}{0.5K^{-0.75}L^{0.75}} = \frac{w}{r},$$

which simplifies to

$$\frac{3K}{L} = \frac{w}{r}.$$

169

Solving for K, we have
$$K = \frac{w}{3r}L.$$

Plugging this into Jared's output, we get
$$q = 2\underbrace{\left(\frac{w}{3r}L\right)}_{K}^{0.25} L^{0.75} = 2\left(\frac{w}{3r}\right)^{0.25} L.$$

Solving for L gives us Jared's input demand for labor
$$L = \frac{q}{2}\left(\frac{3r}{w}\right)^{0.25}.$$

We can plug this into the equation for K from above to get Jared's input demand for capital:
$$K = \frac{w}{3r}\underbrace{\frac{q}{2}\left(\frac{3r}{w}\right)^{0.25}}_{L} = \frac{q}{2}\frac{3r^{0.25-1}}{w^{0.25-1}} = \frac{q}{2}\left(\frac{w}{3r}\right)^{0.75}.$$

To illustrate the results, let's consider that $q = 10$, $w = \$5$, and $r = \$2$. Under these parameters Jared hires
$$L = \frac{10}{2}\left(\frac{3 \times 2}{5}\right)^{0.25} = 5.23 \text{ workers,}$$

and
$$K = \frac{10}{2}\left(\frac{5}{3 \times 2}\right)^{0.75} = 4.36 \text{ units of capital.}$$

Exercise #8.13 - Short-Run Cobb-Douglas Costs[B]

8.13 Jenny produces first-aid kits using labor and capital with the production function $q = 6L^{0.8}K^{0.2}$, where the wage is $5 and rental rate is $3.

(a) Find her total cost function $TC(q)$ if her capital is fixed at 50 units (this is her short-run cost curve).

- When capital is fixed at $\overline{K} = 50$, output is
$$q = 6L^{0.8}50^{0.2}.$$

Solving for L, we can find the firm's demand for labor:

$$L^{0.8} = \frac{q}{6(50)^{0.2}}$$

$$L = \left(\frac{q}{6(50)^{0.2}}\right)^{1/0.8}$$

$$L = \left(\frac{q}{6(50)^{0.2}}\right)^{1.25}.$$

Plugging this into the firm's costs, we get

$$C(q) = 5\underbrace{\left(\frac{q}{6(50)^{0.2}}\right)^{1.25}}_{L} + 3\underbrace{(50)}_{K} = 5\left(\frac{q}{6(50)^{0.2}}\right)^{1.25} + 150.$$

We can simplify this further to find that

$$C(q) = 0.20q^{1.25} + 150.$$

(b) If her capital is fixed at 50 units, what is the total cost of 10, 25, 50, and 100 first-aid kits? Graph this short-run total cost curve.

- We can find the short-run costs by plugging the values directly into the cost function above, $C(q)$, to find that

$$C(10) = 153.56$$
$$C(25) = 161.19$$
$$C(50) = 176.62$$
$$C(100) = 213.32.$$

Figure 8.2 depicts this cost function.

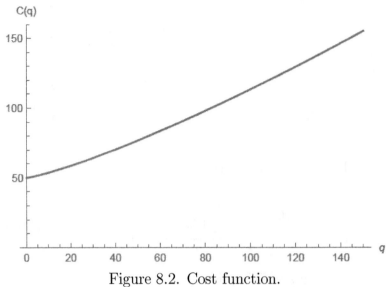

C(q)

Figure 8.2. Cost function.

(c) Graph the short-run average cost and marginal cost curves (at $K = 50$). At what point do these curves cross?

- The average cost is

$$AC = \frac{C(q)}{q} = 0.20q^{0.25} + \frac{150}{q}.$$

The marginal cost is

$$MC = \frac{\partial C(q)}{q} = 0.25q^{0.25}.$$

They cross when $AC = MC$; that is,

$$0.20q^{0.25} + \frac{150}{q} = 0.25q^{0.25}.$$

Simplifying, we have

$$\frac{150}{q} = 0.05q^{0.25}$$
$$q^{1.25} = 3000$$
$$q = 604.92.$$

Figure 8.3 depicts these AC and MC functions, as well as their crossing point at $q = 604.92$ units.

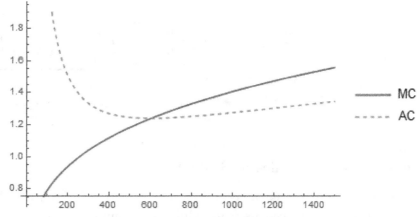

Figure 8.3. Marginal and average cost curves.

Exercise #8.15 - Substitutes in Production[B]

8.15 Hard red winter wheat is planted in the fall in order to be harvested in the spring. Suppose that wheat production uses acres of land A and labor L in its production as follows: $q = \alpha A + L^\beta$, where q is in thousands of bushels. Calculate the total cost function for wheat.

- The tangency condition $\frac{MP_L}{MP_A} = \frac{w}{a}$, where a is the price of land and w is the price of labor, is

$$\frac{\beta L^{\beta-1}}{\alpha} = \frac{w}{a}.$$

Solving for L, we can find the input demand for labor:

$$L^{\beta-1} = \frac{w\alpha}{a\beta}$$

$$L = \left(\frac{w\alpha}{a\beta}\right)^{\frac{1}{1-\beta}}.$$

Plugging this into the output and solving for A, we get our input demand for land:

$$q = \alpha A + \left(\left(\frac{w\alpha}{a\beta}\right)^{\frac{1}{1-\beta}}\right)^\beta$$

$$\alpha A = q - \left(\frac{w\alpha}{a\beta}\right)^{\frac{\beta}{1-\beta}}$$

$$A = \frac{q}{\alpha} - \frac{1}{\alpha}\left(\frac{w\alpha}{a\beta}\right)^{\frac{\beta}{1-\beta}}.$$

173

Plugging these into the firm's costs, we get the firm's cost function for wheat

$$C(q,a,w) = w \underbrace{\left(\frac{w\alpha}{a\beta}\right)^{\frac{1}{1-\beta}}}_{L} + a \underbrace{\left(\frac{q}{\alpha} - \frac{1}{\alpha}\left(\frac{w\alpha}{a\beta}\right)^{\frac{\beta}{1-\beta}}\right)}_{A}$$

$$= w\left(\frac{w\alpha}{a\beta}\right)^{\frac{1}{1-\beta}} + \frac{aq}{\alpha} - \frac{a}{\alpha}\left(\frac{w\alpha}{a\beta}\right)^{\frac{\beta}{1-\beta}}.$$

Exercise #8.17 - Economies of Scale–I[A]

8.17 Suppose that a firm has the cost function $TC(q) = 5q^3 (wr)^{0.5}$. What is the marginal and average cost? Does this firm exhibit economies of scale?

- The marginal and average costs are

$$MC(q) = \frac{\partial TC(q)}{\partial q} = 15q^2 (wr)^{0.5}, \text{ and}$$

$$AC(q) = \frac{TC(q)}{q} = 5q^2 (wr)^{0.5}.$$

To test economies of scale, we take the derivative of the average cost:

$$\frac{\partial AC(q)}{\partial q} = 10q (wr)^{0.5},$$

which is positive for all values of q, w, and r. This means that average cost *increases* in output, so the firm suffers from diseconomies of scale.

Exercise #8.19 - Economies of Scope[A]

8.19 A frozen pizza manufacturer separately produces pepperoni pizzas (p_p) at a total cost of $TC(p_p) = 100 + p_p$, and sausage pizzas (p_s) at a total cost of $TC(p_s) = 100 + 1.5p_s$. Workers have told management there might be some cost savings if the pizzas were produced simultaneously. One worker estimates the total cost of joint production (if the firm produces both types of pizzas in the same plant) as

$$TC(p_p, p_s) = p_p + (1.5 - \alpha)p_s + (100 + \beta).$$

(a) When would the firm prefer to produce both types of pizzas in the same plant?

- The firm should produce the pizzas simultaneously when it benefits from economies of scope; that is,

$$TC(p_p, p_s) < TC(p_p) + TC(p_s)$$
$$p_p + (1.5 - \alpha)p_s + (100 + \beta) < 100 + p_p + 100 + 1.5p_s$$
$$p_p + (1.5 - \alpha)p_s + (100 + \beta) < 200 + p_p + 1.5p_s$$
$$(1.5 - \alpha)p_s + \beta < 100 + 1.5p_s$$
$$1.5p_s - \alpha p_s + \beta < 100 + 1.5p_s$$
$$-\alpha p_s + \beta < 100.$$

When the condition above holds, the firm is better off to simultaneously produce both goods. As α increases, the production of sausage pizzas is relatively cheaper in joint production, and the condition is more likely to be met, while as β increases; that is, the fixed cost of joint production increases, the condition is less likely to be met.

(b) If $\alpha = 0.5$ and the firm wants to produce 150 pepperoni pizzas and 70 sausage pizzas, at what level of β does the manufacturer benefit from economies of scale?

- Plugging $\alpha = 0.5$ into the condition above, we get

$$-\underbrace{0.5}_{\alpha}\underbrace{(70)}_{p_s} + \beta < 100.$$

Simplifying, we find that we need $\beta < 100 + 35 = 135$ to benefit from economies of scope.

Exercise #8.21 - Experience Elasticity–II[A]

8.21 Professor Smith has been teaching for a very long time, and therefore, he has graded many term papers. He has estimated the average time in minutes that he takes to grade a paper is equal to $AT(Y) = 2P \ln Y$, where Y is the number of years he has been teaching and P is how long the paper is in pages. Find Professor Smith's experience elasticity and the slope of his experience curve.

- Professor Smith's experience elasticity is

$$\varepsilon = \frac{\partial AT}{\partial Y}\frac{Y}{AT} = \frac{2P}{Y}\frac{Y}{2P \ln Y}$$
$$= \frac{1}{\ln Y}.$$

The slope of his experience curve is

$$\frac{AT(2Y)}{AT(Y)} = \frac{2P \ln 2Y}{2P \ln Y} = \frac{\ln 2Y}{\ln Y} = \ln 2 + \ln Y - \ln Y = \ln 2 \simeq 0.69.$$

If Professor Smith doubles his experience grading, his average grading time decreases to 69 percent of his original average grading time.

Chapter 9 - Partial and General Equilibrium

9.1 Solutions to Self-Assessment Exercises

Self-assessment exercise #9.1

SA 9.1 Repeat the analysis in example 9.1, but assuming that the firm's total cost function is now $TC(q) = 5 + 40q^2$. Find and depict its supply curve.

- With the new cost function, $TC(q) = 5 + 40q^2$, the firm's marginal cost is

$$MC(q) = \frac{\partial TC(q)}{\partial q} = 80q.$$

  The condition $p = MC(q)$ is $p = 80q$. Solving for q, we find the firm's supply,

$$q = \frac{p}{80}.$$

  This supply curve will have the same shape as figure 9.1b, starting at the origin and with a slope of $\frac{1}{80}$.

Self-assessment exercise #9.2

SA 9.2 Repeat the analysis in example 9.2, but assume that the firm's TC curve is $TC(q) = -5q + 8q^2$. Find $MC(q)$, $AC(q)$, and the firm's supply curve.

- The firm's marginal cost is found by differentiating the new total cost $TC(q) = 4 - 5q + 8q^2$ with respect to q; that is,

$$MC(q) = \frac{\partial TC(q)}{\partial q} = -5 + 16q.$$

  Setting $p = MC(q)$, we obtain $p = -5 + 16q$. Solving for q yields

$$q = \frac{p+5}{16} = \frac{p}{16} + \frac{5}{16}.$$

  To find the firm's supply curve, we also need to find the firm's average cost

$$AC(q) = \frac{TC(q)}{q} = \frac{-5q + 8q^2}{q} = -5 + 8q,$$

  and compare it to the firm's marginal cost to find the firm's shut-down price. The firm's shut-down price is where marginal and average cost curves cross each other, $MC(q) = AC(q)$, or

$$-5 + 16q = -5 + 8q,$$

  which simplifies to $8q = 0$. Solving for output q, we find $q = 0$ units. This is the point where $AC(q)$ and $MC(q)$ cross each other. At this output level, the firm's marginal cost is

$$MC(0) = -5 + (16 \times 0) = -5.$$

Hence, the firm produces positive output levels when facing a positive market price of $p > \$0$, producing $q = \dfrac{p}{16} + \dfrac{5}{16}$; but shuts down, producing zero units when $p = \$0$. Summarizing, the firm's supply function is

$$q(p) = \begin{cases} \dfrac{p}{16} + \dfrac{5}{16} & \text{if } p > \$0 \\ 0 & \text{otherwise.} \end{cases}$$

Self-assessment exercise #9.3

SA 9.3 Consider the supply curve found in self-assessment 9.2. Find the market supply curve, and evaluate it at $N = 100$ firms to obtain the aggregate supply.

- The market supply curve (also known as the aggregate supply curve) is the horizontal summation of all N firms' individual supply curve. From self-assessment 9.2, each firm has the following supply curve

$$q(p) = \begin{cases} \dfrac{p}{16} + \dfrac{5}{16} & \text{if } p > \$0 \\ 0 & \text{otherwise.} \end{cases}$$

The market supply curve is then $Q(p) = N \times q(p)$; that is,

$$Q(p) = \begin{cases} N\left(\dfrac{p}{16} + \dfrac{5}{16}\right) & \text{if } p > \$0 \\ 0 & \text{otherwise.} \end{cases}$$

At $N = 100$ firms, the market supply is

$$Q(p) = \begin{cases} 100\left(\dfrac{p}{16} + \dfrac{5}{16}\right) & \text{if } p > \$0 \\ 0 & \text{otherwise.} \end{cases}$$

Further, at a price of $p = \$10$, the market would supply a total of $100\left(\frac{10}{16} + \frac{5}{16}\right) = 93.75$ units. Note that, at a price of $p = \$0$, no firm supplies any output, $q(0) = 0$, yielding a zero market supply $Q(0) = 0$, regardless of the number of firms in the industry.

Self-assessment exercise #9.4

SA 9.4 Repeat the analysis in example 9.4, but assuming that the firm's fixed costs are distributed differently: only \$2 are sunk while \$8 are non-sunk. Find the firm's short-run supply curve and compare your results against those in example 9.4.

- In this example, the firm's total costs are $TC(q) = 10 - 5q + 2q^2$. The firm's marginal cost remains the same as in example 9.4; that is,

$$MC(q) = \frac{\partial TC(q)}{\partial q} = -5 + 4q.$$

However, the firm's fixed non-sunk costs are now \$8. This means that the firm's non-sunk costs are $NSC = 8 - 5q + 2q^2$, i.e., everything in $TC(q)$ except for \$2 in sunk fixed costs. Therefore, the average non-sunk cost function, $ANSC$, is

$$ANSC = \frac{NSC}{q} = \frac{8 - 5q + 2q^2}{q} = \frac{8}{q} - 5 + 2q.$$

We can now set $MC(q)$ and $ANSC(q)$ equal to each other, to find their crossing point; that is,

$$-5 + 4q = \frac{8}{q} - 5 + 2q,$$

which simplifies to $2q^2 = 8$. Solving for q, we obtain $q = \sqrt{4} = 2$ units. Inserting this output level into the firm's $MC(q)$ curve, we find the shut-down price in the short-run setting, $p = -5 + (4 \times 2) = \$3$. In summary, the firm's short-run supply curve is

$$q(p) = \begin{cases} \frac{p}{4} + \frac{5}{4} & \text{if } p > \$3 \\ 0 & \text{otherwise.} \end{cases}$$

Comparing this to our results in example 9.4, we can see that the firm needs a higher minimal price (\$3 rather than \$1.32) to start producing. This is because the firm faces a larger non-sunk cost, and needs a greater incentive (price) to produce positive units in the short run. Intuitively, the firm has now a larger share of fixed costs that can be avoided (they are non-sunk) than in the setting we analyzed in example 9.4.

Self-assessment exercise #9.5

SA 9.5 Repeat the analysis in example 9.5, but assume that the demand function is now $q^D(p) = 350 - 2p$. How do equilibrium price and quantity change relative to those we found in example 9.5?

- Using the same aggregate supply from example 9.3, $q^S(p) = N\left(\frac{p}{4} + \frac{5}{4}\right)$, aggregate demand and supply cross each other at $q^D(p) = q^S(p)$, or

$$350 - 2p = N\left(\frac{p}{4} + \frac{5}{4}\right),$$

which simplifies to $N(p+5)+8p = 1400$. Solving for price p, we find an equilibrium price of

$$p = \frac{5(280 - N)}{8 + N}.$$

This price crosses the shut-down price of $p = \$1.32$ at $N = 219.85$ firms. Here, aggregate demand is greater than that in example 9.5, as seen by comparing the

178

intercept of the aggregate demand functions since their slopes coincide. Since aggregate supply is the same, the market can support a higher number of firms in the market.

- When $N \leq 219$ firms, equilibrium price is $p = \frac{5(280-N)}{8+N}$, which entails an aggregate output of

$$q = 350 - 2\underbrace{\frac{5(280 - N)}{8 + N}}_{p} = \frac{360N}{8 + N}.$$

This aggregate output is larger than that in example 9.5, for the same number of firms N.

- *Example.* For instance, when $N = 10$ firms enter the industry, the equilibrium price is $p = \frac{5(280-10)}{8+10} = \$75$, and equilibrium quantity is $q = \frac{360N}{8+N} = 200$ units. Relative to example 9.5, the equilibrium price and quantity is greater when there are $N = 10$ firms in the market. The higher equilibrium price and quantity is due to the fact that demand is now stronger than in example 9.5 (graphically, the demand curve in this exercise is shifted upward relative to that in example 9.5).

Self-assessment exercise #9.6

SA 9.6 Repeat the analysis in example 9.6, but assume that the demand function is now $q^D(p) = 350 - 2p$. How do equilibrium price, quantity, and number of firms in the industry, change relative to those we found in example 9.6?

- We have the same total, average, and marginal cost we used in example 9.6, but we face a different market demand curve. Therefore, we have the same long-run equilibrium price $p = \$3.94$ (the shut-down price) and individual firm production of $q = 2.24$ units. This is because the intersection of $MC(q) = AC(q)$ does not depend on market demand.

- We can now move on to finding the second condition (no entry or exit incentive) to obtain the number of firms operating in the industry in equilibrium, N^*. To find N^*, we set aggregate demand equal to aggregate supply, $q^D(p) = q^S(p)$, or

$$350 - 2p = N\left(\frac{p}{4} + \frac{5}{4}\right).$$

Since we have that $p = \$3.94$, we can insert it into the expression above to obtain

$$350 - 2(3.94) = N\left(\frac{3.94}{4} + \frac{5}{4}\right)$$

or, after rearranging,

$$342.12 = 2.235N$$

which, solving for N, yields an equilibrium number of firms of

$$N^* = \frac{342.12}{2.235} = 153.07.$$

Since there cannot be a fractional number of firms in the market, there will be 153 firms active in the industry in the long run. Relative to example 9.6, we can see that the stronger demand firms face in this exercise attracts more firms to the industry than in example 9.6, where only $N = 41$ firms entered the market.

Self-assessment exercise #9.7

SA 9.7 Repeat the analysis in example 9.7, but assume that equilibrium price is $p = \$13$.

- Using the same supply function in example 9.7, $q^S(p) = \frac{p}{4} + \frac{5}{4}$, we can evaluate the producer surplus PS when the market price is $p = \$13$. We can follow the same steps as in example 9.7, by calculating the area of rectangle A plus triangle B in figure 9.7, but at the new price $p = \$13$:

$$
\begin{aligned}
PS &= \text{Area of Rectangle } A + \text{Area of Triangle } B \\
&= \left(p - p^{ShutDown}\right)\left(q^{ShutDown} - 0\right) + \frac{1}{2}\left(p - p^{ShutDown}\right)\left(q^S - q^{ShutDown}\right)
\end{aligned}
$$

where $p = \$13$, $p^{ShutDown} = \$3.94$, and $q^{ShutDown} = 2.24$ units. To find the quantity supplied, q^S, we need to plug our new price $p = \$13$ into our supply function,

$$
q^S(\$13) = \frac{13}{4} + \frac{5}{4} = 4.5 units
$$

which is smaller than the quantity supplied in example 9.7 because the firm is facing a lower price, \$13 rather than \$15.

Using this information, we can calculate the PS:

$$
\begin{aligned}
PS &= \underbrace{(13 - 3.94)(2.24 - 0)}_{\text{Area } A} + \underbrace{\frac{1}{2}(13 - 3.94)(4.5 - 2.24)}_{\text{Area } B} \\
&= 20.29 + 10.24,
\end{aligned}
$$

which yields a producer surplus of $PS = 30.53$.

Self-assessment exercise #9.8

SA 9.8 Repeat the analysis in example 9.8, but assume that the endowment of consumer B changes to $\left(e_1^B, e_2^B\right) = (50, 100)$. How are equilibrium allocations and price affected by this endowment change?

- *Consumer A.* Because consumer A's endowment did not change, we can use her demand for goods 1 and 2 from example 9.8

$$
x_1^A = 50 + 175\frac{p_2}{p_1}, \text{ and}
$$

$$
x_2^A = 175 + 50\frac{p_1}{p_2}.
$$

- *Consumer B.* For consumer B, we can use her tangency condition, $MRS^B_{1,2} = \frac{p_1}{p_2}$, or, after simplifying, $p_1 x^B_1 = p_2 x^B_2$. Inserting this result into consumer B's budget constraint

$$p_1 x^B_1 + p_2 x^B_2 = p_1 50 + p_2 100,$$

  we obtain

$$p_1 x^B_1 + \underbrace{p_1 x^B_1}_{p_2 x^B_2} = p_1 50 + p_2 100,$$

  which, solving for x^B_1, yields into consumer B's demand for good 1

$$x^B_1 = 25 + 50\frac{p_2}{p_1}.$$

  Plugging this back into the tangency condition $p_1 x^B_1 = p_2 x^B_2$, we obtain

$$p_1 \underbrace{\left(25 + 50\frac{p_2}{p_1} \right)}_{x^B_1} = p_2 x^B_2,$$

  and, solving for x^B_2, yields consumer B's demand for good 2,

$$x^B_2 = 50 + 25\frac{p_1}{p_2}.$$

- *Equilibrium prices.* Now, we can find equilibrium prices. Inserting demand for good 1 from consumers A and B into the feasibility condition, $x^A_1 + x^B_1 = 100 + 50$, we obtain

$$\underbrace{\left(50 + 175\frac{p_2}{p_1} \right)}_{x^A_1} + \underbrace{\left(25 + 50\frac{p_2}{p_1} \right)}_{x^B_1} = 150,$$

  which simplifies into $75 + 225\frac{p_2}{p_1} = 150$. Solving for price ratio $\frac{p_2}{p_1}$, we find an equilibrium price ratio of

$$\frac{p_2}{p_1} = \frac{1}{3}.$$

- *Equilibrium quantities.* Finally, we can plug this price ratio into the above demand to find the equilibrium allocation:

  - $x^A_1 = 108.33$ units and $x^A_2 = 325$ units for consumer A, and
  - $x^B_1 = 41.66$ units and $x^B_2 = 125$ units for consumer B.

- Relative to example 9.8, consumer B is endowed with less of good 1 and more of good 2. This changes consumer B's demand for each good and also alters the price ratio. The price ratio changes so that good 1 is more valuable, as it is comparatively more scarce than in example 9.8 (150 units available compared to 200 units in example 9.8). This shift in the price ratio and change in demand lead consumer A to consume more of both goods and consumer B to consume less of good 1 and the same amount of good 2.

SA 9.9 Repeat the analysis in example 9.9, but assume that the endowment of individual B changes to $\left(e_1^A, e_2^B\right) = (50, 100)$. Find the set of efficient allocations. Is it affected by the change in individual B's endowment?

- The tangency condition is the same from example 9.9, $x_2^A x_1^B = x_2^B x_1^A$. The feasibility requirement for good 1 says $x_1^A + x_1^B = 100 + 50$ or, after solving for x_1^B,

$$x_1^B = 150 - x_1^A,$$

while the feasibility requirement for good 2 says $x_2^A + x_2^B = 350 + 100$ or, after solving for x_2^B,

$$x_2^B = 450 - x_2^A.$$

Inserting these equations into the tangency condition, $x_2^A x_1^B = x_2^B x_1^A$, yields

$$x_2^A \underbrace{\left(150 - x_1^A\right)}_{x_1^B} = \underbrace{\left(450 - x_2^A\right)}_{x_2^B} x_1^A,$$

which simplifies to

$$x_2^A = 3x_1^A.$$

- In words, this expression says that, for an allocation to be efficient, consumer A must enjoy three times more units of good 2 than good 1, where $x_1^A = [0, 150]$. Consumer B must then enjoy the remaining $x_1^B = 150 - x_1^A$ units of good 1 and $x_2^B = 450 - x_2^A$ of good 2.

- Comparing this result with that in example 9.9, we can see that the set of efficient allocations is affected by the change in endowments. Specifically, consumer B's endowment in example 9.9 was $(e_1^B, e_2^B) = (100, 50)$. In that context, we found that, for an allocation to be efficient, we need $x_2^A = 2x_1^A$; that is, consumer A must enjoy two times more units of good 2 than good 1. After the endowment change, consumer A needs to enjoy three units of good 2 for every unit of good 1, $x_2^A = 3x_1^A$. Intuitively, while consumer A has the same endowment in both scenarios, good 2 becomes more abundant after B's endowment change, i.e., good 2 increases from $350 + 50 = 400$ units in example 9.9 to $350 + 100 = 450$ units in the current exercise. As a result, consumer A demands more units of good 2 for every unit of good 1 he consumes.

Self-assessment exercise #9.10

SA 9.10 Consider the equilibrium allocation you found in self-assessment 9.8. Is it efficient? *Hint*: It must satisfy the efficiency condition you found in self-assessment 9.9.

- For the allocation to be efficient, condition $x_2^A = 3x_1^A$ must hold. In self-assessment 9.8, we found that the equilibrium allocation satisfied $x_1^A = 108.33$ and $x_2^A = 325$ for consumer A. The equilibrium allocation is then efficient since it satisfies $325 = 3 \times 108.33$. Intuitively, consumer A enjoys three times more units of good 2 than good 1.

9.2 Solutions to End-of-Chapter Exercises

Exercise #9.1 - Identifying Perfectly Competitive Markets[A]

9.1 Are the following markets an example of perfect competition? If not, explain.

(a) The soybean market

- Most agriculture markets are perfectly competitive. They have many producers, all producing soybeans, each having a very small amount of market power (if any), consumers all have pricing information, and each producer has access to the same technology.

(b) The market for cable television provider

- Most local markets for cable television have very few providers. Except in very large cities, many areas may only have one provider, which means this market is not perfectly competitive.

(c) The market for a popular item on the internet

- This market is perfectly competitive (or close to it). Popular items generally have many sellers, all with their pricing information readily available (search engines make this information easy to find).

(d) The market for professional basketball players

- This market is not perfectly competitive. Although there are many professional basketball players, they are not homogeneous and there is not perfect pricing information.

(e) The new car market

- This market is also not perfectly competitive. New cars are not a homogeneous good.

Exercise #9.3 - Long-Run Equilibrium and Subsidies[B]

9.3 Consider a perfectly competitive market with aggregate demand given by $Q(p) = 330 - p$. All firms face the same cost function $C(q_i) = 2q_i^2 - 4q_i + 20$, where q_i denotes the output of firm i.

(a) Assuming that there is free entry and exit in the industry, find the long-run equilibrium: number of firms operating, equilibrium price, and output.

- To find firm i's supply curve, we set marginal and average cost equal to each other, $MC(q_i) = AC(q_i)$; that is,

$$4q_i - 4 = 2q_i - 4 + \frac{20}{q_i}.$$

Recall that in the long run, firms can alter all their inputs, and the shut-down price is found by setting $MC(q_i)$ and $AC(q_i)$ equal to each other. Rearranging, we obtain $2q_i = \frac{20}{q_i}$, or $q_i^2 = 10$. Therefore, long-run equilibrium output is

$$q_i = \sqrt{10} \simeq 3.16 \text{ units.}$$

Figure 9.1 depicts the MC and AC curves, as well as their crossing point at $q_i = 3.16$ units.

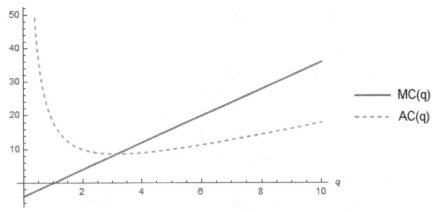

Figure 9.1. Marginal and average cost curves.

Plugging this into the marginal cost, we find the shut-down and long-run equilibrium price is

$$p = 4(\sqrt{10}) - 4 = \$8.65,$$

where each firm will produce 3.16 units. The firm's supply function is found by setting $MC(q_i) = p$ and solving for q:

$$4q_i - 4 = p$$
$$4q_i = p + 4$$
$$q_i(p) = \frac{p}{4} + 1.$$

Figure 9.2 depicts firm i's supply curve, which originates at $q_i = 1$ in the vertical axis, and grows in p at a rate of $\frac{1}{4}$.

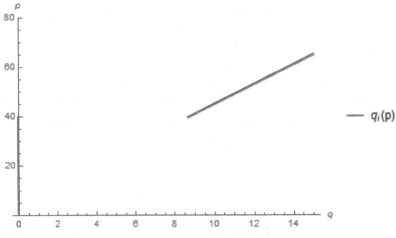

Figure 9.2. Firm i's supply curve.

Recall that firm i's supply is positive for all prices above the shut-down price $p \geq \$8.65$. Next, we can find the number of firms that will operate by setting

184

aggregate demand equal to aggregate supply at the equilibrium price:

$$330 - 8.65 = N\left(\frac{8.65}{4} + 1\right)$$
$$321.35 = N(3.16)$$
$$N^* = 101.69.$$

Therefore, in equilibrium, 101 firms will operate.

(b) The government considers two policies to induce the entry of more firms: (1) a subsidy of $s > 0$ per unit of output sold; or (2) a subsidy of $c > 0$ per unit of output consumed. Compare both policy tools. Which one is more effective at increasing the number of firms in the market (assume $s = c$)?

- *Subsidy to sellers.* First, let us consider the subsidy on output sold. This subsidy would change the firm's marginal cost function to

$$MC(q_i) = 4q_i - 4 - s,$$

and the average cost function to

$$AC(q_i) = 2q_i - 4 - s + \frac{20}{q_i}.$$

Setting these equal to each other, $MC(q_i) = AC(q_i)$, is the first step to finding the shut-down price:[1]

$$4q_i - 4 - s = 2q_i - 4 - s + \frac{20}{q_i},$$

which yields the same quantity as in part (a), $q_i = 3.16$ units. The subsidy has the effect of decreasing both the marginal and average cost curves by the same amount, leaving the value of q_i unaffected. What does change is the shut-down and long-run equilibrium price, as the crossing point of average and marginal cost is lower (by the amount of the subsidy). Plugging $q_i = 3.16$ units into marginal cost gives us the shut-down price (and equilibrium price) of

$$MC(3.16) = 4(3.16) - 4 - s = \$8.65 - s.$$

Next, we can find the number of firms that will operate by setting aggregate

---

[1] Recall that the exercise considers a long-run approach, which implies that $MC(q_i) = AC(q_i)$ provides us with the shut-down price.

demand equal to aggregate supply at the equilibrium price:

$$330 - \underbrace{(8.65 - s)}_{p} = N\left(\frac{\overbrace{8.65 - s}^{p}}{4} + 1\right)$$

$$321.35 + s = N(3.16 - \frac{s}{4})$$

$$N^s = \frac{321.35 + s}{3.16 - \frac{s}{4}}.$$

For example, if $s = 5$, the equilibrium number of firms is

$$N^* = \frac{321.35 + 5}{3.16 - \frac{5}{4}} \simeq 170.86 \text{ firms,}$$

thus increasing the number of firms. If we take a derivative with respect to s, we find that

$$\frac{\partial N^s}{\partial s} = \frac{1335.96}{(s - 12.64)^2} > 0,$$

which means that a larger subsidy increases the number of firms in the market.

- *Subsidy to buyers.* If the subsidy is given to buyers, it impacts the demand curve by decreasing the price each consumer pays, changing it to

$$Q(p) = 330 - (p - c) = 330 - p + c,$$

so firms get the price p for the good while consumers pay $p - c$ for the good. The aggregate supply function is unchanged (from before the subsidy), so we find the equilibrium number firms by solving

$$330 - (8.65 - c) = N\left(\frac{8.65}{4} + 1\right)$$

$$321.35 + c = 3.16N$$

$$N^c = \frac{321.35 + c}{3.16}.$$

If $c = 5$, the equilibrium number of firms is $N^c = \frac{321.35 + 5}{3.16} \simeq 103.26$ firms. We can easily see that the number of firms is increasing in the subsidy by taking a derivative with respect to c:

$$\frac{\partial N^c}{\partial s} = \frac{1}{3.16} > 0,$$

which is always positive. Intuitively, the market becomes more attractive for firms as buyers are more generously subsidized.

- *Comparing policies.* To see which policy increases the number of firms the most, we can compare $N^s > N^c$ when $s = c$:

$$\frac{321.35 + s}{3.16 - \frac{s}{4}} > \frac{321.35 + s}{3.16},$$

which we can rearrange as

$$(321.35 + s)(3.16) > (321.35 + s)(3.16 - \frac{s}{4})$$

$$1015.47 + 3.16s > 1015.47 + 3.16s - \frac{321.35}{4}s - \frac{1}{4}s^2$$

$$80.34s + 0.25s^2 > 0,$$

which holds for all values of $s > 0$. Therefore, if the subsidies per unit coincide, $s = c$, a subsidy given directly to producers increases the number of firms in the market more significantly than a subsidy given to consumers.

Exercise #9.5 - Perfectly Competitive Equilibrium–II[A]

9.5 Consider the perfectly competitive wheat market with aggregate demand given by $Q(p) = 25 - 2p$, where Q is in thousands of pounds of wheat and p is in thousands of dollars. Consider the perfectly competitive wheat market with aggregate demand given by $Q(p) = 25 - 2p$, where Q is in thousands of pounds of wheat and p is in thousands of dollars.

(a) If the marginal cost of wheat is \$2,000, what is the market equilibrium price and quantity sold?

- The market equilibrium will be equal to marginal cost at $p = \$2,000$. Plugging this into the demand for wheat, we get the equilibrium amount of wheat in the market:

$$Q = 25 - 2(2) = 21 \text{ thousand pounds.}$$

(b) One of the more certain things in policy is the so-called farm bill, which subsidizes many agricultural goods. How would a subsidy of \$1 per pound of wheat affect the market equilibrium?

- A subsidy of \$1 per pound will decrease the marginal cost of wheat to \$1,000, which will also be the market equilibrium price. Plugging this into the demand for wheat, we get the equilibrium quantity

$$Q = 25 - 2 = 23 \text{ thousand pounds}$$

which implies an increase from the setting without subsidies.

Exercise #9.7 - Shutdown Price and Short-Run Supply[A]

9.7 Ben is the owner of an on-demand, premade food service. His total cost function is $TC(q) = 50 - 6q + 2q^2$, where his entire fixed cost is sunk (his fixed costs are the kitchen space he leases yearly). Find Ben's shutdown price and short-run supply curve.

- To find Ben's shut-down price, we first need to identify his marginal and average variable costs. Recall that in the short run, firms cannot alter all their inputs, implying that the shut-down price occurs at the point where the marginal cost curve crosses the average variable cost. We first find the equation of each curve:

$$MC(q) = -6 + 4q, \quad \text{and}$$
$$AVC(q) = -6 + 2q.$$

Figure 9.3 depicts the MC and AVC curves.

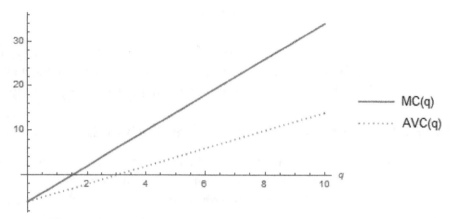

Figure 9.3. Marginal and average variable cost curves.

Setting the marginal cost equal to the average variable costs helps us identify the quantity at the shut-down price:

$$-6 + 4q = -6 + 2q,$$

which simplifies to $q = 0$ units. Plugging this quantity into his marginal cost will give us the shut-down price of $-6 + 4(0) = -\$6$. Therefore, for any price p satisfying $p \geq \$0$, the firm produces positive units. Since price p is zero or negative by assumption, $p \geq \$0$, we can write Ben's short-run supply curve as follows:

$$q(p) = \frac{p}{4} + \frac{3}{2}.$$

Figure 9.4 depicts this supply curve, indicating that Ben offers positive units for all prices $p \geq \$0$.

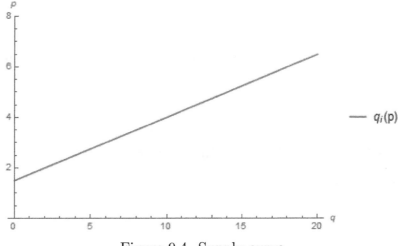

Figure 9.4. Supply curve.

Exercise #9.9 - Finding Aggregate Supply and Equilibrium[A]

9.9 The market for gasoline currently has N firms, each of which faces the cost function $C(q) = 5 + 0.75q^2$, and current market demand is $Q(p) = 500 - 0.1p$.

(a) Find the aggregate supply curve.

- First, we need to find the shut-down price by setting marginal cost $MC(q) = 1.5q$ equal to average cost $AC(q) = \frac{5}{q} + 0.75q$:

$$1.5q = \frac{5}{q} + 0.75q.$$

This results in a shut-down quantity of $0.75q^2 = 5$, or $q = 2.58$ units. Plugging this into the marginal cost gives us the shut-down price

$$p = 5 + 0.75(2.58) = \$6.94.$$

Setting marginal cost equal to price and solving for q will give us the remaining part of the supply curve:
$$p = 1.5q,$$

or $q = \frac{p}{1.5}$. The aggregate supply curve is then

$$Q(p) = \begin{cases} N\frac{p}{1.5} & \text{if } p > \$6.94 \\ 0 & \text{otherwise.} \end{cases}$$

(b) What is the equilibrium price, quantity, and number of firms that will operate in the gasoline market in the long run?

- In the long run, the price will be equal to the shut-down price $p = \$6.94$. To find the number of firms operating, we set demand equal to aggregate supply

189

at the long-run price:

$$500 - 0.1(6.94) = N\frac{6.94}{1.5},$$

which simplifies to $499.31 = 4.63N$, or $N^* = 107.8$ firms. Plugging the price into demand gives us aggregate quantity of

$$Q = 500 - 0.1(6.94) = 499.31 \text{ units.}$$

Exercise #9.11 - Calculating Producer Surplus[A]

9.11 Consider the market for dog treats, which has the aggregate supply of

$$q^S(p) = \begin{cases} \frac{1}{2}p + 5 & \text{if } p > \$5.50 \\ 0 & \text{otherwise.} \end{cases}$$

Aggregate demand in this market is $q^D(p) = 120 - 6p$.

(a) Find the market equilibrium price and quantity.

- Setting supply equal to demand, we find

$$\frac{1}{2}p + 5 = 120 - 6p.$$

Simplifying, we get that $6.5p = 115$, or $p = \$17.69$. Plugging this value back into the demand curve, we find the equilibrium quantity of $120 - 6(17.69) = 13.86$ dog treats.

(b) Identify the producer surplus, PS.

- Before we calculate PS, we need to find the shut-down quantity by plugging the shut-down price into the supply curve:

$$\frac{1}{2}(5.5) + 5 = 7.75.$$

Using the formula for producer surplus,

$$PS = (p - p^{ShutDown})q^{ShutDown} + \frac{1}{2}(p - p^{ShutDown})(q - q^{ShutDown}),$$

we find

$$\begin{aligned} PS &= (17.69 - 5.5)7.75 + \frac{1}{2}(17.69 - 5.5)(13.86 - 7.75) \\ &= 131.71. \end{aligned}$$

(c) A recent report found that dog treats were making dogs overweight, and regulators propose a tax of $2 per unit to decrease the purchase of dog treats. Will the tax have the intended consequences? Find the new producer surplus, PS'.

- The new demand curve is

$$q^D(p+2) = 120 - 6(p+2)$$
$$= 120 - 12 - 6p$$
$$= 108 - 6p.$$

Setting this equal to aggregate supply, we get

$$108 - 6p = \frac{1}{2}p + 5.$$

Simplifying, we get that $6.5p = 103$, and that $p = \$15.85$. Plugging into the demand curve, we find that the equilibrium quantity is $q = 108 - 6(15.85) = 12.9$ treats. The tax did decrease the quantity of treats sold. The new producer surplus, PS', is

$$PS' = (15.85 - 5.5)7.75 + \frac{1}{2}(15.85 - 5.5)(12.9 - 7.75) = 106.86.$$

Exercise #9.13 - Profit versus Producer Surplus[B]

9.13 Is the following statement true or false? Profit is the same as producer surplus. Explain your answer.

- This statement is usually false. Profit is total revenue minus total cost; however, producer surplus is total revenue minus variable cost. The difference between the two is that profit accounts for fixed costs. If the firm has no fixed costs, then they are the same.

Exercise #9.15 - General Equilibrium–I[B]

9.15 Consider two consumers with utility functions $u^i(x_1^i, x_2^i) = \ln x_1^i + x_2^i$, and endowments $(e_1^A, e_2^A) = (50, 100)$ for consumer A and $(e_1^B, e_2^B) = (25, 125)$ for consumer B. What is the equilibrium allocation and price?

- *Consumer A.* We first need the tangency condition for consumer A, $MRS_{1,2}^A = \frac{p_1}{p_2}$, or

$$\frac{1}{x_1^A} = \frac{p_1}{p_2},$$

which simplifies to $x_1^A = \frac{p_2}{p_1}$. This is consumer A's demand for good 1. We can insert this into consumer A's budget constraint $p_1 x_1^A + p_2 x_2^A = p_1 50 + p_2 100$, and we obtain

$$p_1 \frac{p_2}{p_1} + p_2 x_2^A = p_1 50 + p_2 100$$

which simplifies to $p_2 + p_2 x_2^A = p_1 50 + p_2 100$ or $p_2 x_2^A = p_1 50 + p_2 99$, and dividing by p_2 we can get consumer A's demand for good 2

$$x_2^A = 99 + 50 \frac{p_1}{p_2}.$$

- *Consumer B.* Consumer B will have the same tangency condition since she has the same utility function

$$\frac{1}{x_1^B} = \frac{p_1}{p_2},$$

and demand for good 1 of $x_1^B = \frac{p_2}{p_1}$. Plugging this into her budget constraint, $p_1 x_1^B + p_2 x_2^B = p_1 25 + p_2 125$, we get that

$$p_1 \frac{p_2}{p_1} + p_2 x_2^A = p_1 25 + p_2 125,$$

which simplifies to $p_2 x_2^B = 25 p_1 + 124 p_2$, and finally,

$$x_2^B = 124 + 25 \frac{p_1}{p_2},$$

which is consumer B's demand for good 2.

- *Finding equilibrium prices.* To find equilibrium prices, we can insert the demands for good 1 into the feasibility condition $x_1^A + x_1^B = 50 + 25$:

$$\underbrace{\frac{p_2}{p_1}}_{x_1^A} + \underbrace{\frac{p_2}{p_1}}_{x_1^B} = 50 + 25,$$

or, $2\frac{p_2}{p_1} = 75$, and the price ratio is

$$\frac{p_2}{p_1} = \frac{75}{2}.$$

- *Equilibrium quantities.* Plugging this into the demand for good 1 for each consumer, we obtain

$$x_1^A = x_1^B = \frac{75}{2} \text{ units}$$

for each consumer. And for good 2,

$$x_2^A = 99 + 50 \frac{p_1}{p_2} = 99 + 50 \frac{2}{75} = 100.33 \text{ units}$$

for consumer A, and

$$x_2^B = 124 + 25 \frac{p_1}{p_2} = 124 + 25 \frac{2}{75} = 124.67 \text{ units}$$

for consumer B.

Exercise #9.17 - Efficiency in General Equilibrium^B

9.17 Consider two neighbors who trade food from their gardens (f) and groceries (g). Neighbor A has utility $u^A(f^A, g^A) = \ln f^A + 2 \ln g^A$ and neighbor B has utility $u^B(f^B, g^B) = 2 \ln f^B + \ln g^B$. What is the equilibrium allocation and price if each neighbor has 40 units of food and 25 units of groceries? Is this equilibrium efficient?

- *Consumer A.* We first need the tangency condition for neighbor A, $MRS_{f,g}^A = \frac{p_f}{p_g}$, or

$$\frac{g^A}{2f^A} = \frac{p_f}{p_g},$$

which simplifies to $2f^A p_f = g^A p_g$. We can insert this into A's budget constraint

$$p_f f^A + p_g g^A = p_f 40 + p_g 25,$$

to obtain

$$f^A p_f + 2f^A p_f = p_f 40 + p_g 25,$$

which simplifies to $3f^A p_f = p_f 40 + p_g 25$ or

$$f^A = \frac{40}{3} + \frac{25}{3}\frac{p_g}{p_f},$$

which is neighbor A's demand for food from their garden. To find her demand for groceries, we can plug this into the tangency condition $2f^A p_f = g^A p_g$ to find that

$$2\underbrace{\left(\frac{40}{3} + \frac{25}{3}\frac{p_g}{p_f}\right)}_{f^A}p_f = g^A p_g,$$

or, $\frac{80}{3}p_f + \frac{50}{3}p_g = p_g g^A$, and finally we get neighbor A's demand for groceries:

$$g^A = \frac{50}{3} + \frac{80}{3}\frac{p_f}{p_g}.$$

- *Consumer B.* Consumer B has the tangency condition:

$$\frac{2g^B}{f^B} = \frac{p_f}{p_g},$$

which simplifies to $f^B p_f = 2g^B p_g$. We can insert this into B's budget constraint

$$p_f f^B + p_g g^B = p_f 40 + p_g 25,$$

to obtain

$$g^B p_g + 2g^B p_g = p_f 40 + p_g 25,$$

which simplifies to $3g^B p_g = p_f 40 + p_g 25$ or

$$g^B = \frac{25}{3} + \frac{40}{3}\frac{p_f}{p_g},$$

which is neighbor B's demand for groceries. To find her demand for food from their garden, we can plug the result of g^B into the tangency condition $f^B p_f =$

$2g^B p_g$ to find that

$$f^B p_f = 2\underbrace{\left(\frac{25}{3} + \frac{40}{3}\frac{p_f}{p_g}\right)}_{g^B}p_g,$$

or, $f^B p_f = \frac{50}{3}p_g + \frac{80}{3}p_f$, and finally we get neighbor B's demand for food from her garden:

$$f^B = \frac{50}{3}\frac{p_g}{p_f} + \frac{80}{3}.$$

- *Equilibrium prices.* To find equilibrium prices, we can insert the demands for groceries into the feasibility condition $g^A + g^B = 25 + 25$:

$$\underbrace{\left(\frac{50}{3} + \frac{80}{3}\frac{p_f}{p_g}\right)}_{g^A} + \underbrace{\left(\frac{25}{3} + \frac{40}{3}\frac{p_f}{p_g}\right)}_{g^B} = 50,$$

or,

$$\frac{75}{3} + \frac{120}{3}\frac{p_f}{p_g} = 50,$$

or, $25 + 40\frac{p_f}{p_g} = 50$ and the price ratio is

$$\frac{p_f}{p_g} = \frac{25}{40}.$$

- *Equilibrium quantities.* Plugging this equilibrium price into the demand for groceries for each neighbor, obtaining that:
  - Neighbor A consumes $g^A = \frac{50}{3} + \frac{80}{3}\frac{25}{40} = 33.33$ groceries and neighbor B consumes $g^B = \frac{25}{3} + \frac{40}{3}\frac{25}{40} = 16.67$ groceries.
  - Neighbor A will consume $f^A = \frac{40}{3} + \frac{25}{3}\frac{40}{25} = 26.67$ units of food from her garden, and neighbor B will consume $f^B = \frac{50}{3}\frac{40}{25} + \frac{80}{3} = 53.33$ units of food from her garden.

- This is an efficient allocation since we used

$$MRS_{f,g}^A = MRS_{f,g}^B = \frac{p_f}{p_g},$$

to find the equilibrium allocation (by the first welfare theorem).

Exercise #9.19 - Second Welfare Theorem[C]

9.19 Consider the two consumers in exercise 9.18. Propose a second allocation (i.e., not the equilibrium that you found), that satisfies the Second Welfare Theorem. How could this allocation be implemented by a social planner?

- Setting the tangency condition $MRS_{1,2}^A = MRS_{1,2}^B$ yields $\frac{x_2^A}{x_1^A} = \frac{x_2^B}{x_1^B}$, or after cross-multiplying, $x_2^A x_1^B = x_2^B x_1^A$. The feasibility requirement for good 1 says $x_1^A + x_1^B =$

600, or $x_1^B = 600 - x_1^A$, and similarly the feasibility requirement for good 2 says $x_2^A + x_2^B = 450$, or $x_2^B = 450 - x_2^A$. Inserting these feasibility equations into the tangency condition $x_2^A x_1^B = x_2^B x_1^A$, yields

$$x_2^A \underbrace{(600 - x_1^A)}_{x_1^B} = \underbrace{(450 - x_2^A)}_{x_2^B} x_1^A,$$

which simplifies to $600x_2^A - x_1^A x_2^A = 450x_1^A - x_2^A x_1^A$, and finally to $600x_2^A = 450x_1^A$, or

$$x_2^A = \frac{450}{600} x_2^A = \frac{3}{4} x_1^A.$$

Therefore, efficient allocations satisfy

$$x_2^A = \frac{3}{4} x_1^A \quad \text{where } x_1^A \in [0, 600].$$

Here, we can pick any allocation that satisfies these conditions. For example, we could pick $x_1^A = 200$ and $x_2^A = 150$. This leaves consumer B with $x_1^B = 600 - 200 = 400$ units of good 1, and $x_2^B = 450 - 150 = 300$ units of good 2.

- *Consumer A.* Now we need to find the redistribution of initial endowment that can lead to such an allocation emerging in equilibrium. We know that for consumer A that $p_1 x_1^A = p_2 x_2^A$ and for consumer B that $p_1 x_1^B = p_2 x_2^B$. We want to now tax consumer B, $t_B < 0$, with the amount being transferred to consumer A, $t_A > 0$ so that $t_A = -t_B$. Therefore, consumer A's budget constraint after including t_A is

$$p_1 x_1^A + p_2 x_2^A = p_1 e_1^A + p_2 e_2^A + t_A,$$

which, after substituting her original endowment $(e_1^A, e_2^A) = (500, 100)$ and that $p_1 x_1^A = p_2 x_2^A$, becomes

$$2 p_1 x_1^A = 500 p_1 + 100 p_2 + t_A$$

Solving for x_1^A, we obtain

$$x_1^A = 250 + 50 \frac{p_2}{p_1} + \frac{t_A}{2 p_1}.$$

We take this expression for consumer A and insert the specific efficient allocation that we seek to implement; that is, $(x_1^A, x_2^A, x_1^B, x_2^B) = (200, 150, 400, 300)$, insert the price ratio we found in the previous problem; that is, $\frac{p_2}{p_1} = \frac{4}{3}$, and normalize the price of good 2, so that $p_2 = 1$ and $p_1 = \frac{3}{4}$ in equilibrium. Doing this, we obtain:

$$200 = 250 + 50 \frac{4}{3} + \frac{t_A}{2\frac{3}{4}},$$

and now we want to solve for t_A:

$$200 = 250 + 50\frac{4}{3} + \frac{t_A}{2\frac{3}{4}}$$

$$-50 = 66.67 + \frac{t_A}{\frac{3}{2}}$$

$$-116.67 = \frac{2}{3}t_A$$

$$-175 = t_A,$$

which means we tax consumer A, since $t_A < 0$.

- *Consumer B.* We apply a similar argument to consumer B, so her budget constraint as a function of the tax t_B she faces is

$$p_1 x_1^B + p_2 x_2^B = p_1 e_1^B + p_2 e_2^B + t_B,$$

which, after substituting her endowment, and $p_1 x_1^B = p_2 x_2^B$, we get that

$$2p_1 x_1^B = p_1 100 + p_2 350 + t_B.$$

Solving for x_1^B, we get that

$$x_1^B = 50 + 175\frac{p_2}{p_1} + \frac{t_B}{2p_1},$$

and then inserting the specific efficient allocation that we seek to implement; that is, $(x_1^A, x_2^A, x_1^B, x_2^B) = (200, 150, 400, 300)$, insert the price ratio we found in the previous problem; that is, $\frac{p_2}{p_1} = \frac{4}{3}$, and normalize the price of good 2, so that $p_2 = 1$ and $p_1 = \frac{3}{4}$ in equilibrium. Doing this, we obtain:

$$400 = 50 + 175\frac{4}{3} + \frac{t_B}{2\frac{3}{4}},$$

and solving for t_B, we get that

$$350 = 233.33 + \frac{t_B}{\frac{3}{2}}$$

$$116.76 = \frac{2}{3}t_B$$

$$175 = t_B.$$

which is subsidy to consumer B. This coincides with the tax imposed on consumer A.

Exercise #9.21 - First Welfare Theorem with External Effects[C]

9.21 Consider two individuals with utility functions $u^A = x^A y^A$ and $u^B = x^B y^B - 0.5x^A$, and endowments $e^A(e_x^A, e_y^A) = (15, 5)$ and $e^B(e_x^B, e_y^B) = (10, 15)$.

(a) Is individual A's utility affected by individual B's consumption? Is individual B's utility affected by A's consumption? Interpret.

- We can see that individual A is unaffected by individual B's consumption of either good. However, individual B is negatively impacted by individual A's consumption of good x. We can interpret this as individual A's consumption of good x creates a negative externality imposed on individual B.

(b) Find the equilibrium allocation.

- *Consumer A.* The tangency condition for consumer A, $MRS_{x,y}^A = \frac{p_x}{p_y}$, is

$$\frac{y^A}{x^A} = \frac{p_x}{p_y}.$$

Rearranging, we find $p_y y^A = p_x x^A$, which we can insert into consumer A's budget constraint $p_x x^A + p_y y^A = p_x 15 + p_y 5$ to find that

$$p_y y^A + p_y y^A = p_x 15 + p_y 5.$$

Simplifying, we first obtain $2 p_y y^A = p_x 15 + p_y 5$, and solving for y^A, we have consumer A's demand for good y:

$$y^A = \frac{5}{2} + \frac{15}{2} \frac{p_x}{p_y}.$$

Plugging this expression back into the tangency condition $p_y y^A = p_x x^A$, we obtain

$$p_y \underbrace{\left(\frac{5}{2} + \frac{15}{2} \frac{p_x}{p_y} \right)}_{y^A} = p_x x^A.$$

Solving for x^A, we first have

$$x^A = \frac{p_y}{p_x} \left(\frac{5}{2} + \frac{15}{2} \frac{p_x}{p_y} \right),$$

which simplifies to consumer A's demand for good x

$$x^A = \frac{15}{2} + \frac{5}{2} \frac{p_y}{p_x}.$$

- *Consumer B.* The tangency condition for consumer B, $MRS_{x,y}^B = \frac{p_x}{p_y}$ is

$$\frac{y^B}{x^B} = \frac{p_x}{p_y}.$$

Rearranging, we find $p_y y^B = p_x x^B$, which we can insert into consumer B's budget constraint $p_x x^B + p_y y^B = p_x 10 + p_y 15$ to find that

$$p_y y^B + p_y y^B = p_x 10 + p_y 15.$$

Simplifying, we first obtain $2p_y y^B = p_x 10 + p_y 15$, and solving for y^B, we have consumer B's demand for good y:

$$y^B = \frac{15}{2} + 5\frac{p_x}{p_y}.$$

Plugging this expression back into the tangency condition $p_y y^B = p_x x^B$, we obtain

$$p_y \underbrace{\left(\frac{15}{2} + 5\frac{p_x}{p_y}\right)}_{y^B} = p_x x^B.$$

Solving for x^B, we first have

$$x^B = \frac{p_y}{p_x}\left(\frac{15}{2} + 5\frac{p_x}{p_y}\right),$$

which simplifies to consumer B's demand for good x

$$x^B = 5 + \frac{15}{2}\frac{p_y}{p_x}.$$

- *Equilibrium prices.* Inserting the demands for good x from consumers A and B into the feasibility condition $x^A + x^B = 15 + 10$, we obtain

$$\underbrace{\frac{15}{2} + \frac{5}{2}\frac{p_y}{p_x}}_{x^A} + \underbrace{5 + \frac{15}{2}\frac{p_y}{p_x}}_{x^B} = 25,$$

which simplifies to $\frac{25}{2} + \frac{20}{2}\frac{p_y}{p_x} = 25$, and again to $\frac{20}{2}\frac{p_y}{p_x} = \frac{25}{2}$. Solving for $\frac{p_y}{p_x}$, we find an equilibrium price ratio of

$$\frac{p_y}{p_x} = \frac{25}{20} = \frac{5}{4}.$$

- *Equilibrium allocations.* We can plug the price ratio into each consumer's demands for each good to find that consumer A's allocation is

$$x^A = \frac{15}{2} + \frac{5}{2}\frac{p_y}{p_x} = \frac{15}{2} + \frac{5}{2}\frac{5}{4} = \frac{85}{8} = 10.625 \text{ units, and}$$

$$y^A = \frac{5}{2} + \frac{15}{2}\frac{p_x}{p_y} = \frac{5}{2} + \frac{15}{2}\frac{4}{5} = \frac{17}{2} = 8.5 \text{ units.}$$

Consumer B's allocation is

$$x^B = 5 + \frac{15}{2}\frac{p_y}{p_x} = 5 + \frac{15}{2}\frac{5}{4} = \frac{115}{8} = 14.375 \text{ units, and}$$

$$y^B = \frac{15}{2} + 5\frac{p_x}{p_y} = \frac{15}{2} + 5\frac{4}{5} = \frac{23}{2} = 11.5 \text{ units.}$$

(c) Show that the equilibrium allocation is not socially efficient. (*Hint:* Refer to the appendix in this chapter.)

- For an allocation to be efficient, it must solve

$$\max_{x^A, y^A, x^B, y^B \geq 0} x^A y^A$$

subject to

$$x^B y^B - 0.5 x^A \geq \bar{u}^B$$
$$x^A + x^B \leq 25$$
$$y^A + y^B \leq 20.$$

The Lagrangian associated with this maximization problem is

$$\mathcal{L} = x^A y^A + \lambda \left[x^B y^B - 0.5 x^A - \bar{u}^B \right] + \mu_1 [25 - x^A - x^B] + \mu_2 [20 - y^A - y^B].$$

Differentiating with respect to x^A and x^B, we obtain

$$\frac{\partial \mathcal{L}}{\partial x^A} = y^A - 0.5\lambda - \mu_1 = 0$$
$$\frac{\partial \mathcal{L}}{\partial x^B} = \lambda y^B - \mu_1 = 0.$$

Differentiating with respect to y^A and y^B, we obtain

$$\frac{\partial \mathcal{L}}{\partial y^A} = x^A - \mu_2 = 0$$
$$\frac{\partial \mathcal{L}}{\partial y^B} = \lambda x^B - \mu_2 = 0.$$

Combining $\frac{\partial \mathcal{L}}{\partial x^A}$ and $\frac{\partial \mathcal{L}}{\partial y^A}$, we obtain

$$\frac{y^A - 0.5\lambda}{x^A} = \frac{\mu_1}{\mu_2},$$

and combining $\frac{\partial \mathcal{L}}{\partial x^B}$ and $\frac{\partial \mathcal{L}}{\partial y^B}$, we obtain

$$\frac{\lambda y^B}{\lambda x^B} = \frac{y^B}{x^B} = \frac{\mu_1}{\mu_2}.$$

These two equations tell us that optimality requires that

$$\frac{y^A - 0.5\lambda}{x^A} = \frac{y^B}{x^B}.$$

Rearranging, we find that the socially efficient allocation must satisfy $x^B(y^A - 0.5\lambda) = x^A y^B$. This does not coincide with the equilibrium allocation, which requires that $x^B y^A = x^A y^B$. The difference being that, when finding the socially optimal allocation, we consider the negative externality experienced by consumer B.

(d) Does the First Welfare Theorem hold? Interpret your results.

- As we can see in part (b), the First Welfare Theorem does not hold, as the equilibrium allocation and the efficient allocation do not coincide. In the equilibrium allocation, the consumers, who each choose their optimal allocation by setting their marginal rate of substitution equal to the price ratio, do not account for the negative externality. This negative externality is taken into consideration when maximizing joint utility in the efficient allocation, thus leading to a different allocation of the two goods.

Chapter 10 - Monopoly

10.1 Solutions to Self-Assessment Exercises

Self-assessment exercise #10.1

SA 10.1 Consider a monopolist facing an inverse demand $p(q) = 10 - 4q$. Find the marginal revenue curve, its vertical intercept, horizontal intercept, and slope.

- Here, marginal revenue is

$$
\begin{aligned}
MR(q) &= p(q) + \frac{\partial p(q)}{\partial q} q \\
&= \underbrace{10 - 4q}_{p(q)} + \underbrace{(-4)}_{\frac{\partial p(q)}{\partial q}} q \\
&= 10 - 8q.
\end{aligned}
$$

As depicted in figure 10.1, the vertical intercept occurs when $q = 0$ (it is the same as the demand curve) and is at \$10. The horizontal intercept occurs when $p = 0$, or $0 = 10 - 8q$. Simplifying, this becomes $q = \frac{10}{8} = 1.25$ units. The slope of the marginal revenue curve is -8.

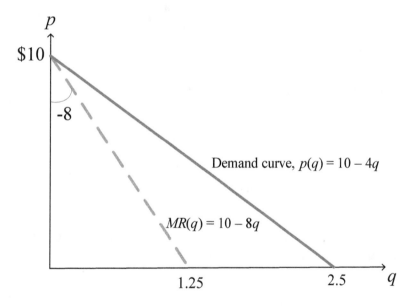

Figure 10.1. Demand and marginal revenue curves.

- Relative to example 10.1, marginal revenue curve $MR(q) = 10 - 8q$ still originates at a height of 10 (same vertical intercept) but decreases faster in output (i.e., the slope is now -8 rather than -6).

SA 10.2 Repeat the analysis in example 10.3, but assume a TC function $TC(q) = cq + \alpha q^2$. Find the monopolist output, price, profits, and consumer surplus. (*Hint*: Marginal cost is now increasing in output, rather than being flat.)

- The monopolist now maximizes profits by solving

$$\max_{q \geq 0} \pi = TR(q) - TC(q) = (a - bq)q - cq - \alpha q^2.$$

Differentiating with respect to output q, yields

$$a - 2bq - c - 2\alpha q = 0,$$

or, rearranging so that $MR(q) = MC(q)$, we obtain

$$a - 2bq = c + 2\alpha q.$$

Next, we need to solve the above equation for q to find the monopolist's profit-maximizing output. The demand and marginal revenue curves coincide with those in example 10.3. However, the marginal cost curve is now $MC(q) = c + 2\alpha q$, thus starting at c (same as the flat $MC(q)$ curve) and increasing at a rate of 2α. Graphically, a larger α makes the $MC(q)$ curve steeper, moving monopoly output in figure 10.2, q^M, closer to the origin (i.e., lower output level). Since marginal cost is increasing, rather than constant, in output q, we say that cost function $TC(q) = cq + \alpha q^2$ is *convex* in output.

The above equation can be rearranged as $a - c = 2bq + 2\alpha q$. After factoring $2q$ on the right-hand side, we obtain $a - c = 2q(b + \alpha)$, and solving for q we find the profit-maximizing output for the monopolist

$$q^M = \frac{a - c}{2(b + \alpha)}.$$

which is increasing in the vertical intercept of the inverse demand function, a, but decreasing in its slope and in the monopolist's production cost (b and α, respectively).

- *Monopoly price.* We can now find the monopoly price by inserting the monopoly output in the inverse demand,

$$p(q^M) = a - bq^M = a - b\left(\overbrace{\frac{a - c}{2(b + \alpha)}}^{q^M} \right)$$
$$= \frac{2a(b + \alpha) - b(a - c)}{2(b + \alpha)},$$

which can be further rearranged and simplified to obtain

$$p^M = \frac{2ab + 2a\alpha - ab + bc}{2(b+\alpha)}$$

$$= \frac{ab + 2a\alpha + bc}{2(b+\alpha)}.$$

We can compare this to the monopoly price under constant marginal cost in example 10.3, where price here is higher than in example 10.3 only if

$$\frac{ab + 2a\alpha + bc}{2(b+\alpha)} > \frac{a-c}{2}.$$

This inequality simplifies to $ab + 2a\alpha + bc > (a-c)(b+\alpha)$, and, expanding, becomes

$$ab + 2a\alpha + bc > ab + a\alpha - bc - c\alpha,$$

then, combining like terms finally becomes

$$a\alpha + 2bc > -c\alpha.$$

This inequality always hold since, by assumption, the left-hand side is always positive and the right-hand side is always negative. Therefore, the price in this example (with convex costs) is greater than that when marginal cost is constant only.

- *Monopoly profits.* Monopoly profits are then

$$\pi^M = p(q^M)q^M - cq^M - \alpha(q^M)^2$$

$$= \left(\overbrace{\frac{ab + 2a\alpha + bc}{2(b+\alpha)}}^{p^M}\right)\frac{a-c}{2(b+\alpha)} - c\left(\frac{a-c}{2(b+\alpha)}\right) - \alpha\left(\frac{a-c}{2(b+\alpha)}\right)^2$$

$$= \frac{(a-c)(ab+2a\alpha+bc)}{4(b+\alpha)^2} - \frac{2c(a-c)(b+\alpha)}{4(b+\alpha)^2} - \frac{\alpha(a-c)^2}{4(b+\alpha)^2}$$

$$= \frac{(a-c)(ab+2a\alpha+bc-2bc-2c\alpha-a\alpha+c\alpha)}{4(b+\alpha)^2}$$

$$= \frac{(a-c)(ab-bc+a\alpha-c\alpha)}{4(b+\alpha)^2}$$

$$= \frac{(a-c)(b(a-c)+\alpha(a-c))}{4(b+\alpha)^2}$$

$$= \frac{(a-c)^2(b+\alpha)}{4(b+\alpha)^2}.$$

We can compare this to monopoly profits under constant marginal cost to find that monopoly profits will be lower under convex costs:

$$\frac{(a-c)^2}{4b} > \frac{(a-c)^2(b+\alpha)}{4(b+\alpha)^2}$$

$$\frac{1}{b} > \frac{(b+\alpha)}{(b+\alpha)^2}$$

$$\frac{1}{b} > \frac{1}{(b+\alpha)}$$

$$b+\alpha > b$$

$$\alpha > 0,$$

which holds by assumption.

- *Consumer surplus.* We can now evaluate consumer surplus under this monopoly:

$$CS^M = \frac{1}{2}\left(a - \frac{ab + 2a\alpha + bc}{2(b+\alpha)}\right)\frac{a-c}{2(b+\alpha)}$$

$$= \frac{1}{2}\frac{2ab + 2a\alpha - ab - 2a\alpha - bc}{2(b+\alpha)}\frac{a-c}{2(b+\alpha)}$$

$$= \frac{1}{2}\frac{ab - bc}{2(b+\alpha)}\frac{a-c}{2(b+\alpha)}$$

$$= \frac{b(a-c)^2}{8(b+\alpha)^2}.$$

We can also show that consumer surplus is lower under convex costs:

$$\frac{b(a-c)^2}{8(b+\alpha)^2} < \frac{(a-c)^2}{8b}.$$

Rearranging, we obtain

$$\frac{b}{(b+\alpha)^2} < \frac{1}{b},$$

which simplifies to $b^2 < (b+\alpha)^2$, and applying square roots on both sides to $b < b+\alpha$, and finally to $0 < \alpha$, which holds by assumption.

- *Numerical example.* For comparison, we can use the same numerical example as example 10.3, where $a = 10$, $b = 1$, $c = 4$, and $\alpha = 1$. We obtain that monopoly output becomes $q^M = \frac{10-4}{2(1+1)} = 1.5$ units, monopoly price is

$$p^M = \frac{10(1) + 2(10)(1) + (1)(4)}{2(1+1)} = \$8.5,$$

profits are

$$\pi^M = \frac{(10-4)^2(1+1)}{4(1+1)^2} = \$4.5,$$

and consumer surplus becomes

$$CS^M = \frac{1(10-4)^2}{8(1+1)^2} = \$1.125.$$

Self-assessment exercise #10.3

SA 10.3 Consider again the monopolist in self-assessment 10.2, but assuming that the monopolist faces a total cost function $TC(q) = 4q^2$. Use your findings from self-assessment 10.2 to evaluate the monopolist price elasticity at q^M.

- *Finding price elasticity.* First, we need to find the demand curve by solving for q in $p(q) = a - bq$ to obtain $q(p) = \frac{a}{b} - \frac{1}{b}p$. We can then find the price elasticity by using its formula, $\varepsilon_{q,p} = \frac{\partial q(p)}{\partial p} \frac{p^M}{q^M}$, as follows

$$\varepsilon_{q,p} = \frac{\partial q(p)}{\partial p} \frac{p^M}{q^M} = -\frac{1}{b} \frac{\frac{ab+2a\alpha+bc}{2(b+\alpha)}}{\frac{a-c}{2(b+\alpha)}},$$

where $\frac{\partial q(p)}{\partial p} = -\frac{1}{b}$ since the demand curve is $q(p) = \frac{a}{b} - \frac{1}{b}p$, monopoly output (as found in self-assessment 10.2) is $q^M = \frac{a-c}{2(b+\alpha)}$, and its corresponding monopoly price is $p^M = \frac{ab+2a\alpha+bc}{2(b+\alpha)}$. Rearranging and simplifying, we obtain a price elasticity of

$$\varepsilon_{q,p} = -\frac{1}{b} \frac{ab+2a\alpha+bc}{2(b+\alpha)} \frac{2(b+\alpha)}{a-c}$$
$$= -\frac{ab+2a\alpha+bc}{b(a-c)}.$$

- *Evaluating price elasticity.* We need to check if the above expression is larger/smaller than 1. Ratio $\frac{ab+2a\alpha+bc}{b(a-c)}$ satisfies $\frac{ab+2a\alpha+bc}{b(a-c)} > 1$ only if

$$ab + 2a\alpha + bc > b(a-c),$$

which simplifies to
$$2a\alpha + 2bc > 0,$$

which holds given our assumption that $a, b, c, \alpha > 0$. As a consequence, the monopolist sets its profit-maximizing price on the *elastic segment* of the demand curve.

- *Numerical example.* Using the numerical example in self-assessment 10.2, where $a = 10$, $b = 1$, $c = 4$, and $\alpha = 1$, the elasticity at the profit-maximizing price is

$$\varepsilon_{q,p} = -\frac{ab+2a\alpha+bc}{b(a-c)}$$
$$= -\frac{10(1) + 2(10)(1) + (1)(4)}{1(10-4)} = -5.67.$$

205

Self-assessment exercise #10.4

SA 10.4 Consider a monopolist facing an inverse demand $p(q) = 10 - 4q$. Following the same steps as in example 10.5, use the Lerner index to find the monopolist's profit-maximizing price.

- After solving for q in inverse demand function $p(q) = 10 - 4q$, we obtain direct demand function $q(p) = \frac{5}{2} - \frac{1}{4}p$. The elasticity is then

$$\varepsilon_{q,p} = \frac{\partial q(p)}{\partial p} \frac{p^M}{q^M} = -\frac{1}{4} \frac{p}{\frac{5}{2} - \frac{1}{4}p} = -\frac{p}{10 - p},$$

since $\dfrac{\partial q(p)}{\partial p} = -\frac{1}{4}$. In this setting, marginal costs are $MC(q) = 4$ (see example 10.5 for details). The Lerner index, $\frac{p - MC(q)}{p} = -\frac{1}{\varepsilon_{q,p}}$, becomes

$$\frac{p - 4}{p} = -\frac{1}{-\dfrac{p}{10 - p}},$$

or, after rearranging, we obtain

$$\frac{p - 4}{p} = -\frac{10 - p}{p},$$

which simplifies to $p - 4 = 10 - p$ or, after solving for price p, $p = \$7$.

Self-assessment exercise #10.5

SA 10.5 Consider a monopolist facing the demand curve $q(p) = 10p^{-\varepsilon}$. Following the same steps as in example 10.6, use the Lerner index to find the monopolist's profit-maximizing price.

- This demand is an example of a "Constant Elasticity" demand function where the price elasticity coincides with the exponent, $-\varepsilon$. The Lerner index to this demand function is
$$\frac{p - MC(q)}{p} = -\frac{1}{-\varepsilon}.$$

If we assume a marginal cost of $MC(q) = \$4$ and $\varepsilon = 2$, then the Lerner index becomes
$$\frac{p - 4}{p} = -\frac{1}{-2},$$

which simplifies to $2p - 8 = p$, or $p = \$8$.

Self-assessment exercise #10.6

SA 10.6 Consider a monopolist facing a marginal cost of $\$3$ and a price elasticity of $\varepsilon_{q,p} = -1.5$. Use the IEPR to find the monopolist's profit-maximizing price.

- The IEPR, $p = \frac{MC(q)}{1+\frac{1}{\varepsilon_{p,q}}}$, provides the optimal price of

$$
\begin{aligned}
p &= \frac{MC(q)}{1+\frac{1}{\varepsilon_{p,q}}} = \frac{3}{1+\frac{1}{-1.5}} \\
&= \frac{3}{1-\frac{2}{3}} = \frac{3}{\frac{1}{3}} = \$9.
\end{aligned}
$$

Self-assessment exercise #10.7

SA 10.7 Consider the multiplant monopolist in example 10.7, but assume that the inverse demand function changes to $p(Q) = 300 - \frac{1}{2}Q$. Follow the steps in example 10.7 to find the optimal output in each plant. How are these results affected by demand increase?

- The total cost of the two plants remains the same as in example 10.7; that is, $TC_1(q_1) = 5 + 12q_1 + 6\left(q_1\right)^2$, and $TC_2(q_2) = 2 + 18q_2 + 3\left(q_2\right)^2$. The monopolist maximizes the joint profits from both plants, as follows,

$$
\begin{aligned}
\max_{q_1 \geq 0,\ q_2 \geq 0} \pi = \pi_1 + \pi_2 = {}& \left(300 - \frac{1}{2}q_1 - \frac{1}{2}q_2\right)q_1 - \left(5 + 12q_1 + 6\left(q_1\right)^2\right) \\
& + \left(300 - \frac{1}{2}q_1 - \frac{1}{2}q_2\right)q_2 - \left(2 + 18q_2 + 3\left(q_2\right)^2\right).
\end{aligned}
$$

Differentiating with respect to output q_1, we obtain

$$
300 - q_1 - \frac{1}{2}q_2 - 12 - 12q_1 =
$$

$$
288 - 13q_1 - \frac{1}{2}q_2 = 0,
$$

or, after solving for q_1, is $q_1 = \frac{288 - \frac{1}{2}q_2}{13}$. Similarly, differentiating with respect to output q_2, we obtain

$$
300 - \frac{1}{2}q_1 - q_2 - 18 - 6q_2 =
$$

$$
282 - \frac{1}{2}q_1 - 7q_2 = 0,
$$

which, after solving for q_2, yields $q_2 = \frac{282 - \frac{1}{2}q_1}{7}$. Inserting this result into $q_1 = \frac{288 - \frac{1}{2}q_2}{13}$, we obtain

$$
q_1 = \frac{288 - \frac{1}{2} \times \frac{282 - \frac{1}{2}q_1}{7}}{13},
$$

which simplifies to $13q_1 = 288 - \frac{282}{14} + \frac{1}{28}q_1$, and further to $\frac{365}{28}q_1 = \frac{1875}{7}$, yielding an output q_1 of $q_1 \simeq 20.55$ units. Therefore, the optimal production q_2 becomes

$$
q_2 = \frac{282 - \frac{1}{2}q_1}{7} = \frac{282 - \frac{1}{2} \times 20.55}{7} \simeq 38.82 \text{ units.}
$$

Relative to example 10.7, the increase in demand causes an increase in production at both plants: q_1 increased from 5 to 20.55 units, and q_2 increased from 4 to 38.82 units.

Self-assessment exercise #10.8

SA 10.8 Consider the monopolist in example 10.8, but assume now that its total cost is $TC(q) = 4q^2$. Repeat the steps in example 10.8 to find the consumer surplus, profits, and welfare under monopoly, and then under perfect competition; and ultimately, find the welfare difference measuring the deadweight loss from monopoly.

- Under perfect competition, output is found at the point where demand crosses supply (the marginal cost curve),

$$10 - q = 8q.$$

Solving for q, we find $q^{PC} = \frac{10}{9} \simeq \$1.11$ units, and a price of $p^{PC} = \frac{80}{9} \simeq \$8.89$, as depicted in figure 10.2. For comparison purposes, the figure also includes output and price under monopoly.

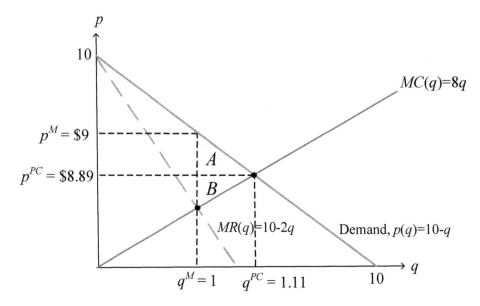

Figure 10.2. Perfect competition vs. monopoly when costs are convex.

- In this context, consumer surplus is

$$CS^{PC} = \frac{1}{2}\left(10 - \frac{80}{9}\right)\frac{10}{9} = \frac{50}{81} \simeq 0.617,$$

and profits are

$$\pi^{PC} = \left(\frac{80}{9} \times \frac{10}{9}\right) - 4\left(\frac{10}{9}\right)^2 = \frac{400}{81} \simeq \$4.94,$$

which generate a total welfare of

$$W^{PC} = CS^{PC} + \pi^{PC} = \frac{50}{81} + \frac{400}{81} = \frac{450}{81} \simeq \$5.56.$$

- This exercise uses the same demand function and cost as self-assessment 10.2, which assumes $a = b = 1$ and $c = 4$, and where we found $\pi^M = \$5$ and $CS^M = \$0.5$. Hence, total welfare is

$$W^M = CS^M + \pi^M = 5 + 0.5 = \$5.5.$$

The difference between the welfare levels across market structures,

$$W^{PC} - W^M = 5.56 - 5.5 = \$0.06,$$

represents the deadweight loss of the monopoly, measured by the sum of areas A and B in figure 10.2.

Self-assessment exercise #10.9

SA 10.9 Consider the monopolist in example 10.9, but assume now that advertising elasticity increases to $\varepsilon_{q,A} = 0.3$. Find the advertising-to-sales ratio $\frac{A}{pq}$, and compare it to that in example 10.9. Interpret your results.

- In this setting, where $\varepsilon_{q,A} = 0.3$ and $\varepsilon_{q,p} = -1.5$, the advertising-to-sales ratio, $\frac{A}{pq} = -\frac{\varepsilon_{q,A}}{\varepsilon_{q,p}}$, becomes

$$\frac{A}{pq} = -\frac{0.3}{-1.5} = 0.2.$$

In words, advertising should account for 20 percent of this monopolist's total revenue. This is higher than the ratio found in example 10.9 because the advertising elasticity is now greater. Since the same percentage increase in advertising increases sales more than in example 10.9, the firm should have a higher advertising-to-sales ratio.

Self-assessment exercise #10.10

SA 10.10 Consider the coal company in example 10.10, but assume now that the price of coal p increases from \$8 to \$10. Use the same steps as in example 10.10 to find the number of workers hired under monopsony, under perfect competition, and also find the corresponding salaries.

- With the new price, the marginal revenue product of labor is

$$MRP_L = pf'(L) = \overbrace{10}^{p} \times \overbrace{100\frac{1}{L}}^{f'(L)} = \frac{1,000}{L}.$$

The increase in the price of coal does not affect the marginal expenditure that the firm incurs when hiring more workers, so that $ME_L = 3 + L$ remains the same.

- *Monopsonistic labor market.* Under a monopsony, MRP_L crosses ME_L curve, so we set $MRP_L = ME_L$ yielding

$$\frac{1,000}{L} = 3 + L,$$

which simplifies to $1,000 = 3L + L^2$, or $L^2 + 3L - 1,000 = 0$. Solving for L in this equation, we find two roots, $L = -33.16$ and $L = 30.16$. Since the firm must hire a positive (or zero) number of workers, we find that the firm hires $L^M = 30$ workers. At $L^M = 30$, wages become

$$w^M = w(30) = 3 + \frac{1}{2}30 = \$18.$$

Figure 10.3 depicts the MRP_L and ME_L curves, their crossing point to obtain the equilibrium number of workers hired, L^M, and the salary that the monopsonist pays them, $w^M = \$18$.

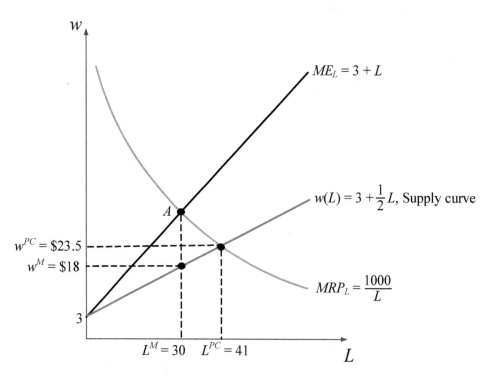

Figure 10.3. Workers hired and salary under monopsony.

- *Perfectly competitive labor market.* Under a perfectly competitive labor market, the number of workers is determined by $MRP_L = w(L)$, which, in this case, becomes

$$\frac{1,000}{L} = 3 + \frac{1}{2}L,$$

which, after expanding, becomes $1,000 = 3L + \frac{1}{2}L^2$. Solving for L we find two roots, $L = -47.82$ and $L = 41.82$; the latter being the optimal number of workers hired under perfect competition in the labor market $L^{PC} = 41$ workers, with wages

$$w^{PC} = w(41) = 3 + \frac{1}{2}41 = \$23.5.$$

The number of workers hired under a perfectly competitive labor market, $L^{PC} = 41$, and their corresponding salary, $w^{PC} = \$23.5$, is also depicted in figure 10.4 to facilitate the comparison with monopsony.

- *Comparison.* When the labor market is competitive, more workers are hired ($L^{PC} = 41$ rather than $L^M = 30$), and workers receive a higher wage ($w^{PC} = \$23.5$ rather than $w^M = \$18$).

10.2 Solutions to End-of-Chapter Exercises

Exercise #10.1 - Monopoly Equilibrium-Linear Costs[B]

10.1 Consider a drug company holding the patent of a new drug for a rare disease (monopoly rights). The firm faces inverse demand function $p(q) = 100 - 0.1q$, and a cost function $C(q) = 4q$.

(a) Find the monopolist profit-maximizing output, its price, and its profits.

- *Monopoly output.* The monopolist maximizes its output when $MR(q) = MC(q)$, where marginal revenue is

$$MR(q) = p(q) + \frac{\partial p(q)}{\partial q} q = \underbrace{100 - 0.1q}_{p(q)} - (0.1)q = 100 - 0.2q,$$

since $\frac{\partial p(q)}{\partial q} = -0.1$. The marginal cost is

$$MC(q) = \frac{\partial C(q)}{\partial q} = 4.$$

Setting marginal revenue equal to marginal cost, $MR(q) = MC(q)$, we have

$$100 - 0.2q = 4.$$

Rearranging, we find $96 = 0.2q$. Solving for q, we obtain that the drug company produces

$$q^M = 480 \text{ units}.$$

Figure 10.4 depicts the above inverse demand curve, $p(q)$, as well as the $MR(q)$ and $MC(q)$ curves.

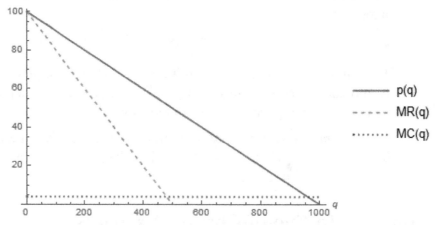

Figure 10.4. Marginal revenue and marginal cost curves with
linear costs.

- *Monopoly price.* We can insert output $q^M = 480$ into the inverse demand curve to find the monopoly price

$$p^M = 100 - 0.1(480) = \$52.$$

- *Monopoly profit.* The monopolist's profit is

$$\begin{aligned}
\pi^M &= p^M q^M - C(q^M) \\
&= (480 \times 52) - (4 \times 480) \\
&= \$21,600.
\end{aligned}$$

(b) Assume now that the government seeks the monopolist to produce the competitive equilibrium output (i.e., where demand crosses the MC function). Find the competitive equilibrium output in this context.

- We find the competitive equilibrium by setting price equal to marginal cost; that is, $p(q) = MC(q)$, or

$$100 - 0.1q = 4.$$

Solving for q, we first simplify to $96 = 0.1q$, or $q^C = 960$ units.
- The competitive price will be equal to marginal cost, or

$$p^C = MC = \$4.$$

Relative to part (a), perfectly competitive output is larger than in monopoly (960 units rather than 480 units) and the price is lower ($4 vs. $52).

(c) Find the subsidy per unit of output that the government needs to offer the monopolist to induce the latter to produce the competitive equilibrium output you identified in part (b).

- A subsidy of s per unit will impact the monopolist's marginal revenue, changing it to

$$MR(q) = p(q) + \frac{\partial p(q)}{\partial q}q + s = \underbrace{100 - 0.1q}_{p(q)} - (0.1)q + s = 100 - 0.2q + s,$$

In the monopoly equilibrium, we know that $MR(q) = MC(q)$, or

$$100 - 0.2q + s = 4.$$

The regulator wants to induce the monopolist to produce $q^C = 960$ units, so we plug this in for q:

$$100 - 0.2(960) + s = 4.$$

Simplifying,

$$-92 + s = 4,$$

that is, a subsidy of $s = \$96$ per unit of output.

(d) What is the total cost that the government incurs with the subsidy? How are profits affected by the subsidy (i.e., the change in profits from parts a to c)?

- The total subsidy can be calculated by multiplying the subsidy per unit of output times the quantity sold,

$$TS = sq^C = 96(960) = \$92,160.$$

The monopolist's profit is calculated as

$$\begin{aligned} \pi &= p^C q^C - C(q^C) + TS \\ &= \underbrace{4(960) - 4(960)}_{\text{zero}} + 92,160 \\ &= \$92,160. \end{aligned}$$

The monopolist's profit if it were induced to produce the competitive equilibrium will be exactly that of the subsidy. Remember that when a firm is in a competitive equilibrium, its economic profit is zero. Therefore, the regulator is inducing the monopolist to produce at a quantity where it will make no profit, but it will have to subsidize the monopolist in order to do so.

Exercise #10.3 - Maximizing Revenue versus Profit[A]

10.3 Consider a monopolist facing linear inverse demand function $p(q) = 20 - 2q$, and constant marginal cost $MC(q) = 1$.

(a) Assume that the monopolist seeks to maximize total revenue rather than profits. Which output does the monopolist choose? What are the equilibrium price and profits?

- *Revenue-maximizing output.* To maximize revenue, the monopolist sets $MR(q) =$

0, or

$$MR(q) = p(q) + \frac{\partial p(q)}{\partial q}q = \underbrace{20 - 2q}_{p(q)} - 2q = 20 - 4q = 0,$$

since $\frac{\partial p(q)}{\partial q} = -2$. Simplifying, we have $20 = 4q$. Solving for q, we ding that revenue is maximized at

$$q^R = 5 \text{ units.}$$

Figure 10.5 depicts demand and marginal revenue in this context.

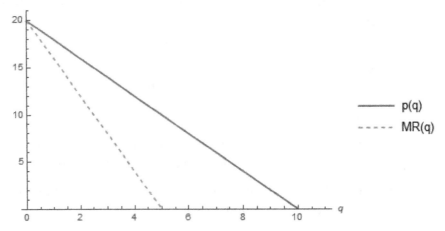

Figure 10.5. Demand and marginal revenue.

- *Revenue-maximizing price.* Plugging this output $q^R = 5$ into the inverse demand, we obtain the price at the revenue maximizing quantity

$$p^R = 20 - 2(5) = \$10.$$

- *Revenue-maximizing profit.* The monopolist's profit is

$$\begin{aligned} \pi^R &= p^R q^R - C(q^R) \\ &= 10(5) - 1(5) \\ &= 50 - 5 = \$45. \end{aligned}$$

(b) Assume now that the monopolist seeks to maximize profits. Show that its optimal output decreases relative to that maximizing total revenue in part (a), that price increases, and that profits increase.

- *Monopoly output.* If the monopolist maximizes profit, it sets marginal revenue equal to marginal cost, $MR(q) = MC(q)$, that is

$$20 - 4q = 1.$$

Solving for q, we first have $19 = 4q$. Solving for q, we obtain the profit-maximizing output for the monopolist,

$$q^M = 4.75 \text{ units.}$$

214

- *Monopoly price.* Plugging this output $q^M = 4.75$ into the inverse demand, we get
$$p^M = 20 - 2(4.75) = \$10.5.$$

- *Monopoly profit.* The monopolist's profit when producing $q^M = 4.75$ units is
$$\begin{aligned} \pi^M &= p^M q^M - C(q^M) \\ &= 10.5(4.75) - 1(4.75) \\ &= \$45.13, \end{aligned}$$

which is greater than if the monopolist maximized revenue.

Exercise #10.5 - Regulating a Natural Monopoly[B]

10.5 Duchess Energy, an electric utility company, provides electricity to Spartanburg. The demand for electricity is $p(q) = 10 - 0.1q$, and this company's costs are $C(q) = 1 + 0.5q$.

(a) Does Duchess Energy exhibit the properties to be a "natural monopoly"?

- As discussed in section 10.2, to be a natural monopoly, Duchess energy must have decreasing average costs. Duchess Energy's average costs are
$$AC(q) = \frac{C(q)}{q} = \frac{1 + 0.5q}{q} = \frac{1}{q} + 0.5.$$

Since q only shows up in the denominator of average costs, it is the case that average costs are decreasing in q, and thus Duchess Energy is a natural monopoly.

(b) Find the unregulated monopolist's profit-maximizing price, output, and profit.

- The monopolist maximizes
$$\max_{q \geq 0} \ (10 - 0.1q)q - (1 + 0.5q).$$

Differentiating with respect to q, we obtain
$$10 - 0.2q - 0.5 = 0,$$

rearranging, we have $9.5 = 0.2q$. Solving for q, we find that the unregulated electric company produces
$$q^U = 47.5 \text{ units.}$$

Inserting this output in the inverse demand function, we obtain that the company charges a price of
$$p^U = 10 - 0.1(47.5) = 10 - 4.75 = \$5.25.$$

As a result, Duchess Energy earns a profit of

$$\pi^U = 5.25(47.5) - [1 + 0.5(47.5)] = 249.38 - 24.75 = \$224.63.$$

(c) The Spartanburg city government passes a law that requires utility and other electricity providers to practice MC pricing (i.e., $p(q^R) = MC(q^R)$). What is the regulated monopolist's output, price, and profit?

- In this case, the monopolist sets its price such that

$$\underbrace{10 - 0.1q}_{p(q)} = \underbrace{0.5}_{MC(q)},$$

rearranging, we first have $0.1q = 9.5$, and solving for q, we find the regulated monopolist produces an output of

$$q^R = 95 \text{ units.}$$

Inserting this output in the inverse demand function, we confirm that the regulated company charges a price equal to marginal cost, $0.5,

$$p^R = 10 - 0.1(95) = 10 - 9.5 = \$0.5,$$

implying that the profits of the regulated monopolist are

$$\pi^R = 0.5(95) - [1 + 0.5(95)] = 47.5 - 48.5 = -\$1.$$

When the regulator enforces marginal cost pricing, the firm cannot recover its fixed costs.

(d) What is the lump-sum subsidy that the regulator must provide the electric utility company to practice MC pricing without operating at a loss?

- When the utility company practices marginal cost pricing, its profit is $-\$1$, as shown in part (c). Therefore, if the regulator offers a lump-sum subsidy of $S = \$1$, the utility company would break even.

(e) Compute the consumer surplus from the pricing strategies in parts (a) and (b).

- *Unregulated monopoly.* Under uniform pricing in the unregulated monopoly, consumer surplus is calculated as $CS = \frac{1}{2}(a - p^U)q^U$, where $a = 10$ is the vertical intercept of the inverse demand, yielding

$$CS^U = \frac{1}{2}(10 - \underbrace{5.25}_{p^U})\underbrace{47.5}_{q^U} = \frac{1}{2}(4.75)(47.5) = \$112.81.$$

- *Marginal cost pricing.* Under marginal cost pricing monopoly, consumer surplus is calculated as $CS = \frac{1}{2}(a - p^R)q^R$, where $a = 10$ is the vertical intercept of the inverse demand, obtaining

$$CS^R = \frac{1}{2}(10 - \underbrace{0.5}_{p^R}) \underbrace{95}_{q^R} = \frac{1}{2}(9.5)(95) = \$451.25.$$

(f) Discuss the pros and cons of MC pricing in natural monopolies.

- If we add total welfare under each pricing scheme, we find that the sum of profit and consumer surplus in the unregulated monopoly is

$$W^U = \pi^U + CS^U = \$224.63 + \$112.81 = \$337.44,$$

while under the marginal cost pricing welfare becomes

$$W^R = \underbrace{(\pi^R + S)}_{\text{Profit after subsidy}} + CS^R - T = (-\$1 + \$1) + \$451.25 - \$1 = \$450.25.$$

The first term represents the firm's profits after receiving the lump-sum subsidy, the second term reflects consumer surplus in this setting, and the last term $T = \$1$ denotes the taxes that the regulator needs to collect to provide the lump-sum subsidy to the monopolist. Overall, welfare is \$450.25, thus being larger than when the firm is left unregulated.

Intuitively, the increase in consumer surplus (from $CS^U = \$112.81$ to $CS^R = \$451.25$) offsets the loss in profits ($\pi^U = \$224.63$ to $\pi^R + S = \$0$) and the cost of the subsidy in terms of tax collection ($T = \$1$). Therefore, an advantage of marginal cost pricing is that it can help increase total welfare.

A major disadvantage is the decrease in profit (to a negative value before subsidies) for the monopolist. Because of this, many regulated natural monopolies are induced to artificially inflate their marginal cost in order to gain some profit. If the monopolist is successful, prices would increase resulting in a decrease in consumer surplus and an increase in deadweight loss. Another important disadvantage is that regulators rarely have accurate information about the monopolist's cost function and set pricing decisions based on expected, rather than true, marginal costs, and lump-sum subsidy decisions based on expected fixed costs.

Exercise #10.7 - Two Parts of Marginal Revenue[A]

10.7 There are two parts to a monopolist's marginal revenue function. Identify the two parts in each of the following demand functions:

(a) $p(q) = 25 - 1.5q$.

- The positive effect is the price at which the next unit is sold, that is $p(q) = 25 - 1.5q$. The negative effect is the loss in revenue from decreasing the price in all previous units, represented by $\frac{\partial p(q)}{\partial q} q = -1.5q$.

- Therefore, marginal revenue for this function is

$$MR = \underbrace{25 - 1.5q}_{p(q)} - 1.5q = 25 - 3q.$$

(b) $p(q) = \frac{1}{q^2} + 50$.

- The positive effect is the price at which the next unit is sold, that is $p(q) = \frac{1}{q^2} + 50$. The negative effect is the loss in revenue from decreasing the price in all previous units, represented by $\frac{\partial p(q)}{\partial q} q = -\frac{2}{q^3} q = -\frac{2}{q^2}$.
- Therefore, marginal revenue for this function is

$$MR = \underbrace{\frac{1}{q^2} + 50}_{p(q)} - \frac{2}{q^2} = 50 - \frac{1}{q^2}.$$

(c) $p(q) = e^{-q}$.

- The positive effect is the price at which the next unit is sold, that is $p(q) = e^{-q}$. The negative effect is the loss in revenue from decreasing the price in all previous units, represented by $\frac{\partial p(q)}{\partial q} q = -e^{-q} q$.
- Therefore, marginal revenue for this function is

$$MR = \underbrace{e^{-q}}_{p(q)} - e^{-q} q = (1 - q)e^{-q}.$$

Exercise #10.9 - Factors of a High Monopoly Price[B]

10.9 A monopolist does not charge an infinitely high price, but certain market conditions can lead to a situation where prices may seem infinitely high. Discuss what the "perfect storm" of market conditions might be.

- A couple of factors may result in a monopoly charging an extremely high price, but the most likely factor is a market with inelastic demand. When a firm faces inelastic demand, they can increase their price and increase total revenue. When a firm increases their price, they sell less, which decreases their costs. Lower costs and higher revenues result in a higher profit. So, if a firm faces a very inelastic demand curve, it has incentive to charge very high prices. An example of this would be the market for pharmaceutical drugs.

Exercise #10.11 - Monopoly with General Linear Demand[C]

10.11 Consider a monopolist with general inverse demand $p(q) = a - bq$ and constant marginal cost c. How does the monopolist's optimal quantity, price, profit, and consumer surplus change as each of the parameters a, b, and c increase?

- From example 10.2, we know that equilibrium output and prices in this case are

$$q^M = \frac{a-c}{2b}$$
$$p^M = \frac{a+c}{2},$$

while equilibrium profits and consumer surplus are

$$\pi^M = \frac{(a-c)^2}{4b}$$
$$CS^M = \frac{(a-c)^2}{8b}.$$

- *Higher parameter a.* Starting with a, it is easy to see that each will increase as a increases. That is, as the intercept of the demand curve increases (or the demand curve shifts up), the monopolist sells more units at a high price for more profit, and consumers enjoy an increase in their surplus.

- *Higher parameter b.* This parameter is in the denominator of all expressions except price, for which it has no impact. An increase in b, which makes the demand curve steeper (indicating that consumers are more sensitive to price increases), decreases equilibrium quantity, profit, and consumer surplus.

- *Higher parameter c.* As marginal cost increases (higher c), equilibrium quantity, profit, and consumer surplus decreases, while the equilibrium price increases.

Exercise #10.13 - Multiplant Monopoly–I^B

10.13 Consider a firm that holds a patent on technology that makes the production of concrete less harmful to the environment (resulting in a monopoly on this technology). The firm has two plants: one domestic (D) and one located in Australia (A). Demand for their technology is $p(Q) = 250 - 10Q$, where $Q = q_D + q_A$ is aggregate output. The domestic plant has total cost $TC_D(q_D) = 5 + 10q_D + 4(q_D)^2$, and the Australian plant has total cost $TC_A(q_A) = 15 + 4q_A + 5(q_A)^2$. Find the optimal output at each plant, and the price it will charge.

- The monopolist maximizes its joint profit in both plants

$$\max_{q_D, q_A} \pi = \pi_D + \pi_A = (250 - 10q_d - 10q_A)q_D - (5 + 10q_D + 4(q_D)^2)$$
$$+ (250 - 10q_d - 10q_A)q_A - (15 + 4q_A + 5(q_A)^2).$$

Differentiating with respect to domestic output q_D, we obtain

$$250 - 20q_D - 10q_A - 10 - 8q_D - 10q_A =$$
$$240 - 28q_D - 20q_A = 0.$$

Solving for q_D, we have that

$$q_D = \frac{240 - 20q_A}{28}.$$

Differentiating profit with respect to Australian production, q_A, we obtain

$$250 - 20q_A - 10q_D - 4 - 10q_A - 10q_D =$$
$$246 - 30q_A - 20q_D = 0.$$

Solving for q_A, we have that

$$q_A = \frac{246 - 20q_D}{30}.$$

Inserting this expression into q_D that we obtained above, we have

$$q_D = \frac{240 - 10 \overbrace{\frac{246 - 20q_D}{30}}^{q_A}}{28}.$$

Rearranging,

$$q_D = \frac{240 - 164 + \frac{400}{30}q_D}{28}$$
$$q_D = \frac{76 + \frac{400}{30}q_D}{28} = \frac{76}{28} + \frac{400}{840}q_D,$$

and further simplifying

$$\frac{440}{840}q_D = \frac{76}{28},$$

or, after solving for q_D, we find $q_D = 5.18$ units. Plugging this output into Australian production we found above

$$q_A = \frac{246 - 20q_D}{30} = \frac{246 - 20(5.18)}{30} = 4.75 \text{ units.}$$

- Therefore, the multiplant monopolist charges a price of

$$\begin{aligned} p &= 250 - 10(q_D + q_A) \\ &= 250 - 10(5.18 + 4.75) \\ &= \$150.70. \end{aligned}$$

Exercise #10.15 - Multiproduct Monopoly[C]

10.15 Consider a pharmaceutical company with a patent on two different prescription drugs, granting them a monopoly in each market. Both drugs (x_1 and x_2) are made in similar ways, with total cost of

$$TC(x_1, x_2) = 50 + 2(x_1 + x_2) + 0.5(x_1 + x_2)^2.$$

Drug x_1 has demand $p_1(x_1) = 500 - x_1$, and drug x_2 has demand $p_2(x_2) = 1,000 - x_2$. Find the monopoly output, price, and profit for each drug.

- Similar to a multiplant monopoly, we can write the monopolist's profit maximization problem as follows:

$$\max_{x_1, x_2} \pi = \overbrace{(500 - x_1)x_1}^{TR_1} + \overbrace{(1,000 - x_2)x_2}^{TR_2} - \underbrace{(50 + 2(x_1 + x_2) + 0.5(x_1 + x_2)^2)}_{TC \text{ from both drugs}},$$

where the first term represents the total revenue from the first drug, the second term the revenue originating from the second drug, and the last term the total costs that the firm incurs from producing both drugs. Differentiating with respect to x_1, we obtain

$$500 - 2x_1 - 2 - (x_1 + x_2) =$$
$$498 - 3x_1 - x_2 = 0.$$

Solving for x_2, yields

$$x_2 = 498 - 3x_1.$$

Differentiating with respect to x_2, we obtain

$$1,000 - 2x_2 - 2 - (x_1 + x_2) =$$
$$998 - 3x_2 - x_1 = 0.$$

Solving for x_1, yields

$$x_1 = 998 - 3x_2.$$

Plugging this result into the expression for x_2, we have

$$x_2 = 498 - 3\overbrace{(998 - 3x_2)}^{x_1},$$

which simplifies to

$$x_2 = 498 - 2,994 + 9x_2,$$

or $x_2 = 312$ units, which is the amount of the second drug the monopoly produces. We plug this into the expression for x_1 to obtain

$$x_1 = 998 - 3(312) = 62 \text{ units},$$

which is the units of drug x_1 the monopolist produces. It will sell each drug at prices

$$p_1(62) = 500 - 62 = \$438$$
$$p_2(312) = 1{,}000 - 312 = \$688.$$

The monopolist's profit is

$$
\begin{aligned}
\pi &= p_1 x_1 + p_2 x_2 - TC(x_1, x_2) \\
&= 438(62) + 688(312) - \left[50 + 2(62 + 312) + 0.5(62 + 312)^2\right] \\
&= \$171{,}076.
\end{aligned}
$$

Exercise #10.17 - Advertising-to-Sales Ratio[A]

10.17 Consider a monopolist with a price elasticity of demand of $\varepsilon_{q,p} = -2.5$ and an advertising elasticity of $\varepsilon_{q,A} = 0.5$. What is the advertising-to-sales ratio? Comment on how price elasticity of demand affects the advertising-to-sales ratio.

- The advertising to sales ratio should be

$$
\frac{A}{pq} = -\frac{\varepsilon_{q,A}}{\varepsilon_{q,p}} = -\frac{0.5}{-2.5} = 0.2.
$$

This means that advertising should account for 20 percent of this monopolist's total revenue. As the price elasticity becomes more elastic (becomes more negative), the ratio decreases and the monopolist should spend less on advertising. This means that the price has a relatively bigger impact on sales than advertising, so the monopolist should do less advertising.

Exercise #10.19 - Identify a Monopsony[A]

10.19 Outside of employers in small towns, describe an example of a real-life monopsony. Be specific about what the good traded is and who the buyers and sellers are.

- An example of this might be professional sports leagues in the United States. Generally, professional athletes are good at one sport for which there is one league they can play (work) in. This makes that professional sports league a single buyer of athletes for that sport, who are selling their talent.

Exercise #10.21 - Monopsony–Two Inputs[B]

10.21 In many rural towns, there may be only one employer. An example of this may be a large, corporation-owned farm. This farm recently bought out many smaller farms in the area, and there is a large surplus of both high- and low-skilled labor (L_h and L_l, respectively). The production function for the farm is

$$q = 10 \ln L_h + 4 \ln L_l.$$

The supply curves for labor are $w_h(L_h) = 5 + 4L_h$ and $w_l(L_l) = 2 + 2L_l$, and the farm's output sells for \$10 per unit. How much of each type of labor will the farm hire, and at what wages? How much output will the farm sell? What is the farm's total profit?

- The farm faces the following problem:

$$\max_{L_l, L_h} \pi = \underbrace{10(10 \ln L_h + 4 \ln L_l)}_{TR} - \underbrace{[(5 + 4L_h)L_h + (2 + 2L_l)L_l]}_{TC}.$$

Differentiating with respect to L_h, we obtain

$$100\frac{1}{L_h} - 5 - 8L_h = 0,$$

multiplying by L_h, we find $100 - 5L_h - 8L_h^2 = 0$. This has two roots, $L_h = -3.86$ and $L_h = 3.24$, and the farm hires the latter amount, $L_h = 3.24$ units of high-skilled labor.

Plugging this value into the wage, the high-skilled workers will earn

$$w_h(3.24) = 5 + 4(3.24) = \$17.96.$$

- Differentiating with respect to L_l, we obtain

$$40\frac{1}{L_l} - 2 - 4L_l = 0,$$

multiplying by L_l, we find $40 - 2L - 4L^2 = 0$, which has two roots, $L_l = -3.42$ and $L_l = 2.92$. The farm will hire a positive amount, $L_l = 2.92$ units of low-skilled labor. The low-skilled laborers earns a wage of

$$w_h(2.92) = 5 + 4(2.92) = \$16.68.$$

- Total farm output will be

$$q = 10 \ln 3.24 + 4 \ln 2.92 = 16.04 \text{ units},$$

and total profits is

$$\begin{aligned} \pi &= pq - w_h L_h - w_l L_l \\ &= 10(16.04) - (17.96)3.24 - 16.68(2.92) \\ &= \$53.50. \end{aligned}$$

Chapter 11 - Price Discrimination and Bundling

11.1 Solutions to Self-Assessment Exercises

Self-assessment exercise #11.1

SA 11.1 Consider the monopolist in example 11.1, but assume that the inverse demand changes to $p(q) = 16 - q$ and the marginal cost $c = 3$. Follow the steps in example 11.1 to find the monopolist's profit if it sets a uniform price, π^M, and if it practices first-degree price discrimination, π^{FD}.

- *Uniform pricing.* First, we find the monopolist profit if it sets a uniform price, p^M. To do this, the monopolist produces where marginal revenue crosses the marginal cost curve, $MR(q) = MC(q)$; that is,

$$16 - 2q = 3.$$

  Solving for q, we find a monopoly output of $q^M = \frac{13}{2} = 6.5$ units, which entails a monopoly price of $p^M = 16 - 6.5 = \$9.5$. Monopoly profit under uniform pricing is

$$\pi^M = (p^M - c)q^M = (9.5 - 3)(6.5) = \$42.25.$$

- *First-degree price discrimination.* If the monopolist practices first-degree price discrimination, it produces an output level where the demand curve crosses the marginal cost (same as under a uniform price), $p(q) = c$, or

$$16 - q = 3.$$

  Solving for q, we obtain an output level of $q^{FD} = 16 - 3 = 13$ units. Since the monopolist charges a price that coincides with each individual's WTP, its profit is

$$\pi^{FD} = \frac{(a-c)^2}{2b} = \frac{(16-3)^2}{2 \times 1} = \frac{169}{2} = \$84.5.$$

  We find that if the monopolist practices first-degree price discrimination, it will obtain twice the amount of profit because of producing two times the amount of the good.

Self-assessment exercise #11.2

SA 11.2 Consider the monopolist in example 11.2, but assume that the inverse demand curve changes to $p(q) = 16 - q$, and its marginal cost is $c = 4$. Follow the steps in example 11.2 to find the units that the monopolist sells to each block, its corresponding prices, and the overall profits from doing so. Also, find the profit that the monopolist obtains from setting a uniform price for all customers, π^M.

- First, we need to write down the monopolist's profit-maximization problem,

$$\max_{q_1, q_2} \ \pi = \underbrace{(16 - q_1)q_1}_{\text{TR from Block 1}} + \underbrace{(16 - q_2)(q_2 - q_1)}_{\text{TR from Block 2}} - \underbrace{4q_2}_{\text{TC}}.$$

224

Differentiating with respect to q_1, we obtain

$$\frac{\partial \pi}{\partial q_1} = 16 - 2q_1 - (16 - q_2) = -2q_1 + q_2 = 0,$$

or, after rearranging, $q_1 = \frac{q_2}{2}$. Differentiating the above profit with respect to q_2, yields

$$\frac{\partial \pi}{\partial q_2} = 16 - 2q_2 + q_1 - 4 = 12 - 2q_2 + q_1 = 0,$$

which simplifies to $q_2 = \frac{12+q_1}{2}$. Inserting $q_1 = \frac{q_2}{2}$ into $q_2 = \frac{12+q_1}{2}$, we find

$$q_2 = \frac{12 + \overbrace{\dfrac{q_2}{2}}^{q_1}}{2},$$

which first simplifies to

$$2q_2 = 12 + \frac{q_2}{2},$$

and then becomes $\frac{3}{2}q_2 = 12$. Solving for q_2 gives

$$q_2 = \frac{24}{3} = 8 \text{ units.}$$

Inserting this output into $q_1 = \frac{q_2}{2}$, we find

$$q_1 = \frac{8}{2} = 4 \text{ units.}$$

Therefore, the first block is $q_1 = 4$ units, while the second block is $q_2 - q_1 = 8 - 4 = 4$ units as well.

- *Prices of each block.* We can now find the optimal prices for each block by plugging these output levels into the inverse demand function, as follows,

$$p(q_1) = 16 - 4 = \$12$$
$$p(q_2) = 16 - 8 = \$8.$$

- *Profits.* Overall profits are then

$$\pi = (12)4 + (8)4 - 8(4) = \$48.$$

- *Uniform pricing.* If, instead, the monopolist charged a uniform price, its optimal output q^M solves $MR(q) = MC(q)$, or

$$16 - 2q = 4.$$

Solving for q, we find an output of $q^M = \frac{12}{2} = 6$ units, a monopoly price of

$p^M = 16 - 6 = \$10$, yielding a monopoly profit from practicing uniform pricing of

$$\pi^U = (10 - 4)6 = \$36.$$

Therefore, the monopolist increases its profit by price discriminating.

Self-assessment exercise #11.3

SA 11.3 Consider the monopolist in example 11.3, but assume that students' inverse demand changes to $p(q) = 16 - q$. Follow the steps in example 11.3 to find the monopolist's sales to each market segment, the corresponding prices, and the profits. Compare your results against those in example 11.3.

- We can treat this as two separate maximization problems:

$$\text{Student group:} \quad \max_{q_1} \pi_1 = (16 - q_1)q_1 - 3q_1, \text{ and}$$

$$\text{Nonstudent group:} \quad \max_{q_2} \pi_2 = (25 - q_2)q_2 - 3q_2.$$

- *Students.* For the students, we set $MR_1 = MC$, or $16 - 2q_1 = 3$, which yields an output level of $q_1 = 6.5$ units, selling them at a price of $p_1 = 16 - 6.5 = \$9.5$. Relative to example 11.3, we can see that the increase in demand increased the quantity and price of the tickets offered to the student group.

- *Nonstudents.* The nonstudent group has the same demand function and costs as in example 11.3, where we found that it was optimal to sell $q_2 = 11$ units at a price of $p_2 = \$14$ per unit.

- Total profit is then calculated as follows

$$\pi = \underbrace{(9.5 - 3) \times 6.5}_{\pi_1} + \underbrace{(14 - 3) \times 11}_{\pi_2} = 42.25 + 121 = \$163.25.$$

Therefore, the increase in student demand also helped the monopolist increase its profit.

Self-assessment exercise #11.4

SA 11.4 Consider the bundling table in example 11.4. Assume now that the average cost of the CPU decreases to \$300. Follow the steps in example 11.4 to find under which conditions the firm chooses to sell different items to each consumer. Compare your results against those in example 11.4.

- *No bundling.* In this case, the firm sells the CPU at either \$500 or \$500α. If the firm sells at the lower price \$500α, then both types of consumers will buy the CPU, earning profits of

$$(2 \times 500\alpha) - (2 \times 300) = 1,000\alpha - 600.$$

If the firm, instead, chooses to set the price equal to consumer 1's WTP for the CPU, $500, its profits are only $500 - 300 = 200$. The firm will choose to entice both consumers only if $1,000\alpha - 600 > 200$, or, solving for α, if $\alpha > 0.8$. This is a less restrictive condition than that needed in example 11.4 because the lower cost increases the potential profit margin when selling the CPU to both types of consumers.

Because the cost and WTP for the monitor did not change, the analysis is the same as that in example 11.4. Therefore, the firm will chose to sell to both consumers if $\beta > 0.9$.

- *Bundling.* With pure bundling, the firm sets a single price for the "combo" of CPU and monitor. The firm has two pricing options to contemplate. First, it can set a price equal to consumer 1's WTP, $500 + 100\beta$, and only entice her, which generates a profit of

$$(500 + 100\beta) - 380 = 120 + 100\beta.$$

Or, the firm can set a price equal to consumer 2's WTP (the lower of the two), inducing both consumers to purchase the computer, yielding profits of

$$2 \times (500\alpha + 100) - (2 \times 380) = 1,000\alpha - 560.$$

Therefore, the firm entices both consumers if $1,000\alpha - 560 > 120 + 100\beta$, or, after solving for α, if $\alpha > 0.68 + 0.1\beta$ (let $\bar{\alpha} = 0.68 + 0.1\beta$ for compactness). Figure 11.1 depicts parameter α in the vertical axis, and parameter β in the horizontal axis, which divides the positive quadrant in Regions I-VI; as in figure 11.3 in the textbook. Relative to that figure, we can identify two changes:

- (1) the horizontal line dividing Regions II and IV (and Regions I and III) shifts down to $\alpha = 0.8$ rather than $\alpha = 0.9$; and
- (2) the diagonal line dividing Regions IV and VI (and Regions III and V), shifts down to $\alpha = 0.68 + 0.1\beta$, which has the same slope as the line depicted in figure 11.3 in the textbook.

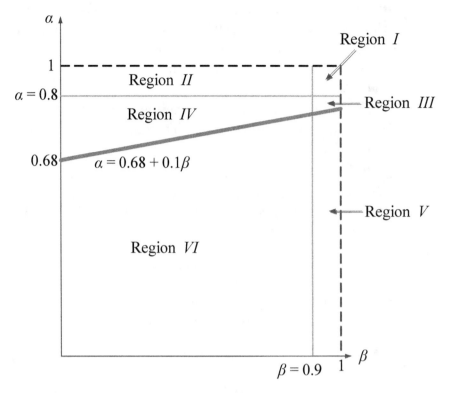

Figure 11.1. Bundling decisions.

Region I. If $\alpha > 0.8$ and $\beta > 0.9$, condition $\alpha > \bar{\alpha}$ holds. In this setting, the firm prefers to sell the CPU, the monitor, and the bundle to both consumers. The firm prefers to sell the bundle rather than their separated items (no bundling) since

$$\underbrace{1,000\alpha - 560}_{\text{Profits from the bundle}} > \underbrace{(1,000\alpha - 600)}_{\text{Profits from the CPU}} + \underbrace{(200\beta - 160)}_{\text{Profits from the monitor}},$$

simplifies to $40 > 200\beta - 160$, or $\beta < 1$; which holds by assumption.

Region II. If $\alpha > 0.8$ but $\beta < 0.9$, condition $\alpha > \bar{\alpha}$ still holds. However, the firm now sells the CPU and the bundle to both customers, and the monitor to customer 2 alone. In this context, the firm offers bundling given that

$$\underbrace{1,000\alpha - 560}_{\text{Profits from the bundle}} > \underbrace{(1,000\alpha - 600)}_{\text{Profits from the CPU}} + \underbrace{20}_{\text{Profits from the monitor}},$$

collapses $-560 > -580$, which is true.

Region III. If $\alpha < 0.8$, $\beta > 0.9$, and $\alpha > \bar{\alpha}$, the firm sells the monitor and bundle to both customers, but the CPU to customer 1 alone. The firm offers bundling if

$$\underbrace{1,000\alpha - 560}_{\text{Profits from the bundle}} > \underbrace{200}_{\text{Profits from the CPU}} + \underbrace{(200\beta - 160)}_{\text{Profits from the monitor}},$$

which yields $1,000\alpha > 600 + 200\beta$, or $\alpha > 0.6 + 0.2\beta$. Figure 11.2 depicts line $\alpha = 0.6 + 0.2\beta$, which originates at 0.6 and reaches a maximum height of 0.8 when

228

$\beta = 1$. This implies that it crosses cutoff $\bar{\alpha}$ at $0.6 + 0.2\beta = 0.68 + 0.1\beta$, or $\beta = 0.8$ (distanced from the left-hand boundary of Region III), thus dividing Region III into two areas: one where condition $\alpha > 0.6 + 0.2\beta$ holds, and the firm offers the bundle; and another where this inequality does not hold, leading the firm to sell the two items separately.

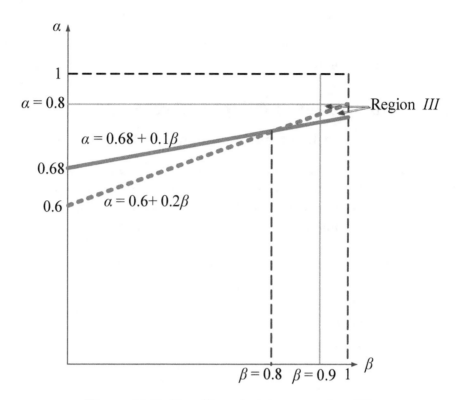

Figure 11.2. Bundling decisions - region III.

Region IV. If $\alpha < 0.8$, $\beta < 0.9$, and $\alpha > \bar{\alpha}$, the firm sells the bundle to both customers, the CPU to customer 1 alone and the monitor to customer 2 alone. The firm offers bundling in this region too given that

$$\underbrace{1,000\alpha - 560}_{\text{Profits from the bundle}} > \underbrace{200}_{\text{Profits from the CPU}} + \underbrace{20}_{\text{Profits from the monitor}},$$

which yields $1,000\alpha > 780$, or $\alpha > 0.78$. Since condition $\alpha > \bar{\alpha}$ is satisfied in this region, and cutoff $\bar{\alpha}$ reaches its highest point at 0.78, condition $\alpha > 0.78$ must hold too.

Region V. If $\alpha < 0.8$, $\beta > 0.9$, and $\alpha < \bar{\alpha}$, the firm sells the monitor to both customers, the CPU to customer 1 alone and the bundle to customer 1 alone. In this setting, the firm does not offer bundling since

$$\underbrace{120 + 100\beta}_{\text{Profits from the bundle}} < \underbrace{200}_{\text{Profits from the CPU}} + \underbrace{(200\beta - 160)}_{\text{Profits from the monitor}},$$

which simplifies to $80 < 100\beta$, or $0.8 < \beta$, which holds in this region. Therefore, the firm does not offer bundling in Region V.

Region VI. If $\alpha < 0.8$, $\beta < 0.9$, and $\alpha < \bar{\alpha}$, the firm sells the CPU to customer 1 alone, the monitor to customer 2 alone, and the bundle to customer 1 alone. In this context, offering bundling is not profitable given that

$$\underbrace{120 + 100\beta}_{\text{Profits from the bundle}} \quad < \quad \underbrace{200}_{\text{Profits from the CPU}} \quad + \quad \underbrace{20}_{\text{Profits from the monitor}},$$

which collapses to $100\beta < 100$, or $\beta < 1$, which holds by assumption (negatively correlated demands).

11.2 Solutions to End-of-Chapter Exercises

Exercise #11.1 - Price Discrimination with Different Demands[B]

11.1 Consider a monopolist selling to two markets. Every market faces a different demand function, which the monopolist can observe, and the monopolist can charge different prices in each market, thus practicing third-degree price discrimination. For simplicity, assume that marginal cost is $c > 0$ in both markets.

(a) *Linear demand.* Consider that the inverse demand in each market i is given by $p_i(q_i) = a_i - b_i q_i$, where $i = \{1, 2\}$. Find the profit-maximizing price and quantity in each market. Under which conditions on the parameters (a_i, b_i, and c) does the monopolist charge the same price in both markets?

- We can write the monopolist's problem as two separate problems, each looking like

$$\max_{q_i} \ \pi = (a_i - b_i q_i)q_i - cq_i.$$

Differentiating with respect to output q_i we find that

$$a_i - 2b_i q_i - c = 0,$$

and solving for q_i, we find the quantity the firm sells in each market

$$q_i = \frac{a_i - c}{2b_i}.$$

- Inserting this output in the inverse demand function of market i, yields a price in this market of

$$
\begin{aligned}
p_i &= a_i - b_i \overbrace{\frac{a_i - c}{2b_i}}^{q_i} \\
&= \frac{2a_i b_i - a_i b_i + b_i c}{2b_i} = \frac{b_i(a + c)}{2b_i} \\
&= \frac{a_i + c}{2}.
\end{aligned}
$$

230

Prices in each market coincide if

$$\frac{a_1 + c}{2} = \frac{a_2 + c}{2},$$

which can only occur if $a_1 = a_2$. This means the monopolist only charges the same price in each market if the vertical intercept of the demand function is the same for both markets.

(b) *Constant elasticity of substitution (CES) demand.* Consider now that the direct demand in each market i is given by $q_i(p_i) = A_i p_i^{-b_i}$, where $i = \{1, 2\}$. (Recall that the exponent $-b_i$ indicates the elasticity of substitution, which is just a number, and thus is constant in q_i.) Find the profit-maximizing price and quantity in each market. Under which conditions on parameters (A_i, b_i, and c) does the monopolist charge the same price in both markets?

- Here, we can use the inverse elasticity pricing rule (IEPR, from chapter 10) to find the price the monopolist charges. The IEPR in market i is

$$p = \frac{MC}{1 + \frac{1}{\varepsilon_{q,p}}} = \frac{c}{1 + \frac{1}{-b_i}} = \frac{c}{\frac{b_i - 1}{b_i}} = \frac{b_i c}{b_i - 1},$$

Setting the price in each market equal to each other, we find

$$\frac{b_1 c}{b_1 - 1} = \frac{b_2 c}{b_2 - 1},$$

or

$$\frac{b_1}{b_1 - 1} = \frac{b_2}{b_2 - 1},$$

cross multiplying, we obtain

$$b_1(b_2 - 1) = b_2(b_1 - 1),$$

which, rearranging, yields

$$b_1 b_2 - b_1 = b_2 b_1 - b_2,$$

which simplifies to $b_1 = b_2$. Therefore, prices in each market coincide when both markets have the same price elasticity.

Exercise #11.3 - Implementing Price Discrimination[A]

11.3 Describe how the following firms could implement price discrimination. Be specific about the degree, which markets/consumers are charged higher or lower prices, and what barriers they may face.

(a) Restaurants

- Restaurants generally price discriminate through different discounts given to seniors, students, military, etc. This would be an example of third-degree price discrimination. To get the discount, you need to prove you meet the criteria, usually by showing your ID. Arbitrage is not usually possible as the meals are eaten in the restaurant and discounts may not be honored for delivery or take-out.

(b) Airlines

- Airlines practice third degree price discrimination by charging a different price for the same seat depending on a number of factors, including how you book the seat, the time you purchase the seat (how close to departure your are), and so on. Airline seats cannot usually be resold as they are nominative and require identification.

(c) Cable providers

- Cable providers generally employ bundling of their services, which may include cable television, internet, and phone service. Though you may share your Wi-Fi password with your neighbor, arbitrage is not generally possible as you cannot resell your cable services to someone else.

(d) Wheat growers

- Wheat growers may not be able to price discriminate, as many are in a perfectly competitive market and have no market power to change prices. Arbitrage is also difficult to prevent in this market.

Exercise #11.5 - When to Price Discriminate[B]

11.5 Consider a monopolist selling to two markets, each with a different demand: (high) $p_H = a_H - b_H q_H$, and (low) $p_L = a_L - b_L q_L$, where $a_H > a_L$ and $b_H \leqslant b_L$, so that demand is greater in the high market for any price. The firm practices third-degree price discrimination and has a constant marginal cost $MC = c > 0$. Is there a level of cost where the monopolist chooses not to sell to the low market?

- Under third-degree price discrimination, the monopolist treats each market as separate monopoly problems. We analyze each market below.
- *Low-demand market.* The monopolist's profit-maximization problem in that market is

$$\max_{q_L} \quad \pi = (a_L - b_L q_L)q_L - cq_L.$$

Differentiating with respect to q_L, we get that

$$a_L - 2b_L q_L - c = 0,$$

and solving for q_L we find that

$$q_L = \frac{a_L - c}{2b_L} \text{ units.}$$

Plugging this output into the market's inverse demand, we find the price in this market; that is,

$$p_L = a_L - b_L \frac{a_L - c}{2b_L} = \frac{a_L + c}{2}.$$

Profit in this market is

$$\pi_L = \frac{a_L + c}{2} \frac{a_L - c}{2b_L} - c \frac{a_L - c}{2b_L} = \frac{(a_L - c)^2}{4b_L}.$$

This is positive only if $a_L - c > 0$, or $a_L > c$. That is, it is only profitable to sell in the low market if the intercept of the demand curve lies above marginal cost, and there are consumers that purchase the good above marginal cost.

- *High-demand market.* The monopolist's profit-maximization problem in this market is

$$\max_{q_H} \quad \pi = (a_H - b_H q_H)q_H - cq_H.$$

Differentiating with respect to q_H, we get that

$$a_H - 2b_H q_H - c = 0,$$

and solving for q_H we find that $q_H = \frac{a_H - c}{2b_H}$ units. Plugging this output into the market's inverse demand, we find the price in this market; that is,

$$p_H = a_H - b_H \frac{a_H - c}{2b_H} = \frac{a_H + c}{2}.$$

Profit in this market is

$$\pi_H = \frac{a_H + c}{2} \frac{a_H - c}{2b_H} - c \frac{a_H - c}{2b_H} = \frac{(a_H - c)^2}{4b_H}.$$

Therefore, the monopolist sells to:

- Both markets if $a_H \geq c$ and $a_L \geq c$. Since $a_H > a_L$ by assumption, then we only need the second condition, $a_L \geq c$, for the monopolist to sell to both markets.
- Only the high-demand market if $a_H \geq c \geq a_L$.
- No market if $a_H < c$.

- *Numerical example.* Let's assume that $a_H = 10$, $b_H = 1$, $a_L = 5$, $b_L = 2$, and $c = 1$. In this case, condition $a_L \geq c$ holds since $5 > 1$ implying that the monopolist sells to both the high-demand and low-demand markets. The price, quantity, and profit in the high-demand market are

$$q_H = \frac{a_H - c}{2b_H} = \frac{10 - 1}{2(1)} = 4.5 \text{ units}$$

$$p_H = \frac{a_H + c}{2} = \frac{10 + 1}{2} = \$5.5$$

$$\pi = \frac{(a_H - c)^2}{4b_H} = \frac{(10 - 1)^2}{4(1)} = \$20.25.$$

233

The price, quantity, and profit in the low-demand market are

$$q_L = \frac{a_L - c}{2b_L} = \frac{5 - 1}{2(2)} = 1 \text{ unit}$$

$$p_L = \frac{a_L + c}{2} = \frac{5 + 1}{2} = \$3$$

$$\pi = \frac{(a_L - c)^2}{4b_L} = \frac{(5 - 1)^2}{4(2)} = \$2.$$

Exercise #11.7 - Willingness to Price Discriminate[B]

11.7 An airline has been collecting data to estimate demand for flights between Greenville, South Carolina, and Seattle, for which it would be the only provider. It has estimated this demand to be $p = 1,000 - 2q$. The total cost (in dollars) of this flight is $TC(q) = 50,000 + 20q$.

(a) *Uniform pricing.* If the airline cannot discriminate, what price does it charge, how many tickets does it sell, and what is its profit?

- Here, the monopolist solves the following profit-maximization problem

$$\max_{q} \quad \pi = (1,000 - 2q)q - (50,000 + 20q).$$

Differentiating with respect to q, we find that

$$1,000 - 4q - 20 = 0.$$

Solving for q, we obtain

$$q = \frac{980}{4} = 245 \text{ tickets.}$$

Plugging this output into the inverse demand, we get a price of

$$p = 1,000 - 2(245) = \$510.$$

Monopoly profit under uniform pricing is then

$$\pi^U = 510(245) - [50,000 + 20(245)] = \$70,050.$$

(b) *First-degree price discrimination.* If the airline can do first-degree price discrimination (based on information it receives through its partners during online booking), how many tickets does it sell, and what is its profit?

- If the airline can practice first-degree price discrimination, it sells tickets to the point where demand is equal to marginal cost, $p(q) = MC$; that is,

$$1,000 - 2q = 20,$$

or $980 = 2q$. Solving for q, we find

$$q = 490 \text{ tickets.}$$

The firm charges a price equal to each consumer's willingness to pay and its profit is calculated as producer surplus net of fixed costs:

$$
\begin{aligned}
\pi^{1st} &= \frac{(a - c)^2}{2b} - FC \\
&= \frac{(1{,}000 - 20)^2}{2(2)} - 50{,}000. \\
&= \$190{,}100
\end{aligned}
$$

(c) *Information acquisition.* If the airline has to pay for the information on prices through its partner in order to practice first-degree price discrimination, how much are they willing to pay for that service?

- The airline pays for the information as long as its profit from first-degree price discrimination net of the information cost (IC) is greater than its profit under uniform pricing, $\pi^{1st} - IC > \pi^U$, or

$$190{,}100 - IC > 70{,}050,$$

which solving for IC yields $IC < 120{,}050$. Therefore, as long as the information cost is less than \$120,050, the monopolist purchases the information and price discriminates.

Exercise #11.9 - Deciding When to Withdraw from a Market[B]

11.9 Clarke's Crisp Croissants has a monopoly on the local market for breakfast pastries, which it makes at zero marginal cost. Demand in the local market is $q_L = 10 - p_L$. The firm also sells croissants in a neighboring town with demand $q_N = 5 - p_N$, where transportation costs are zero.

(a) *Uniform price.* If Clarke chooses to set a uniform price (i.e., the same price in all markets), what is the profit-maximizing price, quantity in each market, and total profit?

- To set a uniform price, we first need to find aggregate demand at a common price $p = p_L = p_N$:

$$Q = q_L + q_N = \underbrace{(10 - p)}_{q_L} + \underbrace{(5 - p)}_{q_N} = 15 - 2p.$$

The monopolist's profit-maximization problem is then

$$\max_{p} \pi = (15 - 2p)p,$$

since the firm produces pastries at no cost. Differentiating with respect to p,

we find
$$15 - 4p = 0,$$
rearranging, $4p = 15$, and solving for p, we find the uniform price set by the monopolist
$$p^U = \frac{15}{4}.$$

At this price, the monopolist locally sells $q_L = 10 - \frac{15}{4} = \frac{25}{4} = 6.25$ units, and $q_N = 5 - \frac{15}{4} = \frac{5}{4} = 1.25$ units to the neighboring town. Clarke's profit under uniform pricing is

$$\pi^U = p^U(q_L + q_N) = \frac{15}{4}\left(\frac{25}{4} + \frac{5}{4}\right) = \frac{225}{8} = \$28.13.$$

(b) *Third-degree price discrimination.* If Clarke employs third-degree price discrimination, what price does it set in each market? How much does the firm sell in each market? What is Clarke's total profit? Is it profitable for it to price discriminate?

- We can treat this situation as Clarke maximizing profit in each market separately.
- *Local Market.* In the local market, Clarke's profit-maximization problem is

$$\max_{p_L} \ \pi_L = (10 - p_L)p_L.$$

Differentiating with respect to p_L, we find

$$10 - 2p_L = 0,$$

rearranging, $2p_L = 10$, and solving for p_L, we find the price Clarke sells croissants at in the local market is

$$p_L = \$5.$$

Clarke will sell $q_L = 10 - 5 = 5$ units for a profit of $\pi_L = 5 \times 5 = \$25$.
- *Neighboring market.* Similarly, in the neighboring town, Clarke's profit-maximization problem is

$$\max_{p_N} \ \pi_N = (5 - p_N)p_N.$$

Differentiating with respect to p_N, we find

$$5 - 2p_N = 0,$$

rearranging, $2p_N = 5$, and solving for p_N, we find the price Clarke sells croissants at in the neighboring market is

$$p_N = \$2.5.$$

Clarke will sell $q_N = 5 - 2.5 = 2.5$ units for a profit of $\pi_N = 2.5 \times 2.5 = \$6.25$.

- *Total profits.* Clarke's total profit from practicing third-degree price discrimination is
$$\pi^{3rd} = \pi_L + \pi_N = 25 + 6.25 = \$31.25.$$

This is an increase in profit over the uniform price, which only yields a profit of \$28.13.

(c) *Demand change.* If the neighboring town's demand falls to $q_N = 2.5 - p_N$, should the monopolist set a uniform price that ignores the neighboring market?

- *Uniform price.* We need to find the new aggregate demand in order to find the uniform price,

$$Q = \underbrace{(10 - p)}_{q_L} + \underbrace{(2.5 - p)}_{q_N} = 12.5 - 2p.$$

The firm's profit-maximization problem is

$$\max_p \ \pi = (12.5 - 2p)p.$$

Differentiating with respect to p, we find

$$12.5 - 4p = 0,$$

rearranging, $4p = 12.5$, and solving for p, we find the uniform price set by the monopolist

$$p^U = \$3.13.$$

At this price, the monopolist locally sells $q_L = 10 - 3.13 = 6.87$ units, and $q_N = 2.5 - 3.13 = -0.63 < 0$. Therefore, no units will be sold in the neighboring town, $q_N = 0$ units. Clarke's profit from charging a uniform price is

$$\pi^U = p^U(q_L + q_N) = 3.13(6.87 + 0) = \$21.5.$$

- *Only selling to the local market.* If Clarke only sells to the local market, he sets a price of \$5 and profit is \$25 (see part (b) of the exercise). This profit is higher than charging a uniform price $p^U = \$3.13$ and selling positive units only to the local market ($\pi^U = \$21.5$). Intuitively, under uniform pricing, the monopolist, in an attempt to sell to both markets (one with a small demand), ends up not even selling in one of the markets and fails to maximize its profit from the market with the larger demand. That is why, in equilibrium, it is profitable for the monopolist to ignore the low-demand market.

Exercise #11.11 - Second-Degree Price Discrimination[A]

11.11 Some local water companies offer a discount to customers who use large quantities of water. Consider a local water utility that faces the inverse demand $p(q) = 100 - 10q$. If the water utility has a marginal cost of \$0.5 per unit of water, find the price and quantity the water utility sells if it practices price discrimination with two blocks, q_1 and $q_2 - q_1$.

- The water utility's profit-maximization problem is

$$\max_{q_1, q_2} \pi = \underbrace{(100 - 10q_1)q_1}_{TR \text{ from first block}} + \underbrace{(100 - 10q_2)(q_2 - q_1)}_{TR \text{ from second block}} - \underbrace{0.5q_2}_{TC}.$$

Differentiating with respect to q_1, we obtain

$$\frac{\partial \pi}{\partial q_1} = 100 - 20q_1 - (100 - 10q_2) = -20q_1 + 10q_2 = 0,$$

which yields $q_1 = \frac{q_2}{2}$. Differentiating the above profits with respect to q_2, we find

$$\frac{\partial \pi}{\partial q_2} = 100 - 20q_2 + 10q_1 - 0.5 = 0.$$

Inserting $q_1 = \frac{q_2}{2}$ into the last expression, we obtain

$$100 - 20q_2 + 10 \underbrace{\frac{q_2}{2}}_{q_1} - 0.5 = 100 - 0.5 - \left(20 - \frac{10}{2}\right) q_2 = 0,$$

which simplifies to $99.5 = 15q_2$. Solving for q_2, yields

$$q_2^* = \frac{99.5}{15} = 6.63 \text{ units.}$$

We can now find q_1 by plugging this output into the equation we found above, $q_1 = \frac{q_2}{2}$, obtaining

$$q_1 = \frac{6.63}{2} = 3.32 \text{ units.}$$

The water utility will sell 3.32 units in each block since $q_1 = 3.32$ units in the first block and $q_2 - q_1 = 6.63 - 3.32 = 3.32$ units in the second block. The price the utility charges in the first block is

$$p_1 = 100 - 10q_1 = 100 - 10(3.32) = \$66.8.$$

In the second block, the monopolist charges

$$p_2 = 100 - 10(6.63) = \$33.7.$$

We can see that the water utility charges the high-use (second-block) customers a price half that of the lower-use (first-block) customers.

- *Total profit.* The total profit the firm makes is

$$\pi = \underbrace{(66.8)3.32}_{TR \text{ from first block}} + \underbrace{(33.7)3.32}_{TR \text{ from second block}} - \underbrace{0.5(6.63)}_{TC} = \$330.35.$$

Exercise #11.13 - Second-Degree Price Discrimination with Three Blocks[C]

11.13 Consider the demand function from example 11.2, $p(q) = 10 - q$, and marginal cost $c = 4$. Consider now that the monopolist wants to add a third block of discounts, $q_3 - q_2$. Set up and solve the monopolist's problem in this case. Compare your answer to the results found in example 11.2, with two blocks.

- The monopolist's problem is now

$$\max_{q_1, q_2, q_3} \quad \pi = \underbrace{(10 - q_1)q_1}_{TR \text{ Block 1}} + \underbrace{(10 - q_2)(q_2 - q_1)}_{TR \text{ Block 2}} + \underbrace{(10 - q_3)(q_3 - q_2)}_{TR \text{ Block 3}} - \underbrace{4q_3}_{TC} \, .$$

Differentiating with respect to q_1, q_2, and q_3, we obtain

$$\frac{\partial \pi}{\partial q_1} = 10 - 2q_1 - (10 - q_2) = -2q_1 + q_2 = 0$$

$$\frac{\partial \pi}{\partial q_2} = 10 - 2q_2 + q_1 - (10 - q_3) = -2q_2 + q_1 + q_3 = 0$$

$$\frac{\partial \pi}{\partial q_3} = 10 - 2q_3 + q_2 - 4 = 0.$$

The first of the three equations yields $q_1 = \frac{q_2}{2}$. Plugging this result into the second equation, we obtain

$$-2q_2 + \underbrace{\frac{q_2}{2}}_{q_1} + q_3 = 0,$$

simplifying, we have that $q_2 = \frac{2}{3}q_3$. Inserting this result into the third equation, we solve for q_3:

$$10 - 2q_3 + \underbrace{\frac{2}{3}q_3}_{q_2} - 4 = 0,$$

simplifying to $\frac{4}{3}q_3 = 6$. Solving for q_3 yields

$$q_3 = 6\frac{3}{4} = 4.5 \text{ units.}$$

This means that

$$q_2 = \frac{2}{3}q_3 = \frac{2}{3}4.5 = 3 \text{ units,}$$

and

$$q_1 = \frac{q_2}{3} = \frac{3}{2} = 1.5 \text{ units.}$$

Therefore, each block is 1.5 units since $q_1 = 1.5$ units, $q_2 - q_1 = 3 - 1.5 = 1.5$ units, and $q_3 - q_2 = 4.5 - 3 = 1.5$ units.

- Using inverse demand curve $p(q) = 10 - q$, we can now find the price that the firm charges in each block. The price of the first block is $p_1 = 10 - 1.5 = \$8.5$, the price in the second block is $p_2 = 10 - 3 = \$7$, and in the third block $p_3 = 10 - 4.5 = \$5.5$.

Total profit is

$$\pi = 8.5(1.5) + 7(1.5) + 5.5(1.5) - 4(4.5) = \$13.5.$$

- *Adding a third block.* With the extra (third) block, the monopolist has slightly smaller blocks (1.5 units in each block rather than 2 units), but sells more units overall (4.5 rather than 4 units) and makes a greater profit ($13 rather than $12). If we continue to add blocks, we eventually reach a point where each block contains a single consumer and our results converge to first-degree price discrimination.

Exercise #11.15 - Bundling Prices[A]

11.15 A fast-food restaurant faces two types of consumers and is deciding on a bundling strategy. The table here reports each consumer's WTP for hamburgers, french fries, and the bundle of both items, as well as the average cost of each good.

	Hamburger	French Fries	Both items (bundle)
Consumer 1	$3	$4	$7
Consumer 2	$5	$2.5	$7.5
Average cost	$2	$2	$4

(a) What prices should the restaurant set for each food item if it sells the items separately? What is its profit in each scenario?

- *Hamburger.* If the restaurant sells the hamburger at $3, both consumer purchase the hamburger and the restaurant earns a profit of $(2 \times 3) - (2 \times 2) = \$2$. If it sets a price equal to $5, consumer 2's WTP, it will earn a profit of $3. Since this strategy maximizes the restaurant's profit, it will only sell the hamburger to consumer 2.

- *French fries.* Here, the restaurant sets a price equal to the highest WTP, $4, sells to consumer 1 and earns a profit of $2. If instead it sells french fries to both consumers, at a maximum price of $2.5, its profit becomes

$$(2 \times \$2.5) - (2 \times \$2) = \$1,$$

which is lower than the profit from selling them only to consumer 1 ($4).

(b) What prices should the restaurant set if it sells the bundle "meal" of a hamburger and french fries?

- *Bundle.* If the restaurant sets a price of $7 for the bundle, it sells to both consumers for a profit of

$$(2 \times \$7) - (2 \times \$4) = \$6.$$

If the restaurant sets the price equal to consumer 2's WTP, it only sells to that consumer for a profit of

$$(1 \times \$7.5) - (1 \times \$4) = \$3.5.$$

240

- *Pricing strategy.* The restaurant sells the bundle of hamburgers and french fries at $7 and sells to both consumers for their highest profit of $6.

(c) How do your answers change if the restaurant's cost of beef increases so that the marginal cost of hamburgers increases to $4?

  - *Separate pricing.* The restaurant will only offer the hamburger to consumer 2 at a price of $5 for a profit of $1, as it is no longer profitable to sell the hamburger at a price that consumer 1 is willing to pay. The pricing of the french fries is unchanged.

  - *Bundling.* The average cost of the bundle is now $6. However, the bundling strategy is unchanged as the restaurant makes the highest profit by selling the bundle at a price of $7 for a profit of $2.

  - *Pricing strategy.* With the increased cost of the hamburger, it is no longer profitable for the firm to offer the bundle. The optimal strategy for the restaurant is to sell the hamburger and french fries separately to both consumers, for a total profit of

$$\underbrace{[(3-4)+(4-2)]}_{\text{Consumer 1}} + \underbrace{[(5-4)+(2.5-2)]}_{\text{Consumer 2}} = \$2.5,$$

which is higher than the bundling profit of $2.

Exercise #11.17 - Bundling-II^B

11.17 TV-Net, a local cable TV and internet provider, is deciding on a bundling strategy. This table reports the WTP for TV alone, internet alone, and the bundle for each customer, as well as the average cost.

	TV	Internet	Both Items (bundle)
Consumer 1	60	50β	$60 + 50\beta$
Consumer 2	60α	50	$60\alpha + 50$
Average cost	10	20	30

where $\alpha, \beta \in (0, 1)$. For simplicity, assume that customer 1 has the highest WTP for the bundle of both goods. Repeat the analysis from example 11.4 to show when the firm should prefer to bundle, sell the items separately, or choose a mixed-bundling strategy.

- *No bundling.* In this case, the firm sells TV at either $60 or 60α. If the firm sells at the lower price 60α, then both types of consumers buy TV, earning profits of

$$(2 \times 60\alpha) - (2 \times 10) = 120\alpha - 20.$$

If the firm, instead, chooses to set the price equal to consumer 1's WTP for TV, $60, its profits are only $60 - 10 = 50$. The firm chooses to entice both consumers only if

$$120\alpha - 20 > 50,$$

241

or, solving for α, if $\alpha > \frac{70}{120} = 0.58$.

The firm sells internet at either \$50 or \$50β. If the firm sells at the lower price \$50β, then both types of consumers buy internet, earning profits of

$$(2 \times 50\beta) - (2 \times 20) = 100\beta - 40.$$

If the firm, instead, chooses to set the price equal to consumer 2's WTP for internet, \$50, its profits are only $50 - 20 = 30$. The firm chooses to entice both consumers only if

$$100\beta - 40 > 30,$$

or, solving for β, if $\beta > \frac{70}{100} = 0.7$.

- *Bundling.* With pure bundling, the firm sets a single price for the "combo" of TV and internet. The firm has two pricing options to contemplate. First, it can set a price equal to consumer 1's WTP, $60 + 50\beta$, and only entice her, which generates a profit of

$$(60 + 50\beta) - 30 = 30 + 50\beta.$$

Or, the firm can set a price equal to consumer 2's WTP (the lower of the two), inducing both consumers to purchase the computer, yielding profits of

$$2 \times (60\alpha + 50) - (2 \times 30) = 120\alpha + 40.$$

Therefore, the firm entices both consumers if $120\alpha + 40 > 30 + 50\beta$, or, after solving for α, if $\alpha > \frac{-10+50\beta}{120} = -0.08 + 0.42\beta$ (let $\bar{\alpha} = -0.08 + 0.42\beta$ for compactness). Figure 11.3 depicts parameter α in the vertical axis, and parameter β in the horizontal axis, which divides the positive quadrant in Regions I-VI. For compactness, the figure denotes these regions as RI-RVI. The upward diagonal line depicts cutoff $\bar{\alpha}$.

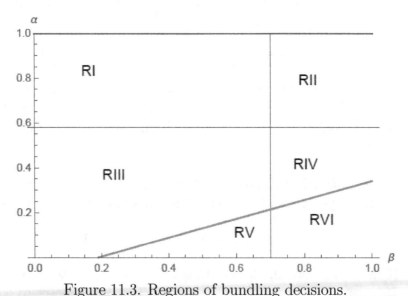

Figure 11.3. Regions of bundling decisions.

Region I (RI). If $\alpha > \bar{\alpha}$ and $\beta < 0.7$, then $\alpha > 0.58$ condition holds. In this setting, the firm prefers to sell TV and the bundle to both consumers, but the internet only to consumer 2. The firm prefers to sell the bundle since

$$\underbrace{120\alpha + 40}_{\text{Profits from the bundle}} > \underbrace{(120\alpha - 20)}_{\text{Profits from TV}} + \underbrace{30}_{\text{Profits from internet}},$$

simplifies to $40 > 10$.

Region II (RII). If $\alpha > 0.58$ and $\alpha > \bar{\alpha}$, then $\beta > 0.7$. The firm now sells TV, internet, and the bundle to both customers. In this context, the firm offers bundling given that

$$\underbrace{120\alpha + 40}_{\text{Profits from the bundle}} > \underbrace{(120\alpha - 20)}_{\text{Profits from TV}} + \underbrace{100\beta - 40}_{\text{Profits from internet}}$$

collapses to $40 > 100\beta - 60$, or $1 > \beta$, which is true.

Region III (RIII). If $\alpha < 0.58$, $\beta < 0.7$, but $\alpha > \bar{\alpha}$, the firm sells TV to customer 1, the internet to customer 2, and a bundle to both customers. The firm offers bundling if

$$\underbrace{120\alpha + 40}_{\text{Profits from the bundle}} > \underbrace{50}_{\text{Profits from TV}} + \underbrace{30}_{\text{Profits from internet}},$$

which yields $120\alpha > 40$, or $\alpha > 0.33$. Since condition $\alpha > \bar{a}$ holds in this region, and cutoff $\bar{\alpha}$ reaches its highest point at 0.33, condition $\alpha > 0.33$ holds for all points of Region III.

Region IV (RIV). If $\alpha < 0.58$, $\beta > 0.7$, and $\alpha > \bar{\alpha}$, the firm sells the bundle and internet to both consumers, and the TV to consumer 1 alone. The firm offers bundling in this region given that

$$\underbrace{120\alpha + 40}_{\text{Profits from the bundle}} > \underbrace{50}_{\text{Profits from TV}} + \underbrace{100\beta - 40}_{\text{Profits from internet}},$$

which yields $120\alpha > 100\beta - 30$, or $\alpha > 0.25 + 0.83\beta$. Comparing this to condition $\alpha > \bar{\alpha}$, that is

$$\alpha > -0.25 + 0.83\beta > \underbrace{-0.08 + 0.42\beta}_{\bar{\alpha}},$$

or $0.17 < 0.41\beta$, which holds by assumption.

Region V (RV). If $\alpha < 0.58$, $\beta < 0.7$, and $\alpha < \bar{\alpha}$, the firm sells TV to consumer 1, internet to consumer 2, and the bundle to consumer 1. In this setting, the firm does not offer bundling since

$$\underbrace{30 + 50\beta}_{\text{Profits from the bundle}} < \underbrace{50}_{\text{Profits from TV}} + \underbrace{30}_{\text{Profits from internet}},$$

which simplifies to $\beta < 1$, which holds by assumption.

Region VI (RVI). If $\alpha < 0.58$, $\beta > 0.7$, and $\alpha < \bar{\alpha}$, the firm sells TV to consumer 1 alone, the internet to both, and the bundle to consumer 1 alone. In this context, offering bundling is profitable given that

$$\underbrace{30 + 50\beta}_{\text{Profits from the bundle}} > \underbrace{50}_{\text{Profits from TV}} + \underbrace{100\beta - 40,}_{\text{Profits from internet}}$$

which collapses to $\beta > -\frac{40}{50} = -0.8$, which holds in this region (recall that in Region VI, β satisfies $\beta > 0.7$).

- In summary, the firm bundles in regions I, II, III, IV, and VI, while electing not to bundle in region V.

Exercise #11.19 - Bundling-III[B]

11.19 TV-Net is deciding on a bundling strategy. This table reports the WTP for TV alone, internet alone, and the bundle for each customer, as well as the average cost.

	TV	Internet	Both items (bundle)
Consumer 1	60	40	100
Consumer 2	40	50	90
Consumer 3	25	60	85
Average cost	10	20	30

(a) If TV-Net only faces consumers 1 and 2, does it prefer to bundle, sell the items separately, or choose a mixed-bundling strategy?

- With full information about consumer's willingness to pay, we can directly compare the profit from each pricing strategy.
- *No bundling.* The firm can sell TV at either $60 or $40. If the firm sells at the lower price, then both consumers buy TV, and its profit is

$$(2 \times 40) - (2 \times 10) = \$60.$$

If the firm, instead, chooses to set the price equal to $60, it earns a profit of

$$\$60 - \$10 = \$50.$$

Therefore, the firm would prefer to set the price at $40 and sell to both consumers for a profit of $60.
The firm can sell internet at either $50 or $40. If the firm sells at the lower price, then both consumers buy internet, and its profit is

$$(2 \times 40) - (2 \times 20) = \$40.$$

If the firm, instead, chooses to set the price equal to $50, it only sells to consumer 2 and earn a profit of

$$\$50 - \$20 = \$30.$$

Therefore, the firm would prefer to set the price at $50 and sell to both customers.

- *Bundling.* TV-Net could offer bundles of both TV and internet for either $100 or $90. If it offers the bundle at $100, it entices only consumer 1 and earns a profit of
$$\$100 - \$30 = \$70.$$

If it offers the bundle at $90, it sells to both consumers and earns profit

$$(2 \times 90) - (2 \times 30) = \$120.$$

Therefore, the firm would price the bundle at $90 and entice both consumers to purchase the bundle.

- *Mixed bundling.* If the firm offers mixed bundling, it could offer the bundle at $100 to consumer 1 for profit $70 and then entice consumer 2 to purchase internet at $50, for an additional profit of $30. This strategy would have a profit of
$$\$70 + \$30 = \$100.$$

- *Comparing profit.* We know the firm's best option in each case; that is,
  - TV: offer to both at $40 for profit $60
  - Internet: offer to both at $40 for profit $40
  - Bundle: offer bundle to both at $90 for profit $120
  - Mixed Bundle: offer bundle to consumer 1 at $100 and internet to consumer 2 for profit $100

Therefore, the firm could offer the TV and internet separately for a total profit of $100, but it would rather offer the bundle at $90 for a profit of $120.

(b) If TV-Net faces all three consumers, does it prefer to bundle, sell the items separately, or choose a mixed-bundling strategy?

- *No bundling.* The firm can sell TV at either $60, $40, or $25. If the firm sells at the lowest price, then all three consumers buy TV, and its profit is

$$(3 \times 25) - (3 \times 10) = \$45.$$

If the firm offers a price of $40, then consumers 1 and 2 buy and its profit is

$$(2 \times 40) - (2 \times 10) = \$60.$$

If the firm, instead, chooses to set the price equal to $60, it earns a profit of

$$\$60 - \$10 = \$50.$$

Therefore, the firm would prefer to price at $40 and sell to consumers 1 and 2 for a profit of $60.
The firm can sell internet at either $60, $50, or $40. If the firm sells at the lowest price, then all consumers buy internet, and its profit is

$$(3 \times 40) - (3 \times 20) = \$60.$$

If the firm, instead, chooses to set the price equal to $50, it only sells to consumers 2 and 3 and earns a profit of

$$(2 \times 50) - (2 \times 20) = \$60.$$

Finally, the firm could set the price equal to $60 and sell to only consumer 3 for a profit of

$$\$60 - \$10 = \$50.$$

Therefore, the firm is indifferent between setting the price at $40 or $50.

- *Bundling.* TV-Net could offer bundles of both TV and internet for either $100, $90, or $85. If it offers the bundle at $100, it entices only consumer 1 and earns a profit of

$$\$100 - \$30 = \$70.$$

If it offers the bundle at $90, it sells to consumers 1 and 2 and earns a profit

$$(2 \times 90) - (2 \times 30) = \$120.$$

The firm could offer the bundle at $85 and sell to all three consumers for a profit of

$$(3 \times 85) - (3 \times 30) = \$165.$$

Therefore, the firm would price the bundle at $85 and entice all consumers to purchase the bundle for a profit of $165.

- *Mixed bundle.* The firm has two options here. It can offer the bundle at $90 to consumer 1 and 2 for a profit of $120 and internet to consumer 3 at $60 for an additional $40 profit. This would be a total profit of $160.
The firm could also offer the bundle to consumer 1 at $100 for a profit of $70. Then it could offer internet at $50 for an additional profit of $60. This would be a total profit of $130.
Of the two mixed-bundle options, the firm would opt for the first, to offer the bundle at $90 to consumer 1 and 2 and internet to consumer 3 at $60 for a total profit of $160.

- *Comparing profit.* We know the firm's best option in each case; that is,

  - TV: offer to consumer 1 and 2 at $40 for a profit of $60
  - Internet: either offer to consumer 2 and 3 at $40 or all three at $50 for a profit of $60
  - Bundle: offer bundle to all three at $90 for a profit of $165
  - Mixed-Bundle: offer the bundle at $90 to consumer 1 and 2 and internet to consumer 3 at $60 for a total profit of $160

Therefore, the firm could offer the TV and internet separately for a total profit of $120, but it would rather offer the bundle at $85 for a profit of $165.

Chapter 12 - Simultaneous-Move Games

12.1 Solutions to Self-Assessment Exercises

Self-assessment exercise #12.1

SA 12.1 Consider Matrix 12.2a again, but assume that the payoff when firms choose technology (B, b), in the lower-right cell of the matrix, is $(3, 3)$, indicating that both firms receive a payoff of \$3, rather than the payoff of \$1 obtained in Matrix 12.2a. Follow the steps in example 12.1 to find if either firm has a dominant strategy. Interpret.

- We can update Matrix 12.2a from the textbook in order to better view the new payoffs associated with each firm's actions to obtain Matrix 12.1.

	Firm 2	
	Tech a	Tech b
Firm 1 Tech A	$5, 5$	$2, 0$
Tech B	$3, 2$	$3, 3$

Matrix 12.1. Technology choice game-III.

In this new situation, neither Tech A nor Tech B strictly dominate one another:

- *Finding dominant strategies for Firm 1.* When Firm 2 chooses a in the left column of Matrix 12.1, Firm 1 prefers Tech A (since $5 > 3$), but when Firm 2 chooses b in the right column, Firm 1 now prefers Tech B (since $3 > 2$).
- *Finding dominant strategies for Firm 2.* Likewise for Firm 2, neither Tech a nor Tech b strictly dominate one another. When Firm 1 chooses A in the top row, Firm 2 prefers Tech a (since $5 > 0$), but when firm 1 chooses B in the bottom row, Firm 2 prefers Tech b (since $3 > 2$).

- Without a dominant strategy for either player, we cannot delete any dominated strategies, and our most precise equilibrium prediction is the game as a whole (all four cells in Matrix 12.1).

Self-assessment exercise #12.2

SA 12.2 Consider Matrix 12.3 again, but assume that the payoff that firms obtain from (High, Medium) is $(3, 4)$ rather than $(1, 4)$ in the top row of the matrix. Which strategy profiles survive IDSDS? Compare your results against those in example 12.2.

- We can update Matrix 12.3 from the textbook in order to analyze how these payoffs affect the outcome of our game to obtain Matrix 12.2.

		Firm 2		
		High	Medium	Low
	High	2, 3	3, 4	3, 2
Firm 1	Medium	5, 1	2, 3	1, 2
	Low	3, 7	4, 6	5, 4

Matrix 12.2. When IDSDS yields more than one equilibrium-IV.

- *First round of deletion of strictly dominated strategies.* For Firm 1 in this setting, High is still strictly dominated by Low. To see this, we can observe that when Firm 2 chooses High, Firm 1 prefers Low to High (since $3 > 2$); when Firm 2 chooses Medium, Firm 1 prefers Low to High (since $4 > 3$); and when Firm 2 chooses Low, Firm 1 still prefers Low to High (since $5 > 3$). Thus, for every possible strategy of Firm 2, Firm 1 prefers Low over High and we can delete the strategy High from Matrix 12.2 (top row), leaving us with Matrix 12.3.

		Firm 2		
		High	Medium	Low
Firm 1	Medium	5, 1	2, 3	1, 2
	Low	3, 7	4, 6	5, 4

Matrix 12.3. When IDSDS yields more than one equilibrium-V.

- *Second round of deletion of strictly dominated strategies.* At this point, Matrix 12.3 is identical to Matrix 12.4 in the textbook, which implies that following the same steps in example 12.2, we arrive at exactly the same solution as before.

- *Comparison.* Intuitively, even though picking High became more attractive in this version of the game compared to the one presented in example 12.2, Firm 1's payoff was not increased enough to overcome the strict dominance that Low has over High. Thus, we reach the same outcome as in example 12.2.

Self-assessment exercise #12.3

SA 12.3 Consider Matrix 12.6 again, but assume that the payoff from both players choosing the same action (i.e., their payoff from (Heads, Heads) or their payoff from (Tails, Tails)), is $(0, 0)$ rather than $(1, -1)$. Which strategy profiles survive IDSDS? Compare your results against those in example 12.3.

- We can update Matrix 12.6 from the textbook in order to analyze this new version of the game to obtain Matrix 12.4.

		Player 2	
		Heads	Tails
Player 1	Heads	0, 0	−1, 1
	Tails	−1, 1	0, 0

Matrix 12.4. Matching Pennies game-II.

- Unfortunately, we find that IDSDS still has "no bite" in this situation:
  - *Finding dominant strategies for Player 1.* When Player 2 chooses Heads, Player 1 prefers Heads (since $0 > -1$); but when Player 2 chooses Tails, Player 1 prefers Tails (since once again, $0 > -1$).
  - *Finding dominant strategies for Player 2.* Likewise, for Player 2, when Player 1 chooses Heads, Player 2 prefers Tails (since $1 > 0$); but when Player 1 chooses Tails, Player 2 prefers Heads (since $1 > 0$ again).
  - Thus, neither heads nor tails strictly dominates the other for either player, and IDSDS does not help us delete any strategies (i.e., rows or columns from Matrix 12.4). In this setting, our most precise equilibrium prediction is the game as a whole (all four cells in Matrix 12.4).

Self-assessment exercise #12.4

SA 12.4 Consider Matrix 12.8 again, but assume that the payoff players obtain from choosing technology (B, b), in the lower right side of the matrix, is $(3, 3)$. Intuitively, coordinating on the superior technology (A, a) is still preferable, yielding a payoff $(5, 5)$, but the payoff difference to (B, b) is now smaller than in Matrix 12.8. Find the NE of the game, and compare your results against those in example 12.4. Interpret.

- Updating Matrix 12.8 from the textbook with our new values, we obtain Matrix 12.5.

		Firm 2	
		Tech a	Tech b
Firm 1	Tech A	$\underline{5,5}$	$2,0$
	Tech B	$3,1$	$\underline{3,3}$

Matrix 12.5. Finding best responses and NE in the Technology game-III.

  - *Firm 1's best responses.* When Firm 2 chooses a, Firm 1's best response is Tech A, $BR_1(a) = A$ (since $5 > 3$). When Firm 2 chooses b, Firm 1's best response is Tech B, $BR_1(b) = B$ (since $3 > 2$).
  - *Firm 2's best responses.* When Firm 1 chooses A, Firm 2's best response is Tech a, $BR_2(A) = a$ (since $5 > 0$). When Firm 1 chooses B, Firm 2's best response is Tech b, $BR_2(B) = b$ (since $3 > 1$).

- These best responses are underlined above in Matrix 12.5, and as can be observed, we have two strategy profiles with the payoffs for both players underlined:

$$(A, a) \quad \text{and} \quad (B, b).$$

- *Comparison.* The difference between this scenario and that in Matrix 12.8 in the textbook is that there is no weak dominance. Neither player is always at least as good by choosing Tech A (a) than by choosing Tech B (b, respectively). In this case, there are two Nash equilibria that are both potential outcomes of the game.

SA 12.5 Consider the Prisoner's Dilemma game from Matrix 12.9a again. However, let us now assume that, when a player confesses while her partner does not, the police do not offer any deal to the confessing player. As a consequence, payoff $(-10, 0)$ becomes $(-10, -1)$; and similarly, payoff $(0, -10)$ becomes $(-1, -10)$. All other payoffs are unaffected. Find the NE of the game, and compare your results against those in example 12.5. Interpret.

- Updating Matrix 12.9a from the textbook with our new values, we obtain Matrix 12.6.

		Player 2	
		Confess	Not confess
Player 1	Confess	$\underline{-5}, \underline{-5}$	$\underline{-1}, -10$
	Not confess	$-10, \underline{-1}$	$\underline{-1}, \underline{-1}$

Matrix 12.6. Prisoner's Dilemma game-II.

  - *Player 1's best responses.* When Player 2 chooses *Confess*, Player 1's best response is also *Confess*, $BR_1(C) = C$ (since $-5 > -10$). When Player 2 chooses *Not confess*, Player 1's best response is to either *Confess* or *Not confess*, $BR_1(NC) = \{C, NC\}$ (since both strategies yield a payoff of -1).
  - *Player 2's best responses.* Similarly, when Player 1 chooses *Confess*, Plater 2's best response is *Confess*, $BR_2(C) = C$ (once again since $-5 > -10$). When Player 1 chooses *Not confess*, Player 2's best response is to either *Confess* or *Not confess*, $BR_2(NC) = \{C, NC\}$ (since both strategies yield a payoff of -1).

- *Comparison.* Now that no benefit is provided for a confessing player when her partner does not confess, there is less incentive for either player to strictly confess. This leads to a situation where *Confess* only weakly dominates *Not confess*, as either player will always be as well off playing *Confess* over *Not confess*, but they may not be strictly better off. As a result, we have two Nash equilibria in this game where the strategy profiles for each player are underlined:

$$\text{(Confess, Confess)} \quad \text{and} \quad \text{(Not confess, Not confess)}.$$

SA 12.6 Consider again the Battle of the Sexes game from Matrix 12.10a. However, let us now assume that Felix started to appreciate opera, changing the payoffs in the second row of Matrix 12.10a to $(3, 2)$ and $(5, 5)$–that is, only Felix's payoffs from going to the opera changed. Find the NE of the game, and compare your results against those in example 12.6. Interpret.

- Updating Matrix 12.10a from the textbook with our new values, we obtain Matrix

$$
\begin{array}{cc}
 & \textit{Ana} \\
 & \begin{array}{cc} \text{Football} & \text{Opera} \end{array}
\end{array}
$$

		Football	Opera
Felix	Football	$\underline{5}, \underline{4}$	$3, 3$
	Opera	$3, 2$	$\underline{5}, \underline{5}$

Matrix 12.7. Battle of the Sexes game-II.

- In this setting, best responses are:

  - *Felix's best responses.* When Ana goes to *Football* (in the left column), Felix's best response is also *Football*, $BR_{Felix}(Football) = Football$, since $5 > 3$. When Ana goes to the *Opera* (in the right-hand column), Felix's best response is to attend the *Opera* too, $BR_{Felix}(Opera) = Opera$, since $5 > 3$.
  - *Ana's best responses.* When Felix goes to *Football* (in the top row), Ana's best response is also *Football*, $BR_{Ana}(Football) = Football$, since $4 > 3$. When Felix goes to the *Opera* (in the bottom row), Ana's best response is to attend the *Opera* too, $BR_{Ana}(Opera) = Opera$, since $5 > 2$.

- This new version of the game has the exact same outcome as example 12.6 in the textbook, where two Nash equilibria exist:

$$(Football,\ Football) \quad \text{and} \quad (Opera,\ Opera).$$

Even though Felix enjoys the opera more than before, he still prefers attending the football game more if he knows Ana will be there, too.[1] Thus, Felix and Ana still encounter the same problem where they cannot independently decide where to go, but Felix is a little bit better off if they end up at the Opera.

Self-assessment exercise #12.7

SA 12.7 Consider again the Coordination game from Matrix 12.11a. Let us now assume that the payoff that depositors obtain when they both withdraw their funds is lower: only $(10, 10)$. Check if the two NEs found in example 12.7 still emerge in this scenario.

- Updating Matrix 12.11a from the textbook with our new values, we obtain Matrix 12.8.

$$
\begin{array}{cc}
 & \textit{Depositor 2} \\
 & \begin{array}{cc} \text{Withdraw} & \text{Not withdraw} \end{array}
\end{array}
$$

		Withdraw	Not withdraw
Depositor 1	Withdraw	$\underline{10}, \underline{10}$	$100, 0$
	Not withdraw	$0, 100$	$\underline{150}, \underline{150}$

Matrix 12.8. Coordination game-II.

- In this setting, best responses are:

---

[1] To clarify, Felix prefers world football (soccer) over opera. Were this game considering American football, Felix would find that opera strictly dominates football.

– *Depositor 1's best responses.* When Depositor 2 chooses to *Withdraw*, Depositor 1's best response is to also *Withdraw*, $BR_1(W) = W$, since $10 > 0$. When Depositor 2 chooses to *Not withdraw*, Depositor 1's best response is to also *Not withdraw*, $BR_1(NW) = NW$, since $150 > 100$.

– *Depositor 2's best responses.* When Depositor 1 chooses to *Withdraw*, Depositor 2's best response is to also *Withdraw*, $BR_2(W) = W$, since $10 > 0$. When Depositor 1 chooses to *Not withdraw*, Depositor 2's best response is to also *Not withdraw*, $BR_2(NW) = NW$, since $150 > 100$.

- Once again, this new game has the exact same outcome as example 12.7 in the textbook. When either depositor chooses to withdraw, the other depositor compares the payoff she receives by also withdrawing against a payoff of 0 if she chooses to not withdraw her funds. Even though the payoff from withdrawing is much lower in this case, any value above 0 will still yield the strategy profile where both depositors withdraw as a Nash equilibrium. Thus, there are still two Nash equilibria in this game:

(Withdraw, Withdraw) and *(Not withdraw, Not withdraw)*.

Self-assessment exercise #12.8

SA 12.8 Consider again the anticoordination game from Matrix 12.12a, but assume that all payoffs are doubled. Show that the two NEs found in example 12.8 still emerge in this scenario.

- Updating Matrix 12.12a from the textbook with our new values,

		Player 2	
		Swerve	Stay
Player 1	Swerve	$-2, -2$	$-20, \underline{20}$
	Stay	$\underline{20}, -20$	$-40, -40$

Matrix 12.9. Anticoordination game-II.

- In this setting, best responses are:
  - *Player 1's best responses.* When Player 2 chooses to *Swerve*, Player 1's best response is to *Stay*, $BR_1(Swerve) = Stay$, since $20 > -2$. When Player 2 chooses to *Stay*, Player 1's best response is to *Swerve*, $BR_1(Stay) = Swerve$, since $-20 > -40$.
  - *Player 2's best responses.* When Player 1 chooses to *Swerve*, Player 2's best response is to *Stay*, $BR_2(Swerve) = Stay$, since $20 > -2$. When Player 1 chooses to *Stay*, Player 2's best response is to *Swerve*, $BR_2(Stay) = Swerve$, since $-20 > -40$.

- As before, the two Nash equilibria in this game are

(Swerve, Stay) and *(Stay, Swerve)*

as in example 12.8 in the textbook. When either player determines his or her best response function, they choose the strategy that provides the larger payoff. The actual value of the payoff does not actually matter; simply whichever payoff is bigger. Doubling the payoffs does not change the ordering of the payoffs for either player, so there are no changes to the result of this game.

Self-assessment exercise #12.9

SA 12.9 Consider again the penalty-kicks scenario from matrix 12.13. Let us now assume, however, that the payoff that players obtain when the kicker scores a goal is $(-2, 30)$ rather than $(-5, 8)$. Intuitively, the kicker is really happy about winning the game, while the goalie is just a bit unhappy. All other payoffs are unaffected. Show that this game does not have a pure strategy (psNE) either, and find the msNE. Compare the mixing probabilities that you find against $p = q = \frac{1}{2}$ in example 12.8. Interpret your results.

- Updating Matrix 12.13a from the textbook with our new values,

		Kicker	
		Aim Left	Aim Right
Goalie	Dive Left	$\underline{0}, \underline{0}$	$-2, \underline{30}$
	Dive Right	$-2, \underline{30}$	$\underline{0}, \underline{0}$

Matrix 12.10. Anticoordination game-II.

- *Pure strategies.* As before in example 12.8, there is no Nash equilibrium in pure strategies in this game.

  - *Goalie's best responses.* When the Kicker chooses *Aim Left*, the Goalie's best response is *Dive Left*, $BR_G(L) = L$ (since $0 > -2$). When the Kicker chooses *Aim Right*, the Goalie's best response is *Dive Right*, $BR_G(R) = R$ (since $0 > -2$).

  - *Kicker's best responses.* Likewise when the Goalie chooses *Dive Left*, the Kicker's best response is *Aim Right*, $BR_K(L) = R$ (since $30 > 0$). When the Goalie chooses *Dive Right*, the Kicker's best response is *Aim Left*, $BR_K(R) = L$ (since $30 > 0$).

  - As a result, neither strategy profile in Matrix 12.10 has both payoffs underlined, so no Nash equilibrium in pure strategies exists.

- *Mixed strategies.* Once again, we can assume that the Goalie dives left with probability p and dives right with probability $1 - p$. Similarly, we assume that the Kicker aims left with probability q and aims right with probability $1 - q$. Once again, we know that since both players are randomizing, that they must be indifferent between the expected payoffs of each of their strategies.

  - Starting with the goalie, his expected payoff from diving left must equal his expected payoff from diving right.

$$EU_{Goalie}(Left) = EU_{Goalie}(Right)$$
$$q0 + (1-q)(-2) = q(-2) + (1-q)0$$
$$-2 + 2q = -2q.$$

Rearranging this expression, we have $4q = 2$. Dividing both sides of this equation by 4 provides the probability that the Kicker aims left, $q = \frac{1}{2}$. In words, the goalie is indifferent between diving left and right if the kicker aims left with 50 percent probability.

- We follow a similar approach to find p, where the Kicker must be indifferent between aiming left and aiming right.

$$EU_{Kicker}(Left) = EU_{Kicker}(Right)$$
$$p0 + (1-p)30 = p30 + (1-p)0$$
$$30 - 30p = 30p.$$

Once again, rearranging this expression gives $60p = 30$. Dividing both sides of this equation by 60 provides the probability that the Goalie dives left, $p = \frac{1}{2}$. Intuitively, the kicker is indifferent between aiming left and right if the goalie dives left with 50 percent probability.

- *Comparison.* Since the payoffs for the Kicker and the Goalie changed symmetrically (i.e., it didn't become better to score a goal or prevent a goal going to the left over going to the right), neither player changes the way that they randomize in this game. Both players randomize between going left and going right with 50 percent probability. The graphical representation of best response functions and the mixed strategy Nash equilibrium would then coincide with that in figure 12.3 of the textbook.

Self-assessment exercise #12.10

SA 12.10 Consider again the Anticoordination game in Matrix 12.12. While we found two psNEs in that game, we can still find one msNE. Repeat the analysis in example 12.9 to find the msNE of the Anticoordination game, and depict the best responses for each player. Show that the best responses cross at three points: (1) at $(p, q) = (0, 1)$ at the corner of the graph, which corresponds to the psNE (*Stay, Swerve*); (2) at $(p, q) = (1, 0)$ at the top-left corner of the graph, corresponding to the psNE (*Swerve, Stay*); and (3) at an interior point where both p and q are strictly between 0 and 1, illustrating the msNE of the game.

- Reproducing Matrix 12.12a from the textbook, we obtain Matrix 12.11.

| | | Player 2 | |
		Swerve	Stay
Player 1	Swerve	$-1, -1$	$-10, 10$
	Stay	$10, -10$	$-20, -20$

Matrix 12.11. Anticoordination game-III.

- *Calculating the msNE.* We assume that Player 1 chooses *Swerve* with probability p and *Stay* with probability $1 - p$. Similarly, we assume that Player 2 chooses *Swerve* with probability q and *Stay* with probability $1 - q$.

  – Since Player 1 is randomizing, we know that he must be indifferent between choosing *Swerve* and *Stay*, so his expected payoff from *Swerve* must be equal to his expected payoff from *Stay*.

$$
\begin{aligned}
EU_1(Swerve) &= EU_1(Stay) \\
q(-1) + (1-q)10 &= q(-10) + (1-q)(-20) \\
10 - 11q &= -20 + 10q.
\end{aligned}
$$

  Rearranging this expression, we have $21q = 10$. Dividing both sides of this equation by 21 provides the probability that Player 2 chooses *Swerve*, $q = \frac{10}{21} = 0.48$. In words, Player 1 is indifferent between swerving and staying if Player 2 swerves with 48 percent probability.

  – We can perform the exact same analysis for player 2 to find that $p = 0.48$ (since the players are symmetric in their payoffs).

- *Building a graphical representation.* Now that we have our point where both players are indifferent between choosing *Swerve* and *Stay*, we can find for which values of their probabilities that they prefer to act in pure strategies. Player 1 prefers *Swerve* over *Stay* if his expected payoff from *Swerve* is greater than his expected payoff from *Stay*,

$$
\begin{aligned}
EU_1(Swerve) &> EU_1(Stay) \\
q(-1) + (1-q)10 &> q(-10) + (1-q)(-20) \\
10 - 11q &> -20 + 10q.
\end{aligned}
$$

Once again, this rearranges to $21q < 10$, which we can solve by dividing both sides of this inequality by 21 to obtain $q < 0.48$. Thus, if Player 2 randomizes by choosing *Swerve* less than 48 percent of the time, Player 1 prefers to choose *Swerve* exclusively. Likewise, if Player 2 chooses *Swerve* more than 48 percent of the time, Player 1 prefers to choose *Stay* exclusively. Again, these results are identical for Player 2. We compile these results in figure 12.1 where we can observe three intersections among the best response functions:

  – one at $(p, q) = (1, 0)$ which corresponds with our pure strategy profile (*Swerve*, *Stay*),

  – one at $(p, q) = (0, 1)$ which corresponds with our pure strategy profile (*Stay*, *Swerve*), and

– one at $(p,q) = (0.48, 0.48)$ which corresponds with our mixed strategy profile where each player randomly chooses *Swerve* 48 percent of the time.

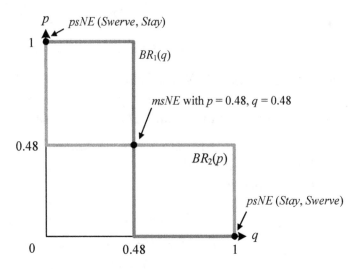

Figure 12.1. Anticoordination game msNE.

12.2 Solutions to End-of-Chapter Exercises

Exercise #12.1 - Strict Dominance[A]

12.1 Apply IDSDS to the game shown here:

		Player 2		
		L	C	R
	U	1, 1	3, 2	5, 3
Player 1	M	2, 3	4, 4	6, 5
	D	3, 5	5, 6	7, 5

- *Player 1.* Starting with player 1, we can see that strategies U and M are both strictly dominated by D. To see this point, note that:

  - When player 2 chooses L in the left column, player 1 obtains a strictly higher payoff from D (3) than from U (1) or M (2).
  - When player 2 chooses C in the middle column, player 1 obtains a strictly higher payoff from D (5) than from U (3) or M (4).
  - When player 2 chooses R in the right-hand column, player 1 obtains a strictly higher payoff from D (7) than from U (5) or M (6).

In summary, player 1 earns a strictly higher payoff with D than with U or M, *regardless* of the strategy that player 2 chooses (that is, regardless of the column player 2 plays). This is exactly the definition of a strictly dominated strategy, so we can delete U and M since player 1 would never pick them.

Deleting the rows corresponding to strategies U and M, we are left with the following reduced-form matrix.

		Player 2	
	L	C	R
Player 1 D	3, 5	5, 6	7, 5

- *Player 2.* Continuing with player 2, we can now delete L and R since they are both strictly dominated by C (6 > 5 when comparing player 2's payoff of C against L, and of C against R). After deleting the columns corresponding to L and R, we are left with the following reduced-form matrix.

	Player 2
	C
Player 1 D	5, 6

- *Summary.* Therefore, the only strategy profile surviving IDSDS is (C, D) with equilibrium payoffs (5, 6). In other words, the application of IDSDS yields a unique equilibrium prediction, where player 1 chooses D and player 2 selects C.

Exercise #12.3 - Strict Dominance – Some Bite[B]

12.3 Apply IDSDS to the game shown here:

		Player 2			
		W	X	Y	Z
	A	1, 1	3, 2	5, 3	3, 3
	B	2, 3	4, 4	6, 5	1, 3
Player 1	C	3, 5	5, 6	7, 5	4, 3
	D	2, 6	6, 4	4, 2	3, 2

- *Player 1.* Starting with player 1, we find that strategy C strictly dominates A and B since:

    - When player 2 chooses the W column, player 1 earns a strictly higher payoff from C (3) than from A (1) or B (2).
    - When player 2 chooses the X column, player 1 earns a strictly higher payoff from C (5) than from A (3) or B (4).
    - When player 2 chooses the Y column, player 1 earns a strictly higher payoff from C (7) than from A (5) or B (6).
    - When player 2 chooses the Z column, player 1 earns a strictly higher payoff from C (4) than from A (3) or B (1).

In summary, player 1 earns a strictly higher payoff with C than with A or B, *regardless* of the strategy that player 2 chooses (that is, regardless of the column player 2 plays). We can then delete the rows corresponding to strategies A and B since player 1 would never pick them, obtaining the following reduced-form matrix.

$$\begin{array}{c} \textit{Player 2} \\ \begin{array}{cccc} \text{W} & \text{X} & \text{Y} & \text{Z} \end{array} \end{array}$$

$$\textit{Player 1}\quad \begin{array}{c} \text{C} \\ \text{D} \end{array} \begin{array}{|c|c|c|c|} \hline 3,5 & 5,6 & 7,5 & 4,3 \\ \hline 2,6 & 6,4 & 4,2 & 3,2 \\ \hline \end{array}$$

- *Player 2.* Moving on to player 2, we can see that strategy X strictly dominates Y and Z since:
  - When player 1 chooses C in the top row, player 2 earns a strictly higher payoff from X (6) than from Y (5) or Z (3).
  - When player 1 chooses D in the bottom row, player 2 earns a strictly higher payoff from X (4) than from Y or Z (both giving player 2 a payoff of 2).

Therefore, player 2 earns a strictly higher payoff with X than with Y or Z, *regardless* of the strategy that player 1 chooses (that is, regardless of the row that player 1 plays). We can then delete the columns corresponding to strategies Y and Z since player 2 would never pick them, obtaining the following reduced-form matrix.

$$\begin{array}{c} \textit{Player 2} \\ \begin{array}{cc} \text{W} & \text{X} \end{array} \end{array}$$

$$\textit{Player 1}\quad \begin{array}{c} \text{C} \\ \text{D} \end{array} \begin{array}{|c|c|} \hline 3,5 & 5,6 \\ \hline 2,6 & 6,4 \\ \hline \end{array}$$

- *Player 1.* We now return to player 1. We do not find any more strictly dominated strategies for him. To see this point, note that:
  - When player 2 chooses the W column, player 1 earns a strictly higher payoff from C (3) than from D (2), but
  - When player 2 chooses the X column, player 1 earns a strictly higher payoff from D (6) than from C (5).

Therefore, there is no strategy that yields unambiguously lower payoffs for player 1 regardless of the strategy that player 2 picks. Since we couldn't find any strictly dominated strategy for player 1 at this point, we cannot delete any rows from the above matrix.

- *Player 2.* Finally, we go back to player 2 to see if we can identify a strictly dominated strategy for him. Like for player 1 above, we cannot find strictly dominated strategies for player 2 at this point since:
  - When player 1 chooses the C row (at the top of the above matrix), player 2 earns a strictly higher payoff from X (6) than from W (5), but...
  - When player 1 chooses the D row (at the bottom of the above matrix), player 2 earns a strictly higher payoff from W (6) than from X (4).

As a result, we cannot delete any strictly dominated strategies for player 2 at this point of our application of IDSDS.

- *Summary.* Therefore, the application of IDSDS provided us with four surviving cells, implying that the equilibrium prediction according to IDSDS is:

$$IDSDS = \{(C, W), (C, X), (D, W), (D, X)\}.$$

In other words, IDSDS had some "bite" since it helped us delete two strategies for player 1 (A and B) and two strategies for player 2 (Y and Z), moving us from 16 potential outcomes in the original matrix to only 4. However, IDSDS in this game didn't provide us with a precise equilibrium prediction since we found four different strategy profiles as possible outcomes.

Exercise #12.5 - Prisoner's Dilemma[B]

12.5 In the Prisoner's Dilemma, why did each player elect to confess when each player would be better off had they both remained silent? Do we see similar behavior like this in the real world? Explain.

- Every player finds Confess to be a strictly dominant strategy, which intuitively means that she obtains a strictly higher payoff confessing than not confessing, *regardless* of what her opponent does. Since both players face this strong incentive to play Confess, they both Confess in equilibrium.

- If both players remain silent, every player's payoff is higher than when they both confess. At first glance, one could think that prisoners recognize this higher payoff from coordinating in remaining silent. However, this outcome cannot emerge in equilibrium (at least when the game is played only once) since every player, despite recognizing that higher payoff, simultaneously and independently chooses whether to confess or not confess. When choosing her strategy, she finds that Confess strictly dominates Not confess since it provides her a strictly higher payoff both when her opponent confesses and when she does not. In other words, (NC, NC) cannot occur in the one-shot game.

- Other settings exhibit similar incentives, with the equilibrium of the game yielding lower payoffs than an alternative outcome. Examples include pricing decisions by firms competing in the same industry (obtaining low profits in equilibrium but being able to coordinate their pricing decisions to charge higher prices) or advertising decisions in politics (spending massive amounts rather than coordinating their advertising decisions to limit their individual advertising).

Exercise #12.7 - Weak Dominance[A]

12.7 Consider the game presented in exercise 12.4.

(a) Identify any weakly dominated strategies.

- For easier reference, we reproduce the game in exercise 12.4.

Player 2

		L	R
Player 1	U	1, 6	5, 7
	D	4, 1	5, 1

- *Player 1.* Starting with player 1, strategy D weakly dominates U since:
  - When player 2 chooses L (in the left column), player 1 earns a strictly higher payoff with strategy D (4) than with U (1).

259

– When player 2 chooses R (in the right column), player 1 earns the same payoff with strategy D (5) as with U (5).

Since strategy D yields the same payoff as strategy U when player 2 chooses column R, but yields a strictly higher payoff at least against one of the strategies of player 2 (when he selects column L), we can claim that strategy D weakly dominates U.

- *Player 2.* Strategy R weakly dominates L since:
  – When player 1 chooses U (in the top row), player 2 earns a strictly higher payoff with strategy R (7) than with L (6).
  – When player 1 chooses D (in the bottom row), player 2 earns the same payoff with strategy R (1) as with L (1).

Since strategy R yields the same payoff as strategy L when player 1 chooses row D, but yields a strictly higher payoff at least against one of the strategies of player 1 (when he selects row U), we can claim that strategy R weakly dominates L.

(b) Does IDWDS provide a unique solution to this game?

- In the application of Iterative Deletion of Weakly Dominated Strategies (IDWDS) we delete the strategies that are weakly dominated for one player, then move to another player, repeating this process until we can no longer find weakly dominated strategies to delete.
- *Player 1.* Let us start deleting weakly dominated strategies for player 1. From part (a), strategy U is weakly dominated for player 1. After deleting row U from the original matrix, we obtain the following reduced-form matrix.

Player 2

		L	R
Player 1	D	4, 1	5, 1

- *Player 2.* We now move to player 2. Since strategy U has been deleted by player 1 via IDWDS, player 2 is indifferent between column L and column R, and neither column weakly dominates the other. (We would reach a similar conclusion if we applied IDWDS to player 2 first.)
- *Summary.* Therefore, we cannot claim that IDWDS provides us with a unique equilibrium prediction.

Exercise #12.9 - Weak Dominance–III[B]

12.9 In several game shows across the US and UK, two players work together to build up a cash prize for the end of the show of size M. At the end of the show, each player must simultaneously choose whether to "Split" or to "Steal" the cash prize.

- If both players choose "Split," each player leaves the show with half the cash price, $\frac{M}{2}$.
- If one player chooses "Split" while the other player chooses "Steal," the player who chooses "Split" receives none of the cash prize, while the player who chooses "Steal" receives the whole cash prize.

- If both players choose "Steal," they both receive none of the cash prize.

(a) Depict the normal-form representation of this game.

- The normal-form representation of this game is the following.

Player 2

		Split	Steal
	Split	$\frac{M}{2}, \frac{M}{2}$	$0, M$
Player 1	Steal	$M, 0$	$0, 0$

(b) Identify any strictly or weakly dominated strategies in this game.

- *Strictly dominated strategies.* Player 1 does not have a strictly dominant strategy. To see this, note that:
  - When player 2 chooses Split (in the left column), player 1 earns a strictly higher payoff with Steal (M) than with Split ($\frac{M}{2}$), but
  - When player 2 chooses Steal (in the right column), player 1 earns the same payoff with Steal (0) as with Split (0).

  Therefore, there is no strategy that yields unambiguously higher payoffs for player 1 regardless of the strategy that player 2 picks. A similar argument applies to player 2 since players are symmetric in their payoffs.

- *Weakly dominated strategies.* Player 1 finds Split to be weakly dominated by Steal since:
  - When player 2 chooses Split (in the left column), player 1 earns a strictly higher payoff with Steal (M) than with Split ($\frac{M}{2}$).
  - When player 2 chooses Steal (in the right column), player 1 earns the same payoff with Steal (0) as with Split (0).

  Since Steal yields the same payoff as Split when player 2 chooses Steal, but yields a strictly higher payoff at least against one of player 2's strategies (when player 2 selects Split), we can claim that strategy Steal weakly dominates Split. A similar argument applies to player 2 since players are symmetric in their payoffs.

(c) Which is your equilibrium prediction after applying IDSDS?

- As shown in part (b) of the exercise, no player has strictly dominated strategies. Therefore, we cannot delete any row for player 1 or column for player 2, implying that IDSDS has no bite. As a result, we find that the four cells in the original payoff matrix are our most precise equilibrium prediction according to IDSDS; that is,

$$IDSDS = \{(Split, Split), (Split, Steal), (Steal, Split), (Steal, Steal)\}.$$

(d) Which is your equilibrium prediction after applying IDWDS?

- As shown in part (b) of the exercise, Split is weakly dominated by Steal for both players.

- *Starting with player 1.* We can delete the row corresponding to Split (top row) obtaining the following reduced-form matrix.

$$
\begin{array}{cc}
 & \textit{Player 2} \\
 & \text{Split} \quad \text{Steal}
\end{array}
$$

		Split	Steal
Player 1	Steal	$M, 0$	$0, 0$

At this point, we cannot delete any weakly dominated strategy for player 2. For that, we need one strategy that provides player 2 with a strictly higher payoff against at least one of his opponent's strategies and earns the same payoff against all other strategies. This definition, however, cannot be satisfied now that player 1 only has one surviving strategy, Steal. Therefore, the above matrix is our most precise equilibrium prediction after applying IDWDS and starting to delete weakly dominated strategies of player 1. That is,

$$IDWDS_{Player1} = \{(Steal, Split), (Steal, Steal)\}.$$

Intuitively, players face a similar strategic situation as in the standard Prisoner's Dilemma game, but with the difference that Steal is here a *weakly* dominant strategy; as opposed to Confess in the Prisoner's Dilemma game which is a strictly dominant strategy.

- *Starting with player 2.* We can show that we obtain the same equilibrium result if we start deleting weakly dominated strategies for player 2. Starting with player 2, we can delete the column corresponding to Split (right-hand column) obtaining the following reduced-form matrix.

$$
\begin{array}{cc}
 & \textit{Player 2} \\
 & \text{Steal}
\end{array}
$$

		Steal
Player 1	Split	$0, M$
	Steal	$0, 0$

By the same argument as above, we cannot delete any weakly dominated strategies for player 1. Therefore, the above matrix is our most precise equilibrium prediction after applying IDWDS and starting to delete weakly dominated strategies of player 2. That is,

$$IDWDS_{Player2} = \{(Split, Steal), (Steal, Steal)\}.$$

which implies that, in this game, IDWDS yields a different equilibrium prediction depending on the deletion order we follow. In other words, if we start deleting weakly dominated strategies for player 1 we find different equilibrium outcomes than if we start deleting weakly dominated strategies for player 2.

Exercise #12.11 - Nash Equilibrium in a 3x3 Matrix[B]

12.11 Find all psNEs in the normal-form representation of the game shown here:

Player 2

		L	C	R
	U	5, 0	1, 9	5, 8
Player 1	M	0, 4	−9, −4	8, 0
	D	1, 6	8, 9	1, 6

- *Player 1 best responses.*

  - If player 2 chooses L (in the left-hand column), player 1's best response is to choose U since his payoff from doing so, 5, is larger than that from choosing M, 0, or D, 1.
  - If player 2 chooses C (in the middle column), player 1's best response is D since his payoff, 8, is larger than that from choosing U, 1, or M, −9.
  - Finally, if player 2 chooses R (in the right-hand column), player 1's best response is to choose M since his payoff from doing so, 8, is larger than that from choosing U, 5, or D, 1.

The following table underlines player 1's payoff from playing the above best responses.

Player 2

		L	C	R
	U	$\underline{5}$, 0	1, 9	5, 8
Player 1	M	0, 4	−9, −4	$\underline{8}$, 0
	D	1, 6	$\underline{8}$, 9	1, 6

- *Player 2 best responses.*

  - If player 1 chooses U (in the top row), player 2's best response is to choose C since her payoff, 9, is larger than that from choosing L, 0, or R, 8.
  - If player 1 chooses M (in the middle row), player 2's best response is L since her payoff, 4, is larger than that from choosing C, −4, or R, 0.
  - Finally, if player 1 chooses D (in the bottom row), player 2's best response is to choose C since her payoff from doing so, 9, is larger than that from choosing L, 6, or R, 6.

The following table underlines player 2's payoff from playing the above best responses.

Player 2

		L	C	R
	U	5, 0	1, $\underline{9}$	5, 8
Player 1	M	0, $\underline{4}$	−9, −4	8, 0
	D	1, 6	8, $\underline{9}$	1, 6

- *Mutual best responses.* The following matrix combines our above results, underlining best response payoffs for both players. We find only one cell where the payoffs of all players are underlined, (C, D), meaning that both players are playing best responses to each other's strategies (mutual best responses). Therefore, (C, D) is the unique Nash equilibrium in this game.

		Player 2		
		L	C	R
Player 1	U	$\underline{5}, 0$	$1, \underline{9}$	$5, 8$
	M	$0, \underline{4}$	$-9, -4$	$\underline{8}, 0$
	D	$1, 6$	$\underline{8}, \underline{9}$	$1, 6$

Exercise #12.13 - Nash Equilibrium in the Split–Steal Game[B]

12.13 Find all psNEs in the game presented in exercise 12.9. Is there ever a reason for a player to choose "Split"?

- We reproduce the normal-form representation that we found in part (a) of exercise 12.9 here for easier reference.

		Player 2	
		Split	Steal
Player 1	Split	$\frac{M}{2}, \frac{M}{2}$	$0, M$
	Steal	$M, 0$	$0, 0$

- *Player 1 best responses.*

  - If player 2 chooses Split (in the left column), player 1's best response is to Steal since his payoff from doing so, M, is higher than from Split, $\frac{M}{2}$. His best response in this case is written as $BR_1(Split) = Steal$.
  - If player 2 chooses Steal (in the right-hand column), player 1 is indifferent between Split and Steal, since his payoff is 0 in both of them. His best response in this case is written as $BR_1(Steal) = \{Split, Steal\}$.

The following table underlines player 1's payoff from playing the above best responses.

		Player 2	
		Split	Steal
Player 1	Split	$\frac{M}{2}, \frac{M}{2}$	$\underline{0}, M$
	Steal	$\underline{M}, 0$	$\underline{0}, 0$

- *Player 2 best responses.*

  - If player 1 chooses Split (in the top row), player 2's best response is to choose Steal since her payoff from doing so, M, is larger than that from Split, $\frac{M}{2}$. Her best response in this case is written as $BR_2(Split) = Steal$.
  - If player 1 chooses Steal (in the bottom row), player 2 is indifferent between Split and Steal since her payoff is 0 in both strategies. Her best response in this case is written as $BR_2(Steal) = \{Split, Steal\}$.

The following table underlines player 2's payoff from playing the above best responses.

Player 2

		Split	Steal
		Split	Steal
Player 1	Split	$\frac{M}{2}, \frac{M}{2}$	$0, \underline{M}$
	Steal	$M, 0$	$0, \underline{0}$

- *Mutual best responses.* The following matrix combines our above results, underlining best response payoffs for both player 1 and 2.

Player 2

		Split	Steal
Player 1	Split	$\frac{M}{2}, \frac{M}{2}$	$0, \underline{M}$
	Steal	$\underline{M}, 0$	$\underline{0}, \underline{0}$

Three cells have all payoffs underlined, (*Split, Steal*), (*Steal, Split*) and (*Steal, Steal*), meaning that both players are choosing best responses to each other's strategies (mutual best responses). Therefore, we found three pure strategy Nash equilibria in this game:

$$NE = \{(Split, Steal), (Steal, Split), (Steal, Steal)\}.$$

Exercise #12.15 - Rock, Paper, Scissors–I[A]

12.15 Suppose that you and a friend engaged in the classic game of Rock, Paper, Scissors. In this game, both players simultaneously choose among "Rock," "Paper," and "Scissors," where "Paper" defeats "Rock," "Scissors" defeats "Paper," and "Rock" defeats "Scissors." Suppose that whoever wins this game receives \$1 from the loser.

(a) Depict the normal-form representation of this game.

- The normal-form representation of the game is the following.

Player 2

		Rock	Paper	Scissors
	Rock	$0, 0$	$-1, 1$	$1, -1$
Player 1	Paper	$1, -1$	$0, 0$	$-1, 1$
	Scissors	$-1, 1$	$1, -1$	$0, 0$

When both players choose the same strategy no player earns or losses money. Otherwise, Rock beats Scissors, Scissors beat Paper, and Paper beats Rock. For instance, in strategy profile (Paper, Rock) in the left column, player 1 earns \$1 from player 2 since Paper beats Rock.

(b) Describe each player's best response.

- *Player 1 best responses (row player).* We take player 2's strategy as given (in columns) finding that player 1's best responses are the following:
  - If player 2 selects Rock (in the left column), player 1's best response is to choose Paper since her payoff from doing so, 1, is larger than from Rock, 0, or Scissors, -1. We write this best response as $BR_1(Rock) = Paper$.

– If player 2 selects Paper (in the middle column), player 1's best response is to choose Scissors since her payoff from doing so, 1, is larger than from Rock, -1, or Paper, 0. We write this best response as $BR_1(Paper) = Scissors$.

– If player 2 selects Scissors (in the right-hand column), player 1's best response is to choose Rock since her payoff from doing so, 1, is larger than from Paper, -1, or Scissors, 0. We write this best response as $BR_1(Scissors) = Rock$.

The following table underlines player 1's payoff from playing the above best responses.

Player 2

		Rock	Paper	Scissors
	Rock	$0,0$	$-1,1$	$\underline{1},-1$
Player 1	Paper	$\underline{1},-1$	$0,0$	$-1,1$
	Scissors	$-1,1$	$\underline{1},-1$	$0,0$

- Player 2's best responses are symmetric to player 1 since players have symmetric payoffs. You can do this as a practice. Recall that in this case, we fix the strategy of player 1 (fixing rows) and find which column provides player 2 with the highest payoff to his opponent's strategy. The following table underlines player 2's payoff from playing the above best responses.

Player 2

		Rock	Paper	Scissors
	Rock	$0,0$	$-1,\underline{1}$	$1,-1$
Player 1	Paper	$1,-1$	$0,0$	$-1,\underline{1}$
	Scissors	$-1,\underline{1}$	$1,-1$	$0,0$

(c) Is there a psNE of this game? If so, what is it? If not, why not?

- Combining the matrices with best response payoffs for players 1 and 2 we found in part (b) of the exercise, we obtain the following matrix.

Player 2

		Rock	Paper	Scissors
	Rock	$0,0$	$-1,\underline{1}$	$\underline{1},-1$
Player 1	Paper	$\underline{1},-1$	$0,0$	$-1,\underline{1}$
	Scissors	$-1,\underline{1}$	$\underline{1},-1$	$0,0$

No cell has the payoffs of both players underlined. Therefore, there is no strategy profile (no cell) where players are selecting mutual best responses to each other's strategies. As a consequence, there is no Nash equilibrium in the Rock-Paper-Scissors game when we restrict players to use pure strategies; that is, to select strategies with 100 percent probability rather than randomizing. This comes at no surprise because, as a player of this game, you would not like to be predictable (e.g., being the player who always selects Rock with 100 percent probability) since being predictable allows your opponent to best

266

respond to your strategy earning a dollar from you. As we show in exercise 12.21, this game has a mixed strategy Nash equilibrium where players randomize between Rock, Paper, and Scissors to avoid being predictable.

Exercise #12.17 - Charitable Contributions[B]

12.17 Suppose that two wealthy donors are considering making a charitable contribution to a public project. This project is costly, and it only reaps benefits if both donors contribute. To contribute (C), a donor must pay a cost of $1, and the project is worth $3 to each donor if both donors contribute, and 0 otherwise. Not contributing (NC) costs nothing.

(a) Depict the normal-form representation of this game.

- The following matrix provides the normal form representation of the game.

		Donor 2	
		C	NC
Donor 1	C	2, 2	−1, 0
	NC	0, −1	0, 0

To understand each entry, note that:

– When both donors contribute to the project, the project is built, with payoff $3 − 1 = 2$ to each donor; as indicated in the (C,C) outcome.

– When only one donor contributes, the project is not implemented, yielding no benefits. In this case, the donor who contributed suffers a cost of 1 while the individual who did not contribute has a payoff of 0. This applies to (NC,C), where donor 2 has a disutility of −1 while donor 1 has a utility of 0, and to (C,NC) where roles and payoffs are switched.

– Finally, when no donor contributes to the project, each of them earns 0.

(b) Describe each donor's best response.

- *Donor 1 best responses (row player).* We take donor 2's strategy as given (in columns) finding that donor 1's best responses are the following:

– If donor 2 selects C (in the left column), donor 1's best response is C since its payoff from doing so, 2, is larger than from NC, 0. We write this best response as $BR_1(C) = C$.

– If donor 2 selects NC (in the left column), donor 1's best response is NC since its payoff from doing so, 0, is larger than from C, −1. We write this best response as $BR_1(NC) = NC$.

Intuitively, donor 1 seeks to mimic donor 2's strategy: contributing when he does, but not contributing when he does not. This is because, once donor 2 has contributed, the project could be built if donor 1 also contributes, increasing 1's payoff. However, when donor 2 does not contribute the project will not be built regardless of 1's decision to contribute or not, so donor 1 is better off avoiding the contribution cost.

The following table underlines donor 1's payoff from playing the above best responses.

		Donor 2	
		C	NC
Donor 1	C	<u>2</u>,2	−1,0
	NC	0,−1	<u>0</u>,0

- *Donor 2 best responses (column player).* We take donor 1's strategy as given (in rows) finding donor 2's best responses. Since donors' payoffs are symmetric, we leave this best responses as a practice for the reader. You should find that, when donor 1 chooses C, donor 2's best response is $BR_2(C) = C$, while when donor 1 selects NC, donor 2's best response is $BR_2(NC) = NC$, thus implying that donor 2's best response is also to imitate the strategy of donor 1.

The following table underlines donor 2's payoff from playing the above best responses.

		Donor 2	
		C	NC
Donor 1	C	2,<u>2</u>	−1,0
	NC	0,−1	0,<u>0</u>

(c) Is there a psNE of this game? If so, what is it? If not, why not?

- Combining the best response payoffs of donors 1 and 2 that we underlined in the matrices of part (b), we obtain the following matrix.

		Donor 2	
		C	NC
Donor 1	C	<u>2</u>,<u>2</u>	−1,0
	NC	0,−1	<u>0</u>,<u>0</u>

There are two cells where both donors' payoffs are underlined, (C, C) and (NC, NC), meaning that both donors are playing best responses to each other's strategies (mutual best responses). Therefore, the two Nash equilibria of the game are

$$NE = \{(C, C), (NC, NC)\}.$$

This game then is strategically equivalent to the Coordination game, where there are two Nash equilibria, but both players are better off in one of them (C, C), where they contribute to the project, than in the other one, (NC, NC), where no player contributes and the project is not built.

Exercise #12.19 - Finding msNE–Coordination Game[B]

12.19 Find the msNE in the Coordination game described in this chapter.

- We reproduce the coordination game below for easier reference.

Depositor 2

		Withdraw	Not Withdraw
Depositor 1	Withdraw	$50, 50$	$100, 0$
	Not Withdraw	$0, 100$	$150, 150$

- *Row player (Depositor 1).* Let q denote the probability that Depositor 2 chooses to withdraw, and $(1 - q)$ the probability that she does not to withdraw. Hence, the expected payoff that Depositor 1 obtains from choosing to withdraw (in the top row) is

$$EU_1(Withdraw) = 50q + 100(1 - q).$$

If instead Depositor 1 does not withdraw (in the bottom row), his expected payoff becomes

$$EU_1(NotWithdraw) = 0q + 150(1 - q).$$

Depositor 1 must be indifferent between choosing withdraw or not to withdraw. Hence, we need that

$$EU_1(Withdraw) = EU_1(NotWithdraw)$$
$$50q + 100(1 - q) = 0q + 150(1 - q),$$

rearranging and solving for probability q yields

$$100 - 50q = 150 - 150q$$
$$q = \frac{1}{2}.$$

That is, Depositor 2 must choose withdraw with 50 percent probability, i.e., $q = \frac{1}{2}$. Otherwise Depositor 1 would not be indifferent.

- *Column player (Depositor 2).* Let p denote the probability that Depositor 1 withdraws, and $(1 - p)$ the probability that he does not. Hence, the expected payoff that Depositor 2 obtains from choosing to withdraw (in the left column) is

$$EU_2(Withdraw) = 50p + 100(1 - p).$$

If instead Depositor 2 does not withdraw (in the right-hand column), her expected payoff becomes

$$EU_2(NotWithdraw) = 0p + 150(1 - p).$$

Therefore, Depositor 2 is indifferent when

$$EU_2(Withdraw) = EU_2(NotWithdraw)$$
$$50p + 100(1 - p) = 0p + 150(1 - p),$$

rearranging and solving for probability p yields

$$100 - 50p = 150 - 150p$$
$$p = \frac{1}{2}.$$

- *Summary.* Hence, the msNE of the Coordination game is given by

$$msNE = \left\{ \left(\frac{1}{2}Withdraw, \frac{1}{2}NotWithdraw \right), \left(\frac{1}{2}Withdraw, \frac{1}{2}NotWithdraw \right) \right\},$$

which is depicted in figure 12.2. That is, every player randomizes between withdraw and not to withdraw half of the time.

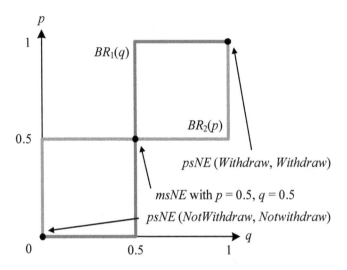

Figure 12.2. msNE of Coordination game.

Exercise #12.21 - Penalty Kicks[A]

12.21 Consider the Penalty Kicks scenario in example 12.9. Suppose that the goalie received information with certainty that the kicker was going to aim right for this shot.

(a) Should he continue to randomly dive? Why or why not?

- We reproduce here the Penalty Kicks game from example 12.9.

		Kicker	
		Aim Left	Aim Right
Goalie	Dive Left	$0,0$	$-5,8$
	Dive Right	$-5,8$	$0,0$

If the goalie received information guaranteeing that the kicker will play Aim

270

Right, the above payoff matrix collapses to the following.

		Kicker Aim Right
		Aim Right
Goalie	Dive Left	−5, 8
	Dive Right	0, 0

In this setting, the goalie's best response to the kicker aiming right is to dive right, and stop the shot, since $0 > -5$. We can write the goalie's best response more formally as $BR_G(AimRight) = DiveRight$.

(b) Suppose now that the kicker knew that the goalie had this information. What should the kicker do?

- If the kicker anticipates that the goalie will dive right, then the original matrix simplifies to the following.

		Kicker	
		Aim Left	Aim Right
Goalie	Dive Right	−5, 8	0, 0

In that context, the kicker's best response to the goalie aiming right with certainty is to aim left, and score, since $8 > 0$. Formally, $BR_K(DiveRight) = AimLeft$.

Chapter 13 - Sequential and Repeated Games

13.1 Solutions to Self-Assessment Exercises

Self-assessment exercise #13.1

SA 13.1 Repeat the analysis in example 13.1, but assume that when the potential entrant joins the industry and the incumbent responds by accommodating, both firms earn a payoff of only 1. Are the results in example 13.1 affected? Interpret.

- Updating figure 13.1a from the textbook with our new values, we obtain figure 13.1.

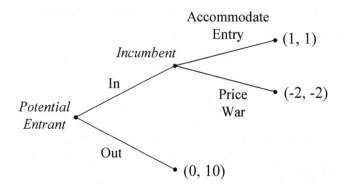

Figure 13.1. Entry game–II.

- In order to analyze the Nash equilibrium of this game, we need to convert it to matrix form. As in example 13.1, each player has only two possible strategies: In and Out for the Entrant, and Accommodate Entry and Price War for the Incumbent. We can organize these strategies into Matrix 13.1.

Potential entrant

		In	Out
Incumbent	Accommodate	1,1	10, 0
	Price war	−2, −2	10,0

Matrix 13.1. Entry game–II in matrix form.

Recall that even though we do not have a situation where the Incumbent accommodates entry after the Entrant decides to stay out of the market, we can still represent that outcome in the matrix form. Intuitively, if the Entrant stays out, it does not matter what the Incumbent decides to do. Now we are prepared to analyze this new game.

- *Incumbent's best responses.* When the Entrant chooses *In*, the Incumbent's best response is to *Accommodate*, $BR_{inc}(In) = Acc$, since $1 > -2$. When the Entrant chooses *Out*, the Incumbent's best response is to either *Accommodate* or *Price war*, $BR_{inc}(Out) = \{Acc, War\}$, since either strategy yields a payoff of 10.

- *Entrant's best responses.* When the Incumbent chooses to *Accommodate*, the Entrant's best response is *In*, $BR_{ent}(Acc) = In$, since $1 > 0$. When the Incumbent chooses *Price war*, the Entrant's best response is *Out*, $BR_{ent}(War) = Out$, since $0 > -2$.

- As we can see, this is the exact same result as in example 13.1. We have two strategy profiles that exist as Nash equilibria,

$$(Acc, In) \quad \text{and} \quad (War, Out).$$

The actual value of the payoffs when the incumbent responds to entry and accommodates really do not matter, as long as they are larger than their alternatives. Since we reduced their payoff by an insufficient amount to make any other strategy more attractive, there is no change in the outcome of this game.

Self-assessment exercise #13.2

SA 13.2 Repeat the analysis in example 13.2, but assume that when the potential entrant joins the industry and the incumbent responds by accommodating, both firms earn a payoff of only 1. Are the results in example 13.2 affected? Interpret.

- Using backward induction on this game (which is represented in figure 13.1), we first examine the decision of the last mover, the incumbent. If the Entrant chooses *In*, they now must choose between accommodating entry with a payoff of 1, and starting a price war with a payoff of -2. Since $1 > -2$, the Incumbent's best response to the Entrant choosing *In* is to *Accommodate*, $BR_{inc}(In) = Acc$, which we denote in figure 13.2.

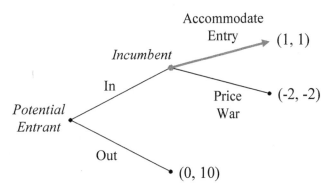

Figure 13.2. Backward induction in the Entry game–II.

Now we move up the game tree to examine the decision of the Entrant. If the Entrant chooses *In*, he knows that the Incumbent will respond with *Accommodate*, and the Entrant will receive a payoff of 1. If the Entrant chooses *Out*, the game ends and he receives a payoff of 0. Since $1 > 0$, the Entrant chooses *In*, knowing that the Incumbent will respond with *Accommodate*. Thus, our subgame perfect equilibrium of this game is (*In, Accommodate*), which results in equilibrium payoffs of (1,1). This result is depicted in figure 13.3.

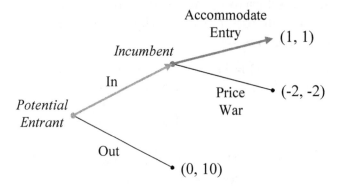

Figure 13.3. Subgame perfect equilibrium in the Entry game–II.

Thus, we end this game with the exact same outcome as in example 13.2 in the textbook. Like before, the actual value of the payoffs does not matter, just the relative ranking of those payoffs. The reduction in the payoff from example 13.2 to our problem did not impact the ranking of any payoffs, and thus our results did not change.

Self-assessment exercise #13.3

SA 13.3 Repeat the analysis in example 13.3, but assume that when firm 1 chooses Up and A, and firm 2 responds with X, their payoff becomes $(5,5)$ rather than $(3,4)$. Find the equilibrium of the game tree, and compare your result against that in example 13.3.

- Updating figure 13.3 from the textbook with our new values, we obtain figure 13.4.

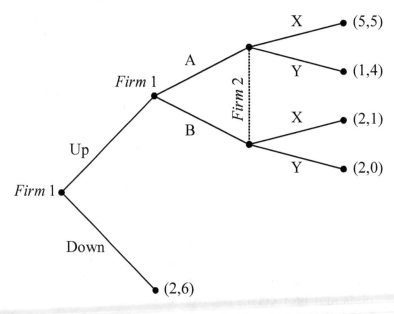

Figure 13.4. A more involved game tree–II.

- *Examining the subgame.* As before, we must utilize backward induction to analyze this game. In this case, our smallest subgame begins when Firm 1 chooses between A and B since creating any other subgame after that point would break an information set. Since Firm 2 cannot observe Firm 1's choice of A or B, we must treat it like a simultaneous move game, which we depict in matrix 13.2.

Firm 2

		X	Y
Firm 1	A	<u>5</u>,<u>5</u>	1, 4
	B	2,<u>1</u>	<u>2</u>, 0

Matrix 13.2. Representing Subgame in matrix form.

- *Firm 1's best responses.* When Firm 2 chooses X, Firm 1's best response is A, $BR_1(X) = A$, since $5 > 2$. When Firm 2 chooses Y, Firm 1's best response is B, $BR_1(Y) = B$, since $2 > 1$.
- *Firm 2's best responses.* When Firm 1 chooses A, Firm 2's best response is X, $BR_1(A) = X$, since $5 > 4$. When Firm 1 chooses B, Firm 2's best response is X, $BR_2(B) = X$, since $1 > 0$.

Thus, we have one Nash equilibrium of this subgame, (A, X), which yields payoffs of $(5, 5)$. Thus, Firm 1 knows that if they choose *Up*, they should also choose A and Firm 2 will respond with X. We represent this reduced game tree in figure 13.5.

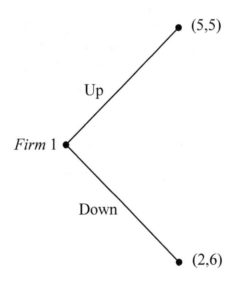

Figure 13.5. Reduced game tree.

- *Game as a whole.* Since Firm 1 anticipates the outcome of the subgame, it knows that if it chooses Up, it receives a payoff of 5. If Firm 1 chooses Down, it receives a payoff of 2. Since $5 > 2$, Firm 1 chooses *Up*, then A, knowing that Firm 2 will respond with X. Thus, our subgame perfect equilibrium of this game is

$$SPE = (Up, (A, X)),$$

which yields payoffs of $(5, 5)$. This is the same result as in example 13.3. Before we changed the payoffs, both firms were already choosing this as their equilibrium outcome. Making this payoff better for both firms just reinforces this outcome even further.

Self-assessment exercise #13.4

SA 13.4 Repeat the analysis in example 13.4 but use the following game: Suppose that two firms could choose to *Cooperate* or *Compete* with one another. If both firms choose *Cooperate*, they both receive a payoff of 5. If one firm chooses *Cooperate* but the other firm chooses *Compete*, the firm that chooses *Cooperate* receives a payoff of 0, while the firm that chooses *Compete* receives a payoff of 7. Last, if both firms choose *Compete*, they both receive a payoff of 1. For which minimal discount factor δ do firms choose *Cooperate*? What if, when one firm chooses *Cooperate* and the other firm chooses *Compete*, the firm that chooses *Compete* receives a payoff of 10 instead? Interpret.

- First, we examine what would happen if the game were only played once in matrix 13.3.

Firm 2

		Cooperate	*Compete*
Firm 1	*Cooperate*	5, 5	0,<u>7</u>
	Compete	<u>7</u>, 0	<u>1</u>,<u>1</u>

Matrix 13.3. Competition Game.

When we analyze this game if it were played only once, we can observe that *Compete* strictly dominates *Cooperate* for both firms. Thus, our only Nash equilibrium in this game is where both firms choose *Compete* and receive a payoff of 1. Unfortunately, this is much worse than if both firms chose *Cooperate*, but the incentive to cheat against the cooperation is simply too strong to ignore for each firm. Now we examine whether we can sustain cooperation in the repeated form of this game by implementing a Grim-Trigger strategy where each firm chooses *Cooperate* until one firm chooses *Compete*, then every firm chooses *Compete* forever after.

- *No previous cheating.* When we implement our Grim-Trigger strategy, as long as no cheating has occurred in the past, each firm continues to choose *Cooperate* earning a payoff of 5 in every period. This leads to the following stream of discounted payoffs

$$5 + \delta 5 + \delta^2 5 + \ldots = 5(1 + \delta + \delta^2 + \ldots) = \frac{5}{1 - \delta},$$

since $1 + \delta + \delta^2 + \ldots = \frac{1}{1-\delta}$. If one firm chose to *Compete* instead, they would receive a payoff of 7 immediately, then a payoff of 1 for every period after as both firms revert to choosing *Compete* in every period. This leads to an alternative stream of discounted payoffs of,

$$7 + \delta 1 + \delta^2 1 + \ldots = 7 + 1(\delta + \delta^2 + \ldots) = 7 + \frac{\delta}{1 - \delta},$$

276

since $\delta+\delta^2+... = \delta(1+\delta+\delta^2+...) = \delta\frac{1}{1-\delta}$. Either firm will prefer to *Cooperate* over *Compete* as long as their stream of discounted payoffs while choosing *Cooperate* are higher than that if they chose *Compete*, i.e.,

$$\frac{5}{1-\delta} \geq 7 + \frac{\delta}{1-\delta}.$$

To solve this, first we multiply both sides of this inequality by $1-\delta$, which gives us $5 \geq 7(1-\delta)+\delta$. Rearranging terms, we have $5 \geq 7 - 6\delta$. Reorganizing terms gives us $6\delta \geq 2$. Last, we divide both sides of this expression by δ to obtain

$$\delta \geq \frac{1}{3},$$

which implies that any value of δ greater than $\frac{1}{3}$ can sustain cooperation in this case. By letting this inequality hold with equality, $\delta = \frac{1}{3}$, we have our minimal discount factor for firms to choose *Cooperate*.

- *Some cheating history.* Now we must examine if firms would want to deviate from their strategy of playing *Compete* when someone has played *Compete* in the past. By continuing to choose Compete, each firm receives a payoff of 1 in each period, leading to the following stream of discounted payoffs,

$$1 + \delta1 + \delta^21 + ... = 1(1 + \delta + \delta^2 + ...) = \frac{1}{1-\delta},$$

since $1+\delta+\delta^2+... = \frac{1}{1-\delta}$. Alternatively, either firm could choose to *Cooperate* for a period, earning 0 for that period and 1 for every period after as they revert back to choosing *Compete*. This leads to an alternative stream of discounted payoffs of,

$$0 + \delta1 + \delta^21 + ... = 0 + 1(\delta + \delta^2 + ...) = \frac{\delta}{1-\delta},$$

since $\delta + \delta^2 + ... = \delta(1 + \delta + \delta^2 + ...) = \delta\frac{1}{1-\delta}$. A firm would prefer to *Compete*, rather than *Cooperate* for a round if its stream of discounted payoffs is higher than that if they played *Cooperate* for that round, i.e.,

$$\frac{1}{1-\delta} \geq \frac{\delta}{1-\delta}.$$

Multiplying both sides by $1-\delta$, we have $\delta \leq 1$, which holds for all possibly values of δ. Thus, as long as $\delta \geq \frac{1}{3}$, our Grim-Trigger Strategy is a subgame perfect Nash equilibrium.

- *More incentive to cheat.* Now with our higher payoff from cheating, our Nash equilibrium in the single round game does not change. For the repeated game, as long as no cheating has occurred in the past, each firm continues to choose *Cooperate* earning a payoff of 5 in every period. This leads to the following stream of discounted payoffs,

$$5 + \delta 5 + \delta^2 5 + \ldots = 5(1 + \delta + \delta^2 + \ldots) = \frac{5}{1-\delta},$$

since $1 + \delta + \delta^2 + \ldots = \frac{1}{1-\delta}$. If one firm chose to *Compete* instead, they would receive a payoff of 10 immediately, then a payoff of 1 for every period after as both firms revert to choosing *Compete* in every period. This leads to an alternative stream of discounted payoffs of

$$10 + \delta 1 + \delta^2 1 + \ldots = 10 + 1(\delta + \delta^2 + \ldots) = 10 + \frac{\delta}{1-\delta},$$

since $\delta + \delta^2 + \ldots = \delta(1 + \delta + \delta^2 + \ldots) = \delta \frac{1}{1-\delta}$. Either firm will prefer to *Cooperate* over *Compete* as long as their stream of discounted payoffs while choosing *Cooperate* are higher than that if they chose *Compete*, i.e.,

$$\frac{5}{1-\delta} \geq 10 + \frac{\delta}{1-\delta}.$$

To solve this, first we multiply both sides of this inequality by $1 - \delta$, which gives us $5 \geq 10(1 - \delta) + \delta$. Rearranging terms, we have $5 \geq 10 - 9\delta$. Reorganizing terms gives us $9\delta \geq 5$. Last, we divide both sides of this expression by δ to obtain

$$\delta \geq \frac{5}{9}.$$

Once again, letting this hold with equality implies that the minimal discount factor to sustain cooperation is $\delta = \frac{5}{9}$. This is much higher than before. Intuitively, firms can make more by cheating on the agreement for a single round, so there is now much more incentive to do so. This makes cooperation much more challenging.

13.2 Solutions to End-of-Chapter Exercises

Exercise #13.1 - Backward Induction–I[A]

13.1 Find the SPE of the extensive-form game depicted in figure 13.7. Player 1's payoff is the top number, whereas player 2's payoff is the bottom number.

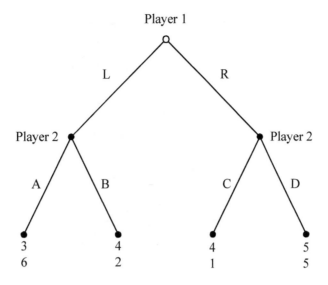

Figure 13.7. Backward Induction–I.

- To solve this game, we must make use of backward induction. We thus focus on player 2 first, as he is the last mover.

- *Player 2's best responses:*

    - When player 1 chooses L, player 2 can respond with A, leading to a payoff of 6, or B, leading to a payoff of 2. Since $6 > 2$, player 2's best response to player 1 choosing L is A, $BR_2(L) = A$.

    - When player 1 chooses R, player 2 can respond with C, leading to a payoff of 1, or D, leading to a payoff of 5. Since $1 < 5$, player 2's best response to player 1 choosing L is D, $BR_2(R) = D$.

    - Thus, player 2's equilibrium strategy is (A, D), which is depicted in figure 13.7a. With player 2's best responses found, we move up the extensive form to analyze player 1's strategy profile.

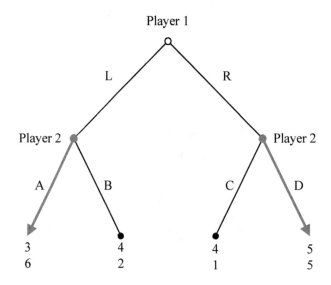

Figure 13.7a. Best responses for Backward Induction–I.

- *Player 1's optimal strategy:*
  - Anticipating player 2's reaction in the second stage, player 1 can choose L, anticipating that player 2 will respond by choosing A, leading to a payoff of 3; or player 1 can choose R, anticipating that player 2 will respond by choosing D, leading to a payoff of 5. Since $3 < 5$, player 1's equilibrium strategy is R.
- *SPE:* With all players' strategies analyzed, the SPE of this game is

$$(R, (A, D)),$$

which is depicted in figure 13.7b.

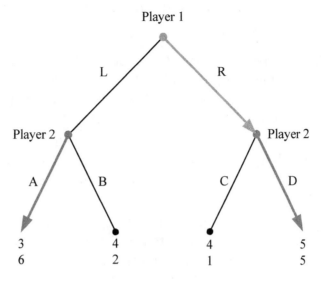

Figure 13.7b. SPE for Backward Induction–I.

Exercise #13.3 - Backward Induction–III^B

13.3 Find the SPE of the extensive-form game depicted in figure 13.9. Player 1's payoff is the top number, whereas player 2's payoff is the bottom number.

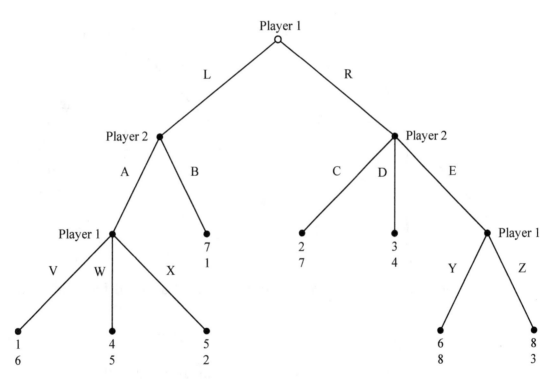

Figure 13.9. Backward Induction–III.

- To solve this game, we must make use of backward induction. We thus focus on player 1 first, as he is the last mover.

- *Player 1's best responses:*

  - When player 1 chooses L and player 2 chooses A, player 1 can respond with V, leading to a payoff of 1, W, leading to a payoff of 4, or X, leading to a payoff of 5. Since $1 < 4 < 5$, player 1's best response to player 1 choosing L and player 2 choosing A is X, $BR_1(L, A) = X$.

  - When player 1 chooses R and player 2 chooses E, player 1 can respond with Y, leading to a payoff of 6, or Z, leading to a payoff of 8. Since $6 < 8$, player 1's best response to player 1 choosing R and player 2 choosing E is Z, $BR_1(R, E) = Z$.

  - Thus, player 1's equilibrium strategy when he reaches his second set of actions is (X, Z), which is depicted in figure 13.9a. With player 1's best responses found, we move up the extensive form to analyze player 2's strategy profile.

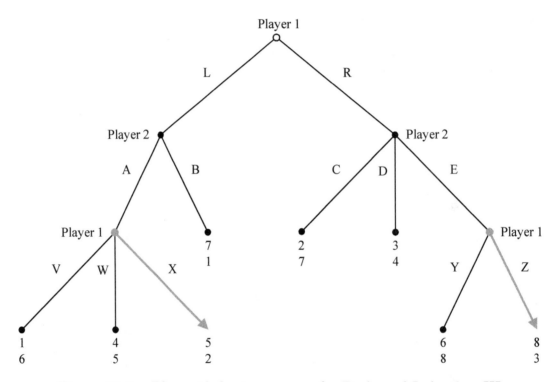

Figure 13.9a. Player 1's best responses for Backward Induction–III.

- *Player 2's best responses:*

  - When player 1 chooses L, player 2 can respond with A, anticipating that player 1 will respond by choosing X, leading to a payoff of 2, or B, leading to a payoff of 1. Since $2 > 1$, player 2's best response to player 1 choosing L is A, $BR_2(L) = A$.

– When player 1 chooses R, player 2 can respond with C, leading to a payoff of 7, D, leading to a payoff of 4, or E, anticipating that player 1 will respond by choosing R, leading to a payoff of 3. Since $7 > 4 > 3$, player 2's best response to player 1 choosing R is C, $BR_2(R) = C$.

– Thus, player 2's equilibrium strategy is (A, C), which is depicted in figure 13.9b. With player 2's best responses found, we move up the extensive form to analyze player 1's strategy profile.

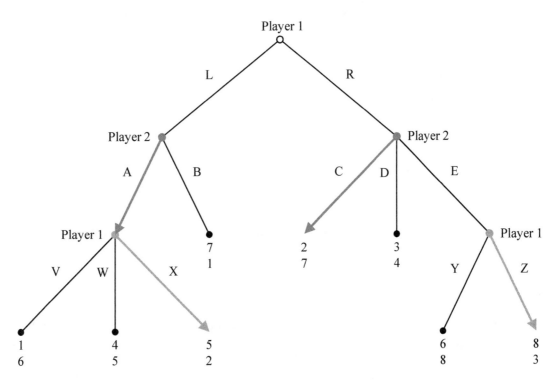

Figure 13.9b. Player 2's best responses for Backward Induction–III.

- *Player 1's optimal strategy:*

  – Anticipating the actions in later rounds by both players, player 1 can choose L, anticipating that player 2 will respond by choosing A and player 1 will respond by choosing X, leading to a payoff of 5; or player 1 can choose R, anticipating that player 2 will respond by choosing C, leading to a payoff of 2. Since $5 > 2$, player 1's equilibrium strategy at his first set of actions is L.

- *SPE:* With all players' strategies analyzed, the SPE of this game is

$$((L, (X, Z)), (A, C)),$$

which is depicted in figure 13.9c.

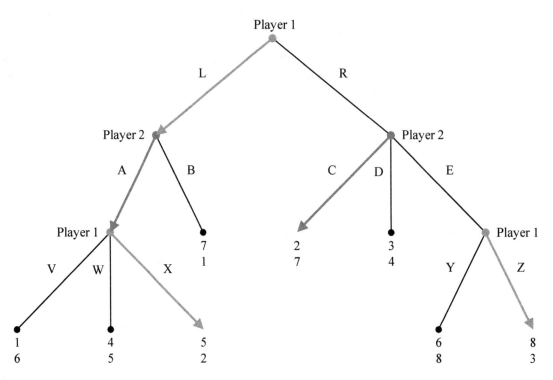

Figure 13.9c. SPE for Backward Induction–III.

Exercise #13.5 - Backward Induction–V^B

13.5 Find the SPE of the extensive-form game in figure 13.11. Player 1's payoff is the top number, whereas player 2's payoff is the bottom number.

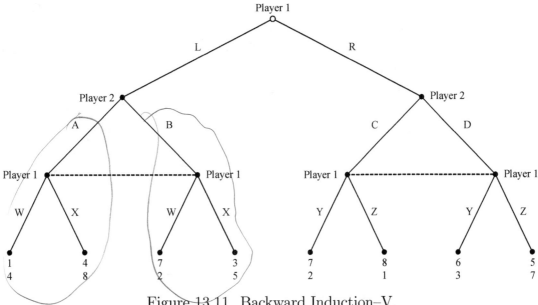

Figure 13.11. Backward Induction–V.

- To solve this game, we must make use of backward induction. We thus focus on player 1 first, as he is the last mover.

- *Player 1's best responses:*

  − We cannot analyze any of player 1's nodes at this level as they are not proper subgames due to them existing in the same information sets. We shall analyze them with player 2's strategy profile.

- *Player 2's best responses:*

  − When player 1 chooses L, player 2's action cannot be properly observed by player 1. This effectively makes the subgame where player 1 chooses L a simultaneous move game with the following normal form representation,

		Player 2	
		A	B
Player 1	W	1, 4	7, 2
	X	4, 8	3, 5

As before with simultaneous move games, we analyze each player's best responses individually.

  * *Player 1's best responses:* When player 2 chooses A, player 1 can respond with W, leading to a payoff of 1, or X, leading to a payoff of 4. Since $1 < 4$, player 1's best response to player 2 choosing A is X, $BR_1(A) = X$. When player 2 chooses B, player 1 can respond with W, leading to a payoff of 7, or X, leading to a payoff of 3. Since $7 > 3$, player 1's best response to player 2 choosing B is W, $BR_1(B) = W$.

* *Player 2's best responses:* When player 1 chooses W, player 2 can respond with A, leading to a payoff of 4, or B, leading to a payoff of 2. Since $4 > 2$, player 2's best response to player 1 choosing W is A, $BR_1(W) = A$. When player 1 chooses X, player 2 can respond with A, leading to a payoff of 8, or B, leading to a payoff of 5. Since $8 > 5$, player 2's best response to player 1 choosing X is A, $BR_2(X) = A$.

* *Nash equilibrium of the subgame:* With the best responses for each player identified, there exists a single Nash equilibrium, (X, A).

- When player 1 chooses R, player 2's action cannot be properly observed by player 1. This effectively makes the subgame where player 1 chooses R a simultaneous move game with the following normal form representation,

Player 2

		C	D
	Y	7, 2	6, 3
Player 1	Z	8, 1	5, 7

As before with simultaneous move games, we analyze each player's best responses individually.

* *Player 1's best responses:* When player 2 chooses C, player 1 can respond with Y, leading to a payoff of 7, or Z, leading to a payoff of 8. Since $7 < 8$, player 1's best response to player 2 choosing C is Z, $BR_1(C) = Z$. When player 2 chooses D, player 1 can respond with Y, leading to a payoff of 6, or Z, leading to a payoff of 5. Since $6 > 5$, player 1's best response to player 2 choosing D is Y, $BR_1(D) = Y$.

* *Player 2's best responses:* When player 1 chooses Y, player 2 can respond with C, leading to a payoff of 2, or D, leading to a payoff of 3. Since $2 < 3$, player 2's best response to player 1 choosing Y is D, $BR_1(Y) = D$. When player 1 chooses Z, player 2 can respond with C, leading to a payoff of 1, or D, leading to a payoff of 7. Since $1 < 7$, player 2's best response to player 1 choosing Z is D, $BR_2(Z) = D$.

* *Nash equilibrium of the subgame:* With the best responses for each player identified, there exists a single Nash equilibrium, (Y, D).

- Thus, player 2's equilibrium strategy is (A, D) and player 1's equilibrium strategy at the final stage of the game is (X, Y), which is depicted in figure 13.11a. With player 2's best responses found, we move up the extensive form to analyze player 1's strategy profile.

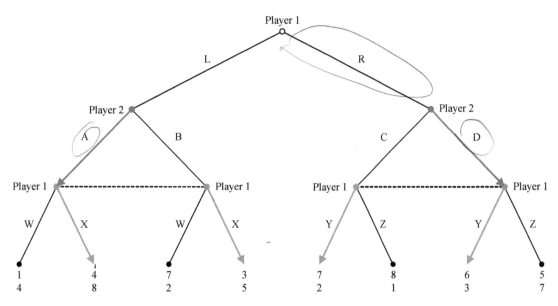

Figure 13.11a. Player 1 and 2's best responses for Backward Induction–V.

- *Player 1's optimal strategy:*
  - Anticipating how players 2 and themselves will react in later rounds of the game, player 1 can choose L, anticipating that player 2 will respond by choosing A and player 1 will respond by choosing X, leading to a payoff of 4; or player 1 can choose R, anticipating that player 2 will respond by choosing D and player 1 will respond by choosing Y, leading to a payoff of 6. Since $4 < 6$, player 1's equilibrium strategy at his first set of actions is R.
- *SPE:* With all players' strategies analyzed, the SPE of this game is

$$((R, (A, D)), (X, Y)),$$

which is depicted in figure 13.11b.

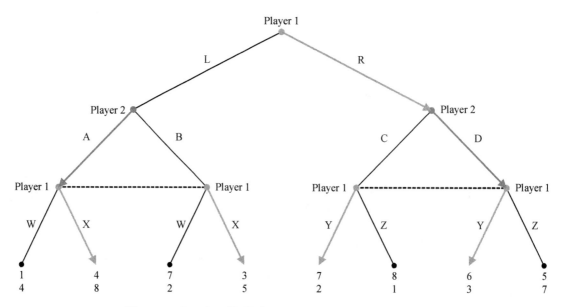

Figure 13.11b. SPE for Backward Induction–V.

Exercise #13.7 - Battle of the Sexes Game[A]

13.7 Consider the Battle of the Sexes game in example 12.6 from chapter 12.

(a) Suppose now that Felix chooses where he goes first, and then Ana observes Felix's choice and decides where to go afterward. Find the SPE of this game.

- First, we must convert the Battle of the Sexes game from the simultaneous version to a sequential version with Felix choosing first. The extensive form of this game is depicted in figure 13.12.

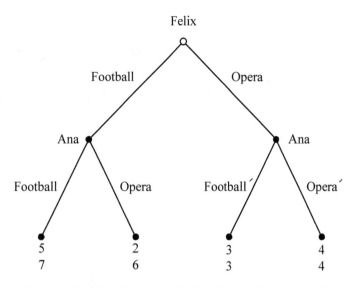

Figure 13.12. Sequential Battle of the Sexes–I.

- To solve this game, we must make use of backward induction. We thus focus on Ana first, as she is the last mover.

- *Ana's best responses:*

  - When Felix chooses *Football*, Ana can respond with *Football*, leading to a payoff of 7, or *Opera*, leading to a payoff of 6. Since $7 > 6$, Ana's best response to Felix choosing *Football* is *Football*, $BR_A(F) = F$.

  - When Felix chooses *Opera*, Ana can respond with *Football'*, leading to a payoff of 3, or *Opera'*, leading to a payoff of 4. Since $3 < 4$, Ana's best response to Felix choosing *Opera* is *Opera'*, $BR_A(O) = O'$.

  - Thus, Ana's equilibrium strategy is (F, O'), which is depicted in figure 13.12a. With Ana's best responses found, we move up the extensive form to analyze Felix's strategy profile.

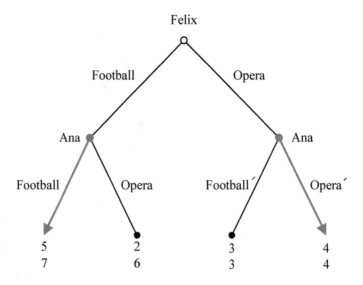

Figure 13.12a. Ana's best responses in sequential Battle of the Sexes–I.

- *Felix's optimal strategy:*
  - Anticipating Ana's reaction in the second stage, Felix can choose *Football*, anticipating that Ana will respond by choosing *Football*, leading to a payoff of 5; or Felix can choose *Opera*, anticipating that Ana will respond by choosing *Opera'*, leading to a payoff of 4. Since 5 > 4, Felix's equilibrium strategy is *Football, F*.
- *SPE:* With all players' strategies analyzed, the SPE of this game is

$$(F, (F, O')),$$

which is depicted in figure 13.12b.

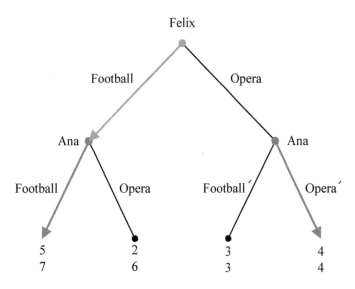

Figure 13.12b. SPE for sequential Battle of the Sexes–I.

(b) Suppose now that Ana chooses where she goes first, and then Felix observes Ana's choice and decides where to go afterward. Find the SPE of this game.

- Now we must convert the Battle of the Sexes game from the simultaneous version to a sequential version with Ana choosing first. The extensive form of this game is depicted in figure 13.13.

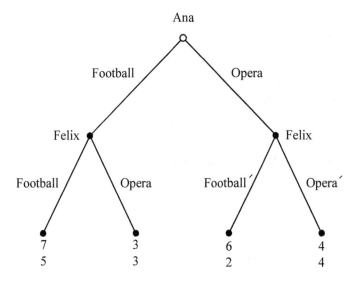

Figure 13.13. Sequential Battle of the Sexes–II.

- To solve this game, we must make use of backward induction. We thus focus on Felix first, as he is the last mover.
- *Felix's best responses:*
  - When Ana chooses *Football*, Felix can respond with *Football*, leading to a payoff of 5, or *Opera*, leading to a payoff of 3. Since $5 > 3$, Felix's best response to Ana choosing *Football* is *Football*, $BR_F(F) = F$.

- When Ana chooses *Opera*, Felix can respond with *Football'*, leading to a payoff of 2, or *Opera'*, leading to a payoff of 4. Since $2 < 4$, Felix's best response to Ana choosing *Opera* is *Opera'*, $BR_F(O) = O'$.
- Thus, Felix's equilibrium strategy is (F, O'), which is depicted in figure 13.13a. With Felix's best responses found, we move up the extensive form to analyze Ana's strategy profile.

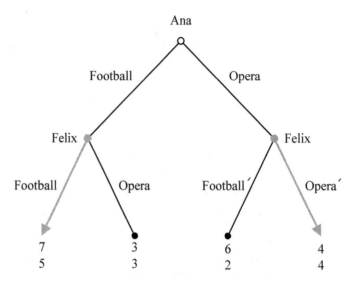

Figure 13.13a. Felix's best responses for sequential Battle of the Sexes–II.

- *Ana's optimal strategy:*
  - Anticipating Felix's reaction in the second stage, Ana can choose *Football*, anticipating that Felix will respond by choosing *Football*, leading to a payoff of 7; or Ana can choose *Opera*, anticipating that Felix will respond by choosing *Opera'*, leading to a payoff of 4. Since $7 > 4$, Ana's equilibrium strategy is *Football*, F.
- *SPE:* With all players' strategies analyzed, the SPE of this game is

$$((F, O'), F),$$

which is depicted in figure 13.13b.

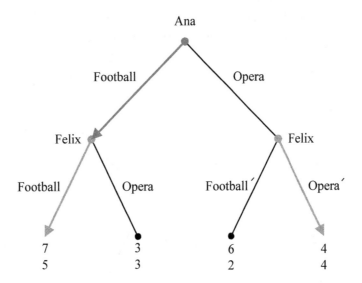

Figure 13.13b. SPE for sequential Battle of the Sexes–II.

(c) Compare the results from parts (a) and (b), and the results from the simultaneous-move version of this game. If they are similar, explain why. If they are different, provide an explanation for any differences.

- The results of the simultaneous-move version game are reproduced here for comparison purposes.

		Ana	
		Football	Opera
Felix	Football	5,7	2,6
	Opera	3,3	4,4

Rather than having two separate Nash equilibria as in the simultaneous-move game, the sequential-move games both arrive at the SPE of (F, F). When either Felix or Ana was able to choose first, they knew that whoever chose second would always pick one of the two Nash equilibria from the simultaneous version of the game. This allows them to choose the Nash equilibria that they prefer the most as the SPE, which happens to be Football for both of them. Notice that the Nash equilibrium (F, F) Pareto dominates (is better for every player) the other Nash equilibrium, (O, O). This means it is the sole outcome regardless of whoever moves first in the sequential-move game.

Exercise #13.9 - Anticoordination Game[A]

13.9 Consider the Anticoordination game in example 12.8 from chapter 12.

(a) Suppose now that player 1 chooses whether to swerve or stay first, and then player 2 observes player 1's choice and responds by staying or swerving. Find the SPE of this game.

- First we must convert the Anticoordination game from the simultaneous version to a sequential version with player 1 choosing first. The extensive form of this game is depicted in figure 13.14.

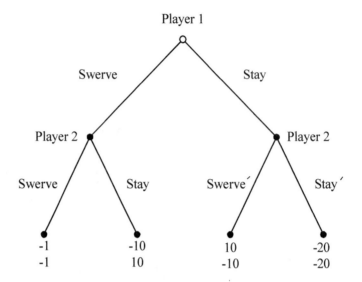

Figure 13.14. Sequential Anticoordination game–I.

- To solve this game, we must make use of backward induction. We thus focus on player 2 first, as he is the last mover.
- *Player 2's best responses:*
    - When player 1 chooses *Swerve*, player 2 can respond with *Swerve*, leading to a payoff of -1, or *Stay*, leading to a payoff of 10. Since $-1 < 10$, player 2's best response to player 1 choosing *Swerve* is *Stay*, $BR_2(Swerve) = Stay$.
    - When player 1 chooses *Stay*, player 2 can respond with *Swerve'*, leading to a payoff of -10, or *Stay'*, leading to a payoff of -20. Since $-10 > -20$, player 2's best response to player 1 choosing *Stay* is *Swerve'*, $BR_2(Stay) = Swerve'$.
    - Thus, player 2's equilibrium strategy is $(Stay, Swerve')$, which is depicted in figure 13.14a. With player 2's best responses found, we move up the extensive form to analyze player 1's strategy profile.

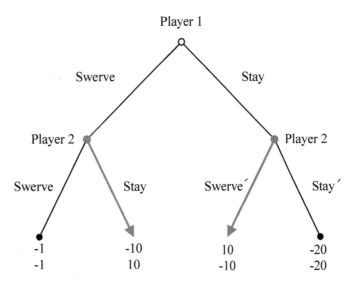

Figure 13.14a. Player 2's best response for sequential Anticoordination game–I.

- *Player 1's optimal strategy:*
  - Anticipating player 2's reaction in the second stage, player 1 can choose *Swerve*, anticipating that player 2 will respond by choosing *Stay*, leading to a payoff of -10; or player 1 can choose *Stay*, anticipating that player 2 will respond by choosing *Swerve'*, leading to a payoff of 10. Since $-10 < 10$, player 1's equilibrium strategy is *Stay*.
- *SPE:* With all players' strategies analyzed, the SPE of this game is

$$(Stay, (Stay, Swerve')),$$

which is depicted in figure 13.14b.

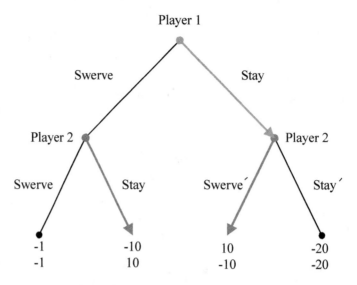

Figure 13.14b. SPE for sequential Anticoordination game–I.

(b) Suppose now that player 2 chooses whether to swerve or stay first, and then player 1 observes player 2's choice and responds by staying or swerving. Find the SPE of this game.

- Now we must convert the Anticoordination game from the simultaneous version to a sequential version with player 2 choosing first. The extensive form of this game is depicted in figure 13.15. (Note that player 1's payoffs are now listed second in the terminal nodes at the bottom of the tree, since he is the second mover in this version of the game.)

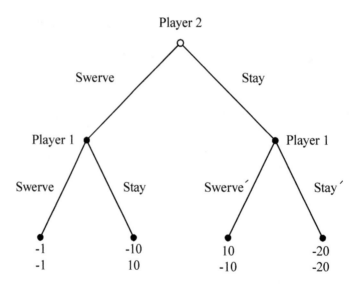

Figure 13.15. Sequential Anticoordination game–II.

- To solve this game, we must make use of backward induction. We thus focus on player 1 first, as he is the last mover.
- *Player 1's best responses:*

296

- When player 2 chooses *Swerve*, player 1 can respond with *Swerve*, leading to a payoff of -1, or *Stay*, leading to a payoff of 10. Since $-1 < 10$, player 1's best response to player 2 choosing *Swerve* is *Stay*, $BR_1(Swerve) = Stay$.

- When player 2 chooses *Stay*, player 1 can respond with *Swerve'*, leading to a payoff of -10, or *Stay'*, leading to a payoff of -20. Since $-10 > -20$, player 1's best response to player 2 choosing *Stay* is *Swerve'*, $BR_1(Stay) = Swerve'$.

- Thus, player 1's equilibrium strategy is $(Stay, Swerve')$, which is depicted in figure 13.15a. With player 1's best responses found, we move up the extensive form to analyze player 2's strategy profile.

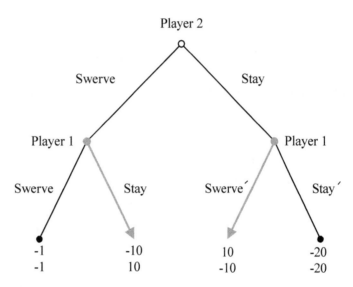

Figure 13.15a. Player 1's best responses for sequential Anticoordination game–II.

- *Player 2's optimal strategy:*
  - Anticipating player 1's reaction in the second stage, player 2 can choose *Swerve*, anticipating that player 1 will respond by choosing *Stay*, leading to a payoff of -10; or player 2 can choose *Stay*, anticipating that player 1 will respond by choosing *Swerve'*, leading to a payoff of 10. Since $-10 < 10$, player 2's equilibrium strategy is *Stay*.

- *SPE:* With all players' strategies analyzed, the SPE of this game is

$$((Stay, Swerve'), Stay)$$

which is depicted in figure 13.15b.

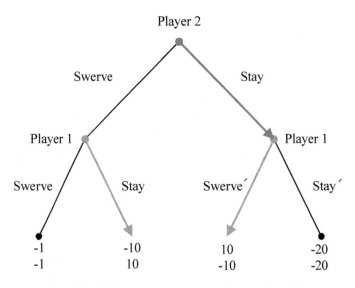

Figure 13.15b. SPE for sequential Anticoordination game–II.

(c) Compare the results from parts (a) and (b), and the results from the simultaneous-move version of this game. If they are similar, explain why. If they are different, provide an explanation for any differences.

- The results of the simultaneous-move version game are reproduced here for comparison purposes.

		Player 2	
		Swerve	Stay
Player 1	Swerve	$-1,-1$	$-10,\underline{10}$
	Stay	$\underline{10},-10$	$-20,-20$

In the Anticoordination game, we find that depending on which player moves first we end up at different Nash equilibria from the simultaneous version of the game. When either of the players was able to choose first, they knew that whoever chose second would always pick one of the two Nash equilibria from the simultaneous version of the game. This allows them to choose the Nash equilibria that they prefer the most as the SPE, which happens to be (*Stay, Swerve*) for player 1 and (*Swerve, Stay*) for player 2. This is a classic game of first-mover's advantage.

Exercise #13.11 - Complementary Pricing[B]

13.11 Consider a situation where two firms of complementary goods are simultaneously deciding whether to price high or low. While not direct competitors in their respective markets, they know that if one firm prices high while the other prices low, that is not beneficial to either firm. The normal-form representation is presented here where the payoffs (in dollars) denote the profits for each firm:

$$
\begin{array}{cc}
 & \textit{Firm 2} \\
 & \begin{array}{cc} \text{High} & \text{Low} \end{array}
\end{array}
$$

		High	Low
Firm 1	High	90, 75	35, 40
	Low	45, 30	60, 60

(a) Find all pure-strategy Nash equilibria of this game. Do the firms know how they should price?

- We can analyze this game by examining each firm's best response to the other firm's pricing strategies.

  - *Firm 1's best responses:* When firm 2 chooses *High*, firm 1 can respond with *High*, leading to a payoff of 90, or *Low*, leading to a payoff of 45. Since $90 > 45$, firm 1's best response to firm 2 choosing *High* is *High*, $BR_1(H) = H$. When firm 2 chooses *Low*, firm 1 can respond with *High*, leading to a payoff of 35, or *Low*, leading to a payoff of 60. Since $35 < 60$, firm 1's best response to firm 2 choosing *Low* is *Low*, $BR_1(L) = L$.

  - *Firm 2's best responses:* When firm 1 chooses *High*, firm 2 can respond with *High*, leading to a payoff of 75, or *Low*, leading to a payoff of 40. Since $75 > 40$, firm 2's best response to firm 1 choosing *High* is *High*, $BR_2(H) = H$. When firm 1 chooses *Low*, firm 2 can respond with *High*, leading to a payoff of 30, or *Low*, leading to a payoff of 60. Since $30 < 60$, firm 2's best response to firm 1 choosing *Low* is *Low*, $BR_2(L) = L$.

  - *Nash equilibrium:* With the best responses for each player identified, there exists two Nash equilibria in pure strategies, (H, H) and (L, L).

- Since there are two Nash equilibria in pure strategies, the firms do not know how they should price. Their best outcomes are when they coordinate with either high or low prices, but since they must choose simultaneously, there is significant room for error.

(b) Suppose now that firm 1 sets their price first, and then firm 2 observes the price and responds. Depict the extensive form of this game and find the SPE.

- First we must convert the Complementary Pricing game from the simultaneous version to a sequential version with firm 1 choosing first. The extensive form of this game is depicted in figure 13.16.

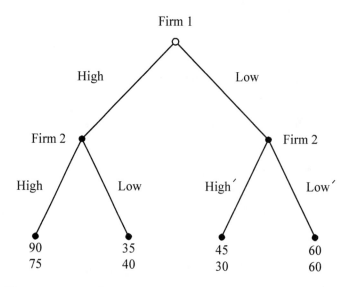

Figure 13.16. Sequential Complementary Pricing–I.

- To solve this game, we must make use of backward induction. We thus focus on firm 2 first, as they are the last mover.

- *Firm 2's best responses:*

  - When firm 1 chooses *High*, firm 2 can respond with *High*, leading to a payoff of 75, or *Low*, leading to a payoff of 40. Since 75 > 40, firm 2's best response to firm 1 choosing *High* is *High*, $BR_2(H) = H$.

  - When firm 1 chooses *Low*, firm 2 can respond with *High'*, leading to a payoff of 30, or *Low'*, leading to a payoff of 60. Since 30 < 60, firm 2's best response to firm 1 choosing *Low* is *Low'*, $BR_2(L) = L'$.

  - Thus, firm 2's equilibrium strategy is (H, L'), which is depicted in figure 13.16a. With firm 2's best responses found, we move up the extensive form to analyze firm 1's strategy profile.

300

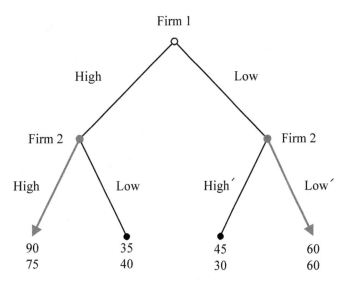

Figure 13.16a. Firm 2's best responses for Sequential Complementary Pricing–I.

- *Firm 1's optimal strategy:*
  - Anticipating firm 2's reaction in the second stage, firm 1 can choose *High*, anticipating that firm 2 will respond by choosing *High*, leading to a payoff of 90; or firm 1 can choose *Low*, anticipating that firm 2 will respond by choosing *Low'*, leading to a payoff of 60. Since 90 > 60, firm 1's equilibrium strategy is *High*, *H*.
- *SPE:* With all players' strategies analyzed, the SPE of this game is

$$(H, (H, L')),$$

which is depicted in figure 13.16b.

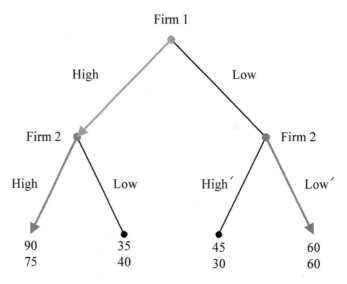

Figure 13.16b. SPE for Sequential Complementary Pricing–I.

(c) Suppose now that firm 2 sets their price first, and then firm 1 observes the price and responds. Depict the extensive form of this game and find the SPE.

- Now we must convert the Complementary Pricing game from the simultaneous version to a sequential version with firm 2 choosing first. The extensive form of this game is depicted in figure 13.17. Note that, at each terminal node at the bottom of the tree, the top payoff now corresponds to the first mover (firm 2) while the bottom payoff denotes that going to the last mover (firm 1).

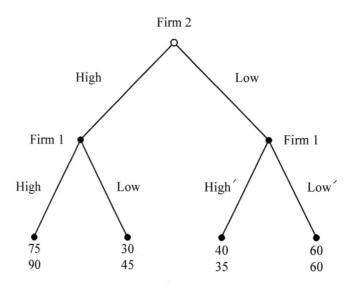

Figure 13.17 Sequential Complementary Pricing–II.

- To solve this game, we must make use of backward induction. We thus focus on firm 1 first, as they are the last mover.
- *Firm 1's best responses:*
  - When firm 2 chooses *High*, firm 1 can respond with *High*, leading to a

302

payoff of 90, or *Low*, leading to a payoff of 45. Since $90 > 45$, firm 1's best response to firm 2 choosing *High* is *High*, $BR_1(H) = H$.

- When firm 2 chooses *Low*, firm 1 can respond with *High'*, leading to a payoff of 35, or *Low'*, leading to a payoff of 60. Since $35 < 60$, firm 1's best response to firm 2 choosing *Low* is *Low'*, $BR_1(L) = L'$.

- Thus, firm 1's equilibrium strategy is (H, L'), which is depicted in figure 13.17a. With firm 1's best responses found, we move up the extensive form to analyze firm 2's strategy profile.

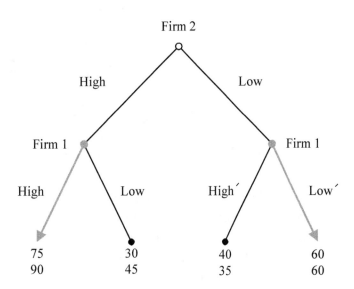

Figure 13.17a. Player 1's best responses for Sequential Complementary Pricing–II.

- *Firm 2's optimal strategy:*
  - Anticipating firm 1's reaction in the second stage, firm 2 can choose *High*, anticipating that firm 1 will respond by choosing *High*, leading to a payoff of 75; or firm 2 can choose *Low*, anticipating that firm 1 will respond by choosing *Low'*, leading to a payoff of 60. Since $75 > 60$, firm 2's equilibrium strategy is *High, H*.

- *SPE:* With all players' strategies analyzed, the SPE of this game is

$$((H, L'), H),$$

which is depicted in figure 13.17b.

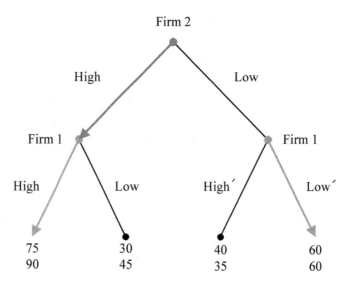

Figure 13.17b. SPE for Sequential Complementary Pricing–II.

(d) Compare the results from parts (a), (b), and (c). If they are similar, explain why. If they are different, provide an explanation for any differences.

- Rather than having two separate Nash equilibria, as in the simultaneous-move game, the sequential move games both arrive at the SPE of (H, H). When either firm was able to choose first, they knew that whoever chose second would always pick one of the two Nash equilibria from the simultaneous version of the game. This allows them to choose the Nash equilibria that they prefer the most as the SPE, which happens to be *High* for both of them. Notice that the Nash equilibrium (H, H) Pareto dominates (is better for every firm) the other Nash equilibrium, (L, L). This means it is the sole outcome regardless of whoever moves first in the sequential move game.

Exercise #13.13 - Centipede Game[C]

13.13 Consider a game where two players take turns deciding whether to take a pile of money. At the start of the game, there are two piles of money, one "large" pile, with $5 and one "small" pile, with $1. Player 1 gets to choose whether to take the large pile or leave both piles alone.

- If player 1 takes the large pile, he receives $5 as his payoff, and player 2 receives the small pile, $1, as his payoff, and the game ends.
- If player 1 leaves both piles alone, both the large and the small piles double ($10, and $2, respectively).
- Player 2 then decides whether to take the large pile or leave both piles alone.
- Every time a player leaves both piles alone, both piles double in size.
- Players take turns deciding whether to take the large pile or leave the piles alone until each player has had three opportunities to take the large pile (six rounds total).

- If, at the end of the game, neither player has taken the large pile, player 1 is awarded the large pile (which will contain $320 at this point), and player 2 is awarded the small pile (which will contain $64).

(a) Depict the extensive form of this game.

- Building the extensive form of this game is straightforward. For each of the six rounds, we double both payoffs and whoever chooses to take the pile receives the larger payoff, while the player who does not receives the smaller payoff. The extensive form tree is depicted in figure 13.18.

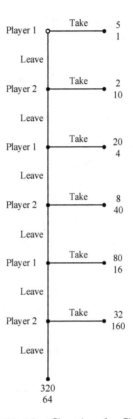

Figure 13.18. Centipede Game–I.

(b) Find the SPE of this game.

- To solve this game, we must make use of backward induction. We thus focus on player 2 first, as he is the last mover.
- *Player 2's best response (Sixth round):*
  - When player 1 chooses Leave in the fifth round, player 2 can respond with Leave, leading to a payoff of 64; or Take, leading to a payoff of 160. Since $64 < 160$, player 2's best response to player 1 choosing Leave in the fifth round is Take, $BR_2(L) = T$.
- *Player 1's best response (Fifth round):*
  - When player 2 chooses Leave in the fourth round, player 1 can respond with Leave, anticipating that player 2 will respond with Take in the sixth round, leading to a payoff of 32, or Take, leading to a payoff of 80. Since

$32 < 80$, player 1's best response to player 2 choosing Leave in the fourth round is Take, $BR_1(L) = T$.

- *Player 2's best response (Fourth round):*
  - When player 1 chooses Leave in the third round, player 2 can respond with Leave, anticipating that player 1 will respond with Take in the fifth round, leading to a payoff of 16, or Take, leading to a payoff of 40. Since $16 < 40$, player 2's best response to player 1 choosing Leave in the third round is Take, $BR_2(L) = T$.

- *Player 1's best response (Third round):*
  - When player 2 chooses Leave in the second round, player 1 can respond with Leave, anticipating that player 2 will respond with Take in the fourth round, leading to a payoff of 8, or Take, leading to a payoff of 20. Since $8 < 20$, player 1's best response to player 2 choosing Leave in the second round is Take, $BR_1(L) = T$.

- *Player 2's best response (Second round):*
  - When player 1 chooses Leave in the first round, player 2 can respond with Leave, anticipating that player 1 will respond with Take in the third round, leading to a payoff of 4, or Take, leading to a payoff of 10. Since $4 < 10$, player 2's best response to player 1 choosing Leave in the first round is Take, $BR_2(L) = T$.

- *Player 1's optimal strategy (First round):*
  - Anticipating player 2's reaction in the second stage, player 1 can choose Leave, anticipating that player 2 responds with Take in the second round, and receive a payoff of 2; or Leave, and receive a payoff of 5. Since $2 < 5$, player 1's equilibrium strategy is Take, T.

- *SPE:* With all players' strategies analyzed, the SPE of this game is

$$((T, T, T), (T, T, T)),$$

which is depicted in figure 13.18a.

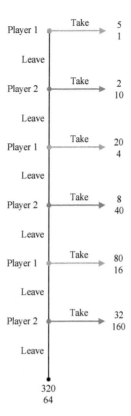

Figure 13.18a. spNE for Centipede Game–I.

Interestingly, had player 1 allowed player 2 to take the large pile of money in the sixth round, he would have received a payoff of 32, over six times his equilibrium payoff of 5. Player 1 takes the large pile of money right away, however, as he fears that player 2 will take the large pile of money as early as round 2.

(c) Suppose that, if at the end of the game no player ever takes the large pile of money, both players are awarded an equal share of both the piles of money, rather than player 1 being awarded the large pile as in previous parts of the exercise. Find the SPE of this game.

- In this case, the final payoff of the game when both players leave the large pile changes to $(192, 192)$. The new extensive form of this game is depicted in figure 13.19.

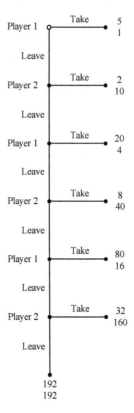

Figure 13.19. Centipede Game–II.

To solve this game, we must make use of backward induction. We thus focus on player 2 first, as he is the last mover.

- *Player 2's best response (Sixth round):*
  - When player 1 chooses Leave in the fifth round, player 2 can respond with Leave, leading to a payoff of 192; or Take, leading to a payoff of 160. Since $192 > 160$, player 2's best response to player 1 choosing Leave in the fifth round is Leave, $BR_2(L) = L$.
- *Player 1's best response (Fifth round):*
  - When player 2 chooses Leave in the fourth round, player 1 can respond with Leave, anticipating that player 2 will respond with Leave in the sixth round, leading to a payoff of 192, or Take, leading to a payoff of 80. Since $192 > 80$, player 1's best response to player 2 choosing Leave in the fourth round is Leave, $BR_1(L) = L$.
- *Player 2's best response (Fourth round):*
  - When player 1 chooses Leave in the third round, player 2 can respond with Leave, anticipating that player 1 will respond with Leave in the fifth round, leading to a payoff of 192; or Take, leading to a payoff of 40. Since $192 > 40$, player 2's best response to player 1 choosing Leave in the third round is Leave, $BR_2(L) = L$.
- *Player 1's best response (Third round):*
  - When player 2 chooses Leave in the second round, player 1 can respond

308

with Leave, anticipating that player 2 will respond with Leave in the fourth and sixth rounds, leading to a payoff of 192, or Take, leading to a payoff of 20. Since $192 > 20$, player 1's best response to player 2 choosing Leave in the second round is Leave, $BR_1(L) = L$.

- *Player 2's best response (Second round):*
  - When player 1 chooses Leave in the first round, player 2 can respond with Leave, anticipating that player 1 will respond with Leave in the third and fifth rounds, leading to a payoff of 192, or Take, leading to a payoff of 10. Since $192 > 10$, player 2's best response to player 1 choosing Leave in the first round is Leave, $BR_2(L) = L$.

- *Player 1's optimal strategy (First round):*
  - Anticipating player 2's reaction in the second, fourth, and sixth rounds and his own reactions in the third and fifth rounds, player 1 can choose Leave, anticipating that player 2 responds with Leave in the second, fourth and sixth rounds, and receive a payoff of 192; or Leave, and receive a payoff of 5. Since $192 > 5$, player 1's equilibrium strategy is Leave, L.

- *SPE:* With all players' strategies analyzed, theSPE of this game is

$$((L, L, L), (L, L, L)),$$

which is depicted in figure 13.19a.

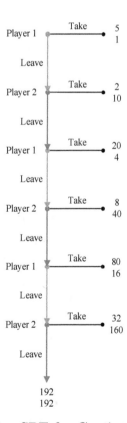

Figure 13.19a. SPE for Centipede Game–II.

With a strong enough prize for cooperating, both players now leave the large pile of money alone until the end of the game. It is interesting to observe how changing a single payoff can change every best response in the game.

Exercise #13.15 - Repeated Dilemmas[B]

13.15 Repeat the infinitely repeated Prisoner's Dilemma game of this chapter, but assume different discount factors for each player, δ_1 for the row player and δ_2 for the column player.

- To analyze the repeated version of this game, we must examine the cheating history.
- *No previous cheating.* When we implement our Grim-Trigger strategy, as long as no cheating has occurred in the past, each player continues to choose *Not Confess* earning a payoff of -1 in every period.. This leads to the following stream of discounted payoffs,

$$-1 + \delta_i(-1) + \delta_i^2(-1) + ... = -1(1 + \delta_i + \delta_i^2 + ...) \quad \text{for } i = 1, 2.$$

Recall that $1 + \delta_i + \delta_i^2 + ...$ is an infinite series that adds up to $\frac{1}{1-\delta_i}$. Substituting this into our expression yields,

$$-1(1 + \delta_i + \delta_i^2 + ...) = \frac{-1}{1 - \delta_i} \quad \text{for } i = 1, 2.$$

If one player chose to *Confess* instead, he would receive a payoff of 0 immediately, then a payoff of -5 for every period after as both players revert to choosing *Confess* in every period. This leads to an alternative stream of discounted payoffs of

$$0 + \delta_i(-5) + \delta_i^2(-5) + ... = -5\delta_i(1 + \delta_i + \delta_i^2 + ...) \quad \text{for } i = 1, 2.$$

Once again, since $1 + \delta_i + \delta_i^2 + ... = \frac{1}{1-\delta_i}$, we can substitute to obtain

$$-5\delta_i(1 + \delta_i + \delta_i^2 + ...) = \frac{-5\delta_i}{1 - \delta_i} \quad \text{for } i = 1, 2.$$

Either player will prefer to *Not Confess* over *Confess* as long as his stream of discounted payoffs while choosing *Not Confess* are higher than that if they chose *Confess*, i.e.,

$$\frac{-1}{1 - \delta_i} \geq \frac{-5\delta_i}{1 - \delta_i} \quad \text{for } i = 1, 2.$$

To solve this, first we multiply both sides of this inequality by $1 - \delta_i$, which gives us $-1 \geq -5\delta_i$. Then we divide both sides of this expression by -5 to obtain

$$\delta_i \geq \frac{1}{5} \quad \text{for } i = 1, 2,$$

which implies that both δ_1 and δ_2 must be greater than or equal to $\frac{1}{5}$ to sustain cooperation in this case. Intuitively, even if player 1 is relatively patient ($\delta_1 \geq \frac{1}{5}$), if player 2 is not, then neither player can sustain the Grim-Trigger strategy.

- *Some cheating history.* Now we must examine if players would want to deviate from their strategy of playing *Confess* when someone has played *Confess* in the past. By continuing to choose *Confess*, each player receives a payoff of -5 in each period, leading to the following stream of discounted payoffs,

$$-5 + \delta_i(-5) + \delta_i^2(-5) + ... = -5(1 + \delta_i + \delta_i^2 + ...) \quad \text{for } i = 1, 2.$$

Once again, since $1 + \delta_i + \delta_i^2 + ... = \frac{1}{1-\delta_i}$, we can substitute to obtain

$$-5(1 + \delta_i + \delta_i^2 + ...) = \frac{-5}{1 - \delta_i} \quad \text{for } i = 1, 2.$$

Alternatively, either player could choose *Not Confess* for a period, earning -10 for that period and -5 for every period after as they revert back to choosing *Confess*. This leads to an alternative stream of discounted payoffs of

$$-10 + \delta_i(-5) + \delta_i^2(-5) + ... = -10 - 5\delta_i(1 + \delta_i + \delta_i^2 + ...) \quad \text{for } i = 1, 2.$$

As before, since $1 + \delta_i + \delta_i^2 + ... = \frac{1}{1-\delta_i}$, we can substitute to obtain,

$$-10 - 5\delta_i(1 + \delta_i + \delta_i^2 + ...) = -10 - \frac{5\delta_i}{1 - \delta_i} \quad \text{for } i = 1, 2.$$

A player would prefer to *Confess*, rather than *Not Confess* for a round if its stream of discounted payoffs is higher than that if they played *Cooperate* for that round, i.e.,

$$\frac{-5}{1 - \delta_i} \geq -10 - \frac{5\delta_i}{1 - \delta_i} \quad \text{for } i = 1, 2.$$

Multiplying both sides by $1 - \delta_i$, we have $-5 \geq -10(1 - \delta_i) - 5\delta_i$. Reorganizing terms, we obtain $5 \geq 5\delta_i$. Last, dividing both sides of this expression by 5, we have $\delta \leq 1$, which holds for all possible values of δ.

- *SPE.* Thus, as long as both δ_1 and $\delta_2 \geq \frac{1}{5}$, our Grim-Trigger Strategy is a subgame perfect Nash equilibrium.

Exercise #13.17 - Alternative Triggers[B]

13.17 Consider the following normal-form game below:

		Player 2 H	M	L
Player 1	H	100, 100	30, 125	20, 80
	M	125, 30	60, 60	30, 50
	L	80, 20	50, 30	40, 40

(a) Find all pure strategy Nash equilibria of this game.

- We can find the pure strategy Nash equilibria of this game by analyzing each player's best responses.

311

– *Player 1's best responses:* When player 2 chooses H, player 1 can respond with H, leading to a payoff of 100, M, leading to a payoff of 125, or L, leading to a payoff of 80. Since $125 > 100 > 80$, player 1's best response to player 2 choosing H is M, $BR_1(H) = M$. When player 2 chooses M, player 1 can respond with H, leading to a payoff of 30, M, leading to a payoff of 60, or L, leading to a payoff of 50. Since $60 > 50 > 30$, player 1's best response to player 2 choosing M is M, $BR_1(M) = M$. When player 2 chooses L, player 1 can respond with H, leading to a payoff of 20, M, leading to a payoff of 30, or L, leading to a payoff of 40. Since $40 > 30 > 20$, player 1's best response to player 2 choosing L is L, $BR_1(L) = L$.

Player 2

		H	M	L
	H	100, 100	30, 125	20, 80
Player 1	M	<u>125</u>, 30	<u>60</u>, 60	30, 50
	L	80, 20	50, 30	<u>40</u>, 40

– *Player 2's best responses:* When player 1 chooses H, player 2 can respond with H, leading to a payoff of 100, M, leading to a payoff of 125, or L, leading to a payoff of 80. Since $125 > 100 > 80$, player 2's best response to player 1 choosing H is M, $BR_1(H) = M$. When player 1 chooses M, player 2 can respond with H, leading to a payoff of 30, M, leading to a payoff of 60, or L, leading to a payoff of 50. Since $60 > 50 > 30$, player 2's best response to player 1 choosing M is M, $BR_1(M) = M$. When player 1 chooses L, player 2 can respond with H, leading to a payoff of 20, M, leading to a payoff of 30, or L, leading to a payoff of 40. Since $40 > 30 > 20$, player 2's best response to player 1 choosing L is L, $BR_1(L) = L$.

Player 2

		H	M	L
	H	100, 100	30,<u>125</u>	20, 80
Player 1	M	125, 30	60,<u>60</u>	30, 50
	L	80, 20	50, 30	40,<u>40</u>

- *Nash equilibrium:* With the best responses for each player identified, there exist two Nash equilibria in pure strategies, (M, M) and (L, L).

Player 2

		H	M	L
	H	100, 100	30,<u>125</u>	20, 80
Player 1	M	<u>125</u>, 30	<u>60</u>,<u>60</u>	30, 50
	L	80, 20	50, 30	<u>40</u>,<u>40</u>

(b) Suppose that each player implements the following GTS: "Choose H in the first round. In every other round, if both players chose H in all previous rounds, choose

H again. Otherwise, choose M forever after." For what minimal discount factor δ do the players cooperate by choosing H?

- To analyze the repeated version of this game, we must examine the cheating history.
- *No previous cheating.* When we implement our Grim-Trigger strategy, as long as no cheating has occurred in the past, each player continues to choose H earning a payoff of 100 in every period. This leads to the following stream of discounted payoffs,

$$100 + \delta 100 + \delta^2 100 + \ldots = 100(1 + \delta + \delta^2 + \ldots).$$

Once again, since $1 + \delta + \delta^2 + \ldots = \frac{1}{1-\delta}$, we can substitute to obtain

$$100(1 + \delta + \delta^2 + \ldots) = \frac{100}{1 - \delta}.$$

If one player chose M instead (their best response to the other firm choosing H), they would receive a payoff of 125 immediately, then a payoff of 60 for every period after as both players revert to choosing M in every period. This leads to an alternative stream of discounted payoffs of,

$$125 + \delta 60 + \delta^2 60 + \ldots = 125 + 60\delta(1 + \delta + \delta^2 + \ldots).$$

As before, since $1 + \delta + \delta^2 + \ldots = \frac{1}{1-\delta}$, we can substitute to obtain

$$125 + 60\delta(1 + \delta + \delta^2 + \ldots) = 125 + \frac{60\delta}{1 - \delta}.$$

Either player will prefer H over M as long as his stream of discounted payoffs while choosing H are higher than if he chose M, i.e.,

$$\frac{100}{1 - \delta} \geq 125 + \frac{60\delta}{1 - \delta}.$$

To solve this, first we multiply both sides of this inequality by $1 - \delta$, which gives us $100 \geq 125(1-\delta)+60\delta$. Rearranging terms, we have $100 \geq 125 - 65\delta$. Reorganizing terms gives us $65\delta \geq 25$. Last, we divide both sides of this expression by 65 to obtain

$$\delta \geq 0.38,$$

which implies that any value of δ greater than 0.38 can sustain cooperation in this case. By letting this inequality hold with equality, $\delta = 0.38$, we have our minimal discount factor for firms to choose H.

- *Some cheating history.* Now we must examine if players would want to deviate from their strategy of playing M when someone has played M in the past. By continuing to choose M, each player receives a payoff of 60 in each period, leading to the following stream of discounted payoffs,

$$60 + \delta 60 + \delta^2 60 + \ldots = 60(1 + \delta + \delta^2 + \ldots).$$

Once again, since $1 + \delta + \delta^2 + \ldots = \frac{1}{1-\delta}$, we can substitute to obtain

$$60(1 + \delta + \delta^2 + \ldots) = \frac{60}{1 - \delta}.$$

Alternatively, either player could choose L for a period (his best alternative), earning 50 for that period and 60 for every period after as he reverts back to choosing M. This leads to an alternative stream of discounted payoffs of

$$50 + \delta 60 + \delta^2 60 + \ldots = 50 + 60\delta(1 + \delta + \delta^2 + \ldots).$$

As before, since $1 + \delta + \delta^2 + \ldots = \frac{1}{1-\delta}$, we can substitute to obtain

$$50 + 60\delta(1 + \delta + \delta^2 + \ldots) = 50 + \frac{60\delta}{1 - \delta}.$$

A player would prefer to M, rather than L for a round if its stream of discounted payoffs is higher than that if they played L for that round, i.e.,

$$\frac{60}{1 - \delta} \geq 50 + \frac{60\delta}{1 - \delta}.$$

To solve this, first we multiply both sides of this inequality by $1 - \delta$, which gives us $60 \geq 50(1 - \delta) + 60\delta$. Rearranging terms, we have $60 \geq 50 + 10\delta$. Reorganizing terms gives us $10\delta \leq 10$. Last, dividing both sides of this expression by 10, we have $\delta \leq 1$, which holds for all possible values of δ.

- *SPE.* Thus, as long as $\delta \geq 0.38$, our Grim-Trigger Strategy is a subgame perfect Nash equilibrium.

(c) Suppose that each player implements the following GTS: "Choose H in the first round. In every other round, if both players chose H in all previous rounds, choose H again. Otherwise, choose L forever after." For what minimal discount factor δ do the players cooperate by choosing H?

- Once again, to analyze the repeated version of this game, we must examine the cheating history.

- *No previous cheating.* When we implement our Grim-Trigger strategy, as long as no cheating has occurred in the past, each player continues to choose H earning a payoff of 100 in every period. This leads to the following stream of discounted payoffs,

$$100 + \delta 100 + \delta^2 100 + \ldots = 100(1 + \delta + \delta^2 + \ldots).$$

Once again, since $1 + \delta + \delta^2 + \ldots = \frac{1}{1-\delta}$, we can substitute to obtain

$$100(1 + \delta + \delta^2 + \ldots) = \frac{100}{1 - \delta}.$$

If one player chose M instead (his best response to the other firm choosing H), he would receive a payoff of 125 immediately, then a payoff of 40 for every period after as both players revert to choosing L in every period. This leads to an alternative stream of discounted payoffs of

$$125 + \delta 40 + \delta^2 40 + ... = 125 + 40\delta(1 + \delta + \delta^2 + ...).$$

As before, since $1 + \delta + \delta^2 + ... = \frac{1}{1-\delta}$, we can substitute to obtain

$$125 + 40\delta(1 + \delta + \delta^2 + ...) = 125 + \frac{40\delta}{1-\delta}.$$

Either player will prefer H over M as long as his stream of discounted payoffs while choosing H is higher than that if he chose M, i.e.,

$$\frac{100}{1-\delta} \geq 125 + \frac{40\delta}{1-\delta}.$$

To solve this, first we multiply both sides of this inequality by $1 - \delta$, which gives us $100 \geq 125(1-\delta) + 40\delta$. Rearranging terms, we have $100 \geq 125 - 85\delta$. Reorganizing terms gives us $85\delta \geq 25$. Last, we divide both sides of this expression by 85 to obtain

$$\delta \geq 0.29,$$

which implies that any value of δ greater than 0.29 can sustain cooperation in this case. By letting this inequality hold with equality, $\delta = 0.29$, we have our minimal discount factor for firms to choose H.

- *Some cheating history.* Now we must examine if players would want to deviate from their strategy of playing L when someone has played M in the past. By continuing to choose L, each player receives a payoff of 40 in each period, leading to the following stream of discounted payoffs,

$$40 + \delta 40 + \delta^2 40 + ... = 40(1 + \delta + \delta^2 + ...).$$

Once again, since $1 + \delta + \delta^2 + ... = \frac{1}{1-\delta}$, we can substitute to obtain

$$40(1 + \delta + \delta^2 + ...) = \frac{40}{1-\delta}.$$

Alternatively, either player could choose M for a period (his best alternative), earning 30 for that period and 40 for every period after as he reverts back to choosing L. This leads to an alternative stream of discounted payoffs of,

$$30 + \delta 40 + \delta^2 40 + ... = 30 + 40\delta(1 + \delta + \delta^2 + ...).$$

As before, since $1 + \delta + \delta^2 + ... = \frac{1}{1-\delta}$, we can substitute to obtain

$$30 + 40\delta(1 + \delta + \delta^2 + ...) = 30 + \frac{40\delta}{1-\delta}.$$

A player would prefer to L, rather than M for a round if its stream of discounted payoffs is higher than if he played L for that round, i.e.,

$$\frac{40}{1-\delta} \geq 30 + \frac{40\delta}{1-\delta}.$$

To solve this, first we multiply both sides of this inequality by $1 - \delta$, which gives us $40 \geq 30(1 - \delta) + 40\delta$. Rearranging terms, we have $40 \geq 30 + 10\delta$. Reorganizing terms gives us $10\delta \leq 10$. Last, dividing both sides of this expression by 10, we have $\delta \leq 1$, which holds for all possible values of δ.

- *SPE.* Thus, as long as $\delta \geq 0.29$, our Grim-Trigger Strategy is a subgame perfect Nash equilibrium.

(d) Compare the results from parts (b) and (c). If they are similar, explain why. If they are different, provide an explanation for any differences.

- The minimal discount factor is lower in part (c) than it is in part (b). Intuitively, the punishment for deviating in part (c) is more severe than the punishment in part (b) (as the Nash equilibrium yields a lower payoff for both firms). Thus, in fear of receiving a lower payoff, each firm has more incentive to cooperate by choosing H in part (c).

Exercise #13.19 - Temporary Punishments^C

13.19 Repeat the infinitely repeated Prisoner's Dilemma game of example 13.4, finding under which conditions you can sustain cooperation under a GTS that temporarily punishes defections for only two periods. Compare your results with those in the chapter (where the GTS has a permanent reversion to NE).

- To analyze the repeated version of this game, we must examine the cheating history.

- *No previous cheating.* When we implement our Grim-Trigger strategy, as long as no cheating has occurred in the past, each player continues to choose *Not Confess* earning a payoff of -1 in every period.. This leads to the following stream of discounted payoffs,

$$-1 + \delta(-1) + \delta^2(-1) + ... = -1(1 + \delta + \delta^2 + ...).$$

Once again, since $1 + \delta + \delta^2 + ... = \frac{1}{1-\delta}$, we can substitute to obtain

$$-1(1 + \delta + \delta^2 + ...) = \frac{-1}{1-\delta}.$$

If one player chose to *Confess* instead, he would receive a payoff of 0 immediately, then a payoff of -5 for two periods after as both players revert to choosing *Confess* in the punishment stage, afterward reverting back to *Not Confess*. This leads to an alternative stream of discounted payoffs of

$$\underbrace{0}_{\text{Cheating}} + \underbrace{\delta(-5) + \delta^2(-5)}_{\text{Punishment}} + \underbrace{\delta^3(-1) + ...}_{\text{Back to coop.}} = -5\delta - 5\delta^2 + -1\delta^3(1 + \delta + \delta^2 + ...).$$

316

As before, since $1 + \delta + \delta^2 + ... = \frac{1}{1-\delta}$, we can substitute to obtain

$$-5\delta - 5\delta^2 + -1\delta^3(1 + \delta + \delta^2 + ...) = -5\delta - 5\delta^2 + \frac{-1\delta^3}{1-\delta}.$$

Either player will prefer to *Not Confess* over *Confess* as long as his stream of discounted payoffs while choosing *Not Confess* are higher than if he chose *Confess*, i.e.,

$$\frac{-1}{1-\delta_i} \geq -5\delta - 5\delta^2 + \frac{-1\delta^3}{1-\delta}.$$

To solve this, it is useful to separate the term on the left-hand side into separate terms

$$\frac{-1}{1-\delta_i} = -1 - 1\delta - 1\delta^2 - ... = -1 - 1\delta - 1\delta^2 - 1\delta^3(1 + \delta + \delta^2 + ...).$$

and reassembling with $1 + \delta + \delta^2 + ... = \frac{1}{1-\delta}$, we can substitute to obtain

$$-1 - 1\delta - 1\delta^2 - 1\delta^3(1 + \delta + \delta^2 + ...) = -1 - 1\delta - 1\delta^2 + \frac{-1\delta^3}{1-\delta}.$$

Canceling out the final terms, our expression becomes

$$-1 - 1\delta - 1\delta^2 \geq -5\delta - 5\delta^2.$$

Rearranging terms yields $4(\delta + \delta^2) \geq 1$. Then we divide both sides of this expression by 4 to obtain

$$\delta + \delta^2 \geq \frac{1}{4},$$

which we can solve using the quadratic formula. Rearranging this expression (and letting it hold with equality), we obtain

$$\delta^2 + \delta - \frac{1}{4} = 0,$$

which corresponds with values of $a = 1$, $b = 1$, and $c = \frac{-1}{4}$ in the quadratic formula. Thus, our two solutions are

$$\begin{aligned}
\delta &= \frac{-b \pm \sqrt{b^2 - 4ac}}{2a} = \frac{-1 \pm \sqrt{1^2 - 4(1)(\frac{-1}{4})}}{2(1)} = \frac{-1 \pm \sqrt{2}}{2} \\
&= (-1.207, 0.207).
\end{aligned}$$

Since one of our solutions is negative, we can discard it, as we are only interested in positive values of δ. Thus, when $\delta \geq 0.207$, players 1 and 2 are able to cooperate by choosing *Not Confess*. By letting this inequality hold with equality, $\delta = 0.207$, we have our minimal discount factor for players to *Not Confess*. Notice that this is slightly higher than the minimum discount factor to sustain cooperation between the two players in the infinitely repeated version of this game from example 13.4.

Intuitively, since the punishment is not as bad, it is slightly harder to convince either player to cooperate and choose *Not Confess*.

- *Some cheating history.* Now we must examine if players would want to deviate from their strategy of playing *Confess* when someone has played *Confess* in the past. By continuing to choose *Confess*, each player receives a payoff of -5 in each period, leading to the following stream of discounted payoffs, as after two additional periods, players revert to *Not Confess*,

$$\underbrace{-5 + \delta(-5)}_{\text{Punishment}} + \underbrace{\delta^2(-1)}_{\text{Back to coop.}} + ... = -5 - 5\delta + \frac{-1\delta^2}{1-\delta}.$$

Alternatively, either player could choose *Not Confess* for a period, earning -10 for that period and -5 for three periods after as he reverts back to choosing *Confess*. This leads to an alternative stream of discounted payoffs of

$$\underbrace{-10}_{\text{Deviation}} + \underbrace{\delta(-5) + \delta^2(-5)}_{\text{Punishment}} + \underbrace{\delta^3(-1)}_{\text{Back to coop.}} + ... = -10 - 5\delta - 5\delta^2 + \frac{-1\delta^3}{1-\delta}.$$

A player would deviate to *Confess*, rather than *Not Confess* for a round if its stream of discounted payoffs is higher than if he played *Cooperate* for that round, i.e.,

$$-5 - 5\delta + \frac{-1\delta^2}{1-\delta} \geq -10 - 5\delta - 5\delta^2 + \frac{-1\delta^3}{1-\delta}.$$

Once again, we can rewrite the left-hand side of this expression as

$$-5 - 5\delta + \frac{-1\delta^2}{1-\delta} = -5 - 5\delta - \delta^2 - 1\delta^3(1 + \delta + \delta^2 + ...).$$

and reassembling with $1 + \delta + \delta^2 + ... = \frac{1}{1-\delta}$, we can substitute to obtain

$$-5 - 5\delta - \delta^2 - 1\delta^3(1 + \delta + \delta^2 + ...) = -5 - 5\delta - \delta^2 + \frac{-1\delta^3}{1-\delta}.$$

Canceling out the final terms, our expression becomes $-5 - 5\delta - \delta^2 \geq -10 - 5\delta - 5\delta^2$. Rearranging terms yields $4\delta^2 \geq -10$. There is no real number value for δ in this situation, which implies that players prefer to continue with the punishment phase of *Confess* for all values of δ. *Note*: For completeness, we would need to analyze this punishment phase for each period of the punishment, but the results are all similar, so are omitted.

- *SPE.* Thus, as long as $\delta \geq 0.207$, our Grim-Trigger Strategy is a subgame perfect Nash equilibrium.

Exercise #13.21 - Punishment Size[B]

13.21 Consider the situation in exercise 13.19. While it is harder to sustain cooperation when the punishment is temporary (i.e., higher δ required), it might be more beneficial to have only small punishments. Why?

- One of the drawbacks to the Grim-Trigger strategy is its permanence. While wanting to punish misbehaving players leaves more room for cooperation, there could be times when a player is forced to deviate from the cooperative agreement temporarily. In the case of a cartel agreement (as in exercise 13.16), it may be necessary to switch from a high price to a low price during changing market conditions. With a permanent reversion, this would make future cooperation impossible, whereas for a temporary punishment, a firm would be able to deviate to a low price temporarily while still being able to return to the cooperative arrangement at a later date.

Exercise #13.23 - Rock, Paper, Scissors–II[B]

13.23 Consider the results of exercises 12.15 and 13.22. A friend of yours approaches you and states that he has found the best strategy for Rock, Paper, Scissors. He claims that he should always pick a random choice for the first round of the game. If he wins, he should stay with his choice; but if he loses, rotate to whatever item beat him previously (e.g., if he lost while playing "Paper," he switches to "Rock"). How would you respond to your friend? Can you describe a strategy that could beat him almost all the time?

- The key to having a strategy exist as a SPE is that it must be the best response in every round of the game. While you friend may win in the first round, by announcing his strategy, you can design a strategy that specifically counters his. For instance, suppose your friend randomly selects *Rock* in the first round of the game. If he wins, you know that he will play *Rock* in the next round, for which your best response is *Paper*. If he loses, you know that he'll play scissors in the next round, for which your best response is *Rock*. Thus, while your friend might win the first round due to randomly choosing an action, all subsequent rounds will be won by you as you can assemble a strategy to calculate theirs. Once your friend has discovered you doing this, he is likely to deviate from his prescribed strategy, returning to the mixed strategy presented in exercise 12.15.

Chapter 14 - Imperfect Competition

14.1 Solutions to Self-Assessment Exercises

Self-assessment exercise #14.1

SA 14.1 Repeat the analysis in example 14.1, but assume that firm 1 faces an inverse demand function $p(q_1, q_2) = 5 - \frac{1}{3}(q_1 + q_2)$ (i.e., $a = 5$ and $b = \frac{1}{3}$). Find the firm's best response function, its vertical and horizontal intercept, and slope.

- Firm 1's profit maximization problem is now

$$\max_{q_1} \pi_1 = p(q_1, q_2)q_1 - cq_1$$

$$= \left[5 - \frac{1}{3}(q_1 + q_2) \right] q_1 - 2q_1.$$

Differentiating with respect to q_1 gives us

$$5 - \frac{2}{3}q_1 - \frac{1}{3}q_2 - 2 = 0.$$

Rearranging, $3 - \frac{1}{3}q_2 = \frac{2}{3}q_1$, and solving for q_1 yields

$$q_1(q_2) = \frac{9}{2} - \frac{1}{2}q_2,$$

which is firm 1's new best response function. As depicted in figure 14.1, the vertical intercept of BRF_1 is $\frac{9}{2}$, the horizontal intercept is $q_2 = 9$, and the slope is $-\frac{1}{2}$.

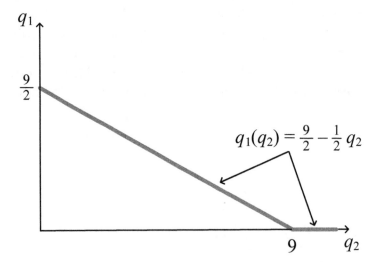

Figure 14.1. Best response function of firm 1.

320

SA 14.2 Repeat the analysis in example 14.1, but assume that the inverse demand function changes to $p(q_1, q_2) = 20 - q_1 - q_2$. Find each firm's best response function, the Cournot equilibrium output, and the corresponding equilibrium price and profits.

- *Firm 1's best response function.* Firm 1's new profit maximization problem is

$$\max_{q_1} \quad \pi_1 = (20 - q_1 - q_2)q_1 - 4q_1.$$

Differentiating with respect to q_1 gives

$$\frac{\partial \pi_1}{\partial q_1} = 20 - 2q_1 - q_2 - 4 = 0.$$

Rearranging, $16 - q_2 = 2q_1$, and solving for q_1 yields

$$q_1(q_2) = 8 - \frac{1}{2}q_2,$$

which is firm 1's best response function. As illustrated in figure 14.2, this best response function originates at 8 units, decreases with a slope of -1/2 as firm 2 increases its production, and hits the horizontal axis at 16 units.

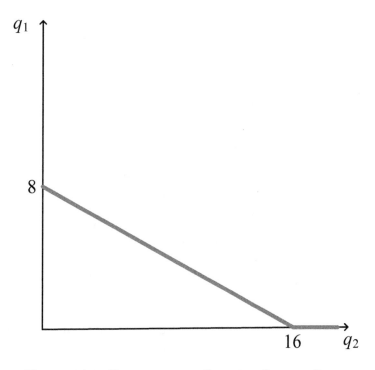

Figure 14.2. Best response function for one firm.

- *Firm 2's best response function.* Firm 2's new profit maximization problem is

$$\max_{q_2} \quad \pi_2 = (20 - q_1 - q_2)q_2 - 4q_2,$$

Differentiating with respect to q_2 gives

$$\frac{\partial \pi_2}{\partial q_2} = 20 - 2q_2 - q_1 - 4 = 0.$$

Rearranging, $16 - q_1 = 2q_2$, and solving for q_2 yields

$$q_2(q_1) = 8 - \frac{1}{2}q_1,$$

which is firm 2's best response function, which originates at 8 units, and decreases with a slope of -1/2 as firm 1 increases its production. It is then symmetric to firm 1's best response function. Figure 14.3 superimposes firm 2's best response function on figure 14.1, so we can simultaneously represent firm 1's and 2's best response functions, as well as identify their crossing point (as we discuss in the next bullet point).

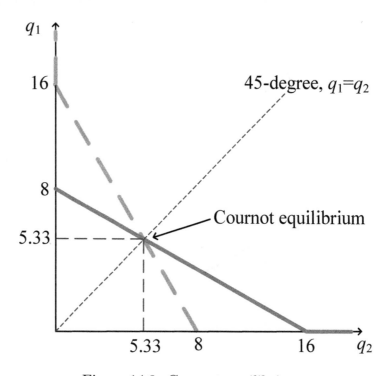

Figure 14.3. Cournot equilibrium.

- *Finding equilibrium output.* In order to solve for the equilibrium output levels of each firm, we can invoke symmetry, i.e., $q_1^* = q_2^* = q^*$. Inserting this into one of

322

the firm's best response functions simplifies it to

$$q^* = 8 - \frac{1}{2}q^*$$

or $\frac{3}{2}q^* = 8$. Solving for q^*, we obtain the equilibrium output for every firm in this Cournot model,

$$q^* = \frac{16}{3} \simeq 5.33 \text{ units.}$$

Equilibrium price is then

$$p^*\left(\frac{16}{3}, \frac{16}{3}\right) = 20 - \frac{16}{3} - \frac{16}{3} = \frac{28}{3} = \$9.33$$

and equilibrium profits are

$$\pi_i^* = \frac{28}{3}\frac{16}{3} - 4\frac{16}{3} = \frac{448}{9} - \frac{64}{3} = \frac{256}{9} = \$28.44.$$

The resulting equilibrium quantity, price, and profit is higher with the new increased demand that each firm faces.

Self-assessment exercise #14.3

SA 14.3 Repeat the analysis in example 14.2 but assuming that firm 2's cost function changes to $TC_2(q_2) = q_2$, thus emphasizing the cost advantage of firm 2 relative to firm 1. Compare your results against those in example 14.2.

- *Firm 1's best response.* We first find firm 1's best response function by solving its profit maximization problem

$$\max_{q_1} \ \pi_1 = (12 - q_1 - q_2)\, q_1 - 4q_1.$$

This problem coincides with that in example 14.2 since firm 1's costs did not change, so firm 1's best response function is

$$q_1(q_2) = 4 - \frac{1}{2}q_2.$$

- *Firm 2's best response.* In contrast, firm 2's profit maximization problem changed relative to example 14.2, becoming now

$$\max_{q_2} \ \pi_2 = (12 - q_1 - q_2)\, q_2 - q_2.$$

Differentiating with respect to its output q_2, yields

$$\frac{\partial \pi_2}{\partial q_2} = 12 - q_1 - 2q_2 - 1 = 0.$$

Rearranging, we find that $11 - q_1 = 2q_2$. Solving for q_2 yields firm 2's best response function, as follows,

$$q_2(q_1) = \frac{11}{2} - \frac{1}{2}q_1.$$

This function has the same slope as that in example 14.2, $-1/2$, but originates at $\frac{11}{2}$ rather than at $\frac{9}{2}$. This indicates that firm 2's best response function experiences a parallel shift upward, as depicted in figure 14.4, when its marginal cost decreases. In words, firm 2 produces a greater amount at each level of firm 1's output.

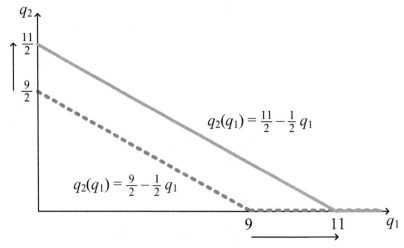

Figure 14.4. Firm 2's best response funciton: new and old.

- *Finding equilibrium output.* In this setting, we cannot invoke symmetry in firms' output in equilibrium since firms face different production costs. As a result, we need to simultaneously solve for q_1 and q_2 in BRF_1 and BRF_2 by, for instance, inserting BRF_2 into BRF_1, as follows

$$q_1 = 4 - \frac{1}{2}\underbrace{\left(\frac{11}{2} - \frac{1}{2}q_1\right)}_{q_2(q_1)}.$$

Rearranging, we find

$$q_1 = 4 - \frac{11}{4} + \frac{1}{4}q_1,$$

or $\frac{3}{4}q_1 = \frac{5}{4}$. Upon solving for q_1, this yields an equilibrium output of

$$q_1^* = \frac{5}{3} \simeq 1.67 \text{ units.}$$

Inserting this output into firm 2's best response function, we find its equilibrium output

$$q_2^* = \frac{11}{2} - \frac{1}{2}\underbrace{\frac{5}{3}}_{q_1^*} = \frac{28}{6} \simeq 4.67 \text{ units}$$

where $q_2^* > q_1^*$ since firm 2's marginal cost is lower than firm 1's, and firm 2 produces more in this case because it has a greater cost advantage than that in example 14.2. Figure 14.5 superimposes firm 1's and 2's best response function, identifying their crossing point as the Cournot equilibrium. Since firm 2 enjoys a substantial cost advantage, the crossing point of firms' best response function happens below the 45-degree line, yielding a larger production for firm 2.

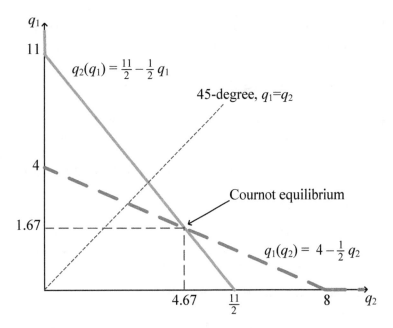

Figure 14.5. Firms' best response function and the
Cournot equilibrium.

- In this setting, equilibrium price is

$$p^* = 12 - \frac{5}{3} - \frac{28}{6} = \frac{34}{6} \simeq \$5.67$$

(lower than example 14.2 since total output is greater), and equilibrium profits are

$$\pi_1^* = \frac{34}{6}\frac{5}{3} - 4\frac{5}{3} = \frac{50}{18} \simeq \$2.77 \text{ for firm 1}$$

and

$$\pi_2^* = \frac{34}{6}\frac{28}{6} - \frac{28}{6} = \frac{784}{36} \simeq \$21.78 \text{ for firm 2.}$$

The greater cost advantage for firm 2 further increases the difference in profits by decreasing firm 1's profit and increasing firm 2's profit.

Self-assessment exercise #14.4

SA 14.4 Repeat the analysis in example 14.3, but assuming that firms face an inverse demand function $p(q_1, q_2) = 20 - q_1 - q_2$. How are the results in example 14.3 affected?

- According to the Bertrand model of price competition, all firms in the industry lower their price until $p = c$. Now, since $p(Q) = 20 - Q$, the equilibrium condition $p = c$ entails

$$20 - Q = 4$$

which, solving for Q, yields $Q = 16$ units, each unit sold at a price of

$$p = 20 - 16 = \$4.$$

Therefore, the price does not change, since cost doesn't change, but aggregate output increases since demand increased.

Self-assessment exercise #14.5

SA 14.5   Repeat the analysis in example 14.4, but assume that firms face an inverse demand function $p(q_1, q_2) = 20 - q_1 - q_2$. How are the results in example 14.4 affected?

- First, we need to find the firms' joint profit if they decide to join a cartel:

$$\max_{q_1, q_2} \pi = \pi_1 + \pi_2$$
$$= \underbrace{(20 - q_1 - q_2) q_1 - 4q_1}_{\pi_1} + \underbrace{(20 - q_1 - q_2) q_2 - 4q_2}_{\pi_2}.$$

Simplifying the expression, we get that

$$\max_{q_1, q_2} (20 - q_1 - q_2)(q_1 + q_2) - 4(q_1 + q_2).$$

Since $20 - q_1 - q_2 = 20 - (q_1 + q_2)$, we obtain

$$\max_{q_1, q_2} [20 - (q_1 + q_2)](q_1 + q_2) - 4(q_1 + q_2).$$

Finally, since $Q = q_1 + q_2$ denotes aggregate output, we can rewrite the cartel's maximization problem more compactly as

$$\max_{Q} [20 - Q]Q - 4Q.$$

In words, the cartel simply needs to choose the aggregate amount of output Q —the total production for all the cartel— to maximize profits as if it was a single firm (a monopolist).

Differentiating with respect to Q, we find

$$20 - 2Q - 4 = 0,$$

which, after solving for Q, yields $Q^* = \frac{16}{2} = 8$ units. Since firms are symmetric, each produces half of $Q^* = 8$ units, i.e., 4 units per firm. In contrast, under Cournot competition (as found in example 14.2) every firm produces $q = \frac{16}{3} \simeq 5.33$ units. Therefore, under the cartel every firm limits its own production to increase market price and profits.

- *Cartel prices.* We can confirm this result by finding that cartel price is

$$p(2,2) = 20 - 4 - 4 = \$12,$$

which is higher than under Cournot competition (\$9.33).

- *Cartel profits.* Similarly, cartel profits for every firm i are

$$\begin{aligned} \pi_i^* &= (20 - q_1 - q_2)\, q_i - 4q_i \\ &= (20 - 4 - 4)\, 4 - (4 \times 4) = \$32, \end{aligned}$$

while under Cournot competition profits were only $\pi_i = \frac{256}{9} \simeq \$28.44$.

Comparing to the cartel in example 14.4, the increased demand increases the output from each firm individually and on aggregate, the price increases, and profits increase.

Self-assessment exercise #14.6

SA 14.6 Repeat the analysis in example 14.5, but assume that firms detect a deviation only after two periods, so a deviating firm earns a profit of \$9 during two periods before the punishment starts. This means that cheating is still detected with certainty, but with a lag of two periods rather than immediately. Find the minimal discount factor δ supporting cooperation in this scenario, and show that cooperation is more difficult to be sustained than in example 14.5.

- *Payoff from cooperating.* The stream of discounted profits from cooperating is unaffected relative to example 14.5, still being $\frac{8}{1-\delta}$.

- *Payoff from deviating.* However, the payoffs from deviating are now

$$\underbrace{9 + \delta 9}_{\text{Deviation}} + \underbrace{\delta^2 \frac{64}{9} + ...}_{\text{Punishment}} = (1+\delta)9 + \frac{64}{9}(\delta^2 + \delta^3 + ...)$$

$$= (1+\delta)9 + \frac{64}{9}\delta^2(1 + \delta + ...)$$

$$= (1+\delta)9 + \frac{64}{9}\frac{\delta^2}{1-\delta}.$$

Here, the firm increases its profit from \$8 to \$9 for two periods before its defection is detected, and the infinite punishment is detected where both firms produce the Cournot output and profit of $\frac{64}{9}$.

- *Comparing profits.* Every firm i prefers to cooperate as long as

$$\frac{8}{1-\delta} \geq (1+\delta)9 + \frac{64}{9}\frac{\delta^2}{1-\delta},$$

multiplying each side by $(1-\delta)$, we obtain $8 \geq (1+\delta)(1-\delta)9 + \frac{64}{9}\delta^2$, and

327

simplifying yields

$$8 \geq (1 - \delta^2)9 + \frac{64}{9}\delta^2$$

$$8 \geq 9 - \delta^2 9 + \frac{64}{9}\delta^2$$

$$8 \geq 9 - \delta^2 \left(9 - \frac{64}{9}\right)$$

$$\delta^2 \geq \frac{9}{17},$$

or, $\delta = \sqrt{9/17} \simeq 0.73$. A cartel output can be sustained with the above GTS if $\delta \geq 0.73$. This value is higher than in example 14.6 (where $\delta = 0.53$) because there is a greater incentive to cheat as now every firm gains deviation profits for two, rather than one, period. Intuitively, firms need to care more about their future payoffs for collusion to be sustained in this setting.

Self-assessment exercise #14.7

SA 14.7 Repeat the analysis in example 14.6, but assume that firms face an inverse demand function $p(q_1, q_2) = 20 - q_1 - q_2$. How are the results in example 14.6 affected?

- Inserting the follower's best response function found in self-assessment 14.2, $q_2(q_1) = 8 - \frac{1}{2}q_1$, into the leader's profit maximization problem yields

$$\max_{q_1} \left[20 - \left(q_1 + \underbrace{\left(8 - \frac{1}{2}q_1\right)}_{q_2(q_1)} \right) \right] q_1 - 4q_1,$$

simplifying, we obtain

$$\max_{q_1} \frac{1}{2}(24 - q_1)q_1 - 4q_1.$$

Differentiating with respect to q_1, we find

$$12 - q_1 - 4 = 0,$$

and solving for q_1 we find the profit-maximizing output for the leader,

$$q_1^* = 8 \text{ units.}$$

The follower's output is then $q_2^* = 8 - \frac{1}{2}8 = 4$ units.

- In this setting, equilibrium price is

$$p^* = 20 - 8 - 4 = \$8,$$

and equilibrium profits become

$$\pi_1^* = (8 \times 8) - (4 \times 8) = \$32,$$

for firm 1 and

$$\pi_2^* = (8 \times 4) - (4 \times 4) = \$16,$$

for firm 2. Relative to example 14.6, the increase in demand increases output for both the leader (from 4 to 8 units) and the follower (from 2 to 4 units), increases the equilibrium price (from \$6 to \$8), and both firms' profit, i.e., the leader's profit increases from \$8 to \$32 while the follower's increases from \$4 to \$16.

Self-assessment exercise #14.8

SA 14.8 Repeat the analysis in example 14.7, but assume that firms experience a higher marginal production cost of $c = 5$ (rather than $c = 3$). How are the results in example 14.7 affected?

- In equilibrium, each firm will produce output $q^* = \frac{a-c}{2b+d}$ units. When $a = 100$, $b = 5$, and $d = 2$, this output becomes

$$q^* = \frac{100 - 5}{2(5) + 2} = \frac{95}{12} \simeq 7.92 \text{ units.}$$

Equilibrium price is then

$$p^* = \frac{ab + c(b+d)}{2b + d} = \frac{100(5) + 5(5+2)}{2(5) + 2} = \frac{535}{12} \simeq \$44.58,$$

and profits are

$$\pi^* = \frac{(a-c)^2 b}{(2b+d)^2} = \frac{(100-5)^2 5}{(2(5)+2)^2} = \frac{45125}{144} \simeq \$313.37.$$

Relative to example 14.3, the increase in cost results in a decrease in quantity produced, an increase in price, and a decrease in profit.

Self-assessment exercise #14.9

SA 14.9 Repeat the analysis in this subsection, but assume that firms face an inverse demand function $p(Q) = 10 - 2Q$, and all N firms have a marginal cost of $c = 3$. Evaluate your results under monopoly, duopoly, and perfect competition.

- In this market, the equilibrium aggregate output with N firms in the market is

$$Q^* = N\left(\frac{1}{N+1}\frac{a-c}{b}\right) = \frac{N}{N+1} \times \frac{10-3}{2} = \frac{N}{N+1} \times \frac{7}{2},$$

while the equilibrium price is

$$p(Q^*) = \frac{a + Nc}{N+1} = \frac{10 + 3N}{N+1}.$$

- *Monopoly.* For a monopoly, $N = 1$, equilibrium output is

$$q^* = \frac{1}{1+1} \times \frac{7}{2} = \frac{7}{4} = 1.75 \text{ units},$$

and equilibrium price is

$$p^* = \frac{10 + 3(1)}{1+1} = \frac{13}{2} = \$6.5.$$

- *Duopoly.* Under a duopoly, $N = 2$, aggregate equilibrium output becomes

$$Q^* = \frac{2}{1+2}\frac{7}{2} = \frac{14}{6} = 2.33 \text{ units},$$

with each firm producing $q^* = \frac{Q^*}{2} = \frac{1}{2}\frac{14}{6} = \frac{14}{12} \simeq 1.17$ units. Equilibrium price is then

$$p^* = \frac{10 + 3(2)}{2+1} = \frac{16}{3} \simeq \$5.33.$$

- *Perfect competition.* Under perfect competition, $N \to +\infty$, aggregate output is

$$Q^* = \frac{a-c}{b} = \frac{10-3}{2} = \frac{7}{2} = 3.5 \text{ units}.$$

In this case, individual firm output approaches zero, or is infinitesimally small; and equilibrium price converges to

$$p^* = c = \$3.$$

Overall, we can see that, as more firms enter the market (the market becomes more competitive), aggregate output increases, individual output decreases to zero, and equilibrium price decreases converging toward the common marginal cost $c = \$3$.

14.2 Solutions to End-of-Chapter Exercises

Exercise #14.1 - Herfindahl-Hirschman Index[A]

14.1 Calculate the HHI in the following markets, where three firms operate under different levels of market share:

(a) Each firm has an equal share of the market (i.e., 33.3 percent).

- The HHI is calculated as

$$
\begin{aligned}
HHI &= (33.3)^2 + (33.3)^2 + (33.3)^2 \\
&= 1,108.89 + 1,108.89 + 1,108.89 \\
&= 3,326.67.
\end{aligned}
$$

(b) One firm captures 50 percent of the market, while the other two each have 25 percent.

- The HHI is calculated as

$$
\begin{aligned}
HHI &= (50)^2 + (25)^2 + (25)^2 \\
&= 2,500 + 625 + 625 \\
&= 3,750.
\end{aligned}
$$

(c) One firm captures 80 percent of the market, while the other two each have 10 percent.

- The HHI is calculated as

$$
\begin{aligned}
HHI &= (80)^2 + (10)^2 + (10)^2 \\
&= 6,400 + 100 + 100 \\
&= 6,600.
\end{aligned}
$$

(d) Two firms have 45 percent of the market, while the other firm has 10 percent.

- The HHI is calculated as

$$
\begin{aligned}
HHI &= (45)^2 + (45)^2 + (10)^2 \\
&= 2,025 + 2,025 + 100 = \\
&4,150.
\end{aligned}
$$

(e) How do these different market shares (in parts a–d) affect the HHI?

- As more of the market share is concentrated in a single firm, the larger the HHI. The market described in part (c), where one firm has 80 percent of the market, the HHI is highest. Whereas when the market share is spread evenly between the three firms, as in part (a), HHI is at its lowest.

Exercise #14.3 - Properties of the Best Response Function[B]

14.3 Consider the best response function of firm 1 in the Cournot model of quantity competition:

$$
q_1(q_2) = \frac{a - c}{2b} - \frac{1}{2} q_2.
$$

Let us do some comparative statics, to understand how this expression changes as we increase one parameter at a time.

(a) How is the best response function $q_1(q_2)$ affected by a marginal increase in the vertical intercept of the inverse demand function, a? Interpret.

- We do this by differentiating with respect to a:

$$\frac{\partial q_1(q_2)}{\partial a} = \frac{1}{2b} > 0.$$

As the vertical intercept of inverse demand increases (as demand increases), the firm increases its output relative to its rival. In other words, for a given level of output by the firm's rival, it will increase its output if a increases. Graphically, firm 1's best response function shifts upward when parameter a increases.

(b) How is the best response function $q_1(q_2)$ affected by a marginal increase in the slope of inverse demand function, b? Interpret.

- We do this by differentiating with respect to b:

$$\frac{\partial q_1(q_2)}{\partial b} = -\frac{a-c}{2b^2} < 0.$$

As the slope of the inverse demand increases, the firm decreases its output relative to its rival's output. Intuitively, price becomes more sensitive to sales as b increases, making every firm less willing to sell positive units when its rival's sales increase. Graphically, firm 1's best response function shifts downward when parameter b increases.

(c) How is the best response function $q_1(q_2)$ affected by a marginal increase in the firm's marginal production cost, c? Interpret.

- We do this by differentiating with respect to c:

$$\frac{\partial q_1(q_2)}{\partial c} = -\frac{1}{2b} < 0.$$

If the firm's marginal cost increases, the firm reduces its output relative to its rival's output. Graphically, firm 1's best response function shifts downward when parameter c increases.

Exercise #14.5 - Symmetric Cournot[A]

14.5 Two medical supply companies are the only two firms that supply stethoscopes to the medical professionals and are competing à la Cournot: Hearts Beat (H) and Lungs Breathe (L). Inverse market demand is $p = 50 - 2(q_H + q_L)$, and each firm has the same total cost of producing stethoscopes of $TC(q_i) = 5q_i$.

(a) Write the PMP for Hearts Beat and Lungs Breathe.

- *Hearts Beat.* Hearts Beat's profit maximization problem is

$$\max_{q_H} \ \pi_H = [50 - 2(q_H + q_L)]\, q_H - 5q_H.$$

- *Lungs Breathe.* Lungs Breathe's profit maximization problem is

$$\max_{q_L} \ \pi_L = [50 - 2(q_H + q_L)]\, q_L - 5q_L.$$

(b) Find each firm's best response function.

- *Hears Beat.* Differentiating Hearts Beat's profit with respect to q_H, we obtain

$$\frac{\partial \pi_H}{\partial q_H} = 50 - 4q_H - 2q_L - 5 = 0,$$

rearranging, $45 - 2q_L = 4q_H$, and solving for q_H yields

$$q_H(q_L) = \frac{45}{4} - \frac{1}{2}q_L,$$

which is Hearts Beat's best response function. This function originates at $\frac{45}{4} = 11.25$ units and decreases at a rate of $\frac{1}{2}$ for each unit its rival produces.

- *Lungs Breathe.* Differentiating Lung Breathe's profit with respect to q_L, we obtain

$$\frac{\partial \pi_L}{\partial q_L} = 50 - 4q_L - 2q_H - 5 = 0,$$

rearranging, $45 - 2q_H = 4q_L$, and solving for q_L yields

$$q_L(q_H) = \frac{45}{4} - \frac{1}{2}q_H,$$

which is Hearts Beat's best response function.

- Comparing both best response functions, we can see they are symmetric since both originate at a vertical intercept of $\frac{45}{4} = 11.25$ units, and decrease at a rate of $\frac{1}{2}$. This symmetry comes at no surprise, since both firms face the same inverse demand function for stethoscopes and the same cost function.

(c) Find the equilibrium quantity that each firm will produce, and the market price.

- In a symmetric equilibrium, both firms produce the same output level, implying $q_H = q_L = q$. Inserting this property in the above best response function, we obtain

$$q = \frac{45}{4} - \frac{1}{2}q.$$

Rearranging, we find $\frac{3}{2}q = \frac{45}{4}$, and solving for q yields the equilibrium output

$$q = \frac{45}{4}\frac{2}{3} = 7.5 \text{ stethoscopes}$$

for every firm. This is a faster approach to find symmetric equilibria in games where firms (or, generally, players) are symmetric. We show below that using the alternative approach—inserting one best response function into its rival's—produces the same equilibrium output.

- Inserting best response function $q_L(q_H)$ into $q_H(q_L)$, we obtain

$$q_H = \frac{45}{4} - \frac{1}{2}\overbrace{\left(\frac{45}{4} - \frac{1}{2}q_H\right)}^{q_L(q_H)}.$$

Simplifying, yields

$$q_H = \frac{45}{4} - \frac{45}{8} + \frac{1}{4}q_H.$$

Rearranging,

$$\frac{3}{4}q_H = \frac{45}{8}.$$

Finally, solving for q_H, we obtain

$$q_H = \frac{45}{8}\frac{4}{3} = \frac{45}{6} = 7.5 \text{ stethoscopes.}$$

We can plug this into Lungs Breathe's best response function to find their equilibrium output q_L, as follows

$$q_L = \frac{45}{4} - \frac{1}{2}(7.5) = 7.5 \text{ stethoscopes.}$$

- The market price will be

$$p = 50 - 2(q_H + q_L) = 50 - 2(7.5 + 7.5) = \$20.$$

Exercise #14.7 - Cournot with Asymmetric Fixed Costs[B]

14.7 Consider the Cournot duopoly in subsection 14.3.1. Assume that firm 1 faces a TC function $TC_1(q_1) = F_1 + cq_1$, where $F_1 > 0$ denotes its fixed cost and $c > 0$ represents its marginal cost. Firm 2's TC function is $TC_2(q_2) = F_2 + cq_2$, where $F_2 > 0$ denotes its fixed cost and satisfies $F_2 > F_1$, and $c > 0$ is the same marginal cost as firm 1. Consider that firms still face a linear inverse demand function $p(Q) = a - bQ$, where parameter a satisfies $a > c$ and $b > 0$. The scenario is therefore analogous to the Cournot duopoly of subsection 14.3.1, except for the fact that both firms now face fixed costs of production.

(a) Find the best response function of each firm, as well as the equilibrium output.

- *Firm 1's best response function.* In this setting, firm 1 chooses its output level q_1 to solve

$$\max_{q_1} \ \pi_1 = (a - bq_1 - bq_2)q_1 - cq_1 - F_1.$$

Differentiating with respect to q_1, we obtain

$$\frac{\partial \pi_1}{\partial q_1} = a - 2bq_1 - bq_2 - c = 0,$$

rearranging, $a - bq_2 - c = 2bq_1$, and solving for q_1 yields

$$q_1(q_2) = \frac{a - c}{2b} - \frac{1}{2}q_2,$$

which is firm 1's best response function. The best response function coincides with that in a Cournot duopoly where firms face no fixed costs. Intuitively, when choosing its optimal output, firm 1 only considers its marginal revenues and costs, but ignores its fixed cost. The fixed cost should only impact its profits and, as a consequence, the conditions under which this firm produces a positive output.

- *Firm 2's best response function.* In this setting, firm 2 chooses its output level q_2 to solve

$$\max_{q_2} \ \pi_2 = (a - bq_1 - bq_2)q_2 - cq_2 - F_2$$

Differentiating with respect to q_2, we obtain

$$\frac{\partial \pi_2}{\partial q_2} = a - 2bq_2 - bq_1 - c = 0$$

rearranging, $a - bq_1 - c_2 = 2bq$, and solving for q_2 yields

$$q_2(q_1) = \frac{a - c}{2b} - \frac{1}{2}q_1$$

which is firm 2's best response function. This best response function is symmetric to firm 1's.

- The best response functions of firm 1 and firm 2 do not differ from the Cournot duopoly with symmetric marginal costs. Therefore, the equilibrium quantity each firm produces is the same as in that situation; that is,

$$q_1^* = q_2^* = \frac{a - c}{3b}.$$

(b) How are the equilibrium results affected? Interpret.

- Given that the best response functions and output do not change relative to the case of symmetric firms, the price in the market will not change, i.e., $p = \frac{a + 2c}{3}$. Profits for the two firms will be altered by the fixed cost:

$$\pi_1 = \frac{(a - c)^2}{9b} - F_1$$

$$\pi_2 = \frac{(a - c)^2}{9b} - F_2.$$

For firm 1, if its fixed cost F_1 satisfies $F_1 > \frac{(a-c)^2}{9b}$, the firm chooses to remain inactive as its overall profits from participating in this market would be negative. A similar argument applies for firm 2 if its fixed cost F_2 satisfies $F_2 > \frac{(a-c)^2}{9b}$. Therefore, four cases arise:

- *Both firms active.* If $F_1, F_2 < \frac{(a-c)^2}{9b}$, both firms produce the equilibrium output found in part (a) and make positive profits.
- *Only firm 1 is active.* If only firm 1 faces a sufficiently low fixed cost; that is, $F_1 < \frac{(a-c)^2}{9b}$ but $F_2 > \frac{(a-c)^2}{9b}$, then firm 1 produces the monopoly output $\frac{a-c}{2b}$, earning monopoly profit $\frac{(a-c)^2}{4b}$, while its rival remains inactive.
- *Only firm 2 is active.* If only firm 2 faces a sufficiently low fixed cost; that is, $F_2 < \frac{(a-c)^2}{9b}$ but $F_1 > \frac{(a-c)^2}{9b}$, then firm 2 produces the monopoly output $\frac{a-c}{2b}$, earning monopoly profit $\frac{(a-c)^2}{4b}$, while its rival remains inactive.
- *No active firms.* If both firms have relatively high fixed costs, that is $F_1, F_2 > \frac{(a-c)^2}{9b}$, then neither firm is active in the market.

Exercise #14.9 - Cournot with Three Firms^C

14.9 Consider a market with three firms producing a homogeneous good and facing a linear demand function $p(Q) = 1 - Q$, where $Q \equiv q_1 + q_2 + q_3$ denotes aggregate output. All firms face a constant marginal cost of production given by c, where $1 > c > 0$.

(a) Set up firm 1's PMP, differentiate with respect to its output q_1, and obtain this firm's best response function. [*Hint*: It should be a function of firm 2's and 3's output, q_2 and q_3.]

- Firm 1's profit maximization problem is

$$\max_{q_1} \pi_1 = (1 - q_1 - q_2 - q_3)q_1 - cq_1.$$

Differentiating with respect to q_1, we obtain

$$\frac{\partial \pi_1}{\partial q_1} = 1 - 2q_1 - q_2 - q_3 - c = 0,$$

rearranging, we find $2q_1 = 1 - q_2 - q_3 - c$, and solving for q_1, we obtain firm 1's best response function

$$q_1(q_2, q_3) = \frac{1 - c}{2} - \frac{1}{2}(q_2 + q_3),$$

which originates at a vertical intercept of $\frac{1-c}{2}$, and decreases at a rate of $\frac{1}{2}$ when either firm 2 or 3 marginally increases its output.

(b) Repeat the process for firms 2 and 3, to obtain their best response functions. [*Hint*: You should find that all firms have symmetric best response functions.]

- *Firm 2.* Firm 2's profit maximization problem is

$$\max_{q_2} \pi_2 = (1 - q_1 - q_2 - q_3)q_2 - cq_2.$$

Differentiating with respect to q_2, we obtain

$$\frac{\partial \pi_2}{\partial q_2} = 1 - q_1 - 2q_2 - q_3 - c = 0,$$

rearranging, we find $2q_2 = 1 - q_1 - q_3 - c$, and solving for q_2, we obtain firm 2's best response function

$$q_2(q_1, q_3) = \frac{1-c}{2} - \frac{1}{2}(q_1 + q_3),$$

which is symmetric to firm 1's best response function. This comes at no surprise since all firms face the same inverse demand function and total cost function.

- *Firm 3.* Firm 3's profit maximization problem is

$$\max_{q_3} \pi_3 = (1 - q_1 - q_2 - q_3)q_3 - cq_3.$$

Differentiating with respect to q_3, we obtain

$$\frac{\partial \pi_3}{\partial q_3} = 1 - q_1 - q_2 - 2q_3 - c = 0,$$

rearranging, we find $2q_3 = 1 - q_1 - q_2 - c$, and solving for q_3, we obtain firm 3's best response function

$$q_3(q_1, q_2) = \frac{1-c}{2} - \frac{1}{2}(q_1 + q_2),$$

which is symmetric to firm 1's best response function. Again, this is not surprising since all firms face the same inverse demand function and total cost function.

(c) Interpret firm 1's best response function: if firm 2 were to marginally increase its output, does firm 1 increase or decrease its own output? Either way, by how much?

- To find this, we differentiate firm 1's best response function with respect to firm 2's output q_2:
$$\frac{\partial q_1(q_2, q_3)}{\partial q_2} = -\frac{1}{2}.$$

For each unit increase in firm 2's output, firm 1 decreases its output by a half unit.

(d) Using the three best response functions for these firms, find the point where they cross. The triplet (q_1^*, q_2^*, q_3^*) characterizes the NE of this Cournot game.

- Since all firms are symmetric, a symmetric equilibrium must exist where all firms produce the same output level $q_1^* = q_2^* = q_3^* = q^*$. We can plug this property into firm 2's to obtain

$$q^* = \frac{1-c}{2} - \frac{1}{2}\left(q^* + q^*\right),$$

which is equivalent to dropping the subscripts of all output levels. Simplifying, we find

$$2q^* = 1 - c - 2q^*,$$

or $4q^* = 1 - c$. Solving for q^*, we find that every firm produces an equilibrium output of

$$q^* = \frac{1-c}{4}.$$

(e) Is the equilibrium output that you found in part (d) increasing or decreasing in marginal cost c?

- Differentiating the equilibrium output with respect to c, we obtain

$$\frac{\partial q^*}{\partial c} = -\frac{1}{4} < 0.$$

Therefore, as marginal cost increases, the equilibrium output for each firm decreases.

(f) Find the price that emerges in equilibrium, along with the profits that every firm earns.

- The price each firm faces is

$$
\begin{aligned}
p &= 1 - q_1 - q_2 - q_3 \\
&= 1 - 3q^* \\
&= 1 - 3\frac{(1-c)}{4} \\
&= \frac{1+3c}{4}.
\end{aligned}
$$

- Each firm earns the same profit in equilibrium; that is,

$$\pi = pq - cq,$$

or, plugging in for p^* and q^*,

$$
\begin{aligned}
\pi &= \left(\frac{1+3c}{4}\right)\frac{1-c}{4} - c\frac{1-c}{4} \\
&= \frac{(1-c)^2}{16},
\end{aligned}
$$

which coincides with the square of the individual output in equilibrium, $\pi = (q^*)^2$.

Exercise #14.11 - Finitely Repeated Grim-Trigger Strategy^B

14.11 Let us repeat example 14.5, but without considering an infinitely repeated game.

(a) Assume that firms interact for $T = 2$ periods. Can the GTS in example 14.5 be sustained as an SPE of the game?

- If the firms collude, their cartel profit is \$8 each. If they deviate and their rival does not, their profit is \$9. The Cournot profit is $\frac{64}{9} \simeq$ \$7.11. In a finitely repeated game, we want to start our analysis in the last period of the game:

- In the second period, both firms play their dominant strategy, which in this case is the Cournot output.

- In the first period, anticipating that both firms produce the Cournot output in the second period, they also play their dominant strategy in the first period; that is, the Cournot equilibrium.

- Therefore, the GTS of example 14.5 cannot be sustained as a SPE since every firm chooses Cournot output in all periods.

(b) Assume that firms interact for $T \geqslant 2$ periods. Can the GTS in example 14.5 be sustained as an SPE of the game?

- We can continue the analysis from part (a), but considering period T as our last period.

- In period T, each firm plays their dominant strategy as described in part (a): Cournot output.

- In period $T - 1$, every firm anticipates that both will produce Cournot output in the next period T, which is unaffected by their production decisions in the current period $T - 1$. Hence, every firm chooses the Cournot output in period $T - 1$.

- In each previous period t, firms anticipate that both choose the Cournot output in all subsequent periods regardless of previous production history (i.e., regardless of the output levels firms choose before period t). Therefore, they both choose Cournot output at period t.

- Therefore, the GTS of example 14.5 cannot be sustained in this finitely repeated game either. In order to sustain the GTS, we need an infinitely repeated game (or a game in which neither firm foresees an end period). This is a common result in games with a unique Nash equilibrium in the unrepeated version of the game where players choose a strictly dominant strategy. As discussed in Chapter 13, this result also applies to the Prisoner's Dilemma game, where cooperation can only be sustained in the infinitely repeated version of the game.

Exercise #14.13 - Collusion with Delayed Detection[B]

14.13 Consider self-assessment 14.6, allowing firms to deviate from the collusive outcome without being detected during *three* periods. This means that cheating is still detected with certainty, but with a lag of three periods rather than immediately. If a firm can deviate and earn a profit of $9 during three periods before the punishment starts, what is the minimal discount factor supporting cooperation? Compare your results with those under immediate detection.

- *Cooperation.* The stream of discounted profits from cooperating is unaffected and remains at $\frac{8}{1-\delta}$.

- *Deviation.* The payoffs from deviating are now

$$\underbrace{9 + \delta 9 + \delta^2 9}_{\text{Deviation}} + \underbrace{\delta^3 \frac{64}{9} + \ldots}_{\text{Punishment}}$$

Here, the firm increases its profit to 9 for three periods before the punishment begins. Rearranging, we obtain

$$(1 + \delta + \delta^2)9 + \frac{64}{9}(\delta^3 + \delta^4 + \ldots)$$

$$= (1 + \delta + \delta^2)9 + \frac{64}{9}\delta^3(1 + \delta + \delta^2)$$

$$= (1 + \delta + \delta^2)9 + \frac{64}{9}\frac{\delta^3}{1 - \delta}.$$

- *Comparing payoffs.* Every firm i prefers to cooperate if

$$\frac{8}{1 - \delta} > (1 + \delta + \delta^2)9 + \frac{64}{9}\frac{\delta^3}{1 - \delta}.$$

Multiplying each side by $(1 - \delta)$, we obtain

$$8 > (1 + \delta + \delta^2)(1 - \delta)9 + \frac{64}{9}\delta^3.$$

Rearranging,

$$8 > (1 - \delta^3)9 + \frac{64}{9}\delta^3$$

$$8 > 9 - 9\delta^3 + \frac{64}{9}\delta^3$$

$$\delta^3 > \frac{9}{17}.$$

Taking the cube root of each side, we find that cooperation is sustained if

$$\delta > \left(\frac{9}{17}\right)^{1/3} \simeq 0.81.$$

This discount factor is higher than that found in self-assessment 14.6 (where we found that cooperation can be sustained if $\delta > 0.73$) because the payoffs from deviating increased. Intuitively, the temptation of deviating becomes more attractive (as the deviating payoff is enjoyed during three, rather than one, period), hindering the emergence of cooperation in equilibrium.

Exercise #14.15 - Colluding Barbecue[B]

14.15 Mike (M) and Jeff (J) each owns a barbecue place in a southern town. Market demand for barbecue is $p = 15 - 0.75Q$, where $Q = q_M + q_J$. Mike's costs are $TC(q_M) =$

340

$10 + 1.5q_M$, and Jeff's are $TC(q_J) = 5 + 3q_J$.

(a) Assuming that Mike and Jeff compete in quantities (à la Cournot), find their best response functions.

- Mike's profit maximization problem is

$$\max_{q_M} \ \pi_M = [15 - 0.75(q_M + q_J)]q_M - (10 + 1.5q_M).$$

Differentiating with respect to q_M, we obtain

$$\frac{\partial \pi_M}{\partial q_M} = 15 - 1.5q_M - 0.75q_J - 1.5 = 0,$$

rearranging, $1.5q_M = 13.5 - 0.75q_J$, solving for q_M we find Mike's best response function

$$q_M(q_J) = 9 - 0.5q_J,$$

which originates at a vertical intercept of 9 units and decreases at a rate of 0.5 when Jeff increases its output by one unit.

- Jeff's profit maximization problem is

$$\max_{q_J} \ \pi_J = [15 - 0.75(q_M + q_J)]q_J - (5 + 3q_J).$$

Differentiating with respect to q_M, we obtain

$$\frac{\partial \pi_J}{\partial q_J} = 15 - 1.5q_J - 0.75q_M - 3 = 0,$$

rearranging, $1.5q_J = 12 - 0.75q_M$, solving for q_J we find Mike's best response function

$$q_J(q_M) = 8 - 0.5q_M,$$

which originates at a vertical intercept of 8 units and decreases at a rate of 0.5 when Jeff increases its output by one unit.

- Comparing Mike's and Jeff's best response functions, we find that they each have the same slope, but Mike's best response has a higher vertical intercept, a direct result of his lower marginal cost. This indicates he will produce more for each unit his rival produces.

(b) Find the equilibrium price and quantity for Mike and Jeff.

- We cannot invoke symmetry in output levels since firms are asymmetric. Instead, we need to insert Jeff's best response function into Mike's, as follows

$$q_M = 9 - 0.5\overbrace{(8 - 0.5q_M)}^{q_J(q_M)},$$

which simplifies to $q_M = 9 - 4 + 0.25q_M$, or $0.75q_M = 5$. Solving for q_M, we obtain

$$q_M = 6.67 \text{ units.}$$

Plugging $q_M = 6.67$ into Jeff's best response, he produces

$$q_J = 8 - 0.5(6.67) = 4.67 \text{ units.}$$

- They will each charge the same price:

$$p = 15 - 0.75(6.67 + 4.67) = \$6.50.$$

(c) If Mike and Jeff form a cartel, how much barbecue product will they sell, and at what price?

- If they form a cartel, their profit maximization problem is similar to a multiplant monopoly (see section 10.6) where they maximize their joint profits, as follows

$$\max_{q_J, q_M} \pi = \pi_M + \pi_J = \underbrace{[15 - 0.75(q_M + q_J)]q_M - (10 + 1.5q_M)}_{\pi_M} +$$

$$\underbrace{[15 - 0.75(q_M + q_J)]q_J - (5 + 3q_J)}_{\pi_J}$$

Differentiating with respect to q_M and q_J, we obtain

$$\frac{\partial \pi}{\partial q_M} = 15 - 1.5q_M - 0.75q_J - 0.75q_M - 1.5 = 0$$

$$\frac{\partial \pi}{\partial q_J} = 15 - 1.5q_J - 0.75q_M - 0.75q_J - 3 = 0.$$

Simplifying the first equation, we find that

$$13.5 - 2.25q_M - 0.75q_J = 0.$$

Rearranging, we obtain $2.25q_M = 13.5 - 0.75q_J$, and solving for q_M,

$$q_M = 6 - 0.33q_J.$$

Plugging this into the second equation, $\frac{\partial \pi}{\partial q_J}$, we find

$$15 - 1.5q_J - 0.75 \underbrace{(6 - 0.33q_J)}_{q_M} - 0.75q_J - 3 = 0,$$

which simplifies to

$$12 - 2.25q_J - 4.5 + 0.25q_J = 0,$$

rearranging, we obtain $2q_J = 7.5$, and solving for q_J, we have that

$$q_J = 3.75 \text{ units.}$$

Plugging this into the equation $q_M = 6 - 0.33q_J$, we have that

$$q_M = 6 - 0.33(3.75) = 4.75 \text{ units.}$$

- Relative to the Cournot equilibrium when firms compete in quantities (part b of the exercise), both firms now restrict their output levels, charging a price of

$$p = 15 - 0.75(3.75 + 4.75) = \$8.63,$$

which is also higher than that in part (b), $p = \$6.50$.

Exercise #14.17 - Properties of the Stackelberg Equilibrium[A]

14.17 Consider the equilibrium output in the Stackelberg game discussed earlier in the chapter, $q_1^* = \frac{a-c}{2b}$ for the leader and $q_2^* = \frac{a-c}{4b}$ for the follower. Let us do some comparative statics in order to understand how this expression changes as we increase one parameter at a time.

(a) How are equilibrium output q_1^* and q_2^* affected by a marginal increase in the vertical intercept of the inverse demand function, a? Interpret.

- Both firms' output increases as the vertical intercept of the inverse demand function increases:

$$\frac{\partial q_1^*}{\partial a} = \frac{1}{2b} > 0, \text{ and}$$

$$\frac{\partial q_2^*}{\partial a} = \frac{1}{4b} > 0.$$

An increase in a is representative of an increase in demand, which increases the equilibrium output from both firms.

(b) How are equilibrium output q_1^* and q_2^* affected by a marginal increase in the slope of inverse demand function, b? Interpret.

- Both firms' output decreases as the slope of the inverse demand function increases:

$$\frac{\partial q_1^*}{\partial b} = -\frac{a-c}{2b^2} < 0, \text{ and}$$

$$\frac{\partial q_2^*}{\partial b} = -\frac{a-c}{4b^2} < 0.$$

As the slope of the inverse demand function increases, the price becomes more sensitive to output. This results in the firms decreasing their output in equilibrium.

(c) How are equilibrium output q_1^* and q_2^* affected by a marginal increase in the firm's marginal production cost, c? Interpret.

- Both firms' output decreases as marginal cost increases since

$$\frac{\partial q_1^*}{\partial c} = -\frac{1}{2b} < 0, \text{ and}$$

$$\frac{\partial q_2^*}{\partial c} = -\frac{1}{4b} < 0.$$

An increase in the marginal cost means that every unit of output is more costly to produce, so both firms reduce their production level.

Exercise #14.19 - Cournot versus Stackelberg[B]

14.19 Consider two neighboring wineries in fierce competition over the production of their specialty wine (where their grapes come from the same vineyard, so we assume that their wines are regarded as identical by customers). One winery is owned by Jill (J), and the other by Ray (R). Each winery produces its wine the same way and have symmetric TC function $TC_i(q_i) = 3 + 0.5q_i$. Inverse market demand for wine is $p = 50 - 2(q_J + q_R)$.

(a) *Cournot competition.* Write down the PMP for each firm if they compete on the basis of quantities.

- Jill's profit maximization problem is

$$\max_{q_J} \ \pi_J = [50 - 2(q_J + q_R)] \, q_J - (3 + 0.5q_J).$$

Ray's maximization problem is

$$\max_{q_R} \ \pi_R = [50 - 2(q_J + q_R)] \, q_R - (3 + 0.5q_R).$$

(b) If the firms compete à la Cournot, what is each winery's equilibrium output and price?

- *Jill's best response function.* If we differentiate Jill's profit with respect to its output q_j, we obtain

$$\frac{\partial \pi_J}{\partial q_J} = 50 - 4q_J - 2q_R - 0.5 = 0,$$

rearranging, we have $4q_J = 49.5 - 2q_R$. Solving for q_J, we obtain Jill's best response function

$$q_J(q_R) = 12.375 - \frac{1}{2}q_R,$$

which originates at a vertical intercept of 12.375 and decreases at a rate of $\frac{1}{2}$ for every unit of Ray's output.

- *Ray's best response function.* Differentiating Ray's profit with respect to its output q_R, we obtain

$$\frac{\partial \pi_R}{\partial q_R} = 50 - 4q_R - 2q_J - 0.5 = 0,$$

rearranging, we have $4q_R = 49.5 - 2q_J$. Solving for q_R, we obtain Ray's best response function

$$q_R(q_J) = 12.375 - \frac{1}{2}q_J,$$

which is symmetric to Jill's best response function. This comes at no surprise since both wineries face the same inverse demand function and total cost function.

- *Finding equilibrium output.* In a symmetric equilibrium, both wineries produce the same output level, $q_J = q_R = q$, which means that the above best response function becomes

$$q = 12.375 - \frac{1}{2}q.$$

Rearranging, we find $\frac{3}{2}q = 12.375$, and solving for q yields equilibrium output

$$q^* = 12.375\frac{2}{3} = 8.25 \text{ units.}$$

- Plugging these quantities into the inverse demand, we find the equilibrium price

$$p^* = 50 - 2(8.25 + 8.25) = \$17,$$

and equilibrium profits are

$$\begin{aligned} \pi^* &= p^*q^* - (3 + 0.5q^*) = (17 \times 8.25) - (3 + 0.5 \times 8.25) \\ &= 140.25 - 7.125 = \$133.125. \end{aligned}$$

(c) *Stackelberg competition.* If Jill was able to get her wine to market first (and become a Stackelberg leader), how will each winery's output and price change?

- *Second stage (follower).* If Jill is able to get to the market first, we start the problem by finding Ray's best response function (since Ray is the follower), which we found in part (b) to be

$$q_R(q_J) = 12.375 - 0.5q_J.$$

- *First stage (leader).* Inserting this best response function into Jill's profit maximization problem, we obtain

$$\max_{q_J} \pi_J = \left[50 - 2(q_J + \underbrace{12.375 - 0.5q_J}_{q_R}) \right] q_J - (3 + 0.5q_J).$$

Before differentiating, we can simplify the profit function

$$\max_{q_J} \pi_J = (25.25 - q_J)q_J - (3 + 0.5q_J).$$

Differentiating with respect to q_J, we obtain

$$\frac{\partial \pi_J}{\partial q_J} = 25.25 - 2q_J - 0.5 = 0.$$

Rearranging, $2q_J = 24.75$, and solving for q_J,

$$q_J = \frac{24.75}{6} = 12.375 \text{ units.}$$

Plugging this into Ray's best response function, we get Ray's equilibrium output

$$q_R(12.375) = 12.375 - 0.5(12.375) = 6.19 \text{ units.}$$

Relative to the Cournot competition we examined in part (b), Jill increases her output when she is the industry leader while Ray decreases his.

- Equilibrium price in the Stackelberg game is

$$p = 50 - 2(12.375 + 6.19) = \$12.87.$$

- Jill's equilibrium profits are

$$\pi_J = 12.87(12.375) - (3 + 0.5 \times 12.375) = \$150.08,$$

and Ray's equilibrium profits are

$$\pi_R = 12.87(6.19) - (3 + 0.5 \times 6.19) = \$73.57.$$

Compared to the Cournot profits of \$133.125 for each firm, Jill (the leader) increases her profit by being first to the market, and Ray (the follower) has a lower profit from being late to the market.

Exercise #14.21 - Product Differentiation[A]

14.21 Two companies sell cell phone cases and compete over quantity. Each firm has a slightly different case, but the two companies, 1 and 2, face symmetric demand as follows:

$$p_i = 25 - 2q_i - q_j,$$

where $i \in \{1, 2\}$ and $j \neq i$. This inverse demand indicates that every firm i is more significantly affected by its own sales, q_i, than by its rival's sales, q_j. Each firm has total cost $TC_i = q_i + 0.5q_i^2$. Assuming that the firms compete over quantity, find the equilibrium output, price, and profit.

- Each firm i solves the following profit maximization problem

$$\max_{q_i} \ \pi_i = (25 - 2q_i - q_j)q_i - \left(q_i + 0.5q_i^2\right).$$

Differentiating with respect to q_i we obtain

$$\frac{\partial \pi_i}{\partial q_i} = 25 - 4q_i - q_j - 1 - q_i = 0.$$

Rearranging, $5q_i = 24 - q_j$, and solving for q_i, we find firm i's best response function

$$q_i = 6.25 - 0.2q_j,$$

which originates at 6.25 units and decreases at a rate of 0.2 in its rival's output.

- Since firms are symmetric, firm j has a symmetric best response function

$$q_j = 6.25 - 0.2q_i.$$

- In a symmetric equilibrium, both firms produce the same output level, $q_i = q_j = q$, which implies that our above best response function becomes

$$q = 6.25 - 0.2q.$$

Rearranging, we find $1.2q = 6.25$. Solving for q, we obtain the equilibrium output

$$q = \frac{6.25}{1.2} = 5.2 \text{ units.}$$

- Therefore, each firm faces a price of

$$p_i = 25 - 2(5.2) - 5.2 = \$9.4.$$

earning an equilibrium profit of

$$\pi_i = 9.4(5.2) - \left[5.2 + 0.5(5.2)^2\right] = \$30.16.$$

Exercise #14.23 - Stackelberg Prices with Homogeneous Goods[A]

14.23 Consider the Bertrand model in subsection 14.3.2, except now firm 1 can set prices first, while firm 2 is the follower. Show that in this Stackelberg version of the Bertrand game, the equilibrium set of prices is $(p_1, p_2) = (c, c)$.

- This situation is not very different from the situation described in subsection 14.3.2. We begin our analysis by looking at firm 2's decision in the second stage.

- *Second stage.* Firm 2's best response to any price firm 1 chooses above marginal cost is to choose a price slightly below that of firm 1, that is firm 2 sets $p_2 = p_1 - \varepsilon$, where ε can be understood as an infinitely small number. In our daily lives, ε would be one cent. In this situation, firm 2 captures the entire market while firm 1, who charges a higher price, has zero sales.

  - If firm 1 sets a price equal to marginal cost, that is, $p_1 = c$, firm 2 cannot set a profitable price below and will also set a price equal to marginal cost $p_2 = p_1 = c$, and the two firms split the market.

- *First stage.* In the first stage, firm 1 anticipates firm 2's pricing strategy, knowing that if firm 1 sets a price above marginal cost, firm 2 will undercut that price, entailing no sales for firm 1. Therefore, firm 1 sets a price equal to marginal cost, firm 2 responds setting the same price, so in equilibrium $(p_1, p_2) = (c, c)$.

- Therefore, the simultaneous and sequential version of the Bertrand game of price competition yield the same outcome, where both firms charge prices equal to their common marginal cost c.

Exercise #14.25 - Reconciling Bertrand and Cournot through Capacity[C]

14.25 A common criticism of the Bertrand model of price competition is that firms face no capacity constraints. In particular, if firm 1 sets the lowest price in the market, it attracts all customers and can serve them regardless of how large demand is. In this exercise, we add a previous stage to the standard Bertrand model of price competition where firms choose a capacity level.

Consider a market with two firms. In the first stage, each firm i chooses a production capacity $\bar{q}_i$ at a cost of $c = \frac{1}{4}$ per unit of capacity, where $0 \leqslant \bar{q}_i \leqslant 1$. In the second stage, the firms observe each other's capacity and respond by competing over prices. Once capacity $\bar{q}_i$ is decided, the firms can produce up to that capacity with zero marginal cost. Each firm faces a demand of $p = 1 - Q$ and chooses prices simultaneously in the second stage, and sales are distributed as in the Bertrand model of price competition.

(a) *Second stage.* Begin in the second stage. Show that both firms set a common price $p_1 = p_2 = p^* = 1 - \bar{q}_1 - \bar{q}_2$ in the second stage.

- Let's start by assuming that firm 1 chooses a price such that $p_1 = p^*$ and show that firm 2 does not have incentives to deviate from that price.
- If firm 2 does not deviate, it sells all of its capacity $\bar{q}_2$.
- If it lowers its price, the firm still sells all of its capacity but will earn less profit, so this is not a profitable deviation.
- If firm 2 increases its price such that $p^* < p_2$, its revenue is its price times the residual demand after all of firm 1's units are sold, or $\hat{Q} = 1 - p_2 - \bar{q}_1$. Revenue is then

$$p_2 \hat{Q} = p_2(1 - p_2 - \bar{q}_1).$$

(Recall that the exercise assumes no production costs, so we only need to consider revenue.) To find the maximum of this revenue, first differentiate with respect to p_2 to obtain

$$1 - 2p_2 - \bar{q}_1 = 0.$$

Solving for p_2, we obtain the revenue maximizing price deviation of

$$p_2 = \frac{1 - \bar{q}_1}{2}.$$

However, this price is larger than firm 1's price of $p^* = 1 - \bar{q}_1 - \bar{q}_2$ if

$$\frac{1 - \bar{q}_1}{2} > 1 - \bar{q}_1 - \bar{q}_2$$
$$1 - \bar{q}_1 > 2 - 2\bar{q}_1 - 2\bar{q}_2$$
$$1 > \bar{q}_1 + 2\bar{q}_2.$$

We know that neither firm can invest in a capacity larger than 1, so condition $1 > \bar{q}_1 + 2\bar{q}_2$ cannot hold. This result means that price $p_2 = \frac{1-\bar{q}_1}{2}$ satisfies $p_2 < p^*$, and firm 2 will earn a lower revenue at the deviating price p_2 than at the equilibrium price p^*.

Hence, each firm has no incentive to deviate from price p^*, and both set a price

$$p_1 = p_2 = p^* = 1 - \bar{q}_1 - \bar{q}_2.$$

(b) *First stage.* In the first stage, every firm i simultaneously and independently chooses its capacity $\bar{q}_i$. How much capacity does each firm invest in?

- In the first stage, firms anticipate equilibrium prices $p^* = 1 - \bar{q}_1 - \bar{q}_2$ in the second stage, and simultaneously choose capacities $\bar{q}_1$ and $\bar{q}_2$. Firm 1's profit maximization problem is

$$\max_{\bar{q}_1} \ p^* \bar{q}_1 - \frac{1}{4} \bar{q}_1,$$

where the second term represents the cost of investing in $\bar{q}_1$ units of capacity. Substituting for p^*, yields

$$\max_{\bar{q}_1} \ \underbrace{(1 - \bar{q}_1 - \bar{q}_2)}_{p^*} \bar{q}_1 - \frac{1}{4} \bar{q}_1.$$

Differentiating with respect to capacity $\bar{q}_1$,

$$1 - 2\bar{q}_1 - \bar{q}_2 - \frac{1}{4} = 0,$$

rearranging, $2\bar{q}_1 = \frac{3}{4} - \bar{q}_2$. Solving for $\bar{q}_1$, we obtain firm 1's best response function

$$\bar{q}_1(\bar{q}_2) = \frac{3}{8} - \frac{1}{2}\bar{q}_2,$$

which originates at a capacity of $\frac{3}{8}$ when firm 2 does not invest in capacity, and decreases at a rate of $\frac{1}{2}$ for every additional unit of capacity of firm 2. Firm 2 has a symmetric best response function; that is

$$\bar{q}_2(\bar{q}_1) = \frac{3}{8} - \frac{1}{2}\bar{q}_1.$$

- In a symmetric equilibrium, both firms invest the same amount in capacity; that is, $\bar{q}_1 = \bar{q}_2 = \bar{q}$. Substituting this condition into either best response function, we obtain:

$$\bar{q} = \frac{3}{8} - \frac{1}{2}\bar{q},$$

rearranging, $\frac{3}{2}\bar{q} = \frac{3}{8}$, and solving for $\bar{q}$, we find the equilibrium capacity each firm chooses

$$\bar{q}^* = \frac{1}{4}.$$

- Plugging this result into the pricing decision from the second stage, we find the equilibrium price to be

$$p^* = 1 - \bar{q}_1^* - \bar{q}_2^* = 1 - \frac{1}{4} - \frac{1}{4} = \$\frac{1}{2},$$

which lies above the marginal capacity cost of $\frac{1}{4}$.

(c) How do your results compare to the standard Cournot model, with two firms competing on the basis of quantities, facing the inverse demand function $p(Q) = 1 - Q$, and marginal cost $c = \frac{1}{4}$?

- The standard Cournot model finds that equilibrium quantity for each firm is

$$q^* = \frac{a - c}{3b} = \frac{1 - \frac{1}{4}}{3} = \frac{1}{4}.$$

This is the same quantity each firm chose in our game above. Which means that the Bertrand game with capacity constraints yields the same results as the Cournot model.

Chapter 15 - Games of Incomplete Information and Auctions

15.1 Solutions to Self-Assessment Exercises

Self-assessment exercise #15.1

SA 15.1 Repeat the analysis in example 15.1, but assuming that firm 1's marginal cost changes to $MC_1 = \$\frac{1}{2}$. Firm 2's costs are still either low, $MC_2 = \$0$, or high, $MC_2 = \$\frac{1}{4}$. How are the results in example 15.1 affected? Interpret.

- *Firm 2's best response - Low costs.* When Firm 2 has low costs ($MC_2 = 0$), it chooses production level q_2^L to maximize its profits as follows

$$\max_{q_2^L \geq 0} \ \pi_2^L = (1 - q_1 - q_2^L)q_2^L$$

Differentiating with respect to q_2^L yields

$$\frac{\partial \pi_2^L}{\partial q_2^L} = 1 - q_1 - 2q_2^L = 0$$

which we can rearrange to solve for Firm 2's best response function when its costs are low,

$$q_2^L(q_1) = \frac{1}{2} - \frac{1}{2}q_1.$$

- *Firm 2's best response - High costs.* When Firm 2 has high costs ($MC_2 = \frac{1}{4}$), it chooses production level q_2^H to maximize its profits as follows

$$\max_{q_2^H \geq 0} \ \pi_2^H = (1 - q_1 - q_2^H)q_2^H - \frac{1}{4}q_2^H$$

Differentiating with respect to q_2^H yields

$$\frac{\partial \pi_2^H}{\partial q_2^H} = 1 - q_1 - 2q_2^H - \frac{1}{4} = 0$$

which again we can rearrange to solve for Firm 2's best response function when its costs are high,

$$q_2^H(q_1) = \frac{3}{8} - \frac{1}{2}q_1.$$

Note that nothing has changed for Firm 2 as compared with example 15.1, so its best response functions remain unchanged.

- *Firm 1's best response.* Firm 1 is only aware of its own costs, so it must maximize its *expected* profits. Firm 1 chooses production level q_1 to maximize

$$\max_{q_1 \geq 0} \ \pi_1 = \frac{1}{2} \underbrace{(1 - q_1 - q_2^L)q_1}_{\text{If firm 2's costs are low}} + \frac{1}{2} \underbrace{(1 - q_1 - q_2^H)q_1}_{\text{If firm 2's costs are high}} - \frac{1}{2}q_1$$

where the first term indicates firm 1's revenue when firm 2's costs are low (and that's why they are evaluated at firm 2's output level in that case, q_2^L), which occurs with probability $\frac{1}{2}$, the second term represents firm 1's revenue when firm 2's costs are high (and thus are evaluated at q_2^H), which happens with probability $\frac{1}{2}$, and the third term reflects firm 1's costs (recall that its marginal cost is 1/2). The above problem simplifies to

$$\max_{q_1 \geq 0} \quad \pi_1 = (1 - q_1 - \frac{1}{2}q_2^L - \frac{1}{2}q_2^H)q_1 - \frac{1}{2}q_1$$

Differentiating with respect to q_1 yields

$$\frac{\partial \pi_1}{\partial q_1} = 1 - 2q_1 - \frac{1}{2}q_2^L - \frac{1}{2}q_2^H - \frac{1}{2} = 0$$

which we can rearrange to solve for Firm 1's best response function,

$$q_1(q_2^L, q_2^H) = \frac{1}{4} - \frac{1}{4}q_2^L - \frac{1}{4}q_2^H.$$

- *Finding our equilibrium.* Our three best response functions serve as a system of three equations and three unknowns. Inserting $q_2^L(q_1)$ and $q_2^H(q_1)$ into Firm 1's best response function,

$$
\begin{aligned}
q_1 &= \frac{1}{4} - \frac{1}{4}\overbrace{\left(\frac{1}{2} - \frac{1}{2}q_1\right)}^{q_2^L(q_1)} - \frac{1}{4}\overbrace{\left(\frac{3}{8} - \frac{1}{2}q_1\right)}^{q_2^H(q_1)} \\
&= \frac{1}{4} - \frac{1}{8} + \frac{1}{8}q_1 - \frac{3}{32} + \frac{1}{8}q_1 \\
&= \frac{1}{32} + \frac{1}{4}q_1.
\end{aligned}
$$

Subtracting $\frac{1}{4}q_1$ from both sides of the equation gives $\frac{3}{4}q_1 = \frac{1}{32}$. Dividing this equation by $\frac{3}{4}$ provides our equilibrium production level for Firm 1,

$$q_1 = \frac{1}{24} = 0.042 \text{ units.}$$

Next, we plug this value back into the best response functions for Firm 2 when either its costs are high or low,

$$q_2^L = \frac{1}{2} - \frac{1}{2}q_1 = \frac{1}{2} - \frac{1}{2}\left(\frac{1}{24}\right) = 0.479 \text{ units, and}$$

$$q_2^H = \frac{3}{8} - \frac{1}{2}q_1 = \frac{3}{8} - \frac{1}{2}\left(\frac{1}{24}\right) = 0.354 \text{ units.}$$

Therefore, the Bayesian Nash equilibrium (BNE) of this duopoly game with incomplete information is

$$(q_1, q_2^L, q_2^H) = (0.042, 0.479, 0.354).$$

- *Comparison with example 15.1.* In this case, firm 1 reduces its production level due to its higher costs. Taking advantage of this situation, firm 2 increases its production both when it has high or low costs.

Self-assessment exercise #15.2

SA 15.2 Consider an SPA with $N = 25$ bidders. If your valuation for the object is $v_i = \$14$, what is your optimal bidding strategy? What if your valuation for the object increases to $v_i = \$17$? What if the number of bidders increases to $N = 120$? Interpret.

- This is a bit of a trick question. In a second-price auction, no bidder has any incentive to bid anything other than her valuation of the good. It does not matter how many other bidders exist or the bidder's preferences for risk. Thus, when bidder i's valuation for the object is $v_i = \$14$, her equilibrium bid is

$$b_i = \$14$$

and likewise, when her valuation for the object increases to $v_i = \$17$, her equilibrium bid increases to
$$b_i = \$17.$$

Self-assessment exercise #15.3

SA 15.3 Consider a first-price auction with $N = 2$ bidders. If your valuation for the object is $v_i = \$14$, which is your optimal bidding strategy? What if your valuation increases to $v_i = \$17$? Interpret.

- *Valuation $v_i = \$14$.* As before, we know that the bidder's expected utility from choosing bid x_i is

$$EU_i(x_i|v_i) = prob(win) \times (14 - x_i) + prob(lose) \times 0.$$

In addition, we know that $prob(win) = \frac{x_i}{a}$, where a is by what proportion the bidder shades her bid (this number in unimportant for now). Thus, bidder i must choose her bid x_i that maximizes her expected utility,

$$\max_{x_i} \quad EU_i(x_i|v_i) = \frac{x_i}{a}(14 - x_i)$$

Differentiating with respect to x_i yields

$$\frac{\partial EU_i(x_i|v_i)}{\partial x_i} = \frac{14 - 2x_i}{a} = 0.$$

Since a is alone in the denominator, it simply cancels out. We are left with $14 - 2x_i = 0$, which we can solve to obtain bidder i's equilibrium bid,

$$x_i = \$7.$$

This implies that bidder i bids half of her valuation ($14).

- *Valuation* $v_i = \$17$. When her valuation increases to 17, we can follow similar steps. Again, bidder i chooses the bid x_i that maximizes her expected utility,

$$\max_{x_i} \quad EU_i(x_i|v_i) = \underbrace{\frac{x_i}{a}}_{prob(win)} (17 - x_i)$$

Differentiating with respect to x_i yields

$$\frac{\partial EU_i(x_i|v_i)}{\partial x_i} = \frac{17 - 2x_i}{a} = 0.$$

Since a is alone in the denominator, it simply cancels out. We are left with $17 - 2x_i = 0$, which we can solve to obtain bidder i's equilibrium bid,

$$x_i = \$8.5.$$

Once again, bidder i shades her bid by half, choosing to bid half of her true valuation when there exists only one other bidder.

Self-assessment exercise #15.4

SA 15.4 Consider a first-price auction with $N = 25$ bidders. If your valuation for the object is $v_i = \$14$, what is your optimal bidding strategy? What if the number of bidders increases to $N = 120$? Interpret.

- Once again, we know that the bidder's expected utility from choosing bid x_i is

$$EU_i(x_i|v_i) = prob(win) \times (14 - x_i) + prob(lose) \times 0.$$

In addition, we know that

$$prob(win) = \left(\frac{x_i}{a}\right)^{N-1} = \left(\frac{x_i}{a}\right)^{24}.$$

Thus, bidder i must choose her bid x_i that maximizes her expected utility,

$$\max_{x_i} \quad EU_i(x_i|v_i) = \underbrace{\left(\frac{x_i}{a}\right)^{24}}_{prob(win)} (14 - x_i)$$

Differentiating with respect to x_i yields

$$\frac{\partial EU_i(x_i|v_i)}{\partial x_i} = 24\left(\frac{x_i}{a}\right)^{23}\frac{1}{a}(14-x_i) - \left(\frac{x_i}{a}\right)^{24} = 0$$

$$= \frac{1}{a^{24}}\left[336x_i^{23} - 25x_i^{24}\right] = 0.$$

Since a^{24} is alone in the denominator, it simply cancels out. We are left with $336x_i^{23} - 25x_i^{24}$, which we can again factor out x_i^{23} and cancel out to obtain

$$336 - 25x_i = 0.$$

We can solve this expression for x_i to obtain bidder i's equilibrium bid,

$$x_i = \frac{336}{25} = \$13.44.$$

- Compared to self-assessment 15.3, our bidder must now increase her bid as there is a much higher chance that one of the other 24 bidders will submit a higher bid. When we again increase the bidders to 125, bidder i must choose her bid x_i that maximizes her expected utility,

$$\max_{x_i} \quad EU_i(x_i|v_i) = \left(\frac{x_i}{a}\right)^{124}(14-x_i)$$

Differentiating with respect to x_i yields

$$\frac{\partial EU_i(x_i|v_i)}{\partial x_i} = 124\left(\frac{x_i}{a}\right)^{123}\frac{1}{a}(14-x) - \left(\frac{x_i}{a}\right)^{124} = 0$$

$$= \frac{1}{a^{124}}\left[1,736x_i^{123} - 125x_i^{124}\right] = 0.$$

Once again, since a^{124} is alone in the denominator, it simply cancels out. We are left with $1,736x_i^{123} - 125x_i^{124}$, which we can again factor out x_i^{123} and cancel out to obtain

$$1,736 - 125x_i = 0.$$

We can solve this expression for x_i to obtain bidder i's equilibrium bid,

$$x_i = \frac{1,736}{125} = \$13.89,$$

which again, we see bidder i increasing her bid to account for more competition among other bidders. With more bidders, we continue to approach bidder i's true valuation of the good.

Self-assessment exercise #15.5

SA 15.5 Consider a FPA with $N = 2$ bidders. If your valuation for the object is $v_i = \$14$ and your utility function is $u(x) = x^{1/3}$, what is your optimal bidding strategy? What if your utility function is $u(x) = x^{1/10}$? Interpret.

- *Utility function $u(x) = x^{1/3}$.* In this situation, bidder i chooses the bid x_i that maximizes her expected utility,

$$\max_{x_i} \quad EU_i(x_i|v_i) = \frac{x_i}{a}(14 - x_i)^{1/3}.$$

Differentiating with respect to x_i yields

$$\frac{\partial EU_i(x_i|v_i)}{\partial x_i} = \frac{1}{a}(14 - x_i)^{1/3} - \frac{1}{3}\frac{x_i}{a}(14 - x_i)^{-2/3} = 0.$$

Rearranging this expression, we obtain

$$\frac{1}{a}(14 - x_i)^{1/3} = \frac{x_i}{3a}(14 - x_i)^{-2/3},$$

from which we can cancel out a, and divide both sides of this expression by $(14 - x_i)^{-2/3}$ to obtain

$$14 - x_i = \frac{x_i}{3}.$$

From here, we add x_i to both sides, and our equation becomes $\frac{4}{3}x_i = 14$, which we solve by dividing both sides of the equation by $\frac{4}{3}$, obtaining bidder i's equilibrium bid,

$$x_i = \$10.5.$$

In this scenario, bidder i is risk averse, and is willing to bid more than our risk neutral bidder in self-assessment 15.2 in hopes of winning the auction.

- *Utility function $u(x) = x^{1/10}$.* When we increase bidder i's degree of risk aversion with the utility function $u(x) = x^{1/10}$, bidder i chooses the bid x_i that maximizes her expected utility,

$$\max_{x_i} \quad EU_i(x_i|v_i) = \frac{x_i}{a}(14 - x_i)^{1/10}.$$

Differentiating with respect to x_i yields

$$\frac{\partial EU_i(x_i|v_i)}{\partial x_i} = \frac{1}{a}(14 - x_i)^{1/10} - \frac{1}{10}\frac{x_i}{a}(14 - x_i)^{-9/10} = 0.$$

Rearranging this expression, we obtain

$$\frac{1}{a}(14 - x_i)^{1/10} = \frac{x_i}{10a}(14 - x_i)^{-9/10},$$

from which we can cancel out a, and divide both sides of this expression by $(14 - x_i)^{-9/10}$ to obtain

$$14 - x_i = \frac{x_i}{10}.$$

Once again, we add x_i to both sides, and our equation becomes $\frac{11}{10}x_i = 14$, which we solve by dividing both sides of the equation by $\frac{11}{10}$, obtaining bidder i's equilibrium bid,

$$x_i = \$12.73.$$

As expected, with a higher degree of risk aversion, bidder i increases her equilibrium bid by more due to her fear of missing out on the auction.

15.2 Solutions to End-of-Chapter Exercises

Exercise #15.1 - Pareto Uncertainty–I[A]

15.1 Two firms are considering the adoption of a new technology that would be mutually beneficial if they both chose to implement it. In the case where only one firm adopted the technology, however, the results could be unpredictable. Firm 1, however, has insider information about whether the technology is useful (with a payoff of 6) or useless (with a payoff of 0) if firm 2 does not adopt the new technology. Firm 2 does not have this information, but it knows that the technology is useful with probability 0.5, and useless otherwise. The payoff for both firms are depicted in the following normal form games:

		Firm 2 New	Firm 2 Old
Firm 1	New	8, 8	0, 0
	Old	0, 0	4, 4

Useless technology

		Firm 2 New	Firm 2 Old
Firm 1	New	8, 8	6, 0
	Old	0, 6	4, 4

Useful technology

(a) Find the best responses of the privately informed player, firm 1, which is type-dependent.

- *Firm 1's best responses when the new technology is useless on its own:* When firm 2 chooses the new technology, firm 1 can respond with the new technology, leading to a payoff of 8, or the old technology, leading to a payoff of 0. Since $8 > 0$, firm 1's best response to firm 2 choosing the new technology is the new technology, $BR_1(N|Useless) = N$. When firm 2 chooses the old technology, firm 1 can respond with the new technology, leading to a payoff of 0, or the old technology, leading to a payoff of 4. Since $0 < 4$, firm 1's best response to firm 2 choosing the old technology is the old technology, $BR_1(O|Useless) = O$.

		Firm 2 N	Firm 2 O
Firm 1	N	<u>8</u>, <u>8</u>	0, 0
	O	0, 0	<u>4</u>, <u>4</u>

- *Firm 1's best responses when the new technology is useful on its own:* When firm 2 chooses the new technology, firm 1 can respond with the new technology, leading to a payoff of 8, or the old technology, leading to a payoff of 0. Since $8 > 0$, firm 1's best response to firm 2 choosing the new technology is the new technology, $BR_1(N|Useful) = N$. When firm 2 chooses the old technology, firm 1 can respond with the new technology, leading to a payoff of 6, or the old technology, leading to a payoff of 4. Since $6 > 4$, firm 1's best response to firm 2 choosing the old technology is the new technology, $BR_1(O|Useful) = N$. Thus, when the new technology is useful on its own, choosing the new technology strictly dominates choosing the old technology for firm 1.

Firm 2

		N	O
		N	O
Firm 1	N	8,8	6,0
	O	0,6	4,4

(b) Find the best response of the uninformed player, firm 2.

- Since firm 2 is not privately informed about whether the new technology is useful on its own, it must consider its expected payoff in each case, which we obtain by multiplying the probability of being in each normal form game with its associated payoff.

  - When firm 1 chooses the new technology (at the top row in both matrices), firm 2's expected payoff of responding with the new technology (left column in both matrices) is $0.5(8) + 0.5(8) = 8$. If instead firm 2 responds with the old technology (right-hand column in both matrices) its expected payoff is $0.5(0) + 0.5(0) = 0$. Since $8 > 0$, firm 2's best response to firm 1 choosing the new technology is the new technology, $BR_2(N) = N$.

  - When firm 1 chooses the old technology (bottom row on both matrices), firm 2 can respond with the new technology, leading to an expected payoff of $0.5(0) + 0.5(6) = 3$, or the old technology, leading to an expected payoff of $0.5(4) + 0.5(4) = 4$. Since $3 < 4$, firm 2's best response to firm 1 choosing the old technology is the old technology, $BR_2(O) = O$.

Firm 2

		New	Old
Firm 1	New	8,8	0,0
	Old	0,0	4,4

Useless Technology

Firm 2

		New	Old
Firm 1	New	8,8	6,0
	Old	0,6	4,4

Useful Technology

(c) Identify the BNE of the game and interpret your results.

- *BNE*: The following payoff matrices illustrate the best responses of both players.

Firm 2

		New	Old
Firm 1	New	8,8	0,0
	Old	0,0	4,4

Useless Technology

Firm 2

		New	Old
Firm 1	New	8,8	6,0
	Old	0,6	4,4

Useful Technology

In this situation, three BNE exist:

- *BNE 1*: $(N_{Useless}, N)$. When the technology is useless on its own, firms only benefit when they both choose the same technology. Thus, when one firm implements the new technology, the other firm's best response is to also implement the new technology.

- *BNE 2: $(O_{Useless}, O)$.* When the technology is useless on its own, firms only benefit when they both choose the same technology. Thus, when one firm sticks with the old technology, the other firm's best response is to also stick with the old technology.

- *BNE 3: (N_{Useful}, N).* When the technology is useful on its own, the privately informed firm adopts the technology regardless of what the uninformed firm does, but due to their uncertainty, the uninformed firm only prefers to adopt the new technology if the privately informed firm implements it, as well.

Exercise #15.3 - Stackelberg Leader Facing Uncertain Costs[A]

15.3 Consider the situation in example 15.1, but suppose that firm 1 acts as a Stackelberg leader. Find the BNE of this duopoly game.

- Since this is a case of Stackelberg competition, we must make use of backward induction. Since firm 2 is the Stackelberg follower, we begin our analysis with them.

  - *Firm 2's best response.* When firm 2 has low costs $(MC_2 = 0)$, it chooses its production level q_2^L (where superscript L indicates that the firm has low costs), to maximize its profits as follows

$$\max_{q_2^L \geq 0} \ \pi_2^L = (1 - q_1 - q_2^L)q_2^L.$$

Differentiating with respect to q_2^L, yields

$$1 - q_1 - 2q_2^L = 0,$$

and solving for q_2^L, we obtain firm 2's best response function when experiencing low costs

$$q_2^L(q_1) = \frac{1}{2} - \frac{1}{2}q_1.$$

On the other hand, when firm 2 has high costs $(MC_2 = \frac{1}{4})$, its profit maximization problem is

$$\max_{q_2^H \geq 0} \ \pi_2^H = (1 - q_1 - q_2^H)q_2^H - \frac{1}{4}q_2^H.$$

Differentiating with respect to q_2^H, yields

$$1 - q_1 - 2q_2^H - \frac{1}{4} = 0,$$

and solving for q_2^H we find firm 2's best response function when experiencing high costs

$$q_2^H(q_1) = \frac{3}{8} - \frac{1}{2}q_1.$$

With firm 2's best responses analyzed for each possible cost, we now analyze the Stackelberg leader, firm 1.

– *Firm 1.* Let us now analyze firm 1. This firm seeks to maximize its expected profits, since firm 1 does not observe whether firm 2 has low or high costs. Then firm 1 solves the following problem, keeping in mind the probability that follower has low (or high) costs is $\frac{1}{2}$:

$$\max_{q_1 \geq 0} \pi_1 = \frac{1}{2}\underbrace{(1 - q_1 - q_2^L)q_1}_{\text{Firm 2 has low costs}} + \frac{1}{2}\underbrace{(1 - q_1 - q_2^H)q_1}_{\text{Firm 2 has high costs}}$$

$$= \left(1 - q_1 - \frac{q_2^L}{2} - \frac{q_2^H}{2}\right)q_1.$$

Since firm 1 is the Stackelberg leader, it also anticipates how firm 2 will react to its production level. To capture this effect, we substitute both of firm 2's best response functions into firm 1's expected profit maximization problem.

$$\max_{q_1 \geq 0} \pi_1 = \left(1 - q_1 - \frac{1}{2}\underbrace{\left(\frac{1}{2} - \frac{1}{2}q_1\right)}_{q_2^L} - \frac{1}{2}\underbrace{\left(\frac{3}{8} - \frac{1}{2}q_1\right)}_{q_1^H}\right)q_1$$

$$= \left(\frac{9}{16} - \frac{q_1}{2}\right)q_1.$$

Differentiating with respect to q_1, yields

$$\frac{9}{16} - q_1 = 0.$$

Solving for output q_1 we obtain $q_1 = \frac{9}{16}$. We can now plug this result into firm 2's best response function, first when having low costs,

$$q_2^L\left(\frac{9}{16}\right) = \frac{1}{2} - \frac{1}{2}\frac{9}{16} = \frac{7}{32} \text{ units,}$$

and when having high costs,

$$q_2^H\left(\frac{9}{16}\right) = \frac{3}{8} - \frac{1}{2}\frac{9}{16} = \frac{3}{32} \text{ units.}$$

• *BNE.* Therefore, the BNE of this duopoly game with incomplete information prescribes production levels

$$\left(q_1, q_2^L, q_2^H\right) = \left(\frac{9}{16}, \frac{7}{32}, \frac{3}{32}\right).$$

Comparing this to example 15.1, notice that firm 1 in this case increases its production by 50 percent, leveraging its Stackelberg leader status, but not quite able to exploit it as it would be able to under complete information. Firm 2 sees its output levels fall in both cases, but not as much when it experiences low costs and is more competitive against firm 1.

Exercise #15.5 - Uncertain Demand–One Uninformed Firm[B]

15.5 Consider a duopoly game where two firms compete on the basis of quantities and face inverse demand function $p = a - q_1 - q_2$. Assume that firm 1 is an incumbent and understands that the size of the market is $a = 100$. Firm 2, the entrant, is unable to accurately observe the size of the market and instead knows that it is low, $a = 80$, with probability 0.5, and high, $a = 100$, with probability 0.5. Assume that marginal costs of production for both firms are 0. Find the BNE of this duopoly game.

- Since firm 1 has private information about the market size and both firms set their output levels simultaneously, we must find the best responses for each firm and see where they cross.

  - *Firm 1's best response under low demand.* When the market size is low ($a = 80$), firm 1 chooses its production level q_1^L (where superscript L indicates that the market size is low), to maximize its profits as follows

  $$\max_{q_1^L \geq 0} \ \pi_1^L = (80 - q_1^L - q_2)q_1^L.$$

  Differentiating with respect to q_1^L, yields

  $$80 - 2q_1^L - q_2 = 0,$$

  and solving for q_1^L, we obtain firm 1's best response function when the market size is low

  $$q_1^L(q_2) = 40 - \frac{1}{2}q_2.$$

  - *Firm 1's best response under high demand.* When the market size is high ($a = 100$), firm 1's profit maximization problem is

  $$\max_{q_1^H \geq 0} \ \pi_1^H = (100 - q_1^H - q_2)q_1^H.$$

  Differentiating with respect to q_1^H, yields

  $$100 - 2q_1^H - q_2 = 0,$$

  and solving for q_1^H we find firm 1's best response function when the market size is high

  $$q_1^H(q_2) = 50 - \frac{1}{2}q_2.$$

  Comparing the best response functions under low and high market size, we can see that, for a given output level of firm 2, q_2, firm 1 responds producing more units when the market size is high than when it is low since $q_1^H(q_2) > q_1^L(q_2)$ for every value of q_2.

– *Firm 2 (uninformed player)*. Let us now analyze firm 2 (the uninformed player in this game). This firm seeks to maximize its expected profits, since firm 2 does not observe whether the market size is low or high. Then firm 2 solves the following problem:

$$\max_{q_2 \geq 0} \pi_2 = \underbrace{\frac{1}{2}(80 - q_1^L - q_2)q_2}_{\text{if market size is low}} + \underbrace{\frac{1}{2}(100 - q_1^H - q_2)q_2}_{\text{if market size is high}}$$

$$= \left(90 - \frac{q_1^L}{2} - \frac{q_1^H}{2} - q_2\right)q_2.$$

Differentiating with respect to q_2, yields

$$90 - \frac{q_1^L}{2} - \frac{q_1^H}{2} - 2q_2 = 0.$$

Solving for q_2, we obtain firm 2's best response function

$$q_2\left(q_1^L, q_1^H\right) = 45 - \frac{1}{4}q_1^L - \frac{1}{4}q_1^H,$$

which is a function of both firm 2's output when the market size is low, q_2^L, and when the market size is high, q_2^H.

- *BNE*. We found three best response functions that we use to obtain the three unknown output levels q_1^L, q_1^H, and q_2. Inserting the best response functions for firm 1, $q_1^L(q_2)$ and $q_1^H(q_2)$, into the expression of firm 2's best response function, $q_2\left(q_1^L, q_1^H\right)$, yields

$$q_2 = 45 - \frac{1}{4}\underbrace{\left(40 - \frac{1}{2}q_2\right)}_{q_1^L} - \frac{1}{4}\underbrace{\left(50 - \frac{1}{2}q_2\right)}_{q_1^H},$$

which simplifies to $q_2 = 22.5 + \frac{1}{4}q_2$. Solving for output q_2 we obtain $q_2 = 30$. We can now plug this result into firm 1's best response function, first when the market size is low,

$$q_1^L(30) = 40 - \frac{1}{2}30 = 25 \text{ units},$$

and when the market size is high,

$$q_1^H(30) = 50 - \frac{1}{2}30 = 35 \text{ units}.$$

Therefore, the BNE of this duopoly game with incomplete information prescribes production levels

$$\left(q_1^L, q_1^H, q_2\right) = (25, 35, 30).$$

15.7 Consider the entry game presented in example 13.1 in chapter 13, but suppose that the incumbent had private information about whether she was crazy or not. A noncrazy incumbent has a game tree exactly as depicted in example 13.1, but a crazy incumbent loves to engage in price wars, and receives a payoff of 6 from doing so. Suppose that the entrant was aware that the probability of an incumbent being crazy is $p = 0.1$.

(a) Find the BNE of this game. Does the entrant still enter this market?

- The Entry game with a Not Crazy and a Crazy incumbent is depicted in figure 15.1.

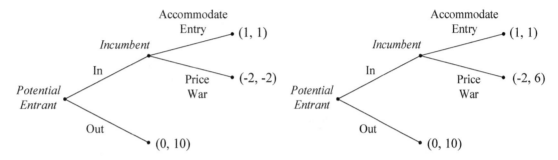

Figure 15.1a. Not Crazy incumbent. Figure 15.1b. Crazy incumbent.

We can combine these two extensive form representations into a single game by adding nature as a first mover, as depicted in figure 15.2. Intuitively, nature begins this game by determining whether the incumbent is crazy or not, but the entrant cannot observe this information, creating an information set.

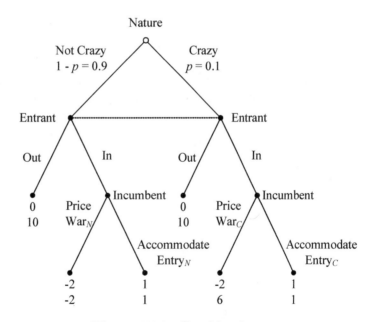

Figure 15.2. Combined game.

To properly analyze this game, we must make use of backward induction.

Since the incumbent is the final mover in this game, we analyze his best responses first.

– *Incumbent's best responses*: If the incumbent is not crazy and observes entry, he can accommodate and receive a payoff of 1, or start a price war and receive a payoff of -2. Since $1 > -2$, the best response for a not crazy incumbent when observing entry is to accommodate, $BR_{I_N}(I) = A_N$. If the incumbent is crazy and observes entry, he can accommodate and receive a payoff of 1, or he can start a price war and receive a payoff of 6. Since $1 < 6$, the best response for a crazy incumbent when observing entry is to start a price war, $BR_{I_C}(I) = W_C$. These best responses are highlighted in figure 15.3.

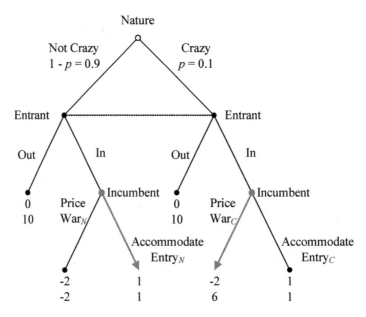

Figure 15.3. Incumbent's best responses.

– Inserting the equilibrium payoff $(1, 1)$ from the left-hand side of the tree and $(-2, 6)$ from the right-hand side, the above game tree becomes that in figure 15.4.

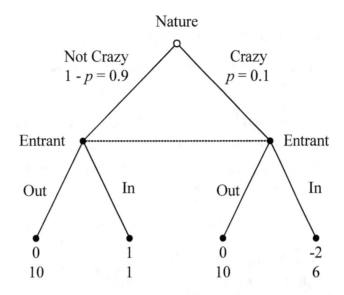

Figure 15.4. Reduced form game.

- *Entrant's optimal strategy*: Since the entrant does not know whether the incumbent is crazy or not, he must evaluate his payoffs based on his anticipation of how each incumbent reacts in the second stage of the game and his expected payoffs. If the entrant stays out of the market, he receives a payoff of 0 with certainty. If the entrant enters the market, he receives a payoff of 1 with a probability of 0.9 (since the incumbent is not crazy), or a payoff of -2 with a probability of 0.1 (since the incumbent is crazy). Thus, the entrants expected payoff from entering the market is,

$$0.9(1) + 0.1(-2) = 0.7.$$

Since $0 < 0.7$, even though the entrant knows there is a chance that the incumbent might be crazy, he still enters the market.

- Therefore, the BNE of this Entry game with incomplete information prescribes strategies

$$(I, (A, W)).$$

(b) For what value of p is the entrant indifferent between entering or staying out of this market?

- The entrant would be indifferent between entering or staying out of the market if his expected payoff from entering the market equals his certain payoff from staying out of the market, 0.

$$p(1) + (1 - p)(-2) = 0.$$

Rearranging this expression, we have $3p = 2$, and dividing both sides of this expression by 3, we obtain our indifference probability level of $p = \frac{2}{3}$. Thus, if the entrant believes that there is a greater than $\frac{2}{3}$ chance that the incumbent is crazy, his optimal strategy is to stay out of the market. (It might be in the best interest of the incumbent to try and make the entrant think he is crazy.)

Exercise #15.9 - First-Price Auction–II^A

15.9 Consider the situation in exercise 15.8, but suppose that Person A's valuation is only $25.

(a) If the seller organizes an FPA, who will be the winner? What will be her winning bid? What price will she pay for the object?

- *Person A's Valuation $v_A = \$25$.* We know that person A's expected utility from choosing bid x_A is

$$EU_A(x_A|25) = prob(win) \times (25 - x_A) + prob(lose) \times 0.$$

In addition, we know that $prob(win) = \frac{x_A}{a}$, where a is by what proportion the bidder shades her bid (this number is unimportant for now). Thus, person A must choose her bid x_A that maximizes her expected utility,

$$\max_{x_A} \quad EU_A(x_A|25) = \frac{x_A}{a}(25 - x_A).$$

Differentiating with respect to x_A yields

$$\frac{\partial EU_A(x_A|25)}{\partial x_A} = \frac{25 - 2x_A}{a} = 0.$$

Since a is alone in the denominator, it simply cancels out. We are left with $25 - 2x_A = 0$, which we can solve to obtain person A's equilibrium bid,

$$x_A = \$12.5.$$

This implies that person A bids half of her valuation ($25).

- *Person B's Valuation $v_B = \$60$.* Similar to person A, person B must choose her bid x_B that maximizes her expected utility,

$$\max_{x_B} \quad EU_B(x_B|60) = \frac{x_B}{a}(60 - x_B).$$

Differentiating with respect to x_B yields

$$\frac{\partial EU_B(x_B|60)}{\partial x_B} = \frac{60 - 2x_B}{a} = 0.$$

Since a is alone in the denominator, it simply cancels out. We are left with $60 - 2x_B = 0$, which we can solve to obtain person B's equilibrium bid,

$$x_B = \$30.$$

Once again, person B shades half of her bid, choosing to bid half of her true valuation when there exists only one other bidder.

- *The winner.* Since person B has the high bid of $30, he wins the auction and pays her bid for the object, $30.

(b) Suppose that Person A were able to observe Person B's private valuation prior to the auction. Would Person A change her bid? If so, how? If not, why not?

- If person A could observe person B's private valuation, she would know that person B would enter a bid of $30 for the object. Thus, person A could simply bid $30.01 for the object and "snipe" the object from person B. This, however, would not be a beneficial strategy for person A, as her net payoff from winning the auction is $25 - $30.01 = -$5.01$, and this is less than her payoff from not winning the auction ($0). Thus, person A would not change her bid.

Exercise #15.11 - Risk Aversion–I^B

15.11 Consider the situation in exercise 15.8, but suppose that both bidders have utility function $u(x) = x^{0.4}$.

(a) If the seller organizes an FPA, who will be the winner? What will be her winning bid? What price will she pay for the object?

- *Person A's valuation $v_A = $50.* We know that person A must choose bid x_A that maximizes her expected utility,

$$\max_{x_A} \quad EU_A(x_A|50) = \frac{x_A}{a}(50 - x_A)^\alpha.$$

where α represents the degree of concavity in her utility function ($\alpha = 0.4$ in this case). Differentiating with respect to x_A yields

$$\frac{\partial EU_A(x_A|50)}{\partial x_A} = \frac{(50 - x_A)^\alpha}{a} - \frac{\alpha x_A}{a}(50 - x_A)^{\alpha-1} = 0.$$

Rearranging our expression, we obtain

$$\frac{(50 - x_A)^\alpha}{a} = \frac{\alpha x_A}{a}(50 - x_A)^{\alpha-1},$$

from which we can cancel out a (not to be confused with α), and divide both sides of this expression by $(50 - x_A)^{\alpha-1}$ to obtain

$$50 - x_A = \alpha x_A.$$

From here, we add x_A to both sides of this expression, and after factoring out x_A, our equation becomes $(1 + \alpha)x_A = 50$, which we solve by dividing both sides of the equation by $1 + \alpha$, obtaining person A's equilibrium bid,

$$x_A = \frac{50}{1 + \alpha}.$$

Plugging in our value for α, we find that person A's equilibrium bid is $x_A = \frac{50}{1+0.4} = \$35.71$. (Note that if $\alpha = 1$ and person A were risk neutral, she would have the same equilibrium bid as in exercise 15.6.)

- *Person B's valuation* $v_B = \$60$. Similarly to person A, person B must choose bid x_B that maximizes her expected utility,

$$\max_{x_B} \ EU_B(x_B|60) = \frac{x_B}{a}(60 - x_A)^\alpha.$$

Differentiating with respect to x_B yields

$$\frac{\partial EU_B(x_B|60)}{\partial x_B} = \frac{(60 - x_B)^\alpha}{a} - \frac{\alpha x_B}{a}(60 - x_B)^{\alpha-1} = 0.$$

Rearranging our expression, we obtain

$$\frac{(60 - x_B)^\alpha}{a} = \frac{\alpha x_B}{a}(60 - x_B)^{\alpha-1},$$

from which we can cancel out a (not to be confused with α), and divide both sides of this expression by $(60 - x_B)^{\alpha-1}$ to obtain

$$60 - x_B = \alpha x_B.$$

From here, we add x_B to both sides of this expression, and after factoring out x_B, our equation becomes $(1 + \alpha)x_B = 60$, which we solve by dividing both sides of the equation by $1 + \alpha$, obtaining person B's equilibrium bid,

$$x_B = \frac{60}{1 + \alpha}.$$

Plugging in our value for α, we find that person B's equilibrium bid is $x_B = \frac{60}{1+0.4} = \$42.86$.

- *The winner.* Since person B has the high bid of $\$42.86$, he wins the auction and pays her bid for the object, $\$42.86$.

(b) Suppose that Person A were able to observe Person B's private valuation prior to the auction. Would Person A change her bid? If so, how? If not, why not?

- If person A could observe person B's private valuation, she would know that person B would enter a bid of $\$42.86$ for the object. Thus, person A could simply bid $\$42.87$ for the object and "snipe" the object from person B. This would be a beneficial strategy for person A, as her net payoff from winning the auction is $\$50 - \$42.87 = \$7.13$, and this exceeds her payoff from not winning the auction ($\$0$). Thus, person A would change her bid.

(c) For what degree of risk aversion (α) would Person A not want to change her bid in part (b)?

- For person A to not want to change her bid, person B must bid at least $\$50$ (because any bid higher than this would yield person A a negative payoff).

368

Thus, we need to find what value of α produces an equilibrium bid of $50 for person B. Setting up our equation,

$$\frac{60}{1+\alpha} \geq 50,$$

and rearranging terms, we obtain $60 \geq 50(1+\alpha)$. Reorganizing terms, we have $50\alpha \leq 10$. Dividing both sides of this expression by 50 yields our range for α, $\alpha \leq 0.2$. Intuitively, if person B is sufficiently risk averse, he will bid higher than person A's total valuation for the object ($50), and person A will have no incentive to outbid person B even if she knows person B's valuation.

Exercise #15.13 - Second-Price Auction–I^A

15.13 Consider the situation in exercise 15.8.

(a) If the seller organizes a second-price auction, who will be the winner? What will be her winning bid? What price will she pay for the object?

- In a second-price auction, no bidder has any incentive to bid anything other than her valuation of the good. It does not matter how many other bidders exist or the bidder's preferences for risk. Thus, person A submits $x_A = \$50$ and person B submits $x_B = \$60$. Person B wins the auction, but pays the second highest bid, $50 for the object.

(b) Suppose that Person A were able to observe Person B's private valuation prior to the auction. Would Person A change her bid? If so, how? If not, why not?

- Person A has no incentive to bid anything other than her valuation in a second-price auction. In order to win the auction, she would have to bid above person B's valuation. This would require person A to pay $60 (person B's bid) for the object, which would yield a negative payoff for person A. Thus, it is better for person A to simply bid her own valuation and nothing else.

Exercise #15.15 - Lottery Allocation–I^B

15.15 Consider a situation where a public all-pay auction takes place for an item, with its allocation determined by a lottery. Each bidder is able to observe all the bids of all the other bidders as they make their own. The probability that bidder i wins the auction is $p = \frac{b_i}{b_i + B_{-i}}$ where B_{-i} denotes the total bids made by all other bidders. Suppose that bidder i has a valuation of $v_i = 9$ for this item, and he knows that bids totaling $B_{-i} = \$4$ have already been submitted. Find the optimal bidding strategy for bidder i, b_i, taking into consideration that he must pay her bid, b_i, regardless of whether he wins the auction.

- Since bidder i can observe all of the other bids, he simply must maximize her own expected payoff,

$$\max_{b_i} \ EU_i(b_i|9) = \left(\frac{b_i}{b_i+4}\right)(9) + \left(1 - \frac{b_i}{b_i+4}\right)(0) - b_i$$

$$= \frac{9b_i}{b_i+4} - b_i.$$

Differentiating this with respect to b_i yields

$$\frac{9(b_i+4) - 9b_i}{(b_i+4)^2} - 1 = 0.$$

Rearranging terms,

$$9(b_i+4) - 9b_i = (b_i+4)^2,$$

and reorganizing the left-hand side yields $(b_i+4)^2 = 36$. Taking the square root of both sides, then subtracting 4, we find bidder i's equilibrium bid $b_i = 2$. (*Note:* $b_i = -10$ is also a solution to this maximization problem, but we assume that only positive bids can be submitted.)

Exercise #15.17 - All-Pay Auction[C]

15.17 Consider the following all-pay auction, with two bidders privately observing their valuations for the object. Valuations are uniformly distributed $v_i \sim U[0,1]$. The player submitting the highest bid wins the object, but all players must pay the bid they submitted. Find the optimal bidding strategy, taking into account that it takes the form $b_i(v_i) = m \times v_i^2$, where m denotes a positive constant.

- *Writing bidder i's problem.* We know that bidder i's expected utility from choosing bid b_i is

$$EU_i(b_i|50) = \underbrace{prob(win) \times v_i}_{\text{if winning}} + \underbrace{prob(lose) \times 0}_{\text{if losing}} - \underbrace{b_i(v_i)}_{\text{always}},$$

where $b_i(v_i)$ is some function that expresses bidder i's valuation as a bid. Since bidder i must pay her bid, $b_i(v_i)$, whether or not she wins the auction, $b_i(v_i)$ enters without being multiplied times the probability of winning or losing.

Since we have a uniform distribution distributed from 0 to 1, we know that $prob(win) = b_i$ (the cumulative density function of $U[0,1]$). Thus, bidder i must choose the bid b_i that maximizes her expected utility,

$$\max_{b_i} \ EU_i(b_i|v_i) = b_i \times v_i - b_i(v_i).$$

- *Finding bidder i's strategy.* Differentiating with respect to b_i yields

$$\frac{\partial EU_i(b_i|v_i)}{\partial b_i} = v_i - b_i'(v_i) = 0.$$

Thus, in equilibrium, we must have that

$$b_i'(v_i) = v_i.$$

Integrating both sides of this expression gives

$$b_i(v_i) = \int v_i dv_i = \frac{1}{2}v_i^2.$$

Therefore, each bidder bids $b_i(v_i) = m \cdot v_i^2$, where $m = 0.5$. More generally, in a scenario with N bidders, the equilibrium bidding function in an all-pay auction is $b_i(v_i) = \frac{N-1}{N}v_i^N$, which is increasing and convex in bidder i's valuation for the object v_i.

Exercise #15.19 - Efficiency with Risk Aversion[B]

15.19 Consider a situation where bidders with heterogeneous attitudes toward risk compete in an FPA. Provide an example of how these bidders can lead to an inefficient allocation of the object.

- Suppose two bidders, Risky Rick and Cautious Carl, were bidding for a common object. Risky Rick has a slightly higher valuation than Cautious Carl, but he is risk loving as opposed to Cautious Carl being risk averse. As such, Rick shades her bid by more than 50 percent while Carl shades her bid by less than 50 percent. Since Rick shades her bid by a higher proportion than Carl, it is possible that Carl could outbid Rick even though Rick has a higher valuation of the object than Carl does. This would lead to an inefficient allocation of the object.

Exercise #15.21 - Comparing Auctions[A]

15.21 Compare and contrast the similarities and differences between an FPA where all bidders can observe everyone's private valuations and an SPA.

- In the case of a first-price auction where all bidders can observe everyone's private valuations, each bidder has incentive to increase her bid up to her valuation in an effort to outbid others. The result is that the bidder with the highest valuation bids the smallest amount above the valuation of the second highest bidder. This is approximately equal to the price the winner pays in a second-price auction where all players simply bid their valuation.

Chapter 16 - Contract Theory

16.1 Solutions to Self-Assessment Exercises

Self-assessment exercise #16.1

SA 16.1 Repeat the analysis in example 16.1, but assume that the worker's reservation utility increases to $\bar{u} = 1/2$. This could happen if, for instance, unemployment benefits become more generous. Find the optimal salaries w_H and w_L in this scenario, and compare them against those in example 16.1. Interpret.

- Since the firm can observe the worker's effort in this case, it simply needs to pay the worker enough to offset the cost of her effort and her reservation utility (which is 0 in this case).

  - *High-effort worker.* For a high-effort worker, her utility from working is $\sqrt{w_H} - 5$, and her effort from not working is equal to her reservation utility, 0. Thus, to get a high-effort worker to accept this job, the firm must set w_H high enough such that a high effort worker's utility from working is at least as large as her reservation utility,

    $$\sqrt{w_H} - 5 \geq 0.$$

    Adding 5 to both sides of this inequality, then squaring both sides yields $w_H \geq 25$. Thus, a high-effort worker will accept any wage at or above \$25. Since the firm wants to maximize its profits, it pays the worker the minimum she will accept, $w_H = \$25$.

  - *Low-effort worker.* For a low-effort worker, her utility from working is $\sqrt{w_L}$, and her effort from not working is equal to her reservation utility, 0. As before, the firm must set the wage for a low-effort worker such that the utility from working is at least as high as her reservation wage,

    $$\sqrt{w_L} \geq 0.$$

    This implies that $w_L \geq 0$, and since the firm wants to maximize its profits, it sets $w_L = \$0$.

- *Comparison with example 16.1* We find that there is no difference between the results of this exercise and those of example 16.1. Since the firm is able to perfectly observe the effort of the worker involved, changing the probabilities of each outcome does not affect the worker's compensation.

Self-assessment exercise #16.2

SA 16.2 Repeat the analysis in example 16.2, but assume that the worker's reservation utility increases to $\bar{u} = 1/2$. Find the optimal salaries w_H^* and w_L^* in this scenario, the worker's information rent, and compare them against your findings in self-assessment 16.1 (the complete information version of this scenario). Interpret.

- Let w_H denote the salary that the worker receives when output is high and w_L when output is low. (Recall that in this scenario the firm cannot condition salaries on the worker's effort, since this effort is unobservable.) The firm's maximization problem in this scenario is

$$\max_{w_H, w_L} \quad \$270 - \underbrace{[0.6 w_H + 0.4 w_L]}_{\text{Expected labor cost}}$$

subject to

$$0.6\sqrt{w_H} + 0.4\sqrt{w_L} - 5 \geq 0 \qquad\qquad (PC)$$

$$\underbrace{0.6\sqrt{w_H} + 0.4\sqrt{w_L} - 5}_{\text{Expected utility from high effort}} \geq \underbrace{0.05\sqrt{w_H} + 0.95\sqrt{w_L}}_{\text{Expected utility from low effort}} . \qquad (IC)$$

As in example 16.2, we know that the incentive compatibility constraint must hold with equality. We can rearrange the second constraint to obtain $0.55\sqrt{w_H} = 0.55\sqrt{w_L} + 5$, or, dividing both sides of this equation by 0.55,

$$\sqrt{w_H} = \sqrt{w_L} + 9.1,$$

or, squaring both sides, $w_H = \left(\sqrt{w_L} + 9.1\right)^2$. From here, we can substitute this expression back into the maximization problem for the firm as well as ignore the participation constraint (it will not bind, as we show below). Thus, the firm's maximization problem becomes

$$\max_{w_L} \quad \$270 - \left[0.6\underbrace{\left(\sqrt{w_L} + 9.1\right)^2}_{w_H} + 0.4 w_L\right].$$

Differentiating with respect to w_L, yields

$$\begin{aligned}
\frac{\partial \pi}{\partial w_L} &= -\left[\frac{0.6}{\sqrt{w_L}}\left(\sqrt{w_L} + 9.1\right) + 0.4\right] \\
&= -0.6 - \frac{5.5}{\sqrt{w_L}} - 0.4 \\
&= -1 - \frac{5.5}{\sqrt{w_L}}.
\end{aligned}$$

which is negative for all possible values of w_L. This implies that the firm will always decrease its profit when it pays a higher wage to the worker after observing a low output level. Thus, upon observing a low output level, the firm pays the worker

$$w_L^* = \$0.$$

Returning to our constraint, we can solve for the wage that the firm pays after observing a high output level is

$$w_H^* = \left(\sqrt{w_L^*} + 9.1\right)^2$$
$$= \left(\sqrt{0} + 9.1\right)^2$$
$$= 9.1^2 = 82.81.$$

- *PC holds.* The worker's PC holds since

$$0.6\sqrt{82.81} + 0.4\sqrt{0} - 5 = 5.46 - 5 = 0.46 > 0.$$

This implies that the worker prefers to exert a high effort level than not participating in the contract at all.

- *Comparison with self-assessment 16.1.* Comparing this value against our solution in self-assessment 16.1, we find that the wage of the high-effort worker, w_H, increases from \$25 to \$82.81. Since the firm can no longer directly observe a worker's effort, it must now pay her more to induce the higher effort from workers, as her effort cannot be directly linked to the profitability of the firm.

Self-assessment exercise #16.3

SA 16.3 Repeat the analysis in subsection 16.3.2, but assume that the car quality is uniformly distributed between 0 and 2 (rather than between 0 and $\frac{3}{2}$). This means that the seller now values a car of quality q as $\frac{q}{2} = \frac{1}{2}q$, rather than at $\frac{q}{\frac{3}{2}} = \frac{2}{3}q$. How are the results in subsection 16.3.2 affected?

- In this situation, the seller maximizes his own profits,

$$\max_p \quad p - \frac{1}{2}q$$
$$\text{subject to} \quad q - p \geq 0. \tag{PC}$$

The buyer's participation constraint ($q - p \geq 0$) will hold with equality since the seller wants to receive as much profit as possible. Thus, we have that $q - p = 0$, or $q = p$. We can substitute this back into the seller's maximization problem to obtain

$$\max_p \quad p - \frac{1}{2}p.$$

Differentiating with respect to p, yields

$$\frac{\partial \pi}{\partial p} = 1 - \frac{1}{2} = \frac{1}{2},$$

which is always positive. Thus, the seller can always increase his price and it will increase his own profits. This implies that the seller sets $p = q$ and charges the buyer the maximum that the buyer is willing to pay (since anything higher than q would violate the seller's participation constraint).

- *Comparison with subsection 16.3.2.* This result coincides with that in subsection 16.3.2. Intuitively, if both the buyer and seller can observe the quality of the car, the seller will charge a price exactly equal to the car's quality and maximize his own profits; it does not matter how the quality of the car is distributed.

Self-assessment exercise #16.4

SA 16.4 Repeat the analysis in subsection 16.3.3, but assume that the car quality is uniformly distributed between 0 and 2 (rather than between 0 and $\frac{3}{2}$). This means that the seller now values a car of quality q as $\frac{q}{2} = \frac{1}{2}q$, rather than at $\frac{q}{\frac{3}{2}} = \frac{2}{3}q$. How are the results in subsection 16.3.3 affected?

- To start, we must first determine the participation constraint for the buyer, which is the expected quality of the car he purchases minus the price he pays,

$$E[q] - p,$$

where the expected quality in this case (due to its uniform distribution) is

$$E[q] = \frac{2 + 0}{2} = 1.$$

Now, setting up the seller's maximization problem, we obtain

$$\max_{p} \quad p - \frac{1}{2}q$$
$$\text{subject to} \quad 1 - p \geq 0.$$

The buyer's participation constraint $(1 - p \geq 0)$ will, again, hold with equality since the seller wants to receive as much profit as possible. Thus, we have that $1 - p = 0$, or $p = \$1$. In this situation, the seller charges a price $p = \$1$, earning positive profits as as long as

$$\pi = p - \frac{1}{2}q = 1 - \frac{1}{2}q \geq 0,$$

which rearranges to $q \leq 2$.

- *Interpretation.* Thus, all qualities of cars are offered for sale in this scenario, and neither the buyer or seller has to worry about a market for "lemons." This occurs because the range of possible qualities for cars in this problem is bounded between 0 and 2, and all of these values lead to positive profits for the seller.

Self-assessment exercise #16.5

SA 16.5 Repeat the analysis in subsection 16.3.5, but assume that the worker's reservation utility is $2 rather than zero (see the right side of her PC). Find the optimal efforts, e_L^{SI} and e_H^{SI}, and the optimal salaries, w_L^{SI} and w_H^{SI}. How are the results in subsection 16.3.5 affected?

- Setting up the firm's maximization problem:

$$\max_{w,e} \quad \log(e) - w$$

$$\text{subject to} \quad w - \theta e^2 \geq 2 \qquad (PC)$$

Looking at the participation constraint for the worker (PC), we know that the firm wants to pay the worker as little as possible to maximize its own profits. Thus, the participation constraint holds with equality, $w - \theta e^2 = 2$, which rearranges to

$$w = 2 + \theta e^2.$$

Substituting this result back into the firm's maximization problem,

$$\max_{e} \quad \log(e) - \underbrace{(2 + \theta e^2)}_{w}.$$

Differentiating with respect to e, yields

$$\frac{\partial \pi}{\partial e} = \frac{1}{e} - 2\theta e = 0.$$

We can rearrange this expression, obtaining $\frac{1}{e} = 2\theta e$ or, cross multiplying, $\frac{1}{2\theta} = e^2$. Applying square roots on both sides, yields

$$e = \left(\frac{1}{2\theta}\right)^{\frac{1}{2}}.$$

Thus, we have our two different effort levels,

$$e_H = \left(\frac{1}{2\theta_H}\right)^{\frac{1}{2}} \quad \text{and} \quad e_L = \left(\frac{1}{2\theta_L}\right)^{\frac{1}{2}}.$$

- Inserting these effort levels in the participation constraint, $w = 2 + \theta e^2$, we obtain the wage levels

$$w_H^{SI} = 2 + \theta_H \overbrace{\left[\left(\frac{1}{2\theta_H}\right)^{\frac{1}{2}}\right]}^{\frac{e_H}{2}} = 2 + \theta_H \left(\frac{1}{2\theta_H}\right) = 2 + \frac{1}{2} = \$2.5 \quad \text{and}$$

$$w_L^{SI} = 2 + \theta_L \underbrace{\left[\left(\frac{1}{2\theta_L}\right)^{\frac{1}{2}}\right]^2}_{e_L} = 2 + \theta_L \left(\frac{1}{2\theta_L}\right) = 2 + \frac{1}{2} = \$2.5.$$

- *Comparison with subsection 16.3.5.* As in subsection 16.3.5, the firm pays both the high and low type workers the same amount, but that amount is higher in this case due to the reservation utility of each worker. The net effect for the firm is that it earns a lower profit due to the higher wages paid.

Self-assessment exercise #16.6

SA 16.6 Repeat the analysis in example 16.4, but assume that the proportion of high-cost workers increases to $\gamma = \frac{1}{2}$. How are the results in example 16.4 affected?

- From example 16.4, we have the following values,

$$
\begin{aligned}
e_L^{AI} &= \left(\frac{1}{2\theta_L}\right)^{\frac{1}{2}} = \left(\frac{1}{2 \times 1}\right)^{\frac{1}{2}} = \frac{1}{\sqrt{2}}. \\
e_H^{AI} &= \left(\frac{\gamma}{2\left[\theta_H - (1-\gamma)\theta_L\right]}\right)^{\frac{1}{2}} = \left(\frac{\frac{1}{2}}{2\left[2 - \left(1 - \frac{1}{2}\right) \times 1\right]}\right)^{\frac{1}{2}} \\
&= \left(\frac{\frac{1}{2}}{3}\right)^{\frac{1}{2}} = \frac{1}{\sqrt{6}}.
\end{aligned}
$$

while optimal wages are

$$
\begin{aligned}
w_L^{AI} &= \frac{(1+\gamma)\theta_H - \theta_L}{2\left[\theta_H - (1-\gamma)\theta_L\right]} = \frac{\left(1 + \frac{1}{2}\right) \times 2 - 1}{2\left[2 - \left(1 - \frac{1}{2}\right) \times 1\right]} \\
&= \frac{\frac{6}{2} - 1}{3} = \$\frac{2}{3}. \\
w_H^{AI} &= \theta_H \frac{\gamma}{2\left[\theta_H - (1-\gamma)\theta_L\right]} = 2\frac{\frac{1}{2}}{2\left[2 - \left(1 - \frac{1}{2}\right) \times 1\right]} \\
&= 2\frac{\frac{1}{2}}{3} = \$\frac{1}{3}.
\end{aligned}
$$

In this case, we find that the high-cost worker exerts more effort compared to that in example 16.4, and as a result, both types of worker receive an increase in wages due to the higher overall productivity of the firm.

16.2 Solutions to End-of-Chapter Exercises

Exercise #16.1 - Moral Hazard[A]

16.1 Give two real-world examples where moral hazard problems exist. In all examples, identify the individuals/firms involved, their order of play, and the available actions.

- *Managing a grocery store.* Typically, a grocery store is owned by an individual or company, but managed by some other person. While the owner would prefer that the manager exerts high effort, effort is not observable on a day-to-day basis. Thus, the owner must offer the manager a lucrative contract to induce her to exert high effort.

- *Teacher and student.* Teachers want their students to exert high effort in their studies. Thus, teachers offer incentives (in the form of grade rewards and penalties) to induce a high effort level (more studying). Students can choose to exert low effort, but they probably won't like their grade at the end of the semester!

Exercise #16.3 - Risk Aversion–II[A]

16.3 Consider the situation in example 16.2.

(a) Suppose now that the worker is risk neutral (i.e., $u(w) = w$). Find the optimal salaries, w_H and w_L in this scenario, and compare them against those in example 16.2.

- Setting up the firm's maximization problem with our new utility function,

$$\max_{w_H, w_L} \quad \$270 - \underbrace{[0.6w_H + 0.4w_L]}_{\text{Expected labor costs}}$$

subject to

$$\underbrace{0.6w_H + 0.4w_L - 5}_{\text{Expected utility from high effort}} \geq 0 \qquad (PC)$$

$$\underbrace{0.6w_H + 0.4w_L - 5}_{\text{Expected utility from high effort}} \geq \underbrace{0.05w_H + 0.95w_L - 0}_{\text{Expected utility from low effort}}. \qquad (IC)$$

As in example 16.2, we know that the incentive compatibility constraint, IC, must hold with equality. We can rearrange the second constraint to obtain $0.55w_H = 0.55w_L + 5$, or, dividing both sides of this equation by 0.55,

$$w_H = w_L + 9.1.$$

From here, we can substitute this expression back into the maximization problem for the firm as well as ignore the participation constraint (it will not bind as we show at the end). Thus, the firm's maximization problem becomes,

$$\max_{w_L} \quad \$270 - \left[0.6 \underbrace{(w_L + 9.1)}_{w_H} + 0.4w_L \right].$$

Differentiating with respect to w_L yields

$$\frac{\partial \pi}{\partial w_L} = -[0.6 + 0.4]$$
$$= -1.$$

Since our result is negative for all possible values of w_L, this implies that the firm will always decrease its profits whenever it pays more money to the worker after a low output is realized. Thus, the wage that the worker receives

378

when the firm observes a low output is

$$w_L^* = \$0.$$

Returning to our constraint, we can solve for the wage that the firm pays when the high output occurs,

$$
\begin{aligned}
w_H &= w_L + 9.1 \\
&= 0 + 9.1 \\
w_H^* &= \$9.1.
\end{aligned}
$$

- *PC holds.* Last, we verify that the participation constraint, PC, holds by plugging in our equilibrium values,

$$
\begin{aligned}
&0.6 w_H + 0.4 w_L - 5 \\
={}& 0.6(9.1) + 0.4(0) - 5 \\
={}& 0.46 > 0,
\end{aligned}
$$

which implies that the worker is better off accepting the contract and exerting high effort than he is by not accepting the contract at all.

- *Comparison.* The salary when the firm observes a high output is much lower in this case relative to example 16.2. Intuitively, since the worker is less risk averse, he does not have to be compensated as much in order for him to bear the risk of his high effort not producing a high output.

(b) Suppose now that the worker is risk loving, with utility function $u(w) = w^2$. Find the optimal salaries, w_H and w_L, in this scenario, and compare them against those in example 16.2.

- Setting up the firm's maximization problem with our new utility function,

$$\max_{w_H, w_L} \quad \$270 - \underbrace{[0.6 w_H + 0.4 w_L]}_{\text{Expected labor costs}}$$

subject to

$$\underbrace{0.6(w_H)^2 + 0.4(w_L)^2 - 5}_{\text{Expected utility from high effort}} \geq 0 \qquad (PC)$$

$$\underbrace{0.6(w_H)^2 + 0.4(w_L)^2 - 5}_{\text{Expected utility from high effort}} \geq \underbrace{0.05(w_H)^2 + 0.95(w_L)^2 - 0}_{\text{Expected utility from low effort}}. \qquad (IC)$$

As in example 16.2, we know that the incentive compatibility constraint, IC, must hold with equality. We can rearrange the second constraint to obtain $0.55(w_H)^2 = 0.55(w_L)^2 + 5$, or, dividing both sides of this equation by 0.55,

$$(w_H)^2 = (w_L)^2 + 9.1,$$

and applying square roots on both sides, we solve for w_H, obtaining

$$w_H = \sqrt{w_L^2 + 9.1}.$$

From here, we can substitute this expression of w_H back into the maximization problem for the firm as well as ignore the participation constraint (it will not bind as we show at the end). Thus, the firm's maximization problem becomes

$$\max_{w_L} \ \$270 - \left[0.6 \underbrace{\sqrt{(w_L)^2 + 9.1}}_{w_H} + 0.4w_L \right].$$

Differentiating with respect to w_L, we find

$$\frac{\partial \pi}{\partial w_L} = - \left[\frac{0.6w_L}{\sqrt{(w_L)^2 + 9.1}} + 0.4 \right],$$

which is negative for all possible values of w_L. Therefore, the firm will always decrease its profits whenever it pays to the worker after observing a low output. Thus, the wage that the worker receives when the firm observes a low output is

$$w_L^* = \$0.$$

Returning to our constraint, we can solve for the wage that the firm pays the high-effort worker,

$$
\begin{aligned}
(w_H)^2 &= (w_L)^2 + 9.1 \\
&= 0^2 + 9.1 \\
&= \$9.1,
\end{aligned}
$$

and taking the square root of both sides of this expression gives a wage

$$w_H^* = \$3.02.$$

- *PC holds.* Last, we verify that the participation constraint, PC, holds by plugging in our equilibrium values,

$$
\begin{aligned}
& 0.6(w_H)^2 + 0.4(w_L)^2 - 5 \\
={}& 0.6(3.02)^2 + 0.4(0)^2 - 5 \\
={}& 0.47 > 0,
\end{aligned}
$$

which implies that the worker is better off accepting the contract and exerting high effort than he is by not accepting the contract at all.
- *Comparison.* The salary that the firm pays after observing a high output is much lower in this case than in either part (a) or example 16.2. Intuitively, since the worker is less risk averse (he is now risk loving), he does not have to be compensated as much for him to bear the risk of his high effort not

producing a high output level.

Exercise #16.5 - Household Chores–I^B

16.5 Ana and Felix have decided that Felix will wash dishes every time Ana prepares a meal. However, Ana cannot observe how careful Felix is when washing them. She knows that when Felix is very meticulous (careless), the probability of having spotless dishes is 0.95 (0.2) and having them dirty is 0.05 (0.8, respectively). Felix's utility is measured by the time he spends watching his favorite TV show each week (i.e., $u(t) = \sqrt{t}$), which depends on his success at washing dishes. If he is very careful when washing dishes, his effort level is represented as $e_H = 1.8$, and if he is careless, it is $e_L = 0$. Ana's expected utility when Felix achieves spotless dishes is 20. Identify the contract that Ana needs to offer Felix in terms of time spent watching his show. (Assume that letting Felix watch his favorite TV show is costly for Ana because there is only one TV in the house, and she does not like this particular TV show.)

- Let t_C denote the TV time that Felix receives when dishes are clean and t_D represent his time when dishes are dirty. Setting up Ana's maximization problem,

$$\max_{t_H, t_L} \quad 20 - \underbrace{[0.95 t_C + 0.05 t_D]}_{\text{Expected labor cost}}$$

subject to Felix's participation and incentive compatibility constraints,

$$\underbrace{0.95\sqrt{t_C} + 0.05\sqrt{t_D} - 1.8}_{\text{Expected utility from high effort}} \geq 0 \qquad (PC)$$

$$\underbrace{0.95\sqrt{t_C} + 0.05\sqrt{t_D} - 1.8}_{\text{Expected utility from high effort}} \geq \underbrace{0.2\sqrt{t_C} + 0.8\sqrt{t_D}}_{\text{Expected utility from low effort}}. \qquad (IC)$$

As in example 16.2, we know that Felix's incentive compatibility constraint, IC, must hold with equality. We can rearrange the second constraint to obtain $0.75\sqrt{t_C} = 0.75\sqrt{t_D} + 1.8$, or, dividing both sides of this equation by 0.75,

$$\sqrt{t_C} = \sqrt{t_D} + 2.4,$$

and applying square roots on both sides, we solve for t_C, obtaining

$$t_C = \left(\sqrt{t_D} + 2.4\right)^2.$$

From here, we can substitute this expression back into the maximization problem for Ana as well as ignore the participation constraint (it will not bind, as we show below). Thus, Ana's maximization problem becomes

$$\max_{t_D} \quad 20 - \left[0.95 \underbrace{\left(\sqrt{t_D} + 2.4\right)^2}_{t_C} + 0.05 t_D \right].$$

Differentiating with respect to t_D,

$$\frac{\partial \pi}{\partial t_D} = -\left[\frac{0.95}{\sqrt{t_D}}\left(\sqrt{t_D} + 2.4\right) + 0.05\right]$$

$$= -0.95 - \frac{2.28}{\sqrt{t_D}} - 0.05$$

$$= -1 - \frac{2.28}{\sqrt{t_D}},$$

which is negative for all possible values of t_D. Therefore, Ana will always decrease her payoff when she increases TV time after observing dirty dishes. Thus, when dishes are dirty, he is allowed

$$t_D^* = 0,$$

or no television time. Returning to Felix's constraint, we can solve for the television time that Ana must offer Felix when dishes are clean,

$$t_C^* = \left(\sqrt{t_D} + 2.4\right)^2 = \left(\sqrt{0} + 2.4\right)^2 = 5.76.$$

- *PC holds.* Last, we verify that the participation constraint, PC, is not violated by plugging in our equilibrium values,

$$0.95\sqrt{t_C} + 0.05\sqrt{t_D} - 1.8$$
$$= 0.95\sqrt{5.76} + 0.05\sqrt{0} - 1.8$$
$$= 0.48 > 0,$$

which implies that Felix is better off accepting the contract and exerting high effort than he is by not accepting the contract at all.

Exercise #16.7 - Basketball–I[A]

16.7 Consider a situation where a star basketball player is in negotiation for a new contract. The player knows that if he exerts high (low) effort in a game, the probability that his team wins the championship is 0.7 (0.3), which is worth \$1 million to the ownership of the team. The basketball player's utility function can be expressed as $u(w) = w^{0.4}$, and he incurs a utility cost of 150 when exerting high effort, and 50 when exerting low effort. Assume that his reservation utility is zero.

(a) Identify the type of contract that the ownership should offer the star basketball player to induce him to exert a high effort level.

- Let w_C denote the salary that the player receives when his team wins the championship and w_{NC} denote his salary when the team does not win. Setting up the team's maximization problem,

$$\max_{w_C, w_{NC}} \quad \$1,000,000 - \underbrace{[0.7w_H + 0.3w_L]}_{\text{Expected labor cost}}$$

subject to

$$\underbrace{0.7 \left(w_C\right)^{0.4} + 0.3 \left(w_{NC}\right)^{0.4} - 150}_{\text{Expected utility from high effort}} \geq 0 \qquad (PC)$$

$$\underbrace{0.7 \left(w_C\right)^{0.4} + 0.3 \left(w_{NC}\right)^{0.4} - 150}_{\text{Expected utility from high effort}} \geq \underbrace{0.3 \left(w_C\right)^{0.4} + 0.7 \left(w_{NC}\right)^{0.4} - 50}_{\text{Expected utility from low effort}}. \qquad (IC)$$

As in example 16.2, we know that the incentive compatibility constraint, IC, must hold with equality. We can rearrange the second constraint to obtain $0.4\sqrt{w_C} = 0.4\sqrt{w_{NC}} + 100$, or, dividing both sides of this equation by 0.4,

$$\left(w_C\right)^{0.4} = \left(w_{NC}\right)^{0.4} + 250,$$

and raising both sides to the 2.5 power, we solve for w_C, obtaining

$$w_C = \left[\left(w_{NC}\right)^{0.4} + 250\right]^{2.5}.$$

From here, we can substitute this expression back into the maximization problem for the firm as well as ignore the participation constraint (it will not bind, as we show below). Thus, the team's maximization problem becomes

$$\max_{w_{NC}} \quad \$1,000,000 - \left[0.7 \underbrace{\left[\left(w_{NC}\right)^{0.4} + 250\right]^{2.5}}_{w_C} + 0.3 w_{NC}\right].$$

Differentiating with respect to w_{NC} yields

$$\frac{\partial \pi}{\partial w_{NC}} = -\left[\frac{0.7}{\left(w_{NC}\right)^{-0.6}}\left[\left(w_{NC}\right)^{0.4} + 250\right]^{1.5} + 0.3\right],$$

which is negative for all possible values of w_{NC}. Therefore, the team will always decrease its profits when paying a higher salary to the player after losing the championship. Thus, the salary after observing that the team loses is

$$w_{NC}^* = \$0.$$

Returning to our constraint, we can solve for the wage that the team pays the player when winning the championship,

$$\begin{aligned}
\left(w_C\right)^{0.4} &= \left(w_{NC}\right)^{0.4} + 250 \\
&= (0)^{0.4} + 250 \\
&= 250,
\end{aligned}$$

and raising both sides of this expression to the 2.5 power gives

$$w_C^* = \$988,211.77.$$

- *PC holds.* Last, we verify that the participation constraint, PC, is not violated by plugging in our equilibrium values,

$$0.7 \left(w_C\right)^{0.4} + 0.3 \left(w_{NC}\right)^{0.4} - 150$$
$$= 0.7(988{,}211.77)^{0.4} + 0.3(0)^{0.4} - 150$$
$$= 25 \geq 0,$$

which implies that the player is better off accepting the contract and exerting high effort than he is by not accepting the contract at all.
- *Optimal contract.* In summary, the optimal contract is

$$(w_C^*, w_L^*) = (\$988{,}211.77, \$0).$$

(b) Find the team's expected profits.

- Plugging our optimal contract back into the team's profit function, we obtain the team's expected profits

$$\$1{,}000{,}000 - [0.7w_H + 0.3w_L]$$
$$= \$1{,}000{,}000 - [0.7(\$988{,}211.77) + 0.3(\$0)]$$
$$= \$308{,}251.76.$$

Exercise #16.9 - Insurance Market–I^B

16.9 Consider a situation where an insurance firm wants to incentivize its policyholder to exert effort in prevention of risky behaviors. Suppose that when a policyholder exerts high effort ($e_H = 10$), she has a probability of 0.1 of experiencing an adverse event (e.g., an accident), which costs the insurance firm \$10,000. A policyholder who exerts low effort ($e_L = 0$) has a probability of 0.2 of the same event happening. The utility function for a policyholder is $d - e^2$, where d represents the size of any policy discounts the insurance company offers her (assume that her reservation utility is equal to $\bar{u} = 0$). If the effort level of policyholders is observable by the insurance firm, identify the type of contract that the insurance firm should offer to induce the policyholder to exert high effort level.

- Since effort is observable in this scenario, the firm simply needs to guarantee that the worker accepts either the high-effort or low-effort contract.

  - *High-effort contract.* The policy holder will accept the high-effort contract as long as $d_H - e_H^2 \geq \bar{u}$, which in this context implies

  $$d_H - 10^2 \geq 0,$$

  since $e_H = 10$ and $\bar{u} = 0$. After rearranging, $d_H \geq 100$. Since the firm seeks to offer the lowest discount, it will offer $d_H = \$100$.

  - *Low-effort contract.* The policy holder will accept the low-effort contract as long as $d_L - e_L^2 \geq \bar{u}$, which in this context implies

$$d_L - 0^2 \geq 0,$$

since $e_L = 0$ and $\bar{u} = 0$. After rearranging, $d_L \geq 0$. Since the firm seeks to offer the lowest discount, it will offer $d_L = \$0$.

- *Optimal salaries.* Therefore, the firm offers a contract

$$(d_H, d_L) = (\$100, \$0)$$

inducing the policy holder to accept it and exert a high effort level.

Exercise #16.11 - Risk-Averse Lemons–I[B]

16.11 Consider the market for lemons presented in subsection 16.3.2. Suppose that while both the buyer and seller can observe the car's quality, the buyer is now risk averse, so her utility from purchasing the car is now $\sqrt{q} - p$.

(a) What price does the seller charge to the buyer in this situation?

- In this situation, the seller maximizes his own profits,

$$\max_{p} \ p - \frac{2}{3}q$$

$$\text{subject to } \sqrt{q} - p \geq 0. \qquad (PC)$$

Once again, the buyer's participation constraint ($\sqrt{q} - p \geq 0$) will hold with equality since the seller wants to receive as much profit as possible. Thus, we have that $\sqrt{q} - p = 0$, or $q = p^2$. We can substitute this back into the seller's maximization problem to obtain

$$\max_{p} \ p - \frac{2}{3}\underbrace{p^2}_{q}.$$

Differentiating with respect to p yields

$$\frac{\partial \pi}{\partial p} = 1 - \frac{4}{3}p = 0.$$

Solving this expression for p, we find that $p = \frac{3}{4}$. Plugging this price back into the participation constraint, we find that the buyer only buys cars of quality

$$q > p^2 = \left(\frac{3}{4}\right)^2 = \frac{9}{16}.$$

This implies that only cars above a quality level of $\frac{9}{16}$ are sold.

(b) Is this sale profitable for the seller? What is the range of qualities that he would be willing to sell to a risk-averse buyer? (Assume that the seller's valuation does not change.)

385

- Since the equilibrium price is $p = \frac{3}{4}$, the firm only makes a profit on cars of quality

$$\pi = p - \frac{2}{3}q = \underbrace{\frac{3}{4}}_{p} - \frac{2}{3}q > 0.$$

Rearranging this expression, we obtain

$$\frac{2}{3}q < \frac{3}{4}.$$

Solving this expression for q yields $q < \frac{9}{8}$. Together with the condition we found in part (a), saying that the buyers only purchase cars of quality $q > \frac{9}{16}$, we can conclude that in equilibrium, only cars of quality $q \in \left[\frac{9}{16}, \frac{9}{8}\right]$ are sold.

Exercise #16.13 - Risk-Averse Lemons–II[B]

16.13 Consider the market for lemons presented in subsection 16.3.3, where the buyer cannot observe car quality. Suppose that the buyer is now risk averse, so her utility from purchasing the car is now $\sqrt{q} - p$.

(a) What price does the seller charge to the buyer in this situation?

- To start, we must first determine the participation constraint for the buyer, which is the expected quality of the car he purchases minus the price he pays,

$$E[q] - p,$$

where the expected quality in this case (due to its uniform distribution) is

$$E[q] = \frac{\frac{3}{2} + 0}{2} = \frac{3}{4}.$$

Now, setting up the seller's maximization problem,

$$\max_{p} \quad p - \frac{2}{3}q$$

$$\text{subject to} \quad \sqrt{\frac{3}{4}} - p \geq 0.$$

Once again, the buyer's participation constraint $\left(\sqrt{\frac{3}{4}} - p \geq 0\right)$ will hold with equality since the seller wants to receive as much profit as possible. Thus, we have that $\sqrt{\frac{3}{4}} - p = 0$, or $p = \$\sqrt{\frac{3}{4}} = \$0.87$.

(b) Is this sale profitable for the seller? What are the range of qualities that he would be willing to sell to a risk-averse buyer? (Assume that the seller's valuation does not change.)

- In this situation, the seller charges a price $p = \$0.87$, earning positive profits as as long as

$$\pi = p - \frac{2}{3}q = 0.87 - \frac{2}{3}q \geq 0,$$

which rearranges to $\frac{2}{3}q \leq 0.87$. Dividing both sides of this expression by $\frac{2}{3}$ yields our upper bound of $q \leq 1.3$.

Exercise #16.15 - Risk Neutrality–II^B

16.15 Repeat exercise 16.14, but assume a risk-averse buyer, with utility function $u(q) = \sqrt{q}$, where $q > 0$ denotes his income.

(a) *Symmetric information.* Suppose that both the sellers and the buyers know the type of each individual car in the market. Explain what will happen in the market.

- *High-quality car.* In this situation, the seller maximizes profits,

$$\max_{p} \quad p - H_s = p - 3$$

$$\text{subject to } \sqrt{H_b} - p = \sqrt{4} - p \geq 0. \qquad (PC)$$

Once again, the buyer's participation constraint ($\sqrt{4} - p \geq 0$) will hold with equality since the seller wants to receive as much profit as possible. Thus, we have that $2 - p = 0$, or $p = \$2$. Thus, the seller charges the maximum price that a risk-neutral buyer is willing to pay for a high-quality car.

- *Low-quality car.* In this situation, the seller maximizes profits,

$$\max_{p} \quad p - L_s = p - 1$$

$$\text{subject to } \sqrt{L_b} - p = 2 - p \geq 0. \qquad (PC)$$

Once again, the buyer's participation constraint ($\sqrt{2} - p \geq 0$) will hold with equality since the seller wants to receive as much profit as possible. Thus, we have that $\sqrt{2} - p = 0$, or $p = \$1.41$. Again, the seller charges the maximum price that a risk-neutral buyer is willing to pay for a low-quality car.

(b) *Asymmetric information.* Now we assume asymmetric information: the seller observes the type of the cars he sells, but the buyers do not. We assume risk-neutral buyers, so they will buy if the price is less than the expected valuation of the car. Suppose that there is no effective way of transmitting the information on the type of the cars to the buyers, so there will be only one price in the used car market. Explain what will happen. In particular, find an expression of the particular value $\widehat{r}$, such that only L cars will be traded if $r < \widehat{r}$. What happens if $r > \widehat{r}$?

- To start, we must first determine the participation constraint for the buyer, which is the expected utility from the car quality he purchases minus the price he pays,

$$E[\sqrt{q}] - p$$

where the expected quality in this case is

$$E[\sqrt{q}] = r \underbrace{\left(\sqrt{H_b}\right)}_{\text{High quality}} + (1-r) \underbrace{\left(\sqrt{L_b}\right)}_{\text{Low quality}}$$

$$= \sqrt{4}r + \sqrt{2}(1-r)$$

$$= \sqrt{2} + \left(2 - \sqrt{2}\right)r.$$

Now, setting up the seller's maximization problem,

$$\max_{p} \quad p - K_s$$

$$\text{subject to} \quad \sqrt{2} + \left(2 - \sqrt{2}\right)r - p \geq 0. \qquad (PC)$$

Once again, the buyer's participation constraint $(\sqrt{2} + (2 - \sqrt{2})r - p \geq 0)$ will hold with equality since the seller wants to receive as much profit as possible. Thus, we have that $\sqrt{2} + (2 - \sqrt{2})r - p = 0$, or

$$p = \sqrt{2} + \left(2 - \sqrt{2}\right)r$$

$$= 1.41 + 0.59r.$$

Intuitively, as the probability of a high-quality car increases, the seller charges a higher price for the car regardless of its true quality.

- *Low-quality sales.* The seller offers low-quality cars if he receives a non-negative profit from their sale; that is,

$$p - L_s = \underbrace{(1.41 + 0.59r)}_{p} - 1$$

$$= 0.41 + 0.59r \geq 0.$$

Rearranging this expression, we find that the seller offers low-quality cars if $\hat{r} > -0.69$, which holds by assumption since r is a probability between 0 and 1. Therefore, for all values of $r \in [0, 1]$, the seller offers low-quality cars.

- *High-quality sales.* The seller offers high-quality cars if he receives a non-negative profit from their sale; that is,

$$p - H_s = \underbrace{(1.41 + 0.59r)}_{p} - 3$$

$$= -1.59 + 0.59r \geq 0.$$

Rearranging this expression, we find that the seller offers high-quality cars if $\hat{r} > 2.69$, which never holds since r is a probability between 0 and 1. Therefore, the seller only offers low-quality cars. Intuitively, even if $r = 1$, the price would only be $1.41 + 0.59(1) = \$2$, which is less than what the seller's value for a high-quality car. Again a market failure ensues from the

388

buyer's incomplete information: despite room for a beneficial exchange of high-quality cars between the seller and the buyer, this market fails to exist.

Exercise #16.17 - Risk Neutrality–II[B]

16.17 Repeat the analysis in example 16.4, but assume that the worker is risk neutral (i.e., her payoff from the contract is $w - \theta e$). How are equilibrium results affected? [*Hint*: Repeat all the steps in subsection 16.3.6 to find the equilibrium effort levels and salaries, and then evaluate your findings at the parameter values considered in example 16.4.]

- Setting up the firm's expected maximization problem:

$$\max_{w_H, e_H, w_L, e_L} \quad \underbrace{\gamma \left[\log(e_H) - w_H \right]}_{\text{If worker is high-type}} + \underbrace{(1 - \gamma) \left[\log(e_L) - w_L \right]}_{\text{If worker is low-type}}$$

subject to

$$w_H - \theta_H e_H \geqslant 0 \tag{PC$_H$}$$

$$w_L - \theta_L e_L \geqslant 0 \tag{PC$_L$}$$

$$w_H - \theta_H e_H \geqslant w_L - \theta_H e_L \tag{IC$_H$}$$

$$w_L - \theta_L e_L \geqslant w_H - \theta_L e_H. \tag{IC$_L$}$$

As before, PC_H and IC_L are our two binding constraints. Rearranging PC_H yields

$$w_H = \theta_H e_H,$$

while rearranging IC_H yields

$$w_L = w_H - \theta_L e_H + \theta_L e_L = \underbrace{\theta_H e_H}_{w_H} - \theta_L e_H + \theta_L e_L$$

$$= \theta_H e_H + \theta_L (e_L - e_H).$$

Substituting these results back into the firm's maximization problem, we obtain

$$\max_{e_H, e_L} \quad \gamma \left[\log(e_H) - \underbrace{\theta_H e_H}_{w_H} \right] + (1 - \gamma) \left[\log(e_L) - \underbrace{[\theta_H e_H + \theta_L (e_L - e_H)]}_{w_L} \right],$$

and differentiating with respect to e_L yields

$$(1 - \gamma) \left[\frac{1}{e_L} - \theta_L \right] = 0.$$

Solving for e_L, we obtain the effort level of the low-cost worker,

$$e_L^{AI} = \frac{1}{\theta_L}.$$

Now, differentiating the firm's maximization problem with respect to e_H yields

$$\gamma \left[\frac{1}{e_H} - \theta_H \right] + (1 - \gamma)\left[\theta_L - \theta_H\right] = 0.$$

Rearranging this expression, we find

$$\frac{1}{e_H} - \theta_H = \frac{(1 - \gamma)}{\gamma}\left[\theta_H - \theta_L\right].$$

Adding θ_H to both sides, then rearranging terms once more yields the equilibrium effort level for the high cost worker,

$$e_H^{AI} = \frac{\gamma}{\gamma\theta_H + (1 - \gamma)\left[\theta_H - \theta_L\right]}.$$

Last, solving for our wage levels, we find

$$w_H^{AI} = \theta_H e_H^{AI} = \frac{\gamma\theta_H}{\gamma\theta_H + (1 - \gamma)\left[\theta_H - \theta_L\right]}.$$

and

$$
\begin{aligned}
w_L^{AI} &= \theta_H e_H^{AI} + \theta_L(e_L^{AI} - e_H^{AI}) \\
&= \frac{\gamma\theta_H}{\gamma\theta_H + (1 - \gamma)\left[\theta_H - \theta_L\right]} + \theta_L \left[\frac{1}{\theta_L} - \frac{\gamma}{\gamma\theta_H + (1 - \gamma)\left[\theta_H - \theta_L\right]} \right] \\
&= 1 - \frac{\gamma\theta_L}{\gamma\theta_H + (1 - \gamma)\left[\theta_H - \theta_L\right]} \\
&= \frac{\gamma\theta_H + (1 - \gamma)\left[\theta_H - \theta_L\right] - \gamma\theta_L}{\gamma\theta_H + (1 - \gamma)\left[\theta_H - \theta_L\right]} \\
&= \frac{\theta_H - \theta_L}{\gamma\theta_H + (1 - \gamma)\left[\theta_H - \theta_L\right]}.
\end{aligned}
$$

- *Evaluation.* Evaluating our results at parameter values $\theta_L = 1$, $\theta_H = 2$ and $\gamma = \frac{1}{3}$, we obtain optimal effort levels

$$
\begin{aligned}
e_L^{AI} &= \frac{1}{\theta_L} = 1, \text{ and} \\
e_H^{AI} &= \frac{\gamma}{\gamma\theta_H + (1 - \gamma)\left[\theta_H - \theta_L\right]} \\
&= \frac{\frac{1}{3}}{\frac{1}{3}(2) + \left(1 - \frac{1}{3}\right)\left[2 - 1\right]} = \frac{1}{4} = 0.25.
\end{aligned}
$$

while optimal wages are

$$
\begin{aligned}
w_L^{AI} &= \frac{\theta_H - \theta_L}{\gamma\theta_H + (1-\gamma)\left[\theta_H - \theta_L\right]} \\
&= \frac{2-1}{\frac{1}{3}(2) + \left(1 - \frac{1}{3}\right)\left[2-1\right]} = \$\frac{3}{4} = \$0.75, \text{ and} \\
w_H^{AI} &= \theta_H e_H^{AI} = \frac{\gamma\theta_H}{\gamma\theta_H + (1-\gamma)\left[\theta_H - \theta_L\right]} \\
&= \frac{\frac{1}{3}(2)}{\frac{1}{3}(2) + \left(1 - \frac{1}{3}\right)\left[2-1\right]} = \$\frac{1}{2} = \$0.5.
\end{aligned}
$$

Thus, we find that when the worker is risk neutral:

- The low-cost worker exerts more effort (1 vs. 0.707 when risk averse) and is paid a higher wage than her risk-averse counterpart ($0.75 vs. $0.625 when risk averse).
- The high-cost worker exerts less effort that her risk-averse counterpart (0.25 vs. 0.35 when risk averse), but is paid a higher wage ($0.5 vs. $0.25 when risk averse).

Exercise #16.19 - Training[A]

16.19 Consider the results of example 16.4. Suppose that the high-cost worker could pay for some training to lower her cost of effort to θ_L. How much would she be willing to pay to achieve this?

- A high-cost worker would be willing to pay up to F to become a low-cost worker. Formally, her utility from being a low-cost worker minus F is weakly higher than her utility when remaining a high-cost worker; that is,

$$
w_L^{AI} - \theta_L \left(e_L^{AI}\right)^2 - F \geq w_H^{AI} - \theta_H \left(e_H^{AI}\right)^2.
$$

Inserting our equilibrium results from example 16.4, yields

$$
\$\frac{5}{8} - 1\left(\frac{1}{\sqrt{2}}\right)^2 - F \geq \$\frac{1}{4} - 2\left(\frac{1}{\sqrt{8}}\right)^2,
$$

which simplifies to

$$
\$\frac{1}{8} - F \geq \$0.
$$

Rearranging this expression, we find $F \leq \$\frac{1}{8}$. Thus, the high-cost worker would only be willing to obtain training to become a low-cost worker if it cost no more than $\$\frac{1}{8}$.

Exercise #16.21 - Adverse Selection[A]

16.21 Give two real-world examples where adverse selection problems exist. In all examples, identify the individuals/firms involved, their order of play, and the available actions.

- *Health insurance.* Insurance companies want to manage their risk pools. While they don't mind insuring high-risk people, they want to ensure that those high-risk individuals pay an appropriately high premium. Thus, insurance companies design policies with different coverage levels and premiums that allow for low-risk and high-risk people to self-select into the one best for them.

- *Choosing a date.* Dating is an adverse selection problem. The bachelor (or bachelorette) doesn't know if his (or her) potential date is a high quality or low quality person. Thus, the daters put their potential dates through a series of effort tests (dinner out, movie night, etc.) while rewarding them with appropriate affection levels for their effort depending on the quality of their potential date. Marriage is also an adverse selection problem, but the stakes are much higher!

Chapter 17 - Externalities and Public Goods

17.1 Solutions to Self-Assessment Exercises

Self-assessment exercise #17.1

SA 17.1 Repeat the analysis in example 17.1, but assume now that the inverse demand function changes to $p(q) = 14 - q$. Compare your results with those in example 17.1.

- With the new demand, the firm maximizes its profits as

$$\max_{q} \quad (14 - q)q - 2q.$$

Differentiating with respect to q yields

$$14 - 2q - 2 = 0,$$

which simplifies to $12 = 2q$. Solving for q, we obtain an output of

$$q^{U} = 6 \text{ units.}$$

Assuming that each unit of output generates $\alpha > 0$ units of pollution, the total pollution that this firm generates when left unregulated is 6α. The firm has no incentive to take its pollution under consideration since it does not impact its profit. If the firm changes its output from 6 units, it will earn less profit.

- Relative to example 17.1, the increased demand induces the firm to increase its output.

Self-assessment exercise #17.2

SA 17.2 Repeat the analysis in example 17.2, but assume the inverse demand function changes to $p(q) = 14 - q$. Show that the socially optimal output q^{SO} is larger than in example 17.2. Interpret.

- Here, the social planner solves the following problem

$$\max_{q} \quad \underbrace{(14 - q)q - 2q]}_{\text{Profits}} - \underbrace{3(\alpha q)^{2}}_{\text{External Cost}}.$$

Differentiating with respect to q yields

$$(14 - 2q - 2) - 6\alpha q = 0,$$

which simplifies to $12 = q(2 + 6\alpha)$. Solving for the output q, we obtain that the social optimum is

$$q^{SO} = \frac{12}{2 + 6\alpha}.$$

393

- *Comparison with example 17.2.* To show that this is greater than that in example 17.2, we need that

$$\frac{12}{2+6\alpha} > \frac{8}{2+6\alpha},$$

which simplifies to $12 > 8$, which always holds. If we break this apart, the marginal profit is $\frac{\partial \pi}{\partial q} = 12 - 2q$ and the marginal damage is $6\alpha q$. Compared to example 17.2, the marginal profit has increased while the marginal damage has remained the same. This increase in marginal profit increases the marginal benefit from producing the good, while the marginal damage is unchanged. This leads the regulator to increase the socially optimal amount of output.

- *Numerical example.* Consider, for instance, that every unit of output generates one unit of emissions, $\alpha = 1$. This leads to a socially optimal output of

$$q^{SO} = \frac{12}{2+6(1)} = 1.5 \text{ units.}$$

In contrast, if output does not generate emissions, $\alpha = 0$, the socially optimal output becomes $q^{SO} = \frac{12}{2+6(0)} = 6$ units, thus coinciding with that produced by the firm under no regulation (see self-assessment 17.1).

Self-assessment exercise #17.3

SA 17.3 Repeat the analysis in example 17.3, but assume that the external cost decreases to $EC = 3\,(e)^2 + 5e$. Find under which values of parameter α the pollution-generating activity should be banned. Interpret.

- Now, the social planner's problem is

$$\max_q \underbrace{(10-q)q - 2q]}_{\text{Profits}} - \underbrace{\left(3\,(\alpha q)^2 + 5\alpha q\right)}_{\text{External Cost}}.$$

Differentiating with respect to q yields

$$(10 - 2q - 2) - (6\alpha q + 5\alpha) = 0,$$

which simplifies to $8 - 5\alpha = q(2 + 6\alpha)$. Solving for output q, we obtain that the social optimum is

$$q^{SO} = \frac{8 - 5\alpha}{2 + 6\alpha}.$$

Socially optimal output can become negative if $q^{SO} = \frac{8-5\alpha}{2+6\alpha} \leq 0$, or $8 - 5\alpha \leq 0$. Solving for α, we find that output should be banned if $\alpha \geq \frac{8}{5} \simeq 1.6$. Intuitively, if every unit of output generates more than 1.6 units of emissions, society is better off prohibiting the production of this good.

- *Comparison with example 17.3.* Cutoff $\alpha \geq \frac{8}{5} \simeq 1.6$ is higher than that found in example 17.3 (where we found that $\alpha \geq \frac{8}{7} \simeq 1.14$). This occurs because the external cost has decreased, from $EC = 3\,(e)^2 + 7e$ in example 17.3 to $EC = 3\,(e)^2 + 5e$ in the current exercise.

394

Self-assessment exercise #17.4

SA 17.4 Consider your results in self-assessment 17.2. Following the steps in example 17.4, find the emission fee t that induces firms to produce the socially optimal output q^{SO}.

- Recall that the new inverse demand is $p(q) = 14 - q$. We consider the same two-period game as in example 17.4, where, in the first stage, the regulator sets the emissions fee t, and, in the second stage, the firm responds by choosing its output q. Operating by backward induction, we start by analyzing the second stage.

- *Second stage.* If the regulator sets a fee t on every unit of output, the monopolist's profit maximization problem becomes

$$\max_{q} \ (14 - q)q - (2 + t)q.$$

Differentiating with respect to q, we obtain

$$14 - 2q - (2 + t) = 0.$$

Solving for q, we find that the monopolist's output is

$$q(t) = \frac{12 - t}{2}.$$

When fees are absent, the monopolist produces the amount we found in self-assessment 17.1, $q = \frac{12-0}{2} = 6$ units. When the fee is positive, the firm reduces its output.

- *First stage.* The regulator sets the emission fee in the first period, while the firm responds to that fee by producing $q(t) = \dfrac{12 - t}{2}$ units in the second period. The regulator anticipates that the firm will respond with output $q(t) = \dfrac{12 - t}{2}$ and sets it equal to the socially optimal output $q^{SO} = 2$ tons of CO_2 that she seeks to induce. That is, $q(t) = q^{SO}$, or

$$\frac{12 - t}{2} = 2,$$

rearranging, we find $12 - t = 4$ and, solving for emission fee t, yields

$$t = \$8.$$

To verify that this fee induces the socially optimal output of 2 tons of CO_2, we can insert the fee we found, $t = \$8$, into the firm's output function to obtain $q(t) = \frac{12-8}{2} = 2$ units. Setting a fee of $8 per unit of output increases the monopolist's costs so that it will produce the socially optimal output.

- *Comparison with example 17.4.* The increase in demand means that the social planner needs to set a higher fee to achieve the same socially optimal output of $q^{SO} = 2$.

Self-assessment exercise #17.5

SA 17.5 Repeat the analysis in example 17.5, but assume that every roommate has only 12 hours (rather than 24), so the benefit of leisure in her utility function decreases to $12 - h_i$. How are the results in example 17.5 affected?

- Now, every roommate i simultaneously and independently chooses the number of hours she spends cleaning, h_i, where $h_i \in [0, 12]$ and her utility from cleaning is given by

$$u_i(h_i, h_j) = (12 - h_i) + \beta h_i(h_i + h_j).$$

Differentiating with respect to h_i, we obtain

$$-1 + 2\beta h_i + \beta h_j = 0.$$

Rearranging, this expression yields $2\beta h_i = 1 - \beta h_j$, and solving for h_i, we find that roommate i's best response function, as follows,

$$h_i(h_j) = \frac{1 - \beta h_j}{2\beta} = \frac{1}{2\beta} - \frac{1}{2} h_j,$$

which is the same as in example 17.5. This means that we will find that

$$h^* = \frac{1}{3\beta}.$$

The decrease in utility did not impact marginal utility, thus the optimal amount of cleaning hours is unaffected. In other words, while the roommate reaches a lower utility level, she still finds it optimal to exert the same amount of hours cleaning (i.e., graphically, the peak of her utility function happens at the same level of h_i but now reaches a lower height).

Self-assessment exercise #17.6

SA 17.6 Repeat the analysis in subsection 17.5.1, but assume $N = 12$ fishermen and a stock of $S = 230$ tons of fish. What if the number of fishermen increases to $N = 14$? What if, still with $N = 12$ fishermen, the stock of fish increases to $S = 250$ tons? Interpret.

- From subsection 17.5.1, we know that the equilibrium appropriation is $q^* = \frac{S}{N+1}$. Therefore, if the stock is $S = 230$ and there are $N = 12$ fishermen exploiting the resource, this appropriation becomes

$$q^* = \frac{230}{12 + 1} \simeq 17.69 \text{ tons},$$

while aggregate appropriation is

$$Q^* = N\frac{S}{N + 1} = 12\frac{230}{12 + 1} = 212.31 \text{ tons}.$$

- *More fishermen.* If the number of fisherman increases to $N = 14$, the equilibrium appropriation is now

$$q^* = \frac{230}{14+1} \simeq 15.33 \text{ tons.}$$

Therefore, the increase in fisherman leads to a decrease in each fisherman's equilibrium appropriation. In this scenario, aggregate appropriation becomes

$$Q^* = N\frac{S}{N+1} = 14\frac{230}{14+1} = 214.67 \text{ tons.}$$

Hence, while individual appropriation decreases, aggregate appropriation increases. In other words, while every fisherman decreases his individual appropriation, the appropriation of the new fishermen increase aggregate appropriation.

- *More abundant stock.* Now, if the stock decreases to $S = 250$ tons (and we still have $N = 12$ fishermen exploiting the commons), the equilibrium appropriation is

$$q^* = \frac{250}{12+1} \simeq 19.23 \text{ tons.}$$

Therefore, the increase in the fish stock increases each fisherman's equilibrium appropriation.

Self-assessment exercise #17.7

SA 17.7 Repeat the analysis in subsection 17.5.2, but assume $N = 12$ fishermen and a stock of $S = 230$ tons of fish. What if the number of fishermen increases to $N = 14$? What if, still with $N = 12$ fishermen, the stock of fish increases to $S = 250$ tons? Interpret.

- For this problem, we can use a model of collusion as a guide (like that in example 14.4). Here, the joint-profit maximization problem is

$$\max_{q_i} \ \pi_1 + ... + \pi_N = \underbrace{\left(q_1 - \frac{q_1(q_1 + ... + q_N)}{S}\right)}_{\pi_1} + ... + \underbrace{\left(q_N - \frac{q_N(q_1 + ... + q_N)}{S}\right)}_{\pi_N}$$

$$= (q_1 + ... + q_N) - \left(\frac{q_1(q_1 + ... + q_N)}{S} + ... + \frac{q_N(q_1 + ... + q_N)}{S}\right)$$

$$= \overbrace{(q_1 + ... + q_N)}^{Q} - \left(\frac{\overbrace{(q_1 + ... + q_N)}^{Q}\overbrace{(q_1 + ... + q_N)}^{Q}}{S}\right)$$

$$= Q - \frac{Q^2}{S}.$$

where Q is the aggregate number of catches; that is, $Q = q_1 + ... + q_N$.

- Differentiating with respect to Q yields

$$1 - \frac{2Q}{S} = 0.$$

Solving for Q, we find that the total amount of fish caught will be

$$Q^{JP} = \frac{S}{2} \text{ tons.}$$

If each fisherman is appropriated the same amount $\frac{Q^{JP}}{N}$, the equilibrium appropriation will be

$$q^{JP} = \frac{Q^{JP}}{N} = \frac{\frac{S}{2}}{N} = \frac{S}{2N} \text{ tons.}$$

We can check our result with $N = 2$ fishermen to find that each firm will catch $q^{JP} = \frac{S}{4}$ tons, the same as was found in subsection 17.5.2.

- Now, if we assume $N = 12$ fishermen and a stock of $S = 230$, each fisherman will appropriate

$$q^{JP} = \frac{230}{2(12)} \simeq 9.58 \text{ tons.}$$

This is less than the 17.7 tons they catch if they act independently.

- *More fishermen.* If, instead, we have $N = 14$ fishermen, each appropriates

$$q^{JP} = \frac{230}{2(14)} \simeq 8.21 \text{ tons,}$$

which is significantly less than appropriation when fishermen act independently (15.3 tons, as found in self-assessment 17.6). Therefore, when fishermen coordinate their fishing to maximize joint profits, they decrease their individual catches relative to when they act independently.

- *More abundant stock.* If the stock increases to $S = 250$ (and we still have $N = 12$ fishermen), each fisherman appropriates

$$q^{JP} = \frac{250}{2(12)} \simeq 10.41 \text{ tons,}$$

which is also substantially less than appropriation when fishermen act independently (19.2 tons, as found in self-assessment 17.6).

17.2 Solutions to End-of-Chapter Exercises

Exercise #17.1 - Regulated Duopoly[B]

17.1 Redo example 17.1 (unregulated equilibrium), but with two firms. Then redo example 17.4 to find the optimal emission fee in a duopoly. Compare this result with that in the monopoly found in example 17.4.

- *Unregulated equilibrium.* Every firm i solves the following problem

$$\max_{q_i} \ \pi_i = (10 - q_i - q_j)q_j - 2q_i.$$

Differentiating with respect to q_i, we obtain

$$\frac{\partial \pi_i}{\partial q_i} = 10 - 2q_i - q_j - 2 = 0,$$

rearranging, $2q_i = 8 - q_j$. Solving for q_i, we obtain every firm i's best response function

$$q_i(q_j) = 4 - \frac{1}{2}q_j.$$

Plugging firm j's best response function $q_j = 4 - \frac{1}{2}q_j$ into the equation above, we obtain

$$q_i = 4 - \frac{1}{2}\underbrace{\left(4 - \frac{1}{2}q_i\right)}_{q_j},$$

which simplifies to $\frac{3}{4}q_i = 2$. Solving for q_i, we obtain the unregulated equilibrium output q^U from every firm i

$$q^U = q_i = 2.67 \text{ units.}$$

- *Social optimum.* To find the fee needed to induce the social optimum (example 17.4), we need the socially optimal output. Assuming that the external cost is the same as in example 17.2, $EC = 3(\alpha q)^2$, where $\alpha = 1/3$, we already have the socially optimal aggregate output

$$Q^{SO} = \frac{8}{2 + 6\alpha} = \frac{8}{2 + 6(1/3)} = 2 \text{ units.}$$

Each firm, in the social optimum, will produce half of this amount:

$$q^{SO} = \frac{1}{2}2 = 1 \text{ unit.}$$

- *Optimal emission fee.* If the regulator sets a fee on every unit of output, every firm i's profit maximization problem becomes

$$\max_{q_i} \pi_i = (10 - q_i - q_j)q_j - (2 + t)q_i.$$

Differentiating with respect to q_i, we obtain

$$\frac{\partial \pi_i}{\partial q_i} = 10 - 2q_i - q_j - 2 - t = 0,$$

rearranging, $2q_i = 8 - t - q_j$. Solving for q_i, we obtain every firm i's best response function

$$q_i(q_j) = 4 - \frac{t}{2} - \frac{1}{2}q_j.$$

Plugging firm j's symmetric best response function into the equation above, we obtain

$$q_i = 4 - \frac{t}{2} - \frac{1}{2}\underbrace{\left(4 - \frac{t}{2} - \frac{1}{2}q_i\right)}_{q_j},$$

simplifying, $\frac{3}{4}q_i = 2 - \frac{t}{4}$, and solving for q_i, we find that every firm i will produce

$$q_i = \frac{8 - t}{3}.$$

The regulator, knowing the two firms set their output level according to this rule, induces them to produce the socially optimal output of one unit each by solving

$$\frac{8 - t}{3} = 1.$$

Multiplying each side by 3 yields $8 - t = 3$. Solving for t, we find the optimal emission fee to be

$$t = \$5.$$

This is greater than the fee set in the case of a monopoly because the two firms have greater aggregate output than the monopolist. This means that the regulator sets a higher fee to offset the extra production.

Exercise #17.3 - Positive Externalities and Social Optimum[A]

17.3 Redo example 17.2, but assume positive externalities, where the external benefit function is $EB = 5(\alpha q)^2 + 3$, where $\alpha \in [0, \frac{1}{5})$. Find the unregulated equilibrium and social optimum.

- The social planner's problem is

$$\max_{q} \quad \underbrace{(10 - q)q - 2q}_{Profits} + \underbrace{5(\alpha q)^2 + 3}_{External\ benefit} .$$

Differentiating with respect to q, we obtain

$$10 - 2q - 2 + 10\alpha q = 0.$$

Rearranging, we obtain $q(2 - 10\alpha) = 8$, and finally, the socially optimal output

$$q^{SO} = \frac{8}{2 - 10\alpha}.$$

The socially optimal output increases in parameter α, as seen in figure 17.1. this means that as the positive externality from production increases, so does the socially optimal output.

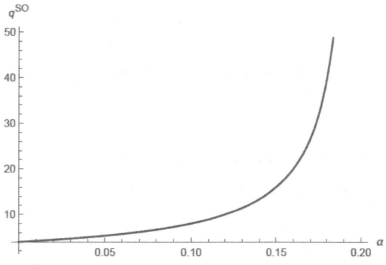

q^{SO}

50

40

30

20

10

0.05   0.10   0.15   0.20 α

Figure 17.1. Socially optimal output with positive
externalities.

Exercise #17.5 - Optimal Emission Fee[B]

17.5 Redo example 17.4, but with the environmental damage function in example 17.3.
Which is the lowest emission fee that achieves this objective?

- Here the optimal output level is:

$$q^{SO} = \frac{8 - 7\alpha}{2 + 6\alpha}.$$

- *Second stage.* This stage is the same as in example 17.4, and we find that the
monopolist's output is

$$q(t) = \frac{8 - t}{2}.$$

- *First stage.* In the first stage, the regulator wants to set a fee that induces the
monopolist to produce q^{SO}, so setting the monopolist's output to the socially
optimal output, we obtain

$$\frac{8 - t}{2} = \frac{8 - 7\alpha}{2 + 6\alpha}.$$

Multiply each side by 2, we obtain $8 - t = \frac{8-7\alpha}{1+3\alpha}$, and solving for t, we obtain the
socially optimal fee

$$t = 8 - \frac{8 - 7\alpha}{1 + 3\alpha} = \frac{8(1 + 3\alpha) - (8 - 7\alpha)}{1 + 3\alpha}$$
$$= \frac{8 + 24\alpha - 8 + 7\alpha}{1 + 3\alpha},$$

which simplifies to

$$t = \frac{31\alpha}{1 + 3\alpha}.$$

401

The emission fee is increasing in parameter α since

$$\frac{\partial t}{\partial \alpha} = \frac{31}{(1+3\alpha)^2} > 0.$$

Intuitively, as α increases, so do the external costs, so the regulator seeks to decrease output. For example, if $\alpha = 0.5$, socially optimal output becomes $q^{SO} = \frac{8-7(0.5)}{2+6(0.5)} = 0.9$ and the emission fee is $t = \frac{31(0.5)}{[1+3(0.5)]^2} = \frac{15.5}{6.25} = \$2.48$ per unit.

Exercise #17.7 - Public Goods and Free-Riding[B]

17.7 Consider two roommates, 1 and 2, who simultaneously choose the number of hours that they spend cleaning their apartment. In particular, assume that roommate i's utility function when he spends h_i hours cleaning and roommate j spends h_j hours cleaning is $u_i(h_i, h_j) = (24 - h_i) + [\beta h_i(h_i + h_j)]^{1/3}$. As in example 17.5, the first term represents the utility that roommate i enjoys from the hours he spends *not* cleaning the apartment, because the day has 24 hours; and the second term measures the utility that he enjoys from a cleaner apartment, which depends on both h_i and h_j, and is increasing in parameter $\beta > 0$.

(a) Suppose that the two roommates choose their hours of cleaning independently. What are the optimal number of hours of cleaning in this context?

- Roommate i's maximization problem is

$$\max_{h_i} \; u_i(h_i, h_j) = (24 - h_i) + [\beta h_i(h_i + h_j)]^{1/3}.$$

Differentiating with respect to h_i, we obtain

$$-1 + \frac{1}{3}[\beta h_i(h_i + h_j)]^{-2/3}(2\beta h_i + \beta h_j) = 0.$$

In a symmetric equilibrium, both individuals choose the same time spent cleaning; that is, $h_i = h_j = h$. Substituting this property into the equation above, yields

$$-1 + \frac{1}{3}[\beta h(h + h)]^{-2/3}(2\beta h + \beta h) = 0,$$

combining terms,

$$-1 + \frac{1}{3}\left[2\beta h^2\right]^{-2/3}(3\beta h) = 0,$$

and rearranging further,

$$3\beta h = 3\left[2\beta\right]^{2/3} h^{4/3}.$$

Dividing both sides of this expression by $3\left[2\beta\right]^{2/3} h$, we obtain

$$\frac{\beta^{1/3}}{2^{2/3}} = h^{1/3},$$

402

and raising both sides of this expression to the third power provides our solution,

$$h = \left(\frac{\beta^{1/3}}{2^{2/3}}\right)^3 = \frac{\beta}{4}.$$

(b) Assume now that the two roommates can coordinate their actions, choosing h_i and h_j to maximize their joint utility $u_i(h_i, h_j) + u_j(h_j, h_i)$. What are the optimal number of hours of cleaning in this context?

- The household's maximization problem is

$$\max_{h_i, h_j} u_i(h_i, h_j) + u_j(h_j, h_i)$$

$$= \underbrace{(24 - h_i) + [\beta h_i(h_i + h_j)]^{1/3}}_{u_i} + \underbrace{(24 - h_j) + [\beta h_j(h_i + h_j)]^{1/3}}_{u_j}.$$

Differentiating with respect to h_i and h_j, we obtain

$$-1 + \frac{1}{3}[\beta h_i(h_i + h_j)]^{-2/3}(2\beta h_i + \beta h_j) + \frac{1}{3}[\beta h_j(h_i + h_j)]^{1/3}(\beta h_j) = 0,$$

$$-1 + \frac{1}{3}[\beta h_i(h_i + h_j)]^{-2/3}(\beta h_i) + \frac{1}{3}[\beta h_j(h_i + h_j)]^{1/3}(\beta h_i + 2\beta h_j) = 0.$$

In a symmetric equilibrium, both individuals choose the same time spent cleaning; that is, $h_i = h_j = h$. Substituting this property into one of the equations above, yields

$$-1 + \frac{1}{3}[\beta h(h + h)]^{-2/3}(2\beta h + \beta h) + \frac{1}{3}[\beta h(h + h)]^{1/3}(\beta h) = 0.$$

Combining terms, we find

$$-1 + \frac{1}{3}[2\beta h^2]^{-2/3}(4\beta h) = 0,$$

and rearranging further,

$$4\beta h = 3[2\beta]^{2/3}h^{4/3}.$$

Dividing both sides of this expression by $3[2\beta]^{2/3}h$, we obtain

$$\frac{4\beta^{1/3}}{3 \times 2^{2/3}} = h^{1/3},$$

and raising both sides of this expression to the third power provides our solution,

$$h = \left(\frac{4\beta^{1/3}}{3 \times 2^{2/3}}\right)^3 = \frac{16\beta}{27}.$$

(c) Compare your results in parts (a) and (b). Interpret your comparison in terms of free-riding incentives.

- When roommates coordinate their hours cleaning the apartment, each of them chooses $\frac{16\beta}{27} \simeq 2.28\beta$, and when they independently choose their cleaning hours, each only exerts $\frac{\beta}{4} \simeq 0.25\beta$. Figure 17.2 illustrates these results. Intuitively, if the roommates coordinate, they both put more time into cleaning since by doing so they internalize the positive externality that each of their cleaning generates on the other roommate. When they act independently, however, every roommates face free-riding incentives, inducing each of them to spend less time cleaning.

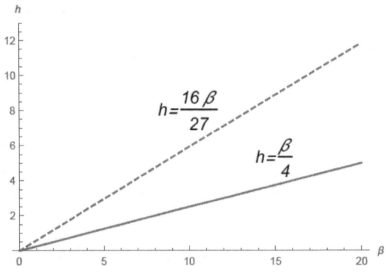

Figure 17.2. Equilibrium cleaning (solid) vs. socially optimal cleaning (dashed).

Exercise #17.9 - Common-Pool Resource–I^B

17.9 Consider a common-pool resource (e.g., a lake) operated by a single firm during two periods, appropriating x units in the first period and q units in the second period. In particular, assume that its first-period cost function is $\frac{x^2}{3}$, while its second-period cost function is

$$\frac{q^2}{3 - (1 - \beta)\,x}.$$

Intuitively, parameter β denotes the regeneration rate of the resource. That is, if regeneration is complete, $\beta = 1$, first- and second-period costs coincide; but if regeneration is null, $\beta = 0$, second-period costs become $\frac{q^2}{3-x}$, and thus every unit of first-period appropriation x increases the firm's second-period costs. For simplicity, assume that every unit of output is sold at a price of $1 at the international market.

(a) Find the profit-maximizing second-period appropriation.

- In the second stage, the firm solves

$$\max_{q} \quad q - \frac{q^2}{3 - (1 - \beta)\, x}.$$

Differentiating with respect to q yields

$$1 - \frac{2q}{3 - (1 - \beta)\, x} = 0,$$

rearranging, $1 = \frac{2q}{3-(1-\beta)x}$, and solving for q we obtain the firm's profit maximizing amount of q in the second-period appropriation as a function of its first period output x:

$$q(x) = \frac{3 - (1 - \beta)\, x}{2},$$

which is decreasing in the amount of the resource taken in the first period, x. Second-period appropriation is, however, increasing in the regeneration rate of the resource, β, since a larger portion of first-period appropriation becomes available again at the beginning of the second period.

(b) Using your result from part (a), find the profit-maximizing first-period appropriation.

- The firm's maximization problem is

$$\max_{x} \pi = \underbrace{x - \frac{x^2}{3}}_{\text{First period profit}} + \underbrace{\frac{3 - (1 - \beta)\, x}{2} - \frac{\left(\frac{3-(1-\beta)x}{2}\right)^2}{3 - (1 - \beta)\, x}}_{\text{Second period profit}}.$$

which first simplifies to

$$\max_{x} \quad \pi = x - \frac{x^2}{3} + \frac{3 - (1 - \beta)\, x}{2} - \frac{3 - (1 - \beta)\, x}{4},$$

and simplifying further yields

$$\max_{x} \pi = x - \frac{x^2}{3} + \frac{3 - (1 - \beta)\, x}{4}.$$

Differentiating with respect to x yields

$$1 - \frac{2}{3}x - \frac{1 - \beta}{4} = 0,$$

rearranging, $\frac{2}{3}x = \frac{3+\beta}{4}$. Solving for x yields the first-period appropriation

$$x^* = \frac{9 + 3\beta}{8}.$$

Substituting this into the second-period appropriation yields

$$q(x) = \frac{3 - (1-\beta)\overbrace{\frac{9+3\beta}{8}}^{x}}{2},$$

which simplifies first to

$$q(x) = \frac{3}{2} - \frac{1}{16}\left(9 - 9\beta - 3\beta^2 + 3\beta\right),$$

and then, the profit-maximizing first-period appropriation

$$q^* = \frac{3}{16}(5 + 2\beta + \beta^2).$$

For verification of intuition, we can plug $\beta = 1$ into both period's appropriations to find that they coincide at

$$x^* = \frac{9 + 3(1)}{8} = \frac{3}{2},$$
$$q^* = \frac{3}{16}\left[5 + 2(1) + (1)^2\right] = \frac{3}{2}.$$

Intuitively, if we have full regeneration of the resource, we expect the firm to appropriate the same amount in each period as it faces the same stock amount, and, as a consequence, the same problem in each period.

(c) How are your results affected by a larger regeneration rate, β?

- We can first investigate how first-period appropriation is affected by a larger β by differentiating with respect to β

$$\frac{\partial x^*}{\partial \beta} = \frac{3}{8} > 0.$$

As the regeneration rate increases, so does the first period appropriation. Since an increase in β lowers the firm's second-period costs (and increases the second-period profits), the firm can now appropriate more in the first period.

Next, we can differentiate second period appropriation q^* with respect to β

$$\frac{\partial q^*}{\partial \beta} = \frac{3}{16}(2 + 2\beta) > 0.$$

A higher regeneration rate lowers the second period costs and increases the profit-maximizing appropriation in the second period.

Exercise #17.11 - Common-Pool Resource–III[B]

17.11 Consider the common-pool resource problem in section 17.5, but with a new cost function $C(q_i, Q_{-i}) = \frac{2q_i(q_i + Q_{-i})}{S}$, where q_i denotes firm i's appropriation and Q_{-i} represents the sum of the appropriation from all firm i's rivals. Assume there are N individuals with access to the fish they can sell on the international market at $1 per unit, which every individual takes as a given.

(a) Find the equilibrium appropriation of fish.

- Every fisherman i chooses its appropriation level q_i to maximize its profits as follow
$$\max_{q_i} \pi_i = q_i - \frac{2q_i(q_i + Q_{-i})}{S}.$$

Differentiating with respect to q_i yields
$$1 - \frac{4q_i + 2Q_{-i}}{S} = 0,$$

rearranging yields $S = 4q_i + 2Q_{-i}$, and solving for q_i, we find
$$q_i(Q_{-i}) = \frac{S}{4} - \frac{1}{2}Q_{-i}.$$

Intuitively, fisherman i appropriates $S/4$ when his rivals do not appropriate, but decreases its appropriation by $1/2$ for every additional unit of aggregate appropriation, Q_{-i}. In a symmetric equilibrium, each fisherman appropriates the same amount of fish, implying that $q_1 = q_2 = ... = q_N = q^*$. Therefore,
$$Q^*_{-i} = \sum_{j \neq i} q^* = (N-1)q^*.$$

Inserting this property into the above best response function yields
$$q^* = \frac{S}{4} - \frac{1}{2} \overbrace{(N-1)q^*}^{Q^*_{-i}}.$$

Combining terms, $(N+1)q^* = \frac{S}{2}$. Solving for q^* yields the equilibrium appropriation of
$$q^* = \frac{S}{2N+2} \text{ units,}$$

which is increasing in the available stock but decreasing in the number of fishermen exploiting the commons.

(b) What is the equilibrium appropriation of fish when there are $N = 10$ fishermen and a stock of $S = 100$ tons of fish.

- Substituting $N = 10$ and $S = 100$ into the equilibrium appropriation yields
$$q^* = \frac{100}{(2 \times 10) + 2} = 4.54 \text{ units of fish.}$$

(c) Find the appropriation of fish if the fishermen were to coordinate their catches?

- Here, the joint maximization problem is

$$\max_{q_1,\dots q_N} \pi_i + \dots + \pi_N = \sum_i \underbrace{q_i - \frac{2q_i(q_i + Q_{-i})}{S}}_{\pi_i}.$$

Differentiating with respect to q_i yields

$$1 - \frac{4q_i + 2Q_{-i}}{S} - \frac{2Q_{-i}}{S} = 0.$$

We obtain a symmetric result after differentiating with respect to the other q_j's. Rearranging, we obtain $4(q_i + Q_{-i}) = S$. Solving for q_i, we find

$$q_i = \frac{S}{4} - Q_{-i}.$$

In a symmetric equilibrium, every firm appropriates the same amount, that is $q_1^{JP} = q_2^{JP} = \dots = q_N^{JP}$, where superscript JP denotes "joint profits" and that $Q_{-i} = (N-1)q^{JP}$. Substituting that into the equation above yields

$$q^{JP} = \frac{S}{4} - (N-1)q^{JP}.$$

Solving for q^{JP}, we find the equilibrium appropriation for each fisherman

$$q^{JP} = \frac{S}{4N} \text{ units.}$$

(d) How much would each of the 10 now-coordinating fishermen catch if there were 100 tons of fish?

- Inserting $N = 10$ and $S = 100$ into our equilibrium appropriation, we find each fisherman catches

$$q^{JP} = \frac{100}{4 \times 10} = 2.5 \text{ units,}$$

which is a smaller catch than if they do not coordinate and catch 4.54 units of fish. More generally, the equilibrium appropriation of fish without coordination is

$$q^* = \frac{S}{2N + 2} \text{ units,}$$

while the equilibrium appropriation when jointly maximizing profit is

$$q^{JP} = \frac{S}{4N} \text{ units.}$$

408

We can tell that condition $q^* > q^{JP}$ holds by showing that

$$\frac{S}{2N+2} > \frac{S}{4N},$$

simplifies to $4N > 2N + 2$, or $2N > 2$. Solving for N, we find that this condition is satisfied when $N > 1$ fishermen. Meaning that when there are multiple fishermen, the joint-profit maximizing appropriation is smaller than the noncooperative appropriation.

Exercise #17.13 - When Does the Coase Theorem Apply?[A]

17.13 Can the following situations be effectively addressed under the Coase theorem? Discuss why or why not.

(a) Air pollution

- Here, the biggest barrier to addressing air pollution under the Coase theorem is that large negotiation costs are present. Because the dispute is between polluting firms and citizens exposed to it, many agents are in play, which makes it hard for the citizens to coordinate and negotiate. This causes a breakdown in the Coase theorem.

(b) A homeowner playing loud music (negatively affecting his neighbors) within a homeowners' association (HOA)

- This situation can likely be settled under the Coase theorem. Property rights are well defined, and the right to play loud music is likely covered under an enforceable contract set by the HOA or local community ordinances. Each of the neighbors is well aware of the benefits and costs at play, and negotiation costs are likely small.

(c) Light pollution in a town with a powerful telescope (that needs surrounding darkness to be effective)

- This situation is a little tricky. Although there are many agents, and negotiation costs may be large, these telescopes are usually in low-population areas, minimizing the amount of people (and houses) nearby, which keeps negotiation costs low. Property rights may not be well defined here, though, as citizens and the telescope operator may both claim a right to the light or dark.

(d) Use of an irrigation ditch between two ranches

- Here, the Coase theorem is very much in play if the water rights are well defined and there is observable (measurable) use of water from the irrigation ditch. With few agents, negotiation costs are low.

Exercise #17.15 - Coase Theorem in Action[A]

17.15 Consider Jordan and Hannah, new neighbors in a nice neighborhood. Each have home businesses, but with different needs. Jordan runs a woodworking business that makes a lot of noise and creates a lot of sawdust, so his garage door has to stay open during the workday. Hannah runs a yoga studio, which needs a quiet environment to be successful. If Jordan runs his shop, he can make $500, while Hannah will have no customers and makes $0. If Jordan does not run his shop, he makes $0, while Hannah makes $600.

(a) Assuming that Jordan has the right to operate his shop, can Hannah induce him to shut down his shop so that she can make a profit? What is the total profit?

- Here, only one of the two neighbors can operate his or her business. Since Jordan has the right to operate his shop, Hannah can only run her studio if she can pay him to keep his shop closed. To do that, she needs to pay him as much as he would make if he operates plus a small amount (say, $1); that is, $501. If she pays that amount, Jordan will shut down his shop, and she can operate her studio for a total profit of $99.

(b) Hannah found out that Jordan can install a dust-collection system in his shop for X dollars, which would allow Jordan to close his garage door and lower the noise enough for her to run her studio. What is the largest amount X that Hannah would be willing to pay for the collection system? What is the total profit?

- Hannah would be willing to pay as much for the dust-collection system as she would to shut down Jordan's shop; that is, $501. If she pays for the system, she will make a total profit of $99, while Jordan will make a profit of $500, for a total overall profit of $599.

(c) Assume that there is an HOA contract (for which Hannah is the HOA president) that does not allow Jordan to make noise. How much would Jordan offer Hannah not to enforce the agreement and allow him to operate with the door open? What would be the total profit?

- Now that Hannah has the right to operate her studio, Jordan could only offer his total profit of $500, which would not cover the lost profit from Hannah if she were to shut down. Therefore, Hannah would not accept any offer Jordan could potentially offer, and she would run her studio for a total profit of $600.

(d) How much would Jordan be willing to pay for a dust-collection system to allow him to operate under the HOA rules? What would be the total profit if he were to invest in the system?

- Here, Jordan would be willing to pay up to his entire profit of $500 in the dust-collection system. If he invests in the system, the total profit would be $600 + $500 − X.

- *Summary.* Though the Coase theorem holds here, we can see that property rights play a large role in the outcome in terms of the payoffs, though the actions negotiated over may not be very dependent on the initial property rights.

Exercise #17.17 - Multiple Polluters[B]

17.17 Two polluting utility companies offer power at a regulated price of $3 per unit but have different cost functions. The first company produces a cheaper but more polluting energy at cost $TC_d = 2 - q_d + 0.5q_d^2$, with emissions $e_d = 2q_d$. The second company produces a less polluting energy, but at a higher cost, $TC_c = 4 - q_c + q_c^2$, with emissions $e_c = q_c$.

(a) Find the amount of energy and emissions that each firm will produce if left un-regulated.

- *Firm d.* The profit maximization problem of firm d is

$$\max_{q_d} \ \pi_d = 3q_d - (2 - q_d + 0.5q_d^2).$$

Differentiating with respect to q_d yields

$$3 + 1 - q_d = 0.$$

Solving for q_d, we find that $q_d = 4$ units. Firm d's total emissions are $e_d = 2(4) = 8$ units in the unregulated equilibrium.

- *Firm c.* The profit maximization problem of firm c is

$$\max_{q_c} \ \pi_c = 3q_c - (4 - q_c + q_c^2).$$

Differentiating with respect to q_c yields

$$3 + 1 - 2q_c = 0.$$

Solving for q_c, we find that $q_c = 2$ units, and their emissions are $e_c = 2$ units in the unregulated equilibrium.

(b) If the external cost of pollution is $EC = \frac{1}{2}(e_d + e_c)^2$ (the regulator cannot directly measure each firm's emissions, but can measure total emissions), find the socially optimal amount of output from each firm.

- The regulator's problem is

$$\max_{q_d, q_c} \ SW = \underbrace{3q_d - (2 - q_d + 0.5q_d^2)}_{\pi_d} + \underbrace{3q_c - (4 - q_c + q_c^2)}_{\pi_c} - \underbrace{\frac{1}{2}(2q_d + q_c)^2}_{EC}.$$

Differentiating with respect to q_d and q_c, we obtain

$$\frac{\partial SW}{\partial q_d} = 3 + 1 - q_d - 4q_d - 2q_c = 0,$$

$$\frac{\partial SW}{\partial q_c} = 3 + 1 - 2q_c - 2q_d - q_c = 0.$$

Simplifying the two equations, we obtain

$$4 - 5q_d - 2q_c = 0,$$
$$4 - 3q_c - 2q_d = 0.$$

Solving the second equation for q_d yields $q_d = 2 - \frac{3}{2}q_c$, which we can plug into the first equation to yield

$$4 - 5\underbrace{\left(2 - \frac{3}{2}q_c\right)}_{q_d} - 2q_c = 0,$$

rearranging $12 = 11q_c$, and solving for q_c gives us the socially optimal output from firm c:

$$q_c^{SO} = \frac{12}{11} \text{ units,}$$

and emissions $e_c = \frac{12}{11}$. Plugging this into the second equation $q_d = 2 - \frac{3}{2}q_c$, we can then the socially optimal output from q_d

$$
\begin{aligned}
q_d^{SO} &= 2 - \frac{3}{2}\left(\frac{12}{11}\right) \\
&= \frac{22 - 18}{11} = \frac{4}{11} \text{ units,}
\end{aligned}
$$

and emissions $e_d = 2\frac{4}{11} = \frac{8}{11}$.

(c) Is it possible to find a single emissions fee t that would induce the market to produce at the social optimum?

- *Emission fee for firm d.* If the social planner uses an emission fee, it solves the two-stage game as described in example 17.4. If the regulator sets a fee t on every unit of output, firm d's profit maximization problem becomes

$$\max_{q_d} \pi_d = 3q_d - (2 - q_d + 0.5q_d^2) - tq_d.$$

Differentiating with respect to q_d yields

$$3 + 1 - q_d - t = 0.$$

Solving for q_d, we find that $q_d(t) = 4 - t$ units. To induce the socially optimal output from firm d, the regulator sets a fee that solves $q_d(t) = q_d^{SO}$, or

$$4 - t = \frac{4}{11},$$

or a fee of

$$t = 4 - \frac{4}{11} = \frac{44 - 4}{11} = \$\frac{40}{11}.$$

- *Emission fee for firm c.* Similarly, for firm c, its profit maximization problem when facing a fee is

$$\max_{q_c} \pi_c = 3q_c - (4 - q_c + q_c^2) - tq_c.$$

Differentiating with respect to q_c yields

$$3 + 1 - 2q_c - t = 0.$$

Solving for q_c, we find that $q_c(t) = 2 - \frac{t}{2}$ units. To induce this firm to produce at the socially optimal level, the regulator finds the fee that solves $q_c(t) = q_c^{SO}$, or

$$2 - \frac{t}{2} = \frac{12}{11},$$

rearranging, $\frac{10}{11} = \frac{t}{2}$, and solving for t we obtain a fee of

$$t = \$\frac{20}{11}.$$

- We can see that the regulator cannot set a uniform fee for both firms to achieve the social optimum; that is, it sets a fee of $\$\frac{40}{11}$ to firm d and $\$\frac{20}{11}$ to firm c. Intuitively, the regulator would like to tax the more polluting firm at a higher rate than the relatively clean firm.

Exercise #17.19 - Common-Pool Refrigerator[A]

17.19 Each year, college students are finding themselves living with new roommates with different lifestyle habits than their own. A potentially frustrating habit is the use of the common refrigerator. Discuss the use, potential problems, and solution to the use of a common refrigerator among a group of two or more roommates.

- We can think of the refrigerator as a common-pool resource, where each roommate uses a particular proportion of the space inside. Each roommate generally has a right to store food in the common refrigerator; however, the right to the space allotted inside the refrigerator may not be well defined. This can lead to conflict and overuse of the resource (by overcrowding), or worse, spoiled food. Although there are relatively few agents involved, there may not be a way to enforce any agreement made over the negotiated use of the refrigerator space.